AMBE

AMBEDKAR
An Overview

RUPA

Published by
Rupa Publications India Pvt. Ltd 2018
7/16, Ansari Road, Daryaganj
New Delhi 110002

Sales Centres:
Allahabad Bengaluru Chennai
Hyderabad Jaipur Kathmandu
Kolkata Mumbai

ISBN: 978-81-291-4993-0

First impression 2018

10 9 8 7 6 5 4 3 2 1

Printed at Thomson Press India Ltd, Faridabad

CONTENTS

INTRODUCTION

INEQUALITY CONTINUES TO perpetuate in India and the rest of the world. India has traversed through the ebbs and flow of a post-colonial era, but the kind of inequality is myriad. Much of it is bequeathed to us from 'timeless' traditions and texts. An interaction with those traditions, texts and history could give us a clue as to how this land weathered the tension and skipped the European course.

Such an interaction is facilitated by the modern texts that intervene with the dominant tradition and history. The text that comes in the written form positions itself best to engage with much of entrenched ideas and belief system. The 'unique' of the inequality has much to do with the course of India's modernity. We appreciate modernity as that of a universalistic value system having its foundation on a sense of equality, we look up for a self-conscious modernist text that India can boast of.

Babasaheb Bhimrao Ambedkar's writings come to us as the moral and ethical succor in India's path to modernity. The moral question he raises is to privilege worth over birth. The ethical question is about the dignity of an individual as an equal citizen before a universal value system. At a more fundamental level, Bhimrao Ambedkar's interventions lead us to a discursive field that links the mode of relations amongst us to the question of community and nation. The erudite and scholarly presentations need to be retrieved and reflected upon as willy-nilly India still grapples with the issue of equality, community and fraternity.

To be sure, till the mid-1990s and beyond, not many Central universities of this country while teaching about Indian society included Ambedkar's works in its core syllabus. The question of caste and social change has been dealt with credible works backed by field studies. While any popular design of a sociology course would include backwardness and Untouchability as a 'problem' in its last section, it is India's tryst with parliamentary democracy, emergent political power and resistance that together form the 'rediscovery' of Ambedkar as far as university syllabi are concerned. Not only that, essential writings of Ambedkar did slowly find its rightful place in all sociology courses, and his popular writings and speeches have caught the imagination of incisive followers of Indian society. It is interesting to note that Ambedkar's works have been complied and organized across platforms as mainstream reading, and not just as text from the margin.

The wide range of themes and issues addressed by Ambedkar confront the dominant understanding of Indian society and its encumbrances. As a leading proponent of depressed classes, Ambedkar agitated academically and canvassed politically through his speeches, pamphlets, scholarly articles and drafting documents for a variety of councils and legislative bodies—a huge body of writings we can identify as couched in liberal modernist thoughts. Such an erudite and in-depth presentation clearly is not to be considered as just a challenge from the margin. It is an alternate mainstream—a centre of reason and rationality. When interwoven together, they could propose a liberal democratic image of India as against the orthodox Indian society.

Such a critic of the orthodoxy could develop only at the cross-section of a personal biography and social history. The everyday life of an 'Untouchable', the mundane regularity of ignominy of early childhood of a Mahar child (Mahar is an Untouchable caste of erstwhile Bombay Presidency) shaped Ambedkar's lived-in experience. As an entry point to an understanding of Bhimrao Ambedkar's works, we may look up to his autobiographical anecdotes. We trace these in his collection 'Waiting for a Visa'.[1] Inter-subjective empathy can only help understand 'Untouchability' in Hinduism to a certain extent and never fully. But a caustic indictment of Hinduism as a religion that rests on certain inegalitarian exclusionary principles can only be expected from Ambedkar, who had in fact encountered the humiliation.

An insider's viewpoint would definitely enrich any sociological appreciation of a vexed issue like that of Untouchability in India. It is

---

[1] See *Waiting for a Visa*, in Dr Babasaheb Ambedkar Writings And Speeches (BAWS), Vol. 12, part V, Bombay, The Education Department Government of Maharashtra, reprinted by Dr. Ambedkar Foundation, 2014, pp 661–92.

all the more necessary now as much of formerly acclaimed sociological research on the caste system has been accused of skipping the role of a participant among the Untouchables in their field-work. Under a satirical title 'Waiting for a Visa', Ambedkar compiled some six anecdotes from his personal life that explored the particular aspects of Untouchability which dehumanizes an entire section of the Indian population. The narrative unfolds a bunch of varied experiences sharing a common thread—the practice of Untouchability. From the lived-in experiences of Ambedkar when he was a nine-year-old boy to his empathy for his kin facing the same conditions as him, on account of him being an Untouchable himself, this compilation may well serve as a diary of the 'condemned'. Drawing partly upon experiences faced by him and partly upon the experiences of others, he graphically illustrates the actuality of the oppressive practices which make a member of the Depressed Classes an outsider to his own society, a bearer of filth whose touch is defiling—one who could never touch or be touched by upper-caste Hindus.

Moving beyond a mere description of the ways Untouchability was practised, Ambedkar empathically presents the experiential world of the Untouchables. The first few anecdotes are about the journey undertaken by him as a child with his elder brother and two cousins. It was a journey to catch up with his father who was posted in Koregaon (now Goregaon) during his summer vacation from Satara. It was a nightmarish experience as in an arduous train and subsequent bullock-cart ride, in which they could not even avail water to drink or wash—due to which the four boys could not even eat the food that they were carrying with them. He experienced a harsh world around him that left an indelible impression on a tender mind. At that tender age itself Ambedkar began understanding that his position in society was challenged by his caste identity. While recollecting his past, he connects such experience with all the discrimination he faced at his school. He realized early on that the outside world was too heartless and cruel.

In another heart-rending episode, Ambedkar puts forward the point that a person who is an Untouchable to a Hindu is also treated as an Untouchable by a Parsi (or, for that matter by a person of any other religion) as well. It was his return from abroad to Baroda in 1918 that opened his eyes to the deeply entrenched practice of Untouchability in India. Availing a scholarship from the Maharaja of Baroda he travelled to Columbia University in the United States of America for higher studies. Those five years in the West completely wiped out of his mind the consciousness of being an Untouchable. Ignoring better opportunities in Indian Education Services, he felt committed to serve the Baroda State which had sponsored his studies abroad. He joined as a probationer in the Accountant General's Office of the Maharaja of Baroda. Once in the Indian soil, again he faced the trials and tribulations of securing a lodging for himself on account of being an Untouchable. Finally, by impersonating as a Parsi he lodged himself in a Parsi inn. But on the eleventh day of his stay he had to face the wrath of a few Parsi youths and had to leave the inn—a wrath that was directed at his caste identity. Out on the street again, he failed to secure shelter even from his close friends—one a caste-Hindu and the other an Indian Christian. Ultimately, he quit Baroda and left for Bombay.

There are other anecdotes, too, that incessantly drive home the point that the ideology and practice of Untouchability could classify and exclude human beings in the worst possible manner. There was a near fatal accident that Ambedkar met with in Chalisgaon in the year 1929. As a member of the Committee to fact-find grievances of the Untouchables, he had to travel in a tonga to a Mahar village at Chalisgaon. A novice had to drive the horse-driven tonga as the owner refused to drive the Untouchable passenger. The untrained driver was unable to drive properly and failed to control the cart. It met with an accident. The Hindu tonga-wallah, who refused to drive the tonga, had the 'dignity' by which he could look upon himself as a person who was superior to even an accomplished Untouchable. These mundane experiences stretched to even cases where caste-Hindu doctors would refuse to treat the wife of an Untouchable schoolteacher who had just delivered. No qualm of conscience worked even with a medical professional, as a result the practice of Untouchability calimed the lives of the teacher's wife and child.

The compilation of the all the disjointed dehumanizing experiences present a picture of a caste-conscious India. Such a repertoire forms the social component of Bhimrao Ambedkar's thought and engagement with Indian society and polity. Modern India has not evolved in a unilinear way. The colonial experience is so dense with layers of engagement that the English-speaking articulate class cannot fathom the news of celebration of Macaulay's birthday by Dalit activists. Thomas Babington Macaulay, as we all know, is credited for the official introduction of English education in colonial India. The appropriation of the 'Western ways' in their favour by the Depressed Classes (Dalits in contemporary India) is resonant with the clue left by Ambedkar. Unabashed, he recorded that the establishment of the rule of the East India Company allowed his forefathers to break away from the hereditary caste occupation and that, his father also could follow suit to seek service in the Army of the Company. The hint is more than sufficient to see the displacement of the orthodox traditional caste custom with the help of the liberal English tradition. No wonder 'English' has an indelible imprint on his persona. His major writings, speeches, lectures and campaigns are all in impeccable English. In cutting English, his work is full of rhetoric as well as reason. Surely, he had his grooming and formative years of academics in the liberal schools of thought.

Born to Ramji Sakpal and Bhimabai on 14 April 1891 in the military cantonment of Mhow in the Central Provinces (now in Madhya Pradesh), Bhimrao Ambedkar belonged to the Mahar caste. Mahar caste was one of many Untouchable castes in Maharashtra. Interestingly, due to the European colonial mercantile and other activities the Mahars of the Ratnagiri district of Maharashtra, had a relatively better social field to debunk their caste predicaments.

On the economic front, Ambedkars could pursue their worth. Ramji Sakpal worked in the local military school. He rose to the rank of an officer and was a subedar when he retired. Post his retirement he took up the job of a cashier in Goregaon, in the Satara district. Nineteenth century reformer Jyotirao Phule's work among the lower classes of Maharashtra had a bearing on Ambedkar's formative years. Although socially mobile, the constant refrain of being born into an Untouchable caste never left his life. How the caste position restricts social interaction, and why commensality is an integral aspect of the dehumanizing caste system, Bhimrao Ambedkar realized right from his childhood days.

However, the avenues opened up by the colonial administration allowed Ramji Sakal to get his son admitted to Elphinstone High School, Bombay. From Elphinstone College itself Bhimrao completed his Bachelor's degree in 1912. In 1913, he secured admission to the Columbia University. He was assisted by the scholarship offered by Maharaja of Baroda for backward class students. Exposed to the liberal tradition of the American University he was drawn to the concepts of objective social science researches.

Having secured his Master's degree from Columbia, Ambedkar went on to obtain his doctoral degree in sociology. His next destination was England. The British empirical as well as liberal intellectual tradition attracted him for pursuing his academic career further. He was fascinated by the idealist thinkers and scholars of London School of Economics. He formally joined the London School in 1920 and completed his second Master's degree from there as well as accomplished yet another doctoral thesis on 'The Problem of the Rupee, Its Origin and Its Solutions'.

Before joining the London School of Economics in 1920, Ambedkar was associated with the formation of the Depressed Classes Forum and organized the First All India Conference of the Depressed Classes in Nagpur. After his exposure to the West in Columbia, he was categorical about the emancipator strategy for the age-old injustices meted out to the Depressed Classes. Instead of a dependency model for liberation he worked to wrest the initiative from upper-caste social reformers and empower the Depressed Classes. His worldview is primarily placed on a pivot which confers agency to the Depressed Classes as the subject.

The British tradition and training prepared Ambedkar to assess the strength of Constitutional State positively. The role of a welfare State to intervene with social justice figures in Ambedkar's thought in all his future public roles. No wonder, after his return to India he initially engaged himself with legal profession and took to teaching law in Government law College, Bombay. Simultaneously, he involved himself with social activism that directly addressed the lives of the

Depressed Classes (the erstwhile Untouchables).

On the one hand, Ambedkar joined and deliberated in the various legislative forums and institutions to further the legal aspects of equality. He realized that the social ostracizing of the Depressed Classes had to be contested with a two-pronged strategy. So, he actively promoted social movement which could challenge the religious restrictions on the ground. Be it the question of access to water resources in the neighbourhood or entry into temples for the Depressed Classes, they were deeply motivated by Ambedkar to take on the Brahmanic texts head-on. He was an active organizer and participant of many such agitating organizations. However, Independent India has preferred to understand Ambedkar as the man behind Indian Constitution. Generally, he is understood as a legal brain and constitutional expert. It is not just because of the fact that he acted as the Chairman of the Drafting Committee of the Constituent Assembly that presented the Indian Constitution. His consistent participation in all such bodies and commissions to advance incisive views and arguments for the Depressed Classes, be it the Simon Commission of 1928 or the Round Table Conferences in the 1930s, resulted in Bhimrao Ambedkar's image in the popular construction.

One can chart out some loosely identifiable phases from Bhimrao Ambedkar's broad expanse of life, world and thought-process. The first two decades of his life are marked by his uneasy embodiment of his ascribed status as an Untouchable as well as his educational achievements. We can see how he struggled for an egalitarian education through the coils of the caste system. The later years from 1910 onwards were instrumental in connecting him intellectually with the rest of the world. He could realize and experience the worth of a free world, once he was out of the Indian soil. The following decades of 1920s and '30s were full of activism for him. He took to popular publications and campaigns to organize the downtrodden Depressed Classes, especially the Untouchables. As a member of the Bombay Legislative Council he took up the fight from the streets to the corridors of power. A major event of this phase (1927) was the Mahad Satyagraha led by him to assert the right of Untouchables to use water in a public tank Chavdar in Mahad (currently in Raigad district), Maharashtra.

He ceremoniously broke the Hindu code and took a drink of water from the tank.

Ambedkar's view on social justice was propelled by an emancipatory aspiration that logically put him to question the Indian National Congress's reformist approach towards Untouchability. Increasingly, he contradicted Gandhian vision of freedom and his conservative position on the question of eradication of the caste system. As a result, the 1930s saw the two iconic figures of India as two contrasting voices of freedom, equality and justice.

The last two decades of his life—the 1940s and '50s—mark the emergence of Ambedkar as an articulate political persona. He conveyed thoughtful ideas on a variety of sensitive topics (such as the demand for Pakistan) in Executive Councils of the then Viceroy as an inducted Labour Member. In Independent India, he became the first Minister for law and was the Chairman of the Drafting Committee for the Constitution. Guiding the Draft Constitution at crucial junctures till its final adoption, Bhimrao Ambedkar's contribution for modern India has been permanently etched in Indian history. The 1950s bear testimony to all the churnings and self-reflections of a thought-provoking crusader of social justice. As an embittered soul, disenchanted with the functioning of the independent government of India, he embraced Buddhism finally. Alongwith, he left a couple of texts on his reconstruction of Buddhism, attempting to explore the liberating potential of Buddhism.

Although Ambedkar finally came out with his conversion to Buddhism in 1956, the very idea of coming out of the fold of Hinduism was floated by him some two decades earlier. Hinduism was a closed option for any amelioration of all the Depressed Classes. He exhorted his followers to renounce such a religion and opt for one that would knit the people together. Hinduism rests on exclusionary principles. So, conversion was very intimate to his thought. In a speech delivered to the Bombay Presidency Mahar Conference in 1936, he brought out the two aspects of conversion—material as well as spiritual.[2] The weapons of boycott and exclusion perpetuated by the caste-Hindus

---

[2] See *What Path to Salvation* in www.columbia.edu/itc/mealac/pritchett/00ambedkar/ txt_ambedkar.salvation.html

on the Untouchables amounted to class-struggle. Denials of varied economic and social activities actually pitted one class against another. He felt that it could be put to successful use as long as the oppressed class failed to stand up with strength against the tyranny.

Apart from the material need, the spiritual need for conversion was put forward by Ambedkar, as he thought individual welfare and progress was the real aim of religion. However, there was no place for an individual in Hindu society. According to him, religion has to impose rules for the maintenance of happiness in society, but the character of the rules has to be based on principles of equality of all individuals. As long as the practice of inequality and injustice goes unabated, all soothing effects of social reformers of Hindu religion could only be a misleading one to perpetuate the system.

The central question raised by Ambedkar is whether the spirit of free enquiry could be accomplished through the Hindu religion. Whether a practitioner is an author of his own life? He is caustic in his assessment of Hindu religion and compares the treatment meted out to the Untouchables as worse than slaves. Surrendering one's freedom one has to refer to the Vedas to seek guidance for action, if it is not forthcoming one falls back upon Smritis, and even when Smritis fail, one must check-in with the path laid by the great saints and sages. So, a series of intermediaries scuttle any chance of free application of one's own reason or thought. The question of Untouchability makes it obvious that salvation involves an escape from the predicaments by quitting the very religious hold.

The term Untouchable is a label. A signifying label by which people are treated as filthy and defiling. What the Untouchables do to escape from the 'label' is to take names borrowed from myths or historical characters to hide the identity. By a mere change of name, e.g. as the the Chamar call themselves Ravidas or the Bhangis renaming themselves as Valmikis would not changed the lived-in world for them. Even a lofty condescending term of 'Harijan' i.e., the children of God would still keep them within the folds of Hinduism. So, he designed salvation as an escape from Hinduism through conversion.

Since his first proclamation in favour of conversion in 1936, Ambedkar had gone through the rigour of polity with his 'protest ideology' and eventually embraced Buddhism in 1956. 'Even thogh I was born in the Hindu religion, I will not die in the Hindu religion…' this oath taken by him in 1936 had to explain 'to which religion'. We find his answer in his 'Buddha and the Future of His Religion'.[3] Buddhism is chosen as the path to escape from the dungeon of blind faith in Hinduism. For him, religion has a role to play in a modern rational society. The question is to opt for an appropriate one. He understands religion as a code of social morality that recognizes the fundamental tenets of liberty, equality and fraternity. Social life stands on these three basic tenets. Primarily every society needs either the sanction of law or the sanction of morality which would hold it together. Religion can instill the sense of morality and act as the governing principle of any society. Crucially, he thinks that in case religion works as anti-reason then it will cease to be functional. Reason for Ambedkar is synonymous with science. He realizes that it is only Buddhism which can stand these tests to be effective and operational for a modern world.

Ambedkar is no less philosophical when he claims that religion stands for hope and that the poor man and the distressed lives on hope. That life is sustained through hope. The hope is for progress and equality. For Ambedkar, progress could only come through Buddhism. He uses the allegory of different rivers flowing into the sea and becoming one and the same, where the Buddhist Sangh is such a sea a repository of equality and progress. Equality as the primary yardstick of progress can be achieved in the Buddhist brotherhood of monk as all the distinctions, be it caste or otherwise, would go like the different rivers meeting the sea. Religion has to be separated from theology if one is interested to appreciate its purpose and social function. Theology is secondary; the practices, usages and observances of a religion are important. There is no god in Buddhism. Morality is god. If a man has to function as a member in any society, in his actions he has to display the values of equality, fraternity and justice. Buddhism emphasizes and universalizes these values and instill them in an individual. By spiritualizing these values Buddhism stands as a

---

[3]See *Buddha and the Future of His Religion*, in BAWS, Vol. 17, part II, pp 97–108.

different religion from any other. He makes it clear in 'Away From the Hindus',[4] that there is no hope for the Untouchables in Hinduism, as Hinduism is Divine dispensation. It follows then that Untouchability is a result of Divine dispensation. The justification for conversation stems from the abject failure of Hinduism to confer the basic self-respect and honour to an Untouchable. The switch over to a nobler religion is supposed to bring immense social gain for the Untouchables, as they become members of a community which has universalized the values of equality in all walks of life. It solves the two essential problems with the Untouchables—that of social isolation and a psychological complex of inferiority.

Prior to his conversion, Ambedkar created a major work on Buddhism. This grand work stands out as his attempt to understand, formulate and reconstruct the ideals of Buddhism before actually embracing it. These are his personal interpretations of Buddha's teachings with which he wishes to invite his followers to the noble path. However, this work—'The Buddha and His Dhamma'—could only be compiled and published posthumously in 1957. Interestingly, prior to his submission to Buddhist idealogies, he was posed with a choice between Marx or Buddha.[5] With his strong conviction in the principles of reason and equality it is quite natural that Marx's ideas had its share of attraction for him. Like any liberal thinking personality of his time, he could not be unaffected by the élan of the great European Marxist tradition. His abiding interest in the philosophy of Marx is expected, as Marxist theory too addresses the issue of historical emancipation of the downtrodden. Despite his appreciation of the communist cause, Ambedkar could not foresee the withering away of the castes with the transformation of only the economic structure of the society. For him religious and cultural factors are more crucial in the Indian context, unlike the orthodox Marxists, who consider them as elements of super-structural epi-phenomenon. For him, the Brahmanical caste order stands as the primary contradiction. A pure economic understanding of class divisions, on the other hand,

---

[4]See *Away From the Hindus*, in BAWS, Vol. 5, pp 403–21.
[5]See *Marx or Buddha*, in BAWS, Vol. 3, pp 441–55.

dominated the analyses of the early Indian Marxists. So, it is an enigmatic relation with the Marxists that we find in Ambedkar. He refutes Marx, while remaining committed to the socialist project. Probably a mix of British Fabian socialism and American thinker, John Dewey's pragmatic philosophy govern his approach towards Marxism. With his 'Marx or Buddha' he provokes us with the idea that in the order of values, liberty should come before equality. He overrides the Marxist penchant for economic equality in favour of social liberty. To be more precise, he underscored the pre-condition of social liberty for any pursuit for economic equality.

Ambedkar's search for social liberty finds its destination in Buddha's ideals. Buddha's teachings are organized as a body of thought by him his last major work—'The Buddha and His Dhamma'.[6] It is his interpretation of Buddha so that the teachings could offer a succour for the distressed. Religion for him has to promise hope, so he is uncomfortable with the four noble truths of Buddhism. In fact he feels that those four truths that, all existence is sorrow, sorrow results from our cravings, cessation of sorrow comes with the cessation of cravings, and a path, Marg (the Noble Eightfold Path) only leads to the ending of sorrow, are the hindrance in the way of non-Buddhists to embrace Buddhism. He is sceptical that these would deny religion its basic goal of offering a hope in the material world. His interpretation of sorrow transcends the individual scope to engage in the transformation of the social world. In his interpretation, the theory of the 'middle path' is more pragmatic as an invitation to embrace Buddhism. He stands for rejection of asceticism on the one hand and indulgence in material luxury on the other.

Similarly, Ambedkar was suspicious of the doctrine of Karma and rebirth. In his scrutiny of Buddha's teachings, he finds it contradictory since Buddha denied the very existence of the soul. If there is no soul, how could there be Karma and rebirth? In fact such a Karma theory would take away from any religion its potential to redeem from their social distress in life. Instead, it would give the social existence of caste a sorted justification. So, he has an alternate understanding

---

[6]See *The Buddha and His Dhamma*, in BAWS, Vol. 17, part 2.

ofKarma. He contends that Buddha's essential teachings can be traced in the Tripitakas.The Tripitaka (called 'Tipitaka' in Pali) is the earliest collection of Buddhist writings. Initially, they were composed orally, but were written down by the third century before the common era. The world has to exist on the law of morality. The rule of law then is intrinsically linked to morality and justice. One can observe such thinking in the Tripitakas where religion is projected as a rational project which moralizes the world. In his own interpretation of 'The Buddha and his Dhamma', he discovers the social function of religion as to reorganize the world instead of searching for its origin. The Buddha's repudiation of supernaturalism makes Buddhism a religion of reason and Ambedkar explores how the worship of the supernatural is not Dhamma at all.

The Dhamma according to Ambedkar, is that morality which knits people together. It has the immense potential to reconstruct the world into a moral order based on the principles of liberty, justice and freedom. His version of Buddhism is a much more 'enlightened' as one which welcomes modernity. He radicalizes the entire concept of salvation ('Nirvana') as not merely a metaphysical or a psychological one. Its foundation has to be on a society that promises peace. Justice and equality are the preconditions of peace. The rational deliberation of the Buddha is so fascinating for him that he feels free to rediscover Buddhism in his own terms and rewrite the scriptures. He insists on the primacy of experience over scriptures and texts. Hence, the project of embracing Buddhism could be made more existential for all his followers.

Ambedkar's exploration of the social function of religion is entwined with his demystification of Hinduism. His in-depth analysis of the caste system and its dynamics is crucially linked to his exposition of Hinduism. Explanation of the caste system remains as one of his major work. Indian sociology in order to capture the reality of Indian social life devoted much of its initial years in researching about caste. The complexity and diversity of caste was being probed with an appealing contention to debunk textual understanding. Attention was drawn to field-based understanding of the very complex reality of the caste system in India. With an underlying postulate of adaptability and flexibility much of such studies ended up with an interpretation of hierarchy which was thought to be merely a reflection of an all-encompassing Brahmanical ideology.

While reading the text does not explain the ground reality of caste dynamics, the field views posit the Jati model as against the varna model. However, the Jati model too is inadequate as long as it presents a single continuous hierarchy. The field view of Jati needs to be counterposed with the textual view of varna. Advance sociological studies have shown that the strength of analysing the system by looking at castes as discrete categories. Such a contemporary research trend not only points out the disjunction between the textual view and the field view, but promises a richer sociology by considering castes as discrete categories. So, as a discrete category every caste has a story to tell about their positions in their specific understanding of hierarchy. Accordingly, a Shudra is best placed to narrate his tale of origin. An alternative way of looking at the Puranic texts and the Shastras are proposed to examine 'How did the Shudras come to occupy the fourth varna in the Indo–Aryan society?' Ambedkar's crucial intervention is to interpret the ascribed position of the Shudras and the Untouchables in the Indian society.

In 1916, Bhimrao Ambedkar read a research paper—'Castes in India: Their Mechanisms, Genesis and Development'[7]—for the Anthropology seminar of Dr A.A. Goldenweizer, at the Columbia University. In his paper, he points out that endogamy that is the prohibition of inter-caste marriage is the essence of caste. He goes on to show how endogamy was superimposed on a pre-existing exogamous society. He argues that essentially India's religion is primitive and it defies the advance of time to operate with its tribal code. Although the prevalence of exogamy—the practice of restricting the field of marriage, lost its efficacy with the passage of time across the world, it still operates in Indian society. He demonstrates it from the law of matrimony. It is not only that blood-kins cannot marry (Sapinda) but a marriage of the same Gotra is also prohibited (Sagotra). The way the custom of endogamy was superimposed on the original practice

---

[7]See *Castes in India*, in BAWS, Vol. 1, pp 3–22.

of exogamy, according to him, reveals the creation of caste.

Evidently, Ambedkar locates the origin of caste in the mechanism for endogamy. He points out at the three singular uxorial Hindu customs—sati, enforced widowhood and child marriage as the means which maintained endogamy. These were the means for creating a strict boundary around a caste group. While the Brahmins initiated the gate-keeping custom, which were later on taken up by other groups.

Demystification of the Brahmanic theory of Shudras is important for Ambedkar. He brings out the historicity of the Shudras through his intelligent reading of the classical Hindu texts. His interpretations stand his critical assessment of the Indian society. So, that its modern jurisprudence could relieve itself from mythological or theocratic deliverance. Before the Constituent Assembly he had to present the cardinal principles of constitutional jurisprudence of equality and liberty. Hence, his reference to the classical texts served the purpose of exposing how inequality in traditional India was institutionalized as the divine dispensation. Such historical research shows how the Brahmanical justification of the caste system negates the very foundation of equality and liberty—by denying the application of reason. The sacred texts curtailed the very possibility of humanity.

Over a period of time, Ambedkar had refined his arguments against the caste system. Through his works we can engage in an unbiased appraisal of the societal norms and realize the requirement for its revision. We give ourselves the Constitution. The Indian Constitution that celebrates the fundamental rights of Indian citizens confers individual autonomy as the unit of social action. It promises to protect an individual from the tyranny of the State or society. From a community-based identity the emergence of an individual identity is the lofty promise of the text of the Constitution. A constitution is a grand norm of legislation.

For the average Indian, Dr Bhimrao Ambedkar's name is etched in history as the prime architect of free India's Constitution. As the law minister of the Nehru government, he was the chairman of the drafting committee of the Constituent Assembly that framed the Constitution. The chairmanship provided Ambedkar with the opportunity to organize his thoughts and arguments over the crucial concepts of democracy, franchise and fundamental rights. The strength of Indian Constitution lies in its listing of the fundamental rights, which envision the individual as independent of all social encumbrances and stigma. Ambedkar's passionate engagement with the drafting committee of the Constitution reveals his deep understanding of the tradition of democracy and constitutional law. We too can appreciate in an unbiased manner the need to revisit our societal norms, revise it where necessary in order to pursue a modern path of ensuring justice, equality and liberty.

With an unflinching faith in constitutional democracy, Ambedkar designed his draft for adoption as the Constitution. With a profound faith in the people he could see beyond the tumultuous years preceding thr Independence, which were marked by intense socio-political divisions amongst its varied population. As a leading figure of the distressed Untouchable class, he wished that the warring communities could self-reflect and move ahead of their exclusionist politics. He reposes all his confidence on the Constitution which could act as a cushion to absorb all the future tension. Constitutional democracy is being understood as the tool to effect reorganization of an unequal society. The constitutional framework and its salient features were presented first on 4 November 1948 as 'Draft Constitution-Discussion'.[8] On being called by the President, Dr Rajendra Prasad, to move the motion as the law minister, Dr Bhimrao Ambedkar introduced the Draft Constitution to the Assembly for consideration.

The principle character that Ambedkar assigns to the draft Constitution is that it is federal in form and unitary in spirit. It envisions a dual polity with the Union at the Centre and the States at the periphery, each endowed with sovereign powers to be exercised in the field assigned to them respectively by the Constitution. The fundamental rights constitute the heart of the Constitution which is justifiable in the court of law. Of all the fundamental rights, 'Equality of Opportunity' was closest to Ambedkar's formulations. While underscoring the necessity of constitutional remedied he proclaimed that fundamental rights are the heart and soul of the Constitution

---

[8]See *Draft Constitution-Discussion*, in BAWS, Vol. 13, pp 49–70.

as they would propel the social system towards equality and liberty. Through the Draft, he spelled out the responsibility of the State towards its citizens. The Directive Principle of State Policy in tandem with the fundamental rights are orchestrated to secure social and economic democracy for a society which has historically been full of inequalities and discriminations. He devised a dynamic Constitution which could evolve with the growth of the nation and adopt to the changing needs of the society by keeping abundant provisions for amendments. He was firm on the question on single citizenship, a single judiciary and uniformity of fundamental laws which would help India to unify as a nation, as it is vulnerable to multiple sources of divisions—be it regions, religions, languages, traditions and customs. At the same time, he was clear in his assessment through the Draft that without economic and social justice, political independence would not bring about the lofty ideals of national integration.

The Draft Constitution presented by Ambedkar evoked varied responses from the members of the Assembly. In response to the lengthy discussion and debate, he replied with his usual calm and composure in his last address to the Constituent Assembly, 'Adoption of the Constitution'.[9] It is interesting as well as instructive for us to look back at the content of his speech and realize how prophetic could be a liberal mind. In his own words, his mind was so full of the future of the country. In his last address to the Constituent Assembly on 25 November 1949, Ambedkar expressed his views on the trials and tribulations ahead for a nascent sovereign State.

The speech represented Ambedkar's concerns for India's forward journey to the realm of a modern constitutional democracy. He explored all the apprehensions and aspects of the Draft Constitution before being adopted by the Assembly. Today, after all these decades of India's engagement with democracy, when we look back at the emotive speech delivered by him, we discover how he could foresee many of the issues that contemporary India is grappling with. And, he cleared the air by claiming that the success of a well-thought-out Constitution would depend finally on the organs of the State such as

---

[9]See, *Adoption of the Constitution*, in BAWS, Vol. 13, pp 1206–18.

the Legislative, the Executive and the Judiciary. In turn the success of these institutions would depend upon the people and the political parties that they would set up as their instruments to accomplish their wishes and hopes. In the true spirit of a liberal democrat, Ambedkar did not wish to say that the principle of parliamentary democracy was the only ideal form of political democracy. He only asserted that all the principles embodied in the Constitution were the views of the then generation. In a changed time, one may have a relook at it but without sabotaging the essence of it.

Ambedkar's incisive thought on the future of the Constitution bears a deep commitment to the principle of justice, liberty and equality. For him, fraternity was the elementary condition for equality. Three things he was worried over, if we wished to maintain democracy not just as a form, but also as a substantive fact of our life. He forewarned us to take guard against three situations. Firstly, along with the old divisive forces like caste and creed, many political parties with diverse and opposing views were bound to function within a parliamentary democracy. We should not allow the parties to place creed above the country. Secondly, he reminded us of the caution that the nineteenth century English liberal thinker John Stuart Mill had voiced—if we are interested to protect our democracy, we should not trust any great man with power and submit our liberties to such a person who could subvert the institutions. Finally, he warned us that political democracy could not last long without social democracy. What did he mean by social democracy? He meant, a way of life which would recognize the worth of liberty, equality and fraternity as the foundational principles of life. These three conditions need to work as a triad to form a union and cannot be separated from each other. The resonance of such a precaution accompanying social movement in India around these building blocks of democracy provoke us to read the essential writings and speeches of one of the finest social thinker of modern India, Babasaheb Bhimrao Ambedkar.

The vast expanse of Bhimrao Ambedkar's writings and speeches is predominantly driven by a feeling of loss of trust. A loss of faith, one may say, from the great struggles that galvanized into the freedom movement. The Constituent Assembly presented him with the scope to organize his worries, hopes and aspirations for a new India. This compilation of Ambedkar's works begins with 'The Failed Promise' as the chapter 1. From the vantage point of view of an Untouchable, he writes about how the very cause of the Depressed Classes was led astray. It chronicles how the pledges made during the Nationalist Movement led by the Indian National Congress to redress the wrongs done to the Untouchables lost its way.

Chapter 2 titled 'Political Safeguards for the Untouchables' enumerates the issues raised by Ambedkar to ensure political agency for the Depressed Classes (this coinage was adopted by him from the colonial administrative literature). It spells out the spirit of political participation. Participation in the legislative bodies is considered as a crucial empowerment for the Untouchables. To operationalize the social upliftment programmes of the Untouchable it is mandatory to engage with the executive power and law, otherwise all such struggles and efforts would remain as abstract goodwill. Chapter 3, 'Freedom From the Governing Class' explores that the fight for freedom from the colonial power led by the governing classes cannot fulfill the aspirations of the Depressed Classes kept heroically in servility by the same classes. Challenging the Hindu nationalist school Ambedkar's thoughts explains why Swaraj would make the governing class of Hindus more powerful and render the Untouchables more helpless.

Chapter 4, 'The Pakistan Question' deals with the political ideologies of the two communities, the Hindus and the Muslims, of the time that witnessed as upsurge in the demand or denial for a separate Pakistan. Chapter 5 titled 'The Common Fate of Hindus and Muslims' discusses how the problem of two separate communities as combatants facing each other overlooks the common reality of a deep malaise afflicting both the communities. It reveals the deep malaise as the aggregate of social stagnation, communal aggression and national frustration. Chapter 6, 'Debunking Pakistan' contains the more substantive views on the possibilities of alternative to Pakistan, for both the Hindus and the Muslims. The writings here are about the limiting conditions of the creation of Pakistan as a separate nation for the Muslims.

In his relentless fight and argument against the caste system Ambedkar makes it clear that one has to re-read the Shastras and the classical texts in an unbiased manner and examine them as the legitimizing texts behind the degrading caste system. A rational scrutiny of the texts reveals how they act as the pillars of a dehumanizing system. Chapter 7, titled as 'The Historicity of the Shudras' carries the essential probing of Ambedkar to demystify the Brahmanic theory of the Shudras in all its aspects. It promises an alternative understanding of the degradation of the Shudras. An overhauling of the caste practices is the ultimate motto of Ambedkar's crusade against Untouchability, which we find so eloquently in chapter 8, 'The Liberation'. Here we find him as the most provocative campaigner against the orthodox system. He discusses how to overcome the social humiliation and oppression beyond mere reformism. As a steady critic of upper-caste led social reformism, he asserts that the mission of doing away with the caste system would remain a distant dream without the absolute repudiation of Hinduism itself. He uses the tool of fierce rationalism to launch a frontal attack on Hindu superstitions. Eager to evolve a unique identity for the Untouchables, he trashes the caste biases in all efforts of conservative upper-class leaders of his time. We read here, how Ambedkar posits Dalit liberation against the social ideal of Gandhism.

Bhimrao Ambedkar and Mohandas Karamchand Gandhi are the two iconic figures of India's freedom struggle. Two contrasting voices of the freedom movement enrich us with two distinct worldviews about social progress. The post-independence discourse on the path ahead of Independent India cannot escape the debate between these two leading voices of India's national independence. As a rational and radical crusader against the pernicious system of caste and other social superstitions, Ambedkar is very clear that to believe in the Hindu Shastras and to simultaneously think of oneself as liberal or moderate is a contradiction in terms. His decisive position and a frontal attack on Hindu religion did provoke Gandhi. As a conservative and moderate, Gandhi appeals to the soul and self-awakening to overcome the degradation. Quite expectedly, such a position results in a profound social, philosophical and political conflict between the two leading personalities of modern India. Chapter 9, 'Critique of Gandhi' contains some excerpts from Ambedkar's arguments which politically and intellectually challenge Gandhian ideas.

Chapter 10 is an extract of Ambedkar's 'Annihilation of caste' which is fiercely critical of Hinduism as a religion itself, it's caste system and holy texts. He also leads the argument that mere inter-dining and inter-marriage among different castes is not sufficient to annihilate the caste system altogether.

We study humanities in classrooms where we look at a classmate as a product of 'reservation', or on the reverse, consider the 'other' as the bearer of social privilege. We debate in the public spheres factoring in ideologies as identity constructed. Identities as denied or designed by birth potentially can separate us permanently. Two different worlds cannot stay in the same house. Two separate worlds cannot appreciate and understand the life of its 'other' respectively. If both can address and consider each other as equal, without actually being rolled into one, possibly then one can think ahead of a fruitful journey for a sovereign independent country towards modern democracy.

Ambedkar's words take new meanings at every corner where India attempts to step out of the older world. Mostly, in popular discourses he has been very selectively appropriated just as a legal-constitutional luminary or as a champion of the Dalit cause. Much ahead of his times, he raised pertinent issues pertaining to the broader cause of nation building process of India. This compilation is an attempt to capture Ambedkar as a modernist thinker with an outstanding intellectual sweep over the major aspects of a newly independent nation. The soul of the suppressed finds an expression in his prolific style of taking on with the orthodox—be it the believer or the reformer. An intelligent reader discerns from him the thread of the rich and tedious tradition of democracy. Democracy is more than a system of government. It has a meaning in a broader sense. Democracy is an ideal of human equality that morally asserts the ultimate worth of the dignity and freedom of the human being. On such a plinth one develops the 'we feeling', the belongingness to one's homeland. Beyond the empty rhetoric, *Ambedkar: An Overview* synoptically captures the materialism of disillusionment through substantive arguments. One gets richer as one weaves through the different themes to be able to relate and answer, why the lost faith in mainstream nationalist movement is intrinsically linked to a paradigm of 'denied by birth'. One gains an alternative perspective to review and reorganize Indian society on the principles of fraternity.

Dr Abhijit Kundu,
Associate Professor, Department of Sociology
Sri Venkateswara College
University of Delhi

Chapter 1

THE FAILED PROMISE

IN THE ANNUAL session of the Indian National Congress held at Calcutta in the year 1917 a strange event took place. In that session the Congress passed the following resolution:

'This Congress urges upon the people of India the necessity, justice and righteousness of removing all disabilities imposed by custom upon the Depressed Classes, the disabilities being of a most vexatious and oppressive character, subjecting those classes to considerable hardship and inconvenience.'

The President of the session was Mrs Annie Besant. The resolution was moved by Mr G.A. Natesan of Madras and was supported by Mr Bhulabhai Desai from Bombay, by Mr Rama Iyer from Malabar and by Mr Asaf Ali from Delhi. In moving the resolution, Mr Natesan said:

'Ladies and Gentlemen, this question has been receiving great attention for years in other platforms; but in view of the unique character of this Congress, the Subjects Committee thought it necessary, after having framed a scheme of self-government for India, that we should complete that by asking us to prepare ourselves for the task of self-government. The first great duty is to see that all inequalities and injustices are removed. You will see that this resolution specially asks you to remove disabilities of a most vexatious and oppressive character. Without injuring your religious feelings, without giving up all that is best in your religious tradition, I think the Congress has a right to ask of you and of me and of others elsewhere that such absurd restrictions as the non-admission of these people to schools should be removed.

'The Congress has also a claim upon all human beings to see that in some portions of the country where these people are refused even the use of common well, these restrictions should disappear. In attempting to elevate ourselves and in trying to remove these galling restrictions we are but elevating Indian manhood; and when Responsible Self-Government is to be given to us we shall be in a position to say that Indians of all classes, of all creeds, have the fullest rights, the commonest social rights, have free access to all schools, to all institutions so that Indian manhood may develop in all its truest, best and noblest traditions.'

Mr Bhulabhai Desai in supporting the resolution pointed out that:

'The disabilities under which some of our brethren suffer are a great blow to the equality and brotherhood of man that we preach. From the great height of the resolution that you have passed this morning, with what face will we approach the British Democracy or any other power if we are unable to uplift our own brethren? They will say, "What lies in your own power, the obliteration of the social degradation of a section of your own people, you have been unable to do!" We can do it by self-help and by self-help alone and in this matter we need not approach any other power but ourselves. That proves the necessity of the great forward step that this Congress has taken in allowing this resolution to be moved before you. The existence of this great bane is an insult to the name of Hinduism. Therefore, both on the ground of necessity and on the ground of justice, as well as on the ground of righteousness, for the truth that you cherish, how can you deny them what this resolution demands, when the justice lies in your own hands? And if you fail to do that, with what justice, with what face, will you demand self-government?'

Mr Rama Iyer said:

'This resolution calls for social freedom by which we shall shatter the shackles that bind the lower classes. They are the foot of the nation and if you and I would climb the hill of Home Rule, we must first shatter the shackles on our feet and then and then only will Home Rule come to us... You cannot be political democrats and at the same time social autocrats. Remember that a man, a social slave, cannot be politically a free man. We all have come here to see the vision of United India, not only politically united but united all along the line...Therefore, let those of us, who are Brahmins, who belong to the higher castes, go to our villages and shatter the shackles of the low castes, people who are struggling against our own men—the social Bureaucrats of our own land.'

Mr Asaf Ali observed that:

'The problem of the Depressed Classes was one of the most difficult of all. They had been crying shame upon the arbitrary and autocratic action of the bureaucratic bunglers, but now it was the turn of the Depressed Classes—the Untouchables—to cover them, Indians, with shame. There were many millions of these victims of misfortune who had been plying their degraded trades in utter muteness for thousands of years, never emerging from the abyss of degradation into which the cruel and utterly unjustified customs of the country had buried them. Whether it was the springtime of hope, or the summer of realization to others, to these unfortunate creatures it was always the winter of black despair. It seemed a cruel irony of fate that those who were vociferously clamouring for the attainment or preservation of human rights themselves were so little mindful of the legitimate rights of others under them. Was it just or fair that a mute section of humanity should be left to suffer the very wrongs for whose redress others were shedding their blood in the battlefield? Why, even the 'Untouchables', in spite of all that cruel custom had subjected them to, were human beings and children of the soil, in whose veins coursed the self-same 'red-blood' as in the veins of those who arrogated superiority to themselves. The Depressed Classes were entitled to the same privileges as their betters in worldly circumstances and could not be debarred from the birthright of man. It was a standing reproach to the Indians that they had any Depressed Classes at all, and it was for the extinction of this reproach that they prayed.'

Many people would wonder why I describe the passing of the Resolution by the Congress moved and supported in such eloquent terms, as a strange event. But those who know the antecedents will admit that it is not an improper description. It was strange for many reasons.

In the first place, the President of the Session was the late Mrs Annie Besant. She was a well-known public figure and had many things for which she will be remembered by the future historians of

India. She was the founder of the Theosophical Society which has its home at Adyar. Mrs Annie Besant was well-known for rearing Mr Krishnamurti, the son of a Brahmin retired Registrar, for a future Messiah. Mrs Annie Besant was known as the founder of the Home Rule League. There may be other things for which friends of Mrs Annie Besant may claim for her a place of honour. But I don't know that she was ever a friend of the Untouchables. So far as I know, she felt great antipathy towards the Untouchables. Expressing her opinion on the question whether the children of the Untouchables should or should not be admitted to the common school, Mrs Annie Besant in an article headed 'The Uplift of the Depressed Classes' which appeared in the Indian Review for February 1909, said:

'In every nation we find, as the basis of the social Pyramid, a large class of people, ignorant, degraded, unclean in language and habits, people, who perform many tasks which are necessary for Society, but who are despised and neglected by the very Society to whose needs they minister. In England, this class is called the '"submerged tenth", forming, as it does, one-tenth of the total population. It is ever on the verge of starvation, and the least extra pressure sends it over the edge. It suffers chronically from under-nutrition, and is a prey to the diseases which spring therefrom. It is prolific, like all creatures in whom the nervous system is of a low type, but its children die off rapidly, ill-nourished, rickety, often malformed. Its better type consists of unskilled labourers, who perform the roughest work, scavengers, sweepers, navvies, casual dock-labourers, costermongers; and into it, forming its worse type, drift all the wastrels of Society, the drunkards, the loafers, the coarsely dissolute, the tramps, the vagabonds, the clumsily criminal, the ruffians. The first type is, as a rule, honest and industrious; the second ought to be under continued control, and forced to labour sufficiently to earn its bread. In India, this class forms one-sixth of the total population, and goes by the generic name of the "Depressed Classes". It springs from the aboriginal inhabitants of the country, conquered and enslaved by the Aryan invaders. It is drunken and utterly indifferent to cleanliness, whether of food, person or dwelling; but marriage is accompanied with some slight formality, children are kindly treated, and there is very little brutality, violence or criminality. Criminal communities, such as hereditary thieves, live apart, and do not mingle with the scavengers, sweepers, husbandmen and the followers of other simple crafts who make up the huge bulk of the Depressed. They are gentle, docile, as a rule industrious, pathetically submissive, merry enough when not in actual want, with a bright though generally very limited intelligence; of truth and the civic virtues they are for the most part utterly devoid—how should they be anything else?—but they are affectionate, grateful for the slightest kindness, and with much "natural religion". In fact, they offer good material for simple and useful though humble civic life...

'What can be done for them by those who feel the barbarity of the treatment meted out to them, by those who feel that the Indians who demand freedoms should show respect to others, and give to others a share of the consideration they claim for themselves?

'Here, as everywhere, education is the lever by which we may hope to raise them, but a difficulty arises at the outset, for one class of the community, moved by noble feeling of compassion and benevolence, but not adding thereto a careful and detailed consideration of the conditions, demands, for the children of the pariah community admission to the schools frequented by the sons of the higher classes, and charges with lack of brotherhood those who are not in favour of this policy. It becomes, therefore, necessary to ask whether brotherhood is to mean levelling down, and whether it is usual in family to treat the elder children and the babies in exactly the same way. It is a zeal not according to knowledge—and not according to nature—which would substitute equality for brotherhood, and demand from the cultured and refined that they should forfeit the hardly won fruits of the education of generations, in order to create an artificial equality, as disastrous to the progress of the future as it would be useless for the improvement of the present. The children of the Depressed Classes need, first of all, to be taught cleanliness, outside decency of behaviour, and the earliest rudiments of education, religion and morality. Their bodies, at present, are ill-odorous and foul with the liquor and strong-smelling food, out of which for generations they have been built up; it will need some generations of purer food and living to make their bodies fit to sit in the close neighbourhood of a school-room with children who have received bodies from an ancestry trained in habits of exquisite personal cleanliness, and fed on pure food-stuffs. We have to reuse the Depressed Classes to a similar level of physical purity, not to drag down the clean to the level of the dirty, and until this is done, close association is undesirable. We are not blaming these children, nor their parents, for being what they are; we are stating a mere palpable fact. The first daily lesson in a school for these children should be a bath, and the putting on of a cleancloth; and the second should be a meal of clean wholesome food; those primary needs cannot be supplied in a school intended for children who take their daily bath in the early morning and who come to school well-fed.

'Another difficulty that faces teachers of these children are the contagious diseases that are bred from first; to take one example, eye-disease, wholly due to neglect, is one of the most common and "catching" complaints among them. In our Panchama schools in Madras, the teachers are ever on the alert to detect and check this, and the children's eyes are daily washed and disease is thus prevented. But is it to be expected that fathers and mothers, whose daily care protects their children from such dirty diseases should deliberately expose them at school to this infection?

'Nor are the manner and habits of these forlorn little ones desirable things to be imitated by gently-nurtured children. Good manners, for instance, are the result of continual and rigid self-control, and of consideration for the comfort and convenience of others; children learn manners chiefly by imitation from well-bred parents and teachers and, secondarily, by suitable precept and reproof. If, at the school, they are to be made to associate with children not thus trained, they will quickly fall into the ways, which they see around them. For, until good habits are rendered fixed by long practice, it is far easier to be slipshod than accurate, to be careless than careful. Ought the children of families in which good manners and courtesy are hereditary, to be robbed of their heritage, a robbery that enriches no one, but drags the whole nation down? Gentle speech, well-modulated voice, pleasant ways, these are the valuable results of long culture, and to let them be swamped out is no true brotherhood...

'In England, it has never been regarded as desirable to educate boys or girls of all classes side by side, and such grotesque equalizing of the unequal would be scouted. Eton and Harrow are admittedly the schools for the higher classes, Hubgy and Winchester are also schools for gentlemen's sons, though somewhat less aristocratic. Then come a number of schools, frequented chiefly by sons of the provincial middle class. Then the Board Schools, where the sons of artisans and the general manual labour classes are taught; and below all these, for the waifs and strays, are the 'ragged schools', the name of which indicates the type of their scholars, and the numerous charitable institutions. An insane in England who proposed that ragged school children should be admitted to Eton and Harrow would not be argued with, but laughed at. Here, when a similar proposition is made in the name of brotherhood, people seem ashamed to point out frankly its absurdity, and they do not realize that the proposal is merely a violent reaction against the cruel wrongs, which have been inflicted on the Depressed Classes, the outcry of an awakened conscience, which has not yet had time to call right reason to guide its emotions. It is sometimes said that government schools pay no attention to social differences; therein they show that they are essentially "foreign" in their spirit. They would not deal so with the sons of their own people, though they may be careless of the sons of Indians, and lump them all together, clean and dirty alike. It is very easy to see the differences of "tone" in the youths when only the sons of the cultured classes are admitted to a school, and it is to the interest of the Indians that they should send their sons where they are guarded from coarse influences as Englishmen guard their own sons in England.'

◆

The second reason why one is justified in describing the passing of this Resolution as a strange event lies in the fact that it was entirely opposed to the declared policy of the Congress. In these days when the 'Constructive Programme' of the Congress is hawked from every street and at all times when the Congress is resting after an active campaign of Non-cooperation and Civil Disobedience, this statement may well cause surprise to present day Congressmen and their friends. The following extracts from the addresses of the Presidents who presided at the Annual Sessions of the Congress will suffice to bring home the fact that the Congress policy was to give no place to questions of social reform in the aims and objects of the Congress.

Social reform to begin with, Mr Dadabhai Naoroji who presided at the Second Session of the Indian National Congress held in Calcutta in the year 1886. In this presidential address he referred to the Congress attitude towards social reform and said:

> 'It has been asserted that this Congress ought to take up questions of social reforms (cheer and cries of "Yes, Yes!") and our failure to do this has been urged as a reproach against us. Certainly no member of this National Congress is more alive to the necessity of social reform than I am; but, gentlemen, for everything there are proper times, proper circumstances, proper parties and proper places (cheer); we are met together as a political body to represent to our rulers our political aspirations, not to discuss social reforms, and if you blame us for ignoring these, you should equally blame the House of Commons for not discussing the abstruse problems of mathematics or meta physics. But, besides this, there are here Hindus of every caste, amongst whom, even in the same province, customs and social arrangements differ widely— there are Mohammedans and Christians of various denominations, Parsis, Sikhs, Brahmins and what not—men indeed of each and of all those numerous classes which constitute in the aggregate the people of India (loudcheer). How can this gathering of all classes discuss the social reforms needed in each individual class? Only the members of that class can effectively deal with the reforms therein needed. A National Congress must confine itself to questions in which the entire nation has a direct participation, and it must leave the adjustment of social reforms and other class questions to Class Congresses...'

The subject was again referred to by the Hon. Mr Badruddin Tyabji who presided over the Third Annual Session of the Congress held in 1887. Mr Tyabji observed:

> '...It has been urged—solemnly urged—as an objection against our proceedings—that this Congress does not discuss the question of social reforms. I must confess that the objection seems to me strange, seeing that this Congress is composed of the representatives, not of any one

class or community, not of one part of India, but of all the different parts, and of all the different classes, and of all the different communities of India. Whereas any question of social reform must of necessity affect some particular part or some particular community of India only and, therefore gentlemen, it seems to me, that although we, Mussalmans, have our own social problems to solve, just as our Hindu and Parsi friends have theirs, yet these questions can be best dealt with by the leaders of the particular communities to which they relate (applause). I, therefore, think, gentlemen, that the only wise and, indeed, the only possible course we can adopt is to confine our discussions to such questions as affect the whole of India at large, and to abstain from the discussion of questions that affect a particular part or a particular community only.'

The third occasion when the subject was referred to was in 1892, when Mr W.C. Bannerjee in his Presidential address to the Eighth Session of the Congress gave expression to the following sentiments:

'Some of our critics have been busy in telling us, thinking they knew our affairs better than we know them ourselves, that we ought not to meddle with political matters, but leaving politics aside devote ourselves to social subjects and so improve the social system of our country; I am one of those who have very little faith in the public discussion of social matters; those are things which, I think, ought to be left to the individuals of a community who belong to the same social organization to do what they can for its improvement. We know how excited people become when social subjects are discussed in public. Not long ago we had an instance of this when what was called the Age of Consent Bill was introduced into the Viceroy Legislative Council. I do not propose to say one word as to the merits of the controversy that arose over that measure, but I allude to it to illustrate how apt the public mind is to get agitated over these social matters if they are discussed in a hostile and unfriendly spirit in public… I may point out that we do not all understand in the same sense what is meant by social reform. Some of us are anxious that our daughters should have the same education as our sons, that they should go to universities, that they should adopt learned professions; others who are more timid would be content with seeing that their children are not given in marriage when very young, and that child widows should not remain widows all the days of their lives. Others more timid still would allow social problems to solve themselves. The Congress commenced and has since remained, and will, I sincerely trust, always remain as a purely political organization devoting its energies to political matters and political matters only. I am afraid that those whether belonging to our own country or to any other country, who find fault with us for not making social subjects a part of our work, cherish a secret wish that we might all be set by the ears, as we are all set by the ears by the Age of Consent Bill, and that thus we might come to an ignominious end. They mean us no good, and when we find critics of that description talking of the Congress as only fit to discuss social problems, I think the wider the berth we give them, the better...

'I, for one, have no patience with those who say we shall not be fit for political reform until we reform our social system. I fail to see any connection between the two. Let me take, for instance, one of the political reforms which we have been suggesting year after year viz., the separation of judicial from executive functions in the same officer. What possible connection can there be between this, which is a purely political reform and social reform? In the same way, take the Permanent Settlement which we have been advocating, the amendment of the law relating to forests and other such measures—and I ask again, what have these to do with social reform? Are we not fit for them because our widows remain unmarried and our girls are given in marriage earlier than in other countries? Because our wives and daughters do not drive about with us visiting our friends? Because we do not send our daughters to Oxford or Cambridge? (Cheers).'

The last occasion when a Congress President is found to refer to this subject was in 1895 when the Congress Session was held in Poona and was presided over by Mr Surendranath Banerjee. Touching upon the subject, in his presidential address, Mr Banerjee said:

'We cannot afford to have a schism in our camp. Already they tell us that it is a Hindu Congress, although the presence of our Mohammedan friends completely contradicts the statement. Let it not be said that this is the Congress of one social party rather than that of another. It is the Congress of United India, of Hindus and Mohammedans, of Christians, of Parsis and of Sikhs, of those who would reform their social customs and those who would not. Here we stand upon a common platform—here we have all agreed to bury our social and religious differences and recognize the one common fact that being subjects of the same Sovereign and living under the same. Government and the same political institutions, we have common rights and common grievances. And we have called forth this Congress into existence with a view to safeguard and extend our rights and redress our grievances. What should we say of a Faculty of Doctors who fell out, because though in perfect accord as to the principles of their science, they could not agree as to the age at which they should marry their daughters, or whether they should remarry their widowed daughters or not. Ours is a political and not a social movement; and it cannot be made a matter of complaint against us that we are not a social organization any more than it can be urged against any of my lawyer friends that they are not doctors. Even in regard to political matters, such is our respect for the opinions of minorities, that so far back as 1887, I think it was at the instance of Mr Badruddin Tyabji, who once was our President and whose elevation to the Bench of the Bombay High Court is a matter of national congratulation, a resolution was passed to the effect that where there is practical unanimity among a class, though in a minority in the Congress, that a question should not be discussed, it should forthwith be abandoned.

'There is special danger to which an organization, such as ours, is exposed and which must be guarded against, the danger of there being developed from within the seeds of dissension and dispute.'

Against this background, the Resolution passed by the Congress about the Depressed Classes in 1917 is obviously a strange event. The Congress had never done such a thing before although it had functioned for thirty-two years. It was even contrary to its declared policy.

Why did the Congress think it necessary to pass such a resolution in the year 1917? What made it take cognizance of the Untouchables? What did it want to gain? Whom did it want to deceive? Was it because of a change in its angle of vision or was it because of some ulterior motive? For answers to these questions, one must turn to the following resolutions passed by the Depressed Classes in the year 1917 at two separate meetings held in the city of Bombay under two different Presidents.

The first of these meetings was held on 11 November 1917 under the Chairmanship of the late Sir Narayan Chandavarkar. In that meeting, the following resolutions[1] were passed:

First Resolution: 'Loyalty—Loyalty to British Government and prayer for victory to the Allies.'

Second Resolution carried [out] at the meeting by an overwhelming majority was: 'The dissentients being about a dozen, *expressed approval of the scheme of reform in the administration of India recommended by the Indian National Congress and the All India Muslim League.*'

Third Resolution carried [out] unanimously was: 'As the population of the Depressed Classes in India considered Untouchable and treated as such, is very large, as their condition is very degraded owing to that treatment and as they are behind the rest of the people in point of education, being unable to secure fair opportunities for their improvement, this public meeting of the Depressed Classes strongly feels that in the scheme of reform and reconstitution of the Legislative Councils which Government may be pleased to adopt, due regard be paid to the interests of the said classes. This meeting, therefore, prays the British Government to be so gracious as to protect those interests by granting to those classes the right to elect their own representatives to the said Councils in proportion to their numbers.'

Fourth Resolution unanimously carried [out] at the meeting was: 'The Government be prayed for the adoption, with all convenient speed, of a compulsory and free system of education rendered necessary by the fact that the social elevation of any community depends upon the universal spread of education among its members and that degradation of the Depressed Classes is due to their illiteracy and ignorance.'

Fifth Resolution carried [out] unanimously was as follows: 'That the Chairman of this public meeting be authorized to *request the*

---

[1]Addresses presented to the Viceroy in India and the Right Hon'ble the Secretary of State for India (1918). Parliamentary Paper Cd. 9178, pp 74–75.

Indian National Congress to pass at its forthcoming session a distinct and independent resolution declaring to the people of India at large the necessity, justice and righteousness of removing all the disabilities imposed by religion and custom upon the Depressed Classes, those disabilities being of a most vexatious and oppressive character, subjecting those classes to considerable hardship and inconvenience by prohibiting them from admission into public schools, hospitals, courts of justice and public offices, and the use of public wells, etc. These disabilities, social in origin, amount in law and practice to political disabilities and as such fall legitimately within the political mission and propaganda of the Indian National Congress.'

Sixth Resolution prays: 'All Hindus of the castes other than the Untouchables and Depressed, especially those of the higher castes, who claim political rights, to take steps for the purpose of removing the blot of degradation from the Depressed Classes, which has subjected those classes to the worst of treatment in their own country.'

The second meeting was also held in November 1917, a week or so after the first meeting. The Chairman was one Bapuji Namdeb Bagade, a leader of the non-Brahmin Party. At this meeting, the following resolutions[2] were unanimously adopted:

(1) Resolution of loyalty to the British throne.

(2) That this meeting cannot give its support to the Congress–League Scheme in spite of its having been declared to have been passed at the meeting of 11th November 1917 by an overwhelming majority.

(3) That it is the sense of this meeting that the administration of India should be largely under the control of the British till all classes, and specially the Depressed Classes, rise up to a condition to effectual by participation in the administration of the country.

(4) That if the British Government has decided to give political concession to the Indian Public, this meeting prays that Government should grant the Untouchables their own representatives in the various legislative bodies to ensure to them

---

[2]Addresses presented to the Viceroy in India and the Right Hon'ble the Secretary of State for India (1918). Parliamentary Paper Cd. 9178, p 75.

their civil and political rights.

(5) That this meeting approves of the objects of the Bahiskrit Bharat Samaj (Depressed India Association) and supports the deputation to be sent on its behalf to Mr Montagu.

(6) That this meeting prays that Government, looking to the special needs of the Depressed Classes, should make primary education both free and compulsory. That the meeting also requests the Government to give special facilities by way of scholarships to the students of the Depressed Classes.

(7) That the meeting authorizes the President to forward the above resolutions to the Viceroy and the Government of Bombay.

It is obvious that there is a close inter-connection between the resolution passed by the Depressed Classes at their meeting in Bombay under the chairmanship of Sir Narayan Chandavarkar and the Congress Resolution of 1917 on the elevation of the Depressed Classes. This inter-connection will be easily understood by adverting to the political events of the year 1917. It will be recalled that it was in 1917 or, to be precise, on the 20 August 1917 the late Mr Montague the then Secretary of State for India announced in the House of Commons the new policy of His Majesty's government towards India, namely, the policy of 'gradual development of self-governing institutions with a view to progressive realization of responsible government in India as an integral part of the British Empire. 'Leading Indian politicians were expecting some such declaration of policy on the part of His Majesty's government and were preparing schemes for changes in the constitutional structure of India in anticipation of such a policy. Of the many schemes that were formulated, there were two around which public attention was centred. One was called 'the Scheme of the Nineteen'. The second was called 'the Congress–League Scheme'. The first was put forth by the nineteen elected additional Members of the then Imperial Legislative Council. The second was an agreed scheme of political reforms supported by the Congress and the League otherwise known as the Lucknow Pact. Both these schemes had come into existence in 1910, a year before the announcement made by Mr Montagu.

Of the two schemes, the Congress was interested in seeing that its own scheme was accepted by His Majesty's government. The Congress, with that purpose in view, was keen on giving the Congress–League scheme the status and character of a national demand. This could happen only if the scheme had the backing of all communities in India. In as much as the Muslim League had accepted the scheme, the problem of securing the backing of the Muslim Community did not arise. Next in numbers came the Depressed Classes. Though not as well-organized as the Muslims, they were politically very conscious as their resolutions show. Not only were they politically conscious but they were all along anti-Congress. Indeed in 1895 when Mr Tilak's followers threatened to burn the Congress pandal if its use was allowed to the Social Conference for ventilating social wrongs, the Untouchables organized a demonstration against the Congress and actually burned its effigy. This antipathy to the Congress has continued ever since. The resolutions passed by both the meetings of the Depressed Classes held in Bombay in 1917 give ample testimony to the existence of this antipathy in the minds of the Depressed Classes towards the Congress. The Congress while anxious to get the support of the Depressed Classes to the Congress–League scheme of reforms knew very well that it had no chance of getting it 'As the Congress did not then practise—it had not learned it then—the art of corrupting people as it does now,' it enlisted the services of the late Sir Narayan Chandavarkar, an Ex-President of the Congress. As the president of the Depressed Classes Mission Society, he exercised considerable influence over the Depressed Classes. It was as a result of his influence and out of respect for him that a section of the Depressed Classes agreed to give support to the Congress–League Scheme.

The Resolution, as its text shows, did not give unconditional support to the Congress–League scheme. It agreed to give support on the condition that the Congress passed are solution for the removal of the social disabilities of the Untouchables. The Congress resolution was a fulfilment of its part of the contract with the Depressed Classes which was negotiated through Sir Narayan Chandavarkar.

This explains the genesis of the Congress Resolution of 1917 on the Depressed Classes and its inter-connection with the Resolutions of the Depressed Classes passed under the Chairmanship of Sir Narayan

Chandavarkar. This explanation proves that there was an ulterior motive behind the Congress Resolution. That motive was not a spiritual motive. It was a political motive.

What happened to the Congress Resolution? The Depressed Classes in their Resolution had called upon the 'higher castes, who claim political rights, to take steps for the purpose of removing the blot of degradation from the Depressed Classes, which has subjected these classes to the worst of treatment in their own country.' What did the Congress do to give effect to this demand of the Depressed Classes? In return for the support it got, the Congress was bound to organize a drive against Untouchability to give effect to the sentiments expressed in its Resolution. The Congress did nothing. The passing of the Resolution was a heartless transaction. It was a formal fulfilment of a condition, which the Depressed Classes had made for giving their support to the Congress–League scheme. Congressmen did not appear to be charged with any qualms of conscience or with any sense of righteous indignation against man's inhumanity to man, which is what Untouchability is. They forgot the Resolution the very day on which it was passed. The Resolution was a dead letter. Nothing came out of it.

Thus ended the first chapter in the history of what the Congress has done to the Untouchables.

◆

Mr Gandhi entered Indian politics in 1919. Very soon thereafter, he captured the Congress. He not only captured it but overhauled it completely and changed it out of recognition. He introduced three main changes. The Old Congress had no sanctions. It only passed a resolution and left it there, hoping that the British Government will take some action on it. If the British Government did not, it merely repeated the resolution next year and year after it. The old Congress was purely a gathering of intellectuals. It did not go down to the masses to secure their active participation in the political movement, as it did not believe in mass action. The old Congress had no machinery and no funds to carry on mass agitation. It did not believe in spectacular political demonstration to impress the British Government of the magnitude of its strength or to attract and interest the masses. The new Congress changed all this. It made the Congress a mass organization by opening its membership to all and sundry. Any one paying four annas a year could be a member of the Congress. It forged sanctions behind its resolutions by adopting the policy of non-cooperation and civil disobedience. It made it a policy to stage demonstration of non-cooperation and civil disobedience and to court gaol. It launched a countrywide organization and propaganda in favour of the Congress. It put out what is called a Constructive Programme of Social Amelioration. To finance these activities it started a fund of one crore of rupees. It was called the Tilak Swaraj Fund. Thus by 1922, the Congress was completely transformed by Mr Gandhi. The new Congress was entirely different from the old, except in name.

The Constructive Programme of social amelioration was an important feature of the Congress. It was outlined by the Working Committee of the Congress at its meeting in Bardoli, held in February 1922. It was also known as the Bardoli Programme. The resolution setting out the details of the programme ran as follows:

'The Working Committee advises all Congress Organizations to be engaged in the following activities:

(1) To enlist at least one crore members of the Congress.
(2) To popularize the spinning wheel and to organize the manufacture of hand-spun and hand-woven khaddar.
(3) To organize national schools.
(4) To organize the Depressed Classes for a better life, to improve their social, mental and moral condition, to induce them to send their children to national schools and to provide for them the ordinary facilities which the other citizens enjoy.
(5) To organize the temperance campaign amongst the people addicted to the drinking habit by house to house visits and to rely more upon appeal to the drinker in his home than upon picketing.
(6) To organize village and town Panchayats for the private settlement of all disputes, reliance being placed solely upon force of public opinion and the truthfulness of Panchayat decisions to ensure obedience to them.

(7) In order to promote and emphasize unity among all classes and races and mutual goodwill, the establishment of which is the aim of the movement of non-cooperation, to organize a social service department that will render help to all, irrespective of differences, in times of illness or accident.

(8) To continue the Tilak Memorial Swaraj Fund collections and call upon every Congressman or Congress sympathizer to pay at least one-hundredth part of his annual income for 1921. Every province to send every month 25 per cent of its income from the Tilak Memorial Swaraj Fund to the All India Congress Committee.'

The resolution was placed before the All India Congress Committee at its meeting held in Delhi on 20 February 1922 for confirmation, which it did. I am not concerned to set out what happened to the different items in this programme of constructive work. I am concerned with only one item, namely that which relates to the Depressed Classes and it is that part of it which I propose to deal with.

I will relate the story of the fate, which overtook this part of the Bardoli resolution relating to the Untouchables, stage by stage. To begin with the story, after the Bardoli resolution was confirmed by the All India Congress Committee, the matter was remitted to the Working Committee for action. The Working Committee took up the matter at its meeting held in Lucknow in June 1922. On that part of the Bardoli problem, which related to the uplift of the Untouchables, the Working Committee passed the following resolutions:

'This Committee hereby appoints a Committee consisting of Swami Shradhanandji, Mrs Sarojini Naidu and Messrs. I.K. Yajnik and G.B. Deshpande to formulate a scheme embodying practical measures to be adopted for bettering the condition of the so-called Untouchables throughout the country and to place it for consideration before the next meeting of this Committee, the amount to be raised for the scheme to be Rs 2 lakhs for the present.'

This resolution of the Working Committee was placed before the All India Congress Committee at its meeting held in Lucknow in June

1922. It accepted the resolution of the Working Committee after making an amendment to it saying that 'the amount to be raised for the scheme should be 5 lakh for the present' instead of two lakh as put forth in the resolution of the Working Committee.

It seems that before the resolution-appointing committee was adopted by the Working Committee, one of its Members Swami Shradhanand tendered his resignation of the membership of the Committee. At the very sitting at which the Working Committee passed the resolution appointing a Committee, another resolution on the same subject and to the following effect was passed by it:

'Read letter from Swami Shradhanandji, dated 8th June 1922 for an advance for drawing up a scheme for Depressed Classes work. Resolved that Mr Gangadhar Rao B. Deshpande be appointed convenor of the Sub-Committee appointed for the purpose and he be requested to convene a meeting at an early date, and that Swami Shradhananda's letter be referred to the Sub-Committee.'

The formation of a Committee marks the second stage in the history of this interesting resolution.

The next reference to the resolution-appointing Committee is found in the proceedings of the Congress Working Committee held in Bombay in July 1922. At that meeting the Committee passed the following resolution:

'That the General Secretary be asked to request Swami Shradhanand to reconsider his resignation and withdraw it and a sum of Rs 500 be remitted to the Convener, Sjt. G.B. Deshpande, for the contingent expenses of the Depressed Classes Sub-Committee.'

Here the matter ended, so far as the year 1922 was concerned. Nothing further seems to have been done. The year 1928 came on. Seeing that nothing was done to set going the Scheme for ameliorating the condition of the Untouchables, the Working Committee which met also at Gaya in January 1928 took up the matter and passed the following resolution:

'With reference to Swami Shradhanand's resignation, resolved that the remaining members of the Depressed Classes Sub-Committee do form the Committee and Mr Yajnik be the convener.'

Thereafter, the All India Congress Committee, which met Bombay in May 1923, passed the following resolution:

'Resolved that the question of the condition of the Untouchables be referred to the Working Committee for necessary action.'

Here ends the second stage in the history of the resolution remitting the question of the Untouchables to a special Committee. The third stage in its history is marked by the resolution of the Working Committee passed in May 1923 at its meeting held in Bombay. This resolution ran as follows:

'Resolved that while some improvement has been effected in the treatment of the so-called Untouchables in response of the policy of the Congress, this Committee is conscious that much work remained yet to be done in this respect and in as much as this question of Untouchability concerns the Hindu community particularly, it requests the All India Hindu Mahasabha also to take up this matter and to make strenuous efforts to remove this evil from amidst the Hindu Community.'

Thus is told the sad tale of the Resolution and how it began and how it ended. What a shameful close to a flaring start!

It will be seen how the Congress washed its hands of the problem of the Untouchables. It need not have added insult to injury by relegating it to the Hindu Mahasabha. There could not be a body most unsuited to take up the work of the upliftment of the Untouchables than the Hindu Mahasabha. If there is any body which is quite unfit for addressing itself to the problem of the Untouchables, it is the Hindu Mahasabha. It is a militant Hindu organization. Its aim and object is to conserve in every way everything that is Hindu, religious and cultural. It is not a social reform association. It is a purely political organization, whose main object and aim are to combat the influence of the Muslims in Indian politics. Just to preserve its political strength, it wants to maintain its social solidarity, and its way to maintain social solidarity is not to talk about caste or Untouchability. How could such a body have been selected by the Congress for carrying on the work of the Untouchables passes my comprehension. This shows that the Congress wanted somehow to get rid of an inconvenient problem and wash its hands of it. The Hindu Mahasabha, of course, did not come forth to undertake the work for it had no urge for it and also because the Congress had merely passed a pious resolution recommending the work to them without making any promise for financial provision. So, the project came to an inglorious and an ignominious end.

Before closing this chapter, it would not be unprofitable to ascertain why the Congress abandoned the work of social amelioration of the Untouchables of which it had made so much show. Was it because the Congress intended that the scheme should be a modest one not costing more than two to five lakh rupees but felt that from that point of view they had made a mistake in including Swami Shradhanand in the Committee and rather than allow the Swami to confront them with a huge scheme which the Congress could neither accept nor reject? The Congress thought it better in the first instance to refuse to make him the convener[3] and subsequently to dissolve the Committee and hand over the work to the Hindu Mahasabha.

Circumstances are not quite against such a conclusion. The Swami was the greatest and the most sincere champion of the Untouchables. There is not the slightest doubt that if he had worked on the Committee he would have produced a very big scheme. That the Congress did not want him in the Committee and was afraid that he would make big demand on Congress funds for the cause of the Untouchables is clear from the correspondence that passed between him and Pandit Motilal Nehru, the then General Secretary of the Congress. If this conclusion is right, then it shows how empty of sincerity were the words of the Congress, which passed that resolution.

Did the Congress abandon the programme because it was revolutionary? The Resolution was in no sense a revolutionary

---

[3]The fact that the Congress was keen on having Mr Deshpande as the convener shows that they did not like to leave matters in the hands of Swami Shradhanand. The choice of Mr Deshpande also indicates that they did not want anything to be done for the simple reason that Mr Deshpande was an orthodox Brahmin who had taken no interest in the welfare of the Untouchables.

resolution. This will be clear from the note which the Working Committee had appended to the resolution and which the All India Congress Committee had approved. The note said:

'Whilst, therefore, in places, where the prejudice against the Untouchables is still strong, separate schools and separate wells must be maintained out of Congress funds, every effort should be made to draw such children to national schools and to persuade the people to allow the Untouchables to use the common wells.'

Obviously, the Congress was not out for the abolition of Untouchability. It had accepted the policy of separate schools and separate wells. The Resolution did no more than to undertake amelioration of the condition of the Untouchables. And even such a timid and mild programme the Congress was unable to carry through and which it gave up without remorse or shame.

◆

Congressmen never hesitate to impress upon the Untouchables that Mr Gandhi is their saviour. Not only do Congressmen all over India hold out Mr Gandhi as a real saviour but they go forth to persuade the Untouchables to accept the fact that he is their only saviour. When pressed for evidence, they tell the Untouchables that if any one ever took a vow to go on a fast unto death for the sake of the Untouchables, it was Mr Gandhi and none else. Indeed, without any compunction, they tell the Untouchables that whatever political rights the Untouchables have got under the Poona Pact, they are the result of Mr Gandhi's efforts. As an illustration of such propaganda, I refer to what one Rai Bahadur Mehrchand Khanna is reported[4] to have said at a meeting of the Untouchables held at Peshawar on April 12, 1945 under the auspices of the Depressed Classes League:

'Your best friend is Mahatma Gandhi who even resorted to a fast for your sake and brought about the Poona Pact, under which you have been enfranchised and given representation on local bodies and legislatures. Some of you, I know, have been running after Dr Ambedkar, who is just

---

[4]*Free Press Journal*, 14 April 1945.

a creation of the British Imperialists and who uses you to strengthen the hands of the British Government in order that India may be divided and the Britishers continue to retain power. I appeal to you in your interests, to distinguish between self-styled leaders and your real friends.'

If I refer to the statement of Rai Bahadur Mehrchand Khanna, it is not because he is worth taking notice of. For, there cannot be any one guilty of bigger blackguardism in Indian politics than this man. In the course of one year—not in very remote time but in 1944—he successfully played three different roles. He started as Secretary of the Hindu Mahasabha, turned agent of British Imperialism, went abroad to explain India's war effort to the British and American people and is now agent of the Congress in N.VV.F. Province. The opinion of a man like Rai Bahadur Khanna, who, to use Dryden's language, is so various as to be everything by starts, and nothing long, and who in the course of one revolving moon, can be a chemist, fiddler, statesman and buffoon, must be beneath contempt. If I refer to him, it is only because I wish to illustrate what sort of propaganda[5] friends of Mr Gandhi are carrying on in order to beguile the Untouchables.

I do not know how many Untouchables will be found prepared to swallow such a lie. But this much I think has been proved by the Nazis that if a lie is a big lie, too big for the common man's intelligence to scrutinize—and if it is repeated continuously, the lie has all the chances of being accepted as truth and if not accepted as truth has all the chances of growing upon the victims of propaganda and win their acquiescence. It is, therefore, necessary for me to expose the part played by Mr Gandhi in the movement of the Untouchables and to warn the Untouchables against succumbing to this propaganda.

◆

That Mr Gandhi's anti-Untouchability campaign has failed is beyond

---

[5]Another illustration of such propaganda is that carried on by one Parsi gentleman by name Prof. A.R. Wadia. The views of Prof. Wadia have been critically examined and exposed by Mr E.J. Sanjana in a series of articles in the *Rast-Rahabar*—a Gujarati weekly published in Bombay—from 29 October 1944 to 15 April 1945 under the heading of 'Sense and Nonsense in Politics'.

cavil. Even the Congress papers admit it. I give below a few quotations from some of them:

On 17 August 1939, Mr B.K. Gaikwad, a member of the Scheduled Castes in the Bombay Legislative Assembly, asked a question as to how many temples in the Bombay Presidency were thrown open to the Untouchables since 1932 when Mr Gandhi started his Temple-Entry movement. According to the figures given by the Congress Minister, the total number of temples thrown open was 142. Of these, 121 were ownerless temples standing on the wayside which were under the care of nobody in particular and which nobody used as places of worship. Another fact revealed was that not a single temple was thrown open to the Untouchables in Gujarat, the district which is the home of Mr Gandhi.

Writing on 10 March 1940 the *Harijan Bandu*, Mr Gandhi's Gujarati paper, said:

'The Untouchability of the "Harijans" in the matter of entry into schools persists nowhere so much still as in Gujarat.'[6]

The Bombay Chronicle in its issue of 27 August 1940 reproduced an extract from a monthly letter of the Harijan Sevak Sangh. It states:

'Harijans of Godhavi in Ahmedabad District were so persecuted by caste Hindus for sending their children to Local Board School that ultimately 42 Harijan families left that place…and went to the Taluka town of Sanand.'

On 27 August 1943, Mr M.M. Nandgaonkar, a leader of the Untouchables residing in Thana in the Bombay Presidency and ex-Vice President of Thana Municipality, was refused tea in a Hindu hotel. *The Bombay Chronicle*, commenting upon this incident in its issue dated 28 August 1948, said:

'When Gandhiji fasted in 1932, some feverish attempts were made to have some temples and hotels opened to Harijans. Now the actual position is nearly what it used to be before with regard to temple-entry

---

[6]Quoted from Sanjana's 'Sense and Nonsense in Politics'.

and access to hotels. The cleanest Harijan is not admitted to temples and hotels. Yet, many anti-Untouchability workers take a complacent view of these disabilities and patronizingly talk of "uplift first" for Harijans, saying that when Harijans learn to be clean, their civic disabilities will fall off automatically. This is rank nonsense.'

Writing on the proceedings of the All India Scheduled Castes Federation held in Cawnpore in January 1944, *The Bombay Chronicle* in its issue of 4 February 1944 said:

'But, such is the passivity of Hindu society that both caste and Untouchability still thrive. Nay, several Hindu leaders…misguided by the interested propaganda by certain Britishers, still plead that there is some mysterious virtue in caste because Hindu culture has remained today. Else, they argue, caste would not have survived the shocks of centuries… It is most tragic to find that, in spite of all that Gandhiji and other reformers have done, Untouchability still persists to no small extent. It is most rampant in villages. Even in a city like Bombay, a person known to be a sweeper, let alone a scavenger, however clean dressed he may be, is not allowed to enter a caste Hindu restaurant, nay, even an Irani's restaurant for tea.'

The Untouchables have always said that Mr Gandhi's anti-Untouchability campaign has failed. After twenty-five years of labour, hotels have remained closed, wells have remained closed, temples have remained closed, and in very many parts of India—particularly in Gujarat—even schools have remained closed. The extracts produced from the papers form, therefore, a very welcome testimony especially because the papers are Congress papers. As they fully corroborate what the Untouchables have been saying on the point, nothing further need be said on the subject except to ask one question.

Why has Mr Gandhi failed? According to me, there are three reasons which have brought about this failure.

The first reason is that the Hindus to whom he makes his appeal for the removal of Untouchability do not respond. Why is this so? It is a common experience that the words a man uses and the effect they produce are not always commensurate. What he says has its momentum indefinitely multiplied, or reduced to nullity, by the impression that the hearer for good reason, or bad, happens to have formed of the spirit of the speaker. This gives a clue to know why Mr Gandhi's sermons on Untouchability have completely failed to move the Hindus, why people hear his after-prayer sermons for few minutes and then go to the comic opera and why there is nothing more to it. The fault is not entirely of the Hindu public. The fault is of Mr Gandhi himself. Mr Gandhi has built up his reputation of being a Mahatma on his being a harbinger of political freedom and not on his being a spiritual teacher. Whatever may be his intentions, Mr Gandhi is looked upon as an apostle of Swaraj. His anti-Untouchability campaign is looked upon as a fad if not a side-show. That is why the Hindus respond to his political biddings but never to his social or religious preaching. The momentum of his anti-Untouchability campaign must, therefore, remain a nullity. Mr Gandhi is a political shoemaker. He must stick to his political task. He thought he could take up the task of solving the social question. That was a mistake. A politician is not the man for it. That is why the hope held out to the Untouchables that Mr Gandhi's sermons will do the trick has failed.

The second reason is that Mr Gandhi does not wish to antagonize the Hindus even if such antagonism was necessary to carry out his anti-Untouchability programme. A few instances will illustrate Mr Gandhi's mentality.

Most of Mr Gandhi's friends give credit to Mr Gandhi for sincerity and earnestness for the cause of the Untouchables and expect the Untouchables to believe in it on the mere ground that Mr Gandhi is the one man who keeps on constantly preaching to the Hindus the necessity of removing Untouchability. They have lost sight of the old proverb that an ounce of practice is worth a ton of preaching, and have never cared to ask Mr Gandhi to explain why does he not cease to preach to the Hindus the necessity of removing Untouchability and launch a campaign of satyagraha or start a fast. If they would ask for such an explanation, they would know why Mr Gandhi merely contents himself with sermons on Untouchability.

The true reasons why Mr Gandhi will not go beyond sermons

were revealed to the Untouchables for the first time[7] in 1929 when the Untouchables in the Bombay Presidency opened a campaign of satyagraha against the Hindus for establishing their civic rights in the matter of temple-entry and taking water from public wells. They hoped to get the blessings of Mr Gandhi in as much as satyagraha was Mr Gandhi's own weapon to get wrongs redressed. When appealed to for support, Mr Gandhi surprised the Untouchables by issuing a statement condemning their campaign of satyagraha against the Hindus. The argument urged by Mr Gandhi was very ingenious. He stated that satyagraha was to be used only against foreigners; it must not be used against one's own kindred or countrymen and as the Hindus were the kindred and countrymen of the Untouchables by rules of satyagraha, the latter were debarred from using the weapon against the former! What a fall from the sublime to the ridiculous! By this Mr Gandhi made nonsense of satyagraha. Why did Mr Gandhi do this? Only because he did not want to annoy and exasperate the Hindus.

As a second piece of evidence, I would refer to what is known as the Kavitha incident. Kavitha is a village in the Ahmedabad District in Gujarat. In 1935, the Untouchables of the village demanded from the Hindus of the village that their children should be admitted in the common school of the village along with other Hindu children. The Hindus were enraged at this outrage and took their revenge by proclaiming a complete social boycott. The events connected with this boycott were reported by Mr A.V. Thakkar, who went to Kavitha to intercede with the Hindus on behalf of the Untouchables. The story told by him runs as follows:

'The Associated Press announced on the 10th inst. that the caste Hindus of Kavitha agreed to admit Harijan boys to the village school in Kavitha and that matters were amicably settled. This was contradicted on the 13th instant by the Secretary of the Ahmedabad Harijan Sevak Sangh, who said in his statement that the Harijans had undertaken (privately

---

[7]In 1924, in the Satyagraha at Vaikom, the object of which was to get a public road in Travancore open to the Untouchables, Mr Gandhi objected to the Sikhs opening a kitchen for the satyagrahis. The reason given by Mr Gandhi was not stated quite so explicitly.

of course) not to send their children to the school. Such an undertaking was not given voluntarily, but was extorted from them by the Caste Hindus, in this case the Garasias of the village, who had proclaimed a social boycott against poor Harijans—weavers, chamars and others, who number over 100 families. They were deprived of agricultural labour, their animals of grazing in the pasture land and their children of buttermilk. Not only this, but a Harijan leader was compelled to take an oath by Mahadev that he and others would not hereafter even make an effort to reinstate their children in the school. The so-called settlement was brought about in this way.

'But, even after the bogus settlement reported on the 10th and the complete surrender by poor Harijans, the boycott was not lifted up to the 19th and partly up to the 22nd from the weavers, it was lifted somewhat earlier from the head of the chamars, as Garasias themselves could not remove the carcasses of their dead animals, and thus had to come to terms with the Chamars earlier. As if the enormities perpetrated so far were not enough, kerosine was poured into the Harijans' well, once on the 15th instant, and again on the 19th instant. One can imagine what terrorism was thus practised on poor Harijans because they had dared to send their children to sit alongside of the princely[8] Garasia boys.

'I met the leaders of the Garasias on the mornirg of the 22nd. They said they could not tolerate the idea of boys of Dheds and Chamars sitting by the side of their own boys. I met also the District Magistrate of Ahmedabad on the 23rd with a view to finding out if he would do something to ease the situation, but without any result.

'Harijan boys are thus practically banned from the village school with nobody to help them. This has caused despondency among the Harijans to such an extent that they are thinking of migration in a body to some other village.'

This was a report made to Mr Gandhi. What did Mr Gandhi do? The following[9] is the advice Mr Gandhi gave to the Untouchables of Kavitha:

---

[8]*Harijan*, 5 October 1935.
[9]*Harijan*, 5 October 1935.

'There is no help like self-help. God helps those who help themselves. If the Harijans concerned will carry out their reported resolve to wipe the dust of Kavitha off their feet, they will not only be happy themselves but they will pave the way for others who may be similarly treated. If people migrate in search of employment, how much more should they do so in search of self-respect? I hope that well-wishers of Harijans will help these poor families to vacate inhospitable Kavitha.'

Mr Gandhi advised the Untouchables of Kavitha to vacate. But why did he not advise Mr Thakkar to prosecute the Hindus of Kavitha and help the Untouchables to vindicate their rights? Obviously, he would like to uplift the Untouchables if he can, but not by offending the Hindus. What good can such a man do to promote the cause of the Untouchables? All this shows that Mr Gandhi is most anxious to be good to the Hindus. That is why he opposes satyagraha against the Hindus. That is why he opposed the political demands of the Untouchables as he believed that they were aimed against them. He is anxious to be so good to the Hindus that he does not care if he is thereby becoming good for nothing for the Untouchables. That is why Mr Gandhi's whole programme for the removal of Untouchability is just words, words and words, and why there is no action behind it.

The third reason is that Mr Gandhi does not want the Untouchables to organize and be strong. For, he fears that they might thereby become independent of the Hindus and weaken the ranks of Hindus. This is best illustrated by the activities of the Harijan Sevak Sangh. The whole objective of the Sangh is to create a slave mentality among the Untouchables towards their Hindu masters. Examine the Sangh from any angle one may like, and the creation of slave mentality will appear to be its dominant purpose.

The work of the Sangh reminds one of the mythological demoness Putana described in the Bhagvad—a companion to the Mahabharata. Kamsa, the king of Mathura, wanted to kill Krishna, as it was predicted that Kamsa will die at the hands of Krishna. Having come to know of the birth of Krishna, Kamsa asked Putana to undertake the mission to kill Krishna while he was yet a baby. Putana took the form of a beautiful woman and went to Yashoda, the foster mother of Krishna, and having applied liquid poison to her breast pleaded to be employed as a wet nurse for suckling the baby Krishna and thus have the opportunity to kill it. The rest of the story it is unnecessary to pursue. The point of the story is that the real purpose is not always the same as the ostensible purpose and a nurse can be a murdress. The Sangh is to the Untouchables what Putana was to Krishna. The Sangh, under the pretence of service, is out to kill the spirit of independence from among the Untouchables. The Untouchables, in the early stages of their agitation, had taken the support of some well-meaning Hindus and had followed their leadership. By the time of the Round Table Conference, the Untouchables had become completely self-reliant and independent. They were no longer satisfied with charity from the Hindus. They demanded what they said was their right. There is no doubt that it is to kill this spirit of independence among the Untouchables that Mr Gandhi started the Harijan Sevak Sangh. The Harijan Sevak Sangh, by its petty services, has collected a swarm of grateful Untouchables who are employed to preach that Mr Gandhi and the Hindus are the saviours of the Untouchables. Daniel O'Connel, the Irish leader, once said that no man can be grateful at the cost of his honour, no woman can be grateful at the cost of her chastity, and no country can be grateful at the cost of its liberty. The Untouchables are too simple-minded to know that the cost of the service which the Harijan Sevak Sangh offers to render is loss of independence. This is exactly what Mr Gandhi wants.

The worst part of the activities of the Harijan Sevak Sangh is the help rendered to the Untouchable students kept in the hostels maintained by the Sangh. These Untouchable students remind me of Bhishma and Kacha, two prominent characters which figure in the Mahabharata. Bhishma proclaimed with great show that the Pandavas were right and the Kauravas wrong. Yet, when it came to a war between the two, he fought on the side of the Kauravas and against the Pandavas. When asked to justify his conduct, he was not ashamed to say that he fought for the Kauravas because they fed him. Kacha belonged to the community of the Devas who were engaged in a war against the Rakshasas. The spiritual head of the Rakshasas knew a mantra (incantation) by which he could revive a dead Rakshasa. The Devas were losing the battle since their head did not know the mantra and could not revive their dead. The Devas planned to send Kacha to the head of the Rakshasas with instructions somehow to learn the mantra and come back. Kacha in the beginning could not succeed. Ultimately, he entered into an agreement with Devayani, the daughter of the spiritual head of the Rakshasas that if she helped him to acquire the mantra, he would be prepared to marry her. Devayani succeeded in fulfilling her part of the contract. But Kacha refused to perform his part alleging that the interests of his community were more important than his promise to her.

Bhishma and Kacha, in my opinion, are typical of the morally depraved characters who know no other purpose but to serve their own interests for the time being. The Untouchable students in the Harijan hostels are acting the part of both Bhishma and Kacha. During their stay in the hostels, they play the part of Bhishma by singing the praises of Mr Gandhi and the Congress. When they come out of the hostels, they play the part of Kacha and denounce Mr Gandhi and the Congress. I am extremely pained to see this. Nothing worse could happen to the youth of the Untouchables than this moral degeneration. But, this is the greatest disservice which his Harijan Sevak Sangh has done to the Untouchables. It has destroyed their character. It has destroyed their independence. This is what Mr Gandhi wants to happen.

Take a fourth illustration. The Sangh is run by the Caste Hindus. There are some Untouchables who have demanded that the institution should be handed over to the Untouchables and should be run by them. Others have demanded that the Untouchables should have representation on the Governing Board. Mr Gandhi has flatly refused to do either on two very ingenious grounds which no man with the greatest cunning could improve. Mr Gandhi's first argument is that the Harijan Sevak Sangh is an act of penance on the part of the Hindus for the sin of observing Untouchability. It is they who must do the penance. Therefore, the Untouchable can have no place in running the Sangh. Secondly, Mr Gandhi says the money collected by him is given by the Hindus and not by the Untouchables, and as the money is not of the Untouchables, the Untouchables have no right to be on the Governing Body. The refusal of Mr Gandhi may be tolerated, but his argument's are most insulting and a respectable an Untouchable will be forgiven if he refuses to have anything to do with the Sangh. One should have thought that the Harijan Sevak Sangh was a Trust and the Untouchables its beneficiaries. Any trio in law would admit that the beneficiaries have every right to know the aims and objects of the Trust, its funds and whether the objectives are properly carried out or not. The beneficiaries have even the right to have the Trustees removed for breach of trust. On that basis, it would be impossible to deny the claim of the Untouchables for representation on the Managing Board. Evidently, Mr Gandhi does not wish to accept this position. A self-respecting Untouchable who has no desire to cringe and who does not believe in staking the future of the Untouchables on the philanthropy of strangers cannot have any quarrel with Mr Gandhi. He is quite prepared to say that if meanness is a virtue, then Mr Gandhi's logic is superb and Mr Gandhi is welcome to the benefit of it. Only he must not blame the Untouchables if they boycott the Sangh.

These, however, could not be the real reasons for not allowing the Untouchables to run the Sangh. The real reasons are different. In the first place, if the Sangh was handed over to the Untouchables, Mr Gandhi and the Congress will have no means of control over the Untouchables. The Untouchables will cease to be dependent on the Hindus. In the second place, the Untouchables having become independent will cease to be grateful to the Hindus. These consequences will be quite contrary to the aim find object, which have led Mr Gandhi to found the Sangh. He wants to create among the Untouchables what is known among Indian Christians as the mission compound mentality. That is why Mr Gandhi does not wish to hand over the Sangh to the control and management of the Untouchables. Is this consistent with a genuine desire for the emancipation of the Untouchables? Can Mr Gandhi be called a liberator of the Untouchables? Does this not show that Mr Gandhi is more anxious to tighten the tie which binds the Untouchables to the apron strings of the Hindus than to free them from the thraldom of the Hindus?

These are the reasons why Mr Gandhi's anti-Untouchability campaign has failed.

To sum up, can it be said that Mr Gandhi has recovered the title deeds to humanity which the Untouchables have lost? Obviously not. Those title deeds are still with the Hindus. He has done nothing to recover them. Nor has he helped the Untouchables to recover them.

On the contrary, Mr Gandhi has put every obstacle in their way. The Untouchables feel that their title deeds to humanity—'which means their emancipation from their thraldom of the Hindus'—can be secured by them by political power, and by nothing else. Mr Gandhi, on the other hand, believes that his preaching and the charity and zeal of the Hindus are sufficient panacea for all the ills of the Untouchables. Can the Untouchables rely on a sustained flow of Hindu charity and Hindu zeal? Charity, which has its fury, is worth talking about. Zeal, which has its vengeance, is worth building upon. But, which friend of the Untouchables can ask them to depend upon the miserable measure of Hindu charity and the Hindu zeal? Untouchability has been in existence for the last two thousand years, during which period the Hindus have day in and day out sucked the very blood of the Untouchables and have mutilated them and trodden upon them in every way. During these two thousand years, what amount of charity have the Hindus done to the Untouchables? Only 8 lakh and that too when Mr Gandhi personally went round the country with a begging bowl! Having put his programme to test, Mr Gandhi might have shown his willingness to concede the Untouchables' demand for political power as their only means of salvation. Indeed, so obvious is the justice of this demand that a man with no more than common sense could have understood that executive power in the hands of the Untouchables could do more in a year than the whole order of preaching friars could be relied upon to do in a century. But, the very idea of political power to the Untouchables is hateful to Mr Gandhi. Why should not the Untouchables say 'Beware of Mr Gandhi' when they know that he would not allow the use of political processes for the emancipation of the Untouchables, though Mr Gandhi is fully alive to the fact that the social processes on which he laid so much store for helping them have completely failed.

In this connection one is reminded of the attitude of President Lincoln in the American Civil War towards the two questions of union and slavery. This attitude is well-revealed by the correspondence[10] that passed in 1862 between Mr Horace Greeleyand President Lincoln. In, a letter addressed to the President entitled 'The Prayer of Twenty Millions', Mr Greeley said:

> 'On the face of this wide earth, Mr President, there is not one disinterested, determined, intelligent champion of the Union cause who does not feel that all attempts to put down the rebellion and at the same time uphold its inciting cause (namely slavery) are preposterous and futile.'

To this, President Lincoln's reply was:

> 'If there be those who would not save the Union unless they could at the same time save slavery, I do not agree with them.
>
> 'If there be those who would not save the Union unless they could at the same time destroy slavery, I do not agree with them.
>
> 'My paramount object is to save the Union, and not either to save or to destroy slavery.
>
> 'If I could save the Union without freeing any slave, I would do it. If I could save it by freeing all the slaves, I would do it—and if I could do it by freeing some and leaving others alone, I would also do that.'

These were the views of President Lincoln about Negro slavery and its relation to the question of Union. They certainly throw a very different light on one who is reputed to be the liberator of the Negroes. As a matter of fact, he did not believe in the emancipation of the Negroes as a categorical imperative. Obviously, the author of the famous Gettysberg oration about 'government of the people, by the people and for the people' would not have minded if his statement had taken the shape of government of the black people by the white people and for the white people provided there was union. Mr Gandhi's attitude towards Swaraj and the Untouchables resembles very much the attitude of President Lincoln towards the two questions of the Negroes and the Union. Mr Gandhi wants Swaraj as did President Lincoln want Union. But, he does not want Swaraj at the cost of disrupting the

---

[10] *The Collected Works of Abraham Lincoln*, Vol. XI, pp xii–xiii.

structure of Hinduism which is what political emancipation of the Untouchables means as President Lincoln did not want to free the slaves if it was not necessary to do so for the sake of the Union. There is, of course, this difference between Mr Gandhi and President Lincoln. President Lincoln was prepared to emancipate the Negro slaves if it was necessary to preserve the Union. Mr Gandhi's attitude is in marked contrast. He is not prepared for the political emancipation of the Untouchables even if it was essential for winning Swaraj. Mr Gandhi's attitude is: let Swaraj perish if the cost of it is the political freedom of the Untouchables.

Some Untouchables are probably under the impression that all this is a matter of the dead past and that Mr Gandhi, having accepted the Poona Pact, cannot now oppose the political demands of the Untouchables, for, as a party to the Poona Pact, Mr Gandhi must be assumed to have conceded that the Untouchables are a separate element in the national life of India. This is a complete misunderstanding. For, there are grounds to believe that the Poona Pact has made no difference on Mr Gandhi's view and he still maintains the same attitude to the Untouchables' claim for political safeguards as he did at the Round Table Conference and before the Poona Pact. These grounds have their foundation in the fact that when His Majesty's government declared in 1940 that the Untouchables are a separate element in the National life of India and that their consent to the Constitution is necessary, Mr Gandhi came out with a protest. When the Viceroy Lord Linlithgow referred to the Untouchables as a separate element and said that their consent to the Constitution was necessary, Mr Gandhi said:[11]

> 'I felt that the putting up by the Viceroy, and then the Secretary of State, of want of agreement by the Congress with the Princes, the Muslim League and even the Scheduled Classes as a barrier to the British recognition of India's right to freedom was more than unjust to the Congress and the people.
>
> 'The introduction of the Scheduled Classes in the controversy has made the unreality of the case of the British Government doubly unreal.

---

[11] *Harijan*, 13 October 1940.

They know that these are the special care of the Congress, and that the Congress is infinitely more capable of guarding their interests than the British Government. Moreover, the Scheduled Classes are divided into as many castes as the caste Hindu Society. No single Scheduled Classes member could possibly and truthfully represent the innumerable castes.'

The argument advanced by Mr Gandhi is puerile. It may be pointed out that in the hurry he made in stating his opposition to the position assigned to the Scheduled Castes by the Viceroy, Mr Gandhi forgot that if the Scheduled Castes are divided into many castes and no single caste could represent them all, the case of the Muslims and the Indian Christians is in no way different. The Muslims are divided into three groups: (1) Sunnis, (2) Shias, and (3) Momins, each of which consists of many castes who inter-dine but do not inter-marry. Indian Christians are divided into: (1) Catholics, and (2) Protestants. Catholics are again sub-divided into: (1) Caste Christians, and (2) Non-caste Christians. Both Catholics and Protestants have castes which do not inter-marry and Caste Christians and non-caste Christians do not even inter-dine or go to the same church. This shows that Mr Gandhi, notwithstanding his being a party to the Poona Pact, is determined not to allow the Scheduled Castes being given the status of a separate element and that he is prepared to adopt any argument, however desperate, to justify his attitude of opposition.

In short, Mr Gandhi is still on the war path so far as the Untouchables are concerned. He may start the trouble over again. The time to trust him has not arrived. The Untouchables must still hold that the best way to safeguard themselves is to say: 'Beware of Mr Gandhi.'

Chapter 2

POLITICAL SAFEGUARDS FOR
THE UNTOUCHABLES

IN THE GOVERNMENT of India Act of 1919, there was a provision which had imposed an obligation on His Majesty's government to appoint at the end of ten years a Royal Commission to investigate into the working of the Constitution and report upon, such changes as may be found necessary. Accordingly, in 1928 a Royal Commission was appointed under the Chairmanship of Sir John Simon. Indians expected that the Commission would be mixed in its personnel. But Lord Birkenhead, who was then the Secretary of State for India, was opposed to the inclusion of Indians and insisted on making it a purely Parliamentary Commission. At this, the Congress and the Liberals took great offence and treated it as an insult. They boycotted the Commission and carried on a great agitation against it. To assuage this feeling of opposition, it was announced, by His Majesty's government, that after the work of the Commission was completed representative Indians would be assembled for a discussion before the new Constitution for India is settled. In accordance with this announcement, representative Indians were called to London at a Round Table Conference with the Representatives of Parliament and of His Majesty's government.

On the 12 November 1930, His late Majesty King George V formally inaugurated the Indian Round Table Conference. From the point of view of Indians, the Round Table Conference was an event of great significance. Its significance lay in the recognition by His Majesty's government of the right of Indians to be consulted in the matter of framing a constitution for India. For the Untouchables, it was a landmark in their history. For, the Untouchables were for the first time allowed to be represented separately by two delegates who happened to be myself and Dewan Bahadur R. Srinivasan. This meant that the Untouchables were regarded not merely a separate element from the Hindus but also of such importance as to have the right to be consulted in the framing of the Constitution for India.

The work of the Conference was distributed among nine committees. One of these committees was called the Minorities Committee to which was assigned the most difficult work of finding a solution of the Communal question. Anticipating that this Committee was the most important committee, the Prime Minister, the late Mr Ramsay MacDonald, himself assumed its chairmanship. The proceedings of the Minorities Committee are of the greatest importance to the Untouchables. For, much of what happened between the Congress and the Untouchables and which has led to bitterness between them will be found in the proceedings of that Committee.

When the Round Table Conference met, the political demands of communities other than the Untouchables were quite well-known. Indeed, the Constitution of 1919 had recognized them as statutory minorities and provisions relating to their safety and security were embodied in it. In their case, the question was of expanding those provisions or altering their shape. With regard to the Depressed Classes, the position was different. The Montagu–Chelmsford Report which preceded the Constitution of 1919 had said in quite unmistakable terms that provision must be made in the Constitution for their protection. But unfortunately when the details of the Constitution were framed, the Government of India found it difficult to devise any provisions for their protection except to give them token representation in the legislatures by nomination. The first thing that was required to be done was to formulate the safeguards deemed necessary by the Untouchables for their protection against the tyranny and oppression of the Hindus. This I did by submitting a Memorandum to the Minorities Committee of the Round Table Conference. To give an idea of the safeguards that were formulated by me, I reproduce below the text of the Memorandum:

A Scheme of Political Safeguards for the Protection of the Depressed Classes in the Future Constitution of a self-governing India, submitted to the Indian Round Table Conference.

The following are the terms and conditions on which the Depressed

Classes will consent to place themselves under a majority rule in a self-governing India.

Condition No. I

Equal Citizenship

The Depressed Classes cannot consent to subject themselves to majority rule in their present state of hereditary bondsmen. Before majority rule is established, their emancipation from the system of Untouchability must be an accomplished fact. It must not be left to the will of the majority. The Depressed Classes must be made free citizens entitled to all the rights of citizenship in common with other citizens of the State.

(A) To secure the abolition of Untouchability and to create the equality of citizenship, it is proposed that the following fundamental right shall be made part of the Constitution of India.

Fundamental Right

'All subjects of the State in India are equal before the law and possess equal civic rights. Any existing enactment,' regulation, order, custom or interpretation of law by which any penalty, 'disadvantage, disability is imposed upon or any discrimination is made against any subject of the State on account of Untouchability shall, as from the day on which this Constitution comes into operation, cease to have any effect in India.'

(B) To abolish the immunities and exemptions now enjoyed by executive officers by virtue of Sections 110 and 111 of the Government of India Act 1919 and their liability for executive action be made co-extensive with what it is in the case of a European British Subject.

Condition No. II

Free Enjoyment of Equal Rights

It is no use for the Depressed Classes to have a declaration of equal rights. There can be no doubt that the Depressed Classes will have to face the whole force of orthodox society if they try to exercise the equal rights of citizenship. The Depressed Classes, therefore, feel that if these declarations of rights are not to be mere pious pronouncements, but are to be realities of everyday life, then they should be protected by adequate pains and penalties from interference in the enjoyment of these declared rights.

(A) The Depressed Classes therefore propose that the following section should be added, to Part XI of the Government of India Act 1919, dealing with Offers, Procedure and Penalties:

(i) Offence of infringement of Citizenship.

'Whoever denies to any person except for reasons by law applicable to persons of all classes and regardless of any previous condition of Untouchability the full enjoyment of any of the accomodations, advantages, facilities, privileges of inns, educational institutions, roads, paths, streets, tanks, wells and other watering places, of public conveyances on land, air or water, theatres or other places of *public amusement, resort or convenience whether they are dedicated to or maintained or licenced for the use of the public shall be punished with imprisonment of either description for a term which may extend to five years and shall also be liable to fine.'*

(B) Obstruction by orthodox individuals is not the only menace to the Depressed Classes in the way of peaceful enjoyment of their rights. The commonest form of obstruction is the social boycott. It is the most formidable weapon in the hands of the orthodox classes with which they beat down any attempt on the part of the Depressed Classes to undertake any activity if it happens to be unpalatable to them. The way it works and the occasions on which it is brought into operation are well-described in the Report of the Committee appointed by the Government of Bombay in 1928 'to enquire into the educational, economic and social condition of the Depressed Classes (Untouchables) and of the Aboriginal Tribes in the Presidency and to recommend measures for their uplift.' The following is an extract from the same:

Depressed Classes and Social Boycott

'Although we have recommended various remedies to secure to the Depressed Classes their rights to all public utilities, we fear that there will be difficulties in the way of their exercising them for a long time to come. The first difficulty is the fear of open violence against them by the orthodox classes. It must be noted that the Depressed Classes form a small minority in every village, opposed to which is a great majority of the orthodox who are bent on protecting their interests and dignity from any supposed invasion by the Depressed Classes at any cost. The danger of prosecution by the Police has put a limitation upon the use of violence by the orthodox classes and consequently such cases are rare.

'The second difficulty arises from the economic position in which the Depressed Classes are found today. The Depressed Classes have no economic independence in most parts of the Presidency. Some cultivate the lands of the orthodox classes as their tenants at will. Others live on their earnings as farm labourers employed by the orthodox classes and the rest subsist on the food or grain given to them by the orthodox classes in lieu of service rendered to them as village servants. We have heard of numerous instances where the orthodox classes have used their economic power as a weapon against those Depressed Classes in their villages, when the latter have dared to exercise their rights, and have evicted them from their land, and stopped their employment and discontinued their remuneration as village servants. This boycott is often planned on such an extensive scale as to include the prevention of the Depressed Classes from using the commonly used paths and the stoppage of sale of the necessaries of life by the village Bania. According to the evidence, sometimes small causes suffice for the proclamation of a social boycott against the Depressed Classes. Frequently, it follows on the exercise by the Depressed Classes of their right to the use of the common well, but cases have been by no means rare where a stringent boycott has been proclaimed simply because a Depressed Class man has put on the sacred thread, has bought a piece of land, has put on good clothes or ornaments, or has carried a marriage procession with the bridegroom on the horse through the public street.

'We do not know of any weapon more effective than this social boycott which could have been invented for the suppression of the Depressed Classes. The method of open violence pales away before it, for it has the most far-reaching and deadening effects. It is more dangerous because it passes as a lawful method consistent with the theory of freedom of contact. We agree that this tyranny of the majority must be put down with a firm hand, if we are to guarantee the Depressed Classes the freedom of speech and action necessary for their uplift.'

In the opinion of the Depressed Classes, the only way to overcome this kind of menace to their rights and liberties is to make social boycott an offence punishable by law. They are therefore bound to insist that the following sections should be added to those included in Part XI, of the Government of India Act 1919, dealing with Offences, Procedure and Penalties.

I. Offence of Boycott Defined

(i) A person shall be deemed to boycott another who—

(a) *refuses to let or use or occupy any house or land, or to deal with, work for hire, or do business with another person, or to render to him or receive from him any service, or refuses to do any of the said things on the terms on which such things should commonly be done in the ordinary course of business, or*

(b) *abstains from such social, professional or business relations as he would, having regard to such existing customs in the community which are not inconsistent with any fundamental right or other rights of citizenship declared in the Constitution ordinarily maintain with such person, or*

(c) *in any way injures, annoys or interferes with such other person in the exercise of his lawful rights.*

II. Punishment for Boycotting

Whoever, in consequence of any person having done any act which he was legally entitled to do or of his having omitted to do any act which he was legally entitled to omit to do, or with intent to cause any person to do any act which he is not legally bound to do or to omit to do any act which he is legally entitled to do, or with intent to cause, harm to such person in body, mind, reputation or property, or in his business or means of living, boycotts such person or any person in whom such person is interested, shall be punished with imprisonment of either description which may extend to seven years or with fine or with both.

Provided that no offence shall be deemed to have been committed under this Section, if the Court is satisfied that the accused person has not acted at the instigation of or in collusion with any other person or in pursuance of any conspiracy or of any agreement or combination to boycott.

III. Punishment for Instigating or Promoting a Boycott

Whoever—

(a) *publicly makes or publishes or circulates a proposal for, or*
(b) *makes, publishes or circulates any statement, rumour or report with intent to, or which he has reason to believe to be likely to cause or*
(c) *in any other way instigates or promotes the boycotting of any person or class of persons, shall be punished with imprisonment which may extend to five years, or with fine or with both.*

Explanation: An offence under this section shall be deemed to have been committed although the person affected or likely to be affected by any action of the nature referred to herein is not designated by name or class but only by his acting or abstaining from acting in some specified manner.

IV. Punishment for Threatening a Boycott

Whoever, in consequence of any person having done any act which he was legally entitled to do or of his having omitted to do any act which he was legally entitled to omit to do, or with intent to cause any person to do any act which he is not legally bound to do, or to omit to do any act which he is legally entitled to do, threatens to cause such person or any person in whom such person is interested, to be boycotted shall be punished with imprisonment, of either description for a term which may extend to five years or with fine or with both.

Exception—It is not boycott

(i) *to do any act in furtherance of a bona fide labour dispute,*
(ii) *to do any act in the ordinary course of business competition.*

N.B.—All these offences shall be deemed to be cognizable offences.

Condition No. III

Protection Against Discrimination

The Depressed Classes entertain grave fears of discrimination either by legislation or by executive order being made in the future. They cannot, therefore, consent to subject themselves to majority rule unless it is rendered impossible in law for the legislature or the executive to make any invidious discrimination against the Depressed Classes.

It is, therefore, proposed that the following Statutory provision be made in the constitutional law of India:

'It shall not be competent for any Legislature or Executive in India to pass a law or issue an order, rule or regulation so as to violate the rights of the Subjects of the State, regardless of any previous condition of Untouchability, in all territories subject to the jurisdiction of the dominion of India,

(1) *to make and enforce contracts, to sue, be parties, and give evidence, to inherit, purchase, lease, sell, hold and convey real and personal property,*

(2) *to be eligible for entry into the civil and military employ and to all educational institutions except for such conditions and limitations as may be necessary to provide for the due and adequate representation of all classes of the subjects of the State,*

(3) *to be entitled to the full and equal enjoyment of the accommodations, advantages, facilities, educational institutions, privileges of inns, rivers, streams, wells, tanks, roads, paths, streets, public conveyances on land, air and water, theatres, and other places of public resort or amusement except for such conditions and limitations applicable alike to all subjects of every race, class, caste, colour or creed,*

(4) *to be deemed fit for and capable of sharing without distinction the benefits of any religious or charitable trust dedicated to or created, maintained or licenced for the general public or for persons of the same faith and religion,*

(5) *to claim full and equal benefit of all laws and proceedings for the security of person and property as is enjoyed by other subjects regardless of any previous condition of Untouchability and be subject to like punishment pains and penalties and to none other.*

Condition No. IV

Adequate Representation in the Legislatures

The Depressed Classes must be given sufficient political power to influence legislative and executive action for the purpose of securing their welfare. *In view of this they demand that the following provisions shall be made in the electoral law so as to give them:*

(1) *Right to adequate representation in the Legislatures of the Country, Provincial and Central.*

(2) *Right to elect their own men as their representatives,*
    (a) *by adult suffrage, and*
    (b) *by separate electorates for the first ten years and thereafter by joint electorates and reserved seats, it being understood that joint electorates shall not be forced upon the Depressed Classes against their will unless such joint electorates are accompanied by adult suffrage.*

N.B.—Adequate Representation for the Depressed Classes cannot be defined in quantitative terms until the extent of representation allowed to other communities is known. But it must be understood that the Depressed Classes will not consent to the representation of any other community being settled on better terms than those allowed to them. They will not agree to being placed at a disadvantage in this matter. In any case the Depressed Classes of Bombay and Madras must have weightage over their population ratio of representation irrespective of the extent of representation allowed to other minorities in the Provinces.

Condition No. V

Adequate Representation in the Services

The Depressed Classes have suffered enormously at the hands of the high caste officers who have monopolized the Public Services by abusing the law or by misusing the discretion vested in them in administering it to the prejudice of the Depressed Classes and to the advantage of the Caste Hindus without any regard to justice, equity or good conscience. This mischief can only be avoided by destroying the monopoly of Caste

Hindus in the Public Services and by regulating the recruitment to them in such a manner that all communities including the Depressed will have an adequate share in them. For this purpose, the Depressed Classes have to make the following proposals for statutory enactment as part of the constitutional law:

(1) *There shall be established in India and in each Province in India a Public Services Commission to undertake the recruitment and control of the Public Services.*

(2) *No member of the Public Service Commission shall be removed except by a resolution passed by the Legislature nor shall he be appointed to any office under the Crown after his retirement.*

(3) *It shall be the duty of the Public Service Commission, subject to the tests of efficiency as may be prescribed*

(a) *to recruit the Services in such a manner as will secure due and adequate representation of all communities, and*

(b) *to regulate from time to time priority in employment in accordance with the existing extent of the representation of the various communities in any particular service concerned.*

Condition No. VI

Redress Against Prejudicial Action or Neglect of Interests

In view of the fact that the Majority Rule of the future will be the rule of the orthodox, the Depressed Classes fear that such a Majority Rule will not be sympathetic to them and that the probability of prejudice to their interests and neglect of their vital needs cannot be overlooked. It must be provided against particularly because, however adequately represented, the Depressed Classes will be in a minority in all legislatures. The Depressed Classes think it very necessary that they should have the means of redress given to them in the Constitution. *It is, therefore, proposed that the following provision should be made in the Constitution of India:*

(1) *In and for each Province and in and for India it shall be the duty and obligation of the Legislature and the Executive or any other Authority established by law to make adequate provision for the*

education, sanitation, recruitment in Public Services and other matters of social and political advancement of the Depressed Classes and to do nothing that will prejudicially affect them.

(2) *Where in any Province, or in India, the provisions of this section are violated, an appeal shall lie to the Governor-General in Council from any act or decision of any Provincial Authority and to the Secretary of State from any act or decision of a Central Authority affecting the matter.*

(3) *In every such case where it appears to the Governor-General in Council or to the Secretary of State that the Provincial Authority or Central Authority does not take steps requisite for the due execution of the provisions of this Section, then and in every such case, and as far only as the circumstances of each case require, the Governor-General in Council or the Secretary of State acting as an appellate authority may prescribe, for such period as they may deem fit, take remedial measures for the due execution of the provisions of this Section and of any of its decisions under this Section and which shall be binding upon the authority appealed against.'*

Condition No. VII

Special Departmental Care

The helpless, hapless and sapless condition of the Depressed Classes must be entirely attributed to the dogged and determined opposition of the whole mass of the orthodox population which will not allow the Depressed Classes to have equality of status or equality of treatment. It is not enough to say of their economic condition that they are poverty-stricken or that they are a class of landless labourers, although both these statements are statements of fact. It has to be noted that the poverty of the Depressed Classes is largely due to the social prejudices in consequence of which many an occupation for earning a living is closed to them. This is a fact which differentiates the position of the Depressed Classes from that of the ordinary caste labourer and is often a source of trouble between the two. It has also to be borne in mind that the forms of tyranny and oppression practised against the Depressed Classes are very various and the capacity of the Depressed Classes to protect themselves is extremely limited. The facts, which obtain in this connection and which are of common occurrence throughout India, are well-described in the Abstracts of Proceedings of the Board of Revenue of the Government of Madras dated 5 November 1892, No. 723, from which the following is an extract:

'There are forms of oppression only hitherto hinted at which must be at least cursorily mentioned. To punish disobedience of Pariahs, their masters—

(a) Bring false cases in the village court or in the criminal courts.
(b) Obtain, on application, from government waste lands lying all round the paracheri, so as to impound the Pariahs' cattle or obstruct the way to their temple.
(c) Have mirasi names fraudulently entered in the government account against the paracheri.
(d) Pull down the huts and destroy the growth in the backyards.
(e) Deny occupancy right in immemorial sub-tenancies.
(f) Forcibly cut the Pariahs' crops, and on being resisted, charge them with theft and rioting.
(g) Under misrepresentations, get them to execute documents by which they are afterwards ruined.
(h) Cut off the flow of water from their fields.
(i) Without legal notice, have the property of sub-tenants attached for the landlords' arrears of revenue.

'It will be said there are civil and criminal courts for the redress of any of these injuries. There are the courts indeed; but India does not breed village Hampdens. One must have courage to go to the courts; money to employ legal knowledge and meet legal expenses; and means to live during the case and the appeals. Further, most cases depend upon the decision of the first court; and these courts are presided over by officials who are sometimes corrupt and who generally, for other reasons, sympathize with the wealthy and landed classes to which they belong.

'The influence of these classes with the official world can hardly be exaggerated. It is extreme with natives and great even with Europeans. Every office, from the highest to the lowest, is stocked with their representatives, and there is no proposal affecting their interests but they can bring a score of influence to bear upon it in its course from inception to execution.'

There can be no doubt that in view of these circumstances the uplift of the Depressed Classes will remain a pious hope unless the task is placed in the forefront of all governmental activities and unless equalization of opportunities is realized in practice by a definite policy and determined effort on the part of government. *To secure this end, the proposal of the Depressed Classes is that the constitutional law should impose upon the Government of India a statutory obligation to maintain at all times a department to deal with their problems by the addition of a section in the Government of India Act to the following effect:*

(1) *Simultaneously with the introduction of this Constitution and as part thereof there shall be created in the Government of India a Department to be incharge of a Minister for the purpose of watching the interests of the Depressed Classes and promoting their welfare.*

(2) *The Minister shall hold office so long as he retains the confidence of the Central Legislature.*

(3) *It shall be the duty of the Minister in the exercise of any powers and duties conferred upon him or transferred to him by law, to take all such steps as may be desirable to secure the preparation, effective carrying out and coordination of measures preventative of acts of social injustice, tyranny or oppression against the Depressed Classes and conducive to their welfare through out India.*

(4) *It shall be lawful for the Governor-General—*

    (a) *to transfer to the Minister all or any powers or duties in respect of the welfare of the Depressed Classes arising from any enactment relating to education, sanitation, etc.*

    (b) *to appoint Depressed Classes welfare bureaus in each province to work under the authority of and in cooperation with the Minister.'*

Condition No. VIII

Depressed Classes and the Cabinet

Just as it is necessary that the Depressed Classes should have the power to influence governmental action by seats in the Legislature so also it is desirable that the Depressed Classes should have the opportunity to frame the general policy of the government. This they can do only if they can find a seat in the cabinet. The Depressed Classes, therefore, claim that in common with other minorities, their moral rights to be represented in the cabinet should be recognized. With this purpose in view, *the Depressed Classes propose:*

> *that in the Instrument of Instructions an obligation shall be placed upon the Governor and the Governor-General to endeavour to secure the representation of the Depressed Classes in his cabinet.*

◆

Before the first session of the Round Table Conference was concluded, the reports of both the Committees were placed before the Conference and were passed by the Conference. It will be noticed that although agreement on details was lacking it was unanimously accepted that the Untouchables were entitled to recognition as a separate entity for political and constitutional purposes.

The only party in the country whose attitude to this decision of the Round Table Conference was not known when the First Session of the Round Table Conference was closed, was the Congress. This was because the Congress had boycotted the Round Table Conference and was busy in carrying on civil disobedience against the government. By the time the Second Session of the Round Table Conference became due, a compromise between His Majesty's government and the Congress was reached, as a result of which the Congress agreed to participate in it and make its contribution to the solution of the many problems confronting the Conference. Everybody, who had witnessed the good temper, happy relationship and the spirit of give and take shown by the delegates at the first session of the Round Table Conference, hoped that the progress made would be maintained from session to session.

Indeed the rate of progress in forging an agreement was expected to be much more rapid as a result of the advent of the Congress. In fact, friends of Congress were alleging that if the session did not produce an agreement it was because of the absence of the Congress.

Everybody was, therefore, looking forward to the Congress to lead the Conference to success. Unfortunately, the Congress chose Mr Gandhi as its representative. A worse person could not have been chosen to guide India's destiny. As a unifying force, he was a failure. Mr Gandhi presents himself as a man full of humility. But his behaviour at the Round Table Conference showed that in the flush of victory Mr Gandhi can be very petty-minded. As a result of his successful compromise with the government just before he came, Mr Gandhi treated the whole non-Congress delegation with contempt. He insulted them whenever an occasion furnished him with an excuse by openly telling them that they were nobodies and that he alone, as the delegate of the Congress, represented the country. Instead of unifying the Indian delegation, Mr Gandhi widened the breach. From the point of view of knowledge, Mr Gandhi proved himself to be a very ill-equipped person. On the many constitutional and communal questions with which the Conference was confronted, Mr Gandhi had many platitudes to utter but no views or suggestions of a constructive character to offer. He presented a curious complex of a man who in, some cases would threaten to resist in every possible way any compromise on what he regarded as a principle though others regarded it as a pure prejudice but in other cases would not mind making the worst compromises on issues which appeared to others as matters of fundamental principle on which no compromise should be made.

Mr Gandhi's attitude to the demands of the Untouchables at the second session of the Round Table Conference furnishes the best illustration of this rather queer trait in his character. When the delegates assembled for the second session of the Round Table Conference, the Federal Structure Committee met first. In the very first speech which he made in the Federal Structure Committee on 15 September 1931, Mr Gandhi referred to the question of the Untouchables. Mr Gandhi said:

'The Congress has, from its very commencement, taken up the cause of the so-called "Untouchables". There was a time when the Congress had at every annual session as its adjunct the Social Conference, to which the late Ranade dedicated his energies, among his many other activities. Headed by him you will find, in the programme of the Social Conference, reform in connection with the "Untouchables" taking a prominent place. But, in 1920, the Congress took a large step and brought in the question of the removal of Untouchability as a plank on the political platform, making it an important item of the political programme. Just as the Congress considered the Hindu–Muslim unity—thereby meaning unity amongst all the classes—to be indispensable for the attainment of Swaraj, so also did the Congress consider the removal of the curse of Untouchability as an indispensable condition for the attainment of full freedom. The position the Congress took up in 1920 remains the same today; and so you will see the Congress has attempted from its very beginning to be what it described itself to be, namely, national in every sense of the term.'

Those, who were friends of Mr Gandhi, could not understand Mr Gandhi's attitude to the demands of the Untouchables. To give recognition to the Muslims and the Sikhs and to refuse it to the Untouchables came to them as a surprise and a puzzle. Whenever they asked for an explanation, Mr Gandhi did nothing except to get angry. Mr Gandhi himself could not give a logical and consistent defence of his opposition to the Untouchables. Inside the Round Table Conference his defence was that the Hindus had seriously taken up the cause of the Untouchables and that, therefore, there was no reason to give them political safeguards. Outside the Round Table Conference, he gave totally different reasons. In a speech in defence of his position Mr Gandhi said:

'Muslims and Sikhs are all well-organized. The "Untouchables" are not. There is very little political consciousness among them and they are so horribly treated that I want to save them against themselves. If they had separate electorates, their lives would be miserable in villages which are the strongholds of Hindu orthodoxy. It is the superior class of Hindus who have to do penance for having neglected the "Untouchables" for ages. That penance can be done by active social reform and by making the lot of the "Untouchables" more bearable by acts of service, but not by asking for separate electorates for them. By giving them separate electorates, you will throw the apple of discord between the "Untouchables" and the orthodox. You must understand I can tolerate the proposal for special representation of the Musalmans and the Sikhs only as a necessary evil. It would be a positive danger for the "Untouchables". I am certain that the question of separate electorates for the "Untouchables" is a modern manufacture of government. The only thing needed is to put them on the voters' list, and provide for fundamental rights for them in the Constitution. In cases they are unjustly treated and their representative is deliberately excluded they would have the right to special election tribunal which would give them complete protection. It should be open to these tribunals to order the unseating of an elected candidate and the election of the excluded men.

'Separate electorates to the "Untouchables" will ensure them bondage in perpetuity. The Musalmans will never cease to be Musalmans by having separate electorates. Do you want the "Untouchables" to remain "Untouchables" forever? Well, the separate electorates would perpetuate the stigma. What is needed is destruction of Untouchability, and when you have done it, the bar-sinister which has been imposed by an insolent "superior" class upon an "inferior" class will be destroyed. When you have destroyed the bar-sinister, to whom will you give the separate electorates? Look at the history of Europe. Have you got separate electorates for the working classes or women? With adult franchise, you give the "Untouchables" complete security. Even the orthodox would have to approach them for votes.

'Now then you ask, does Dr Ambedkar, their representative, insist on separate electorates for them? I have the highest regard for Dr Ambedkar. He has every right to be bitter. That he does not break our heads is an act of self-restraint on his part. He is today so much saturated with suspicion that he cannot see anything else. He sees in every Hindu a determined opponent of the "Untouchables" and it is quite natural. The same thing happened to me in my early days in South Africa, where I was bounded out by Europeans wherever I went. It is quite natural for him to vent his wrath. But the separate electorates that he seeks will not give him social reform. He may himself mount to power and position but nothing good will accrue to the '"Untouchables".' I can say all this with authority, having lived with the "Untouchables" and having shared their joys and sorrows all these years.'

Mr Gandhi at the Round Table Conference was not satisfied with mere propaganda. When he found that the propaganda was not succeeding as well as he expected, he resorted to intrigue. When Mr Gandhi heard that at the suggestion of the Prime Minister the minorities were about to produce a settlement and that this settlement would have the effect of the Untouchables getting the support of the other minorities and particularly of the Muslims, Mr Gandhi felt considerably disturbed. He devised a scheme to isolate the Untouchables. For this, Mr Gandhi planned to buy out the Musalmams by giving to the Musalmans their fourteen demands, which Mr Gandhi was not in the beginning prepared to agree. When he found the Musalmans were lending their support to the Untouchables, Mr Gandhi agreed to them their fourteen points on condition that they withdrew their support from the Untouchables.

Having been disgusted with the Round Table Conference where there were critics but no devotees, Mr Gandhi was the first to return to India. On account of a statement which he is alleged to have made in an interview he gave to a newspaper correspondent in Rome wherein he threatened to revive his campaign of civil disobedience, Mr Gandhi on his arrival was arrested and put in jail. Though in jail, not Swaraj but the Untouchables were on his brain. He feared that, notwithstanding his threat to resist it with his life, the Prime Minister as a sole arbitrator might accept the claims made on behalf of the Untouchables at the Round Table Conference. Long before any decision was given by the Prime Minister, Mr Gandhi on 11 March 1932 addressed from jail a letter to Sir Samuel Hoare, the then Secretary of State for India, reminding him of his opposition to the claim of the Untouchables. The following is the text of that letter:

'Dear Sir Samuel,

You will perhaps recollect that at the end of my speech at the Round Table Conference when the Minorities' claim was presented, I had said that I should resist with my life the grant of separate electorates to the Depressed Classes. This was not said in the heat of the moment nor by way of rhetoric. It was meant to be a serious statement. In pursuance of that statement, I had hoped on my return to India to mobilize public opinion against separate electorates, at any rate, for the Depressed Classes. But it was not to be.

'From the newspapers I am permitted to read, I observe that any moment His Majesty's government may declare their decision. At first, I had thought, if the decision was found to create separate electorates for the Depressed Classes, I should take such steps as I might then consider necessary to give effect to my vow. But I feel it would be unfair to the British Government for me to act without giving previous notice. Naturally, they could not attach the significance I give to my statement.

'I need hardly reiterate all the objections I have to the creation of separate electorates for the Depressed Classes. I feel as if I was one of them. Their case stands on a wholly different footing from that of others. I am not against their representation in the legislatures. I should favour everyone of their adults, male and female, being registered as voters irrespective of education or property qualification, even though the franchise test may be stricter for others. But I hold that separate electorate is harmful for them and for Hinduism, whatever it may be from the purely political standpoint. To appreciate the harm that separate electorate would do them, one has to know how they are distributed amongst the so-called Caste Hindus and how dependent they are on the latter. So far as Hinduism is concerned, separate electorates would simply vivisect and disrupt it.

'For me, the question of these classes is predominantly moral and religious. The political aspect, important though it is, dwindles into insignificance compared to the moral and religious issue.

'You will have to appreciate my feelings in this matter by remembering that I have been interested in the condition of these classes from my boyhood and have more than once staked my all for their sake. I say this not to pride myself in any way. For, I feel that no penance that the Hindus may do can in any way compensate for the calculated degradation to which they have consigned the Depressed Classes for centuries.

'But I know that separate electorate is neither a penance nor any remedy for the crushing degradation they have groaned under. I, therefore, respectfully inform His Majesty's government that in the event of their decision creating separate electorate for the Depressed Classes, I must fast unto death.

'I am painfully conscious of the fact that such a step, whilst I am a prisoner, must cause grave embarrassment to His Majesty's government, and that it will be regarded by many as highly improper on the part of one holding my position to introduce into the political field methods which they would describe as hysterical if not much worse. All I can urge in defence is that for me the contemplated step is not a method, it is part of my being. It is the call of conscience which I dare not disobey, even though it may cost whatever reputation for sanity I may possess. So far as I can see now my discharge from imprisonment would not make the duty of fasting any the less imperative. I am hoping, however, all my fears are wholly unjustified and the British Government have no intention whatever of creating separate electorate for the Depressed Classes.'

The following reply was sent to Mr Gandhi by the Secretary of State:

'India Office, Whitehall,
April 13, 1932.

Dear Mr Gandhi,

I write this in answer to your letter of 11th March, and I say at once I realize fully the strength of your feeling upon the question of separate electorates for the Depressed Classes. I can only say that we intend to give any decision that may be necessary solely and only upon the merits of the case. As you are aware, Lord Lothian's Committee has not yet completed its tour and it must be some weeks before we can receive any conclusions at which it may have arrived. When we receive that report we shall have to give most careful consideration to its recommendations, and we shall not give a decision until we have taken into account, in addition to the view expressed by the Committee, the views that you and those who think with you have so forcibly expressed. I feel sure if you were in our position you would be taking exactly the same action we intend to take. You would admit the Committee's report, you would then give it your fullest consideration, and before arriving at a final decision, you would take into account the views that have been expressed on both sides of the controversy. More than this I cannot say. Indeed I do not imagine you would expect me to say more.'

After giving this warning, Mr Gandhi slept over the matter thinking that a repetition of his threat to fast unto death was sufficient to paralyse the British Government and prevent them from accepting the claim of the Untouchables for special representation. On the 17 August 1932, the decision of the Prime Minister on the communal question was announced.

That part of the decision which relates to the Untouchables is produced below:

'Communal Decision by His Majesty's government, 1932.

- In the statement made by the Prime Minister on 1st December last on behalf of His Majesty's government at the close of the second session of the Round Table Conference, which was immediately afterwards endorsed by both Houses of Parliament, it was made plain that if the communities in India were unable to reach a settlement acceptable to all parties on the communal questions which the Conference had failed to solve, His Majesty's government were determined that India's constitutional advance should not on that account be frustrated, and that they would remove this obstacle by devising and applying themselves a provisional scheme.

- On the 19th March last, His Majesty's government, having been informed that the continued failure of the communities to reach agreement was blocking the progress of the plans for the framing of a new Constitution, stated that they were engaged upon a careful re-examination of the difficult and controversial questions which arise. They are now satisfied that without a decision of at least some aspects of the problems connected with the position of minorities under the new Constitution, no further progress can be made with the framing of the Constitution.

- His Majesty's government has accordingly decided that they will include provisions to give effect to the scheme set out below in the proposals relating to the Indian Constitution to be laid in due course before the Parliament. The scope of this scheme is purposely confined to the arrangements to be made for the representation of the British Indian communities in the Provincial Legislatures, consideration of representation in the Legislature at the Centre. The decision to limit the scope of the scheme implies no failure to realize that the framing of the Constitution will necessitate the decision of a number of other problems of great importance to minorities, but has been taken in the hope that once a pronouncement has been made upon the basic questions of method and proportions of representation the communities themselves may find it possible to arrive at modus vivendi on other communal problems, which have not received the examination they require.

- His Majesty's government wish it to be most clearly understood that they themselves can be no parties to any negotiations which may be initiated with a view to the revision of their decision, and will not be prepared to give consideration to any representation aimed at securing the modification of it which is not supported by all the parties affected. But they are most desirous to close no door to an agreed settlement should such happily be forthcoming. If, therefore, before a new Government of India Act has passed into law, they are satisfied that the communities who are concerned are mutually agreed upon a practicable alternative scheme, either in respect of my one or more of the Governors' Provinces or in respect of the whole of the British India, they will be prepared to recommend to the Parliament that that alternative should be substituted for the provisions now outlined.

- Members of the "Depressed Classes" qualified to vote will vote in a general constituency. In view of the fact that for a considerable period these classes would be unlikely, by this means alone, to secure any adequate representation in the Legislature, a number of special seats will be assigned to them as shown in the table. These seats will be filled by election from special constituencies in which only members of the "Depressed Classes" electorally qualified will be entitled to vote. Any person voting in such a special constituency will, as stated above, be also entitled to vote in a general constituency. It is intended that these constituencies should be formed in selected areas where the depressed classes are most numerous, and that, except in Madras, they should not cover the whole area of the Province.'

In Bengal it seems possible that in some general constituencies a majority of the voters will belong to the Depressed Classes. Accordingly, pending further investigation, no number has been fixed for the members to be returned from the special Depressed Class constituencies in that province. It is intended to secure that the Depressed Classes should obtain not less than ten seats in the Bengal Legislature.

The precise definition in each province of those who (if electoral by qualified) will be entitled to vote in the special Depressed Class constituencies has not yet been finally determined. It will be based as a rule on the general principles advocated in the Franchise Committee's Report. Modification may, however, be found necessary in some provinces in Northern India where the application of the general criteria of Untouchability might result in a definition unsuitable in some respects to the special conditions of the province.

His Majesty's government does not consider that these special Depressed Classes constituencies will be required for more than limited time. They intend that the Constitution shall provide that they shall come to an end after twenty years if they have not previously been abolished under the general powers of electoral revision.

◆

Mr Gandhi found that his threat had failed to have any effect. He did not care that he was a signatory to the requisition asking the Prime Minister to arbitrate. He forgot that as a signatory he was bound to accept the award. He started to undo what the Prime Minister had done. He first tried to get the terms of the Communal Award revised. Accordingly, he addressed the following letter to the Prime Minister:

'Yeravda Central Prison,
August 18,1932.

Dear Friend,

There can be no doubt that Sir Samuel Hoare has showed you and the cabinet my letter to him of 11th March on the question of the representation of the Depressed Classes. That letter should be treated as part of this letter and be read together with this.

'I have read the British Government's decision on the representation of minorities and have slept over it. In pursuance of my letter to Sir Samuel Hoare and my declaration at the meeting of the Minorities Committee of the Round Table Conference on 13th November, 1931, at St James' Palace, I have to resist your decision with my life. The only way I can do so is by declaring a perpetual fast unto death from food of any kind save water with or without salt and soda. This fast will cease if during its progress the British Government, of its own motion or under pressure of public opinion, revise their decision and withdraw their scheme of communal electorates for the Depressed Classes, whose representatives should be elected by the general electorate under the common franchise, no matter how wide it is.

'The proposed fast will come into operation in the ordinary course from the noon of 20 September next, unless the said decision is meanwhile revised in the manner suggested above.

'I am asking the authorities here to cable the text of this letter to you so as to give you ample notice. But in any case, I am leaving sufficient time for this letter to reach you in time by the slowest route.

'I also ask that this letter and my letter to Sir Samuel Hoare already referred to be published at the earliest possible moment. On my part, I have scrupulously observed the rule of the jail and have communicated my desire or the contents of the two letters to no one, save my two companions, Sardar Vallabhbhai Patel and Mr Mahadev Desai. But I want, if you make it possible, public opinion to be affected by my letters. Hence, my request for their early publication.

'I regret the decision I have taken. But as a man of religion that I hold myself to be, I have no other course left open to me. As I have said in my letter to Sir Samuel Hoare, even if His Majesty's government decided to release me in order to save themselves from embarrassment, my fast will have to continue. For, I cannot now hope to resist the decision by any other means; and I have no desire whatsoever to compass my release by any means other than honourable.

'It may be that my judgement is warped and that I am wholly in error in regarding separate electorates for the Depressed Classes as harmful to them or to Hinduism. If so, I am not likely to be in the right with reference to other parts of my philosophy of life. In that case, my death by fasting will be at once a penance for my error and a lifting of a weight from off these numberless men and women who have childlike faith in my wisdom. Whereas if my judgement is right, as I have little doubt it is, the contemplated step is but due to the fulfilment of the scheme of life which I have tried for more than a quarter of a century, apparently not without considerable success.

I remain,
Your faithful friend,
M.K. Gandhi.'

Finding that the Prime Minister would not yield, he sent him the following letter informing him that he was determined to carry out his threat of fast unto death:

'Yeravda Central Prison,
September 9th, 1932.

Dear Friend,

I have to thank you for your frank and full letter telegraphed and received this day. I am sorry, however, that you put upon the contemplated step an interpretation that never crossed my mind. I have claimed to speak on behalf of the very class, to sacrifice whose interests you impute to me a desire to fast myself to death. I had hoped that the extreme step itself would effectively prevent any such selfish interpretation. Without arguing, I affirm that for me this matter is one of pure religion. The mere fact of the Depressed Classes having double votes does not protect them or Hindu society in general from being disrupted. In the establishment of separate electorate at all for the Depressed Classes, I sense the injection of poison that is calculated to destroy Hinduism and do no good whatever to the Depressed Classes. You will please permit me to say that no matter how sympathetic you may be, you cannot come to a correct decision on a matter of such vital and religious importance to the parties concerned.

'I should not be against even over-representation of the Depressed Classes. What I am against is their statutory separation even in a limited form, from the Hindu fold, so long as they choose to belong to it. Do you realize that if your decision stands and the Constitution comes into being, you arrest the marvellous growth of the work of Hindu reformers, who have dedicated themselves to the uplift of their suppressed brethren in every walk of life?

'I have, therefore, been compelled reluctantly to adhere to the decision conveyed to you.

'As your letter may give rise to a misunderstanding, I wish to state that the fact of my having isolated for special treatment the Depressed Classes not in any way mean that I approve of or am reconciled to other parts of the decision. In my opinion, many other parts are open to very grave objection. Only, I do not consider them to be any warrant for calling from me such self-immolation as my conscience has promoted me to in the matter of the Depressed Classes.

I remain,
Your Faithful Friend.
M.K. Gandhi.'

Accordingly, on the 20 September 1932, Mr Gandhi commenced his 'fast unto death' as a protest against the grant of separate electorates to the Untouchables.

The story of this fact has been told by Mr Pyarelal in a volume which bears the picturesque and flamboyant title of 'The Epic Fast'. The curious may refer it. I must, however, warn him that it is written by a Boswell and has all the faults of a Boswelliana. There is another side to it, but there is neither time nor space to present it here. All I can do is to invite attention to the statement I issued to the Press on the eve of Mr Gandhi's fast exposing his tactics. Suffice it to say that although Mr Gandhi declared a fast unto death, he did not want to die. He wanted very much to live.

The fast nonetheless created a problem, and that problem was how to save Mr Gandhi's life. The only way to save his life was to alter the Communal Award which Mr Gandhi said hurt his conscience so much. The Prime Minister had made it quite clear that the British cabinet would not withdraw it or alter it of its own, but that they were ready to substitute for it a formula that may be agreed upon by the Caste Hindus and the Untouchables. As I had the privilege of representing the Untouchables at the Round Table Conference, it was assumed that the assent of the Untouchables would not be valid unless I was a party to it. The surprising fact is that my position as the leader of the Untouchables of India was not only not questioned by Congressmen but it was accepted as a fact. All eyes naturally turned to me as the man of the moment or rather as the villain of the piece.

As to myself it is no exaggeration to say that no man was placed in a greater and graver dilemma than I was then. It was a baffling situation. I had to make a choice between two different alternatives. There was before me the duty, which I owed as a part of common humanity, to save Gandhi from sure death. There was before me the problem of saving for the Untouchables the political rights which the Prime Minister had given them. I responded to the call of humanity and saved the life of Mr Gandhi by agreeing to alter the Communal Award in a manner satisfactory to Mr Gandhi. This agreement is known as the Poona Pact.

TEXT OF POONA PACT

The following is the text of the agreement:

(1) There shall be seats reserved for the Depressed Classes out of the general electorate seats in the Provincial Legislatures as follows: Madras 30; Bombay with Sind 15; Punjab 8; Bihar and Orissa 18; Central Provinces 20; Assam 7; Bengal 30; United Provinces 20; Total 148.
These figures are based on the total strength of the Provincial Councils, announced in the Prime Minister's decision.

(2) Election of these seats shall be by joint electorates subject, however, to the following procedure:
All the members of the Depressed Classes, registered in the general electoral roll in a constituency, will form an electoral college, which will elect a panel off our candidates belonging

to the Depressed Classes for each of such reserved seats, by the method of the single vote; the four persons getting the highest number of votes in such primary election shall be candidates for election by the general electorate.

(3) Representation of the Depressed Classes in the Central Legislature shall likewise be on the principle of joint electorates and reserved seats by the method of primary election in the manner provided for in clause 2 above, for their representation in the Provincial Legislatures.

(4) In the Central Legislature, 18 per cent of the seats allotted to the general electorate for British India in the said legislature shall be reserved for the Depressed Classes.

(5) The system of primary election to a panel of candidates for election to the Central and Provincial Legislatures, as herein before mentioned, shall come to an end after the first ten years, unless terminated sooner by mutual agreement under the provision of clause 6 below.

(6) The system of representation of the Depressed Classes by reserved seats in the Provincial and Central Legislatures as provided for in clauses 1 and 4 shall continue until determined by mutual agreement between the communities concerned in the settlement.

(7) Franchise for the Central and Provincial Legislatures for the Depressed Classes shall be as indicated in the Lothian Committee Report.

(8) There shall be no disabilities attaching to any one on the ground of his being a member of the Depressed Classes in regard to any elections to local bodies or appointment to the Public Services. Every endeavour shall be made to secure fair representation of the Depressed Classes in these respects, subject to such educational qualifications as may be laid down for appointment to the Public Services.

(9) In every province out of the educational grant, an adequate sum shall be earmarked for providing educational facilities to the members of the Depressed Classes.

The terms of the Pact were accepted by Mr Gandhi and given effect to by the government by embodying them in the Government of India Act. The Poona Pact had produced different reactions. The Untouchables were sad. They had every reason to be. There are, however, people who do not accept this. They never fail to point out that the Poona Pact gave the Untouchables larger number of seats than what was given to them by the Prime Minister in his Communal Award. It is true that the Poona Pact gave the Untouchables 148 seats, while the Award had only given them 78. But to conclude from this that the Poona Pact gave them more than what was given by the Award is to ignore what the Award had in fact given to the Untouchables.

The Communal Award gave the Untouchables two benefits: (i) a fixed quota of seats to be elected by separate electorate of the Untouchables and to be tilled by persons belonging to the Untouchables (ii) double vote, one to be used through separate electorates and the other to be used in the general electorates.

Now, if the Poona Pact increased the fixed quota of seats it also took away the right to the double vote. This increase in seats can never be deemed to be a compensation for the loss of the double vote. The second vote given by the Communal Award was a priceless privilege. Its value as a political weapon was beyond reckoning. The voting strength of the Untouchables in each constituency is one to ten. With this voting strength free to be used in the election of caste Hindu candidates, the Untouchables would have been in a position to determine, if not to dictate, the issue of the General Election. No caste Hindu candidate could have dared to neglect the Untouchable in his constituency or be hostile to their interest if he was made dependent upon the votes of the Untouchables. Today, the Untouchables have a few more seats than were given to them by the Communal Award. But this is all that they have. Every other member is indifferent, if not hostile. If the Communal Award with its system of double voting had remained, the Untouchables would have had a few seats less but every other member would have been a member for the Untouchables. The increase in the number of seats for the Untouchables is no increase at all and was no recompense for the loss of separate electorate and the double vote. The Hindus, although they did not celebrate the Poona Pact, did not like it. Throughout their commotion to save Mr Gandhi's life, there was a definite current of conscious feeling that the cost of terms of the Pact, they very definitely disliked it, although they had not the courage to reject it. Disliked by the Hindus and disfavoured by the Untouchables, the Poona Pact was given recognition by both parties and was embodied in the Government of India Act.

The deprivation of the Untouchables by the Congress of their right to representation in the cabinet has the appearance of malice aforethought. One of the grounds, urged by the Congress for the non-inclusion of representatives of the minorities in their cabinets, was that a cabinet must be a party cabinet if it is to take collective responsibility and that the Congress was quite ready to include members of the Minority communities in its cabinet provided they were prepared to join the Congress and sign the Congress pledge. Whatever may be the value of such argument against other minorities, it had absolutely no value against the Untouchables. The Congress could not use it to defend its conduct in excluding the Untouchables from the cabinet for two reasons. In the first place, the Congress was bound by the terms of the Poona Pact to give representation to the Untouchables in the cabinet. In the second place, the Congress could not say that there were no Untouchables in the Legislatures who were not members of the Congress Party. On the contrary, there were as many as 78 Untouchables returned on the Congress ticket and pledged to the Congress policy. Why then did the Congress not include them in the cabinet? The only answer is that it was a part of the Congress policy not to admit the right of the Untouchables to be represented in the cabinet and that this policy had the support of Mr Gandhi. Those who may have any doubt as to the correctness of this statement may well consider the evidence set out below.

The first piece of evidence lies imbedded in the story of the expulsion of the Hon'ble Dr Khare from the Congress. As is well-known, Dr Khare was the prime minister in the Congress Ministry in the Central Provinces. Owing to internal quarrels among the members of his cabinet, Dr Khare to get rid of those that were inconvenient, adopted the perfectly normal course of tendering his own resignation and that of the other ministers to the Governor with a view to form a new cabinet. Thereafter, the Governor, in full conformity with constitutional practice, recalled Dr Khare and asked him to form another cabinet with himself as the Premier. Dr Khare accepted the invitation and formed a new cabinet dropping old and inconvenient hands and taking in some new ones. Dr Khare's new cabinet was different from the old in one important respect, namely, that it included Mr Agnibhoj, an Untouchable, who was a member of the Central Provinces, who belonged to the Congress Party and who by his education was well-qualified to be a minister. On 26 July 1938, the Congress Working Committee met in Wardha and passed a resolution condemning Dr Khare on the ground that in tendering the resignation of his colleagues in the old ministry he was guilty of a grave error of judgement and that in forming a new ministry he was guilty of indiscipline. In explaining what was behind this charge of indiscipline in forming a new ministry, Dr Khare openly said that according to Mr Gandhi the act of indiscipline consisted in the inclusion of an Untouchable in the Ministry. Dr Khare also said that Mr Gandhi told him that it was wrong on his part to have raised such aspirations and ambitions in the Untouchables and it was such an act of bad judgement that he would never forgive him. This statement was repeatedly made by Dr Khare from platforms. Mr Gandhi has never contradicted it.

There is, however, more direct evidence on this point. In 1942, there was held All India Conference of the Untouchables. In that Conference, resolutions setting out the political demands of the Untouchables were passed. An Untouchable of the Congress Party who attended the Conference went to Mr Gandhi to ascertain what Mr Gandhi had to say about these demands and put him the following five questions:

'1. What will be the position of the Harijans in the future Constitution to be framed?
2. Will you advise the government and the Congress to agree to fix the five seats from a Panchayat Board upwards to the State Council on population basis?
3. Will you advise the Congress and the leaders of the various majority parties in the legislatures in the provinces to nominate the cabinet members from among the Scheduled caste legislators who enjoy the confidence of the majority of Scheduled caste members?

4. In view of the backwardness of the Harijans, will you advise the government to make a provision in the Act that Executive posts in the Local Boards and Municipal Councils be held on communal rotation, so as to enable the Harijans to become Presidents and Chairmen?

5. Why do you not fix some percentage of seats for Harijans from District Congress Committee upwards to the Working Committee of the Congress?'

Mr Gandhi gave his answers in the issue of the Harijan dated 2 August 1942. This is what Mr Gandhi said:

'1. The Constitution, which I could influence, would contain a provision making the observance of Untouchability in any shape or form an offence. The so-called "Untouchables" would have seats reserved for them in all elected bodies according to their population within the elected area concerned.

2. You will see that the answer is covered by the foregoing.

3. I cannot. The principle is dangerous. Protection of its neglected classes should not be carried to an extent which will harm them and harm the country. A cabinet minister should be a topmost man commanding universal confidence. A person after he has secured a seat in an elected body should depend upon his intrinsic merit and popularity to secure coveted positions.

4. In the first place, I am not interested in the present Act which is as good as dead. But I am opposed to your proposal on the ground already mentioned.

5. I am opposed for the reasons mentioned. But I should like to compel large elective Congress organizations to ensure the election of Harijan members in proportion to their numbers on the Congress register. If Harijans are not interested enough in the Congress to become 4 anna members, they may not expect to find their names in elective bodies. But I would strongly advise Congress workers to see that they approach Harijans and induce them to become members of the Congress.'

Is there any doubt that Mr Gandhi and the Congress were determined on principle not to recognize the right of the Untouchables to be represented in the cabinet? As to the question of qualifications, there would have been some sense if Mr Gandhi had that limiting condition applicable to all minorities. Dare Mr Gandhi say that about the Muslim demand? What is the use in shutting it out in the case of the Untouchables only? Nobody has claimed that an unqualified Untouchable should be made a minister. It only confirms the inner feeling of opposition that lies locked in the heart of Mr Gandhi.

In the series of acts which the Congress perpetrated in order to nullify the Poona Pact, there remain two more to mention. First relates to the policy adopted by the Congress Parliamentary Board in selecting candidates for election. Unfortunately, this question has not been studied as deeply as its importance demands. I have examined this question, and I hope to publish the results along with the evidence in a separate treatise. Here, all I can do is to set out the general principles which seem to have been adopted by these Boards in selecting candidates for election. Communal principle played a very great part in it. In a constituency where there were two candidates to choose from, the Congress did not feel it necessary to choose the one more worthy. It chose the one who belonged to a caste which was more numerous. Considerations of wealth also played their part. A wealthier candidate was often preferred to a poor and a better qualified candidate. These considerations were unjustifiable. But they could be understood as the object was to adopt a safe candidate who will pull through. But, there were other principles followed which reveal a deep-seated plot. Different classes of qualifications were set down for different classes of candidates. From candidates who came from high-caste Hindus as Brahmins and the allied communities, those with the highest qualifications were selected. In the case of the non-Brahmins, those with low qualifications were preferred to those with higher qualifications. And in the case of the Untouchables, those with little or no qualifications were selected in preference to those who had. I don't say that is true in every case. But, the general result was that of the candidates selected by the Congress, the candidates from the Brahmin and allied communities were the most highly educated, candidates from the non-Brahmins were moderately educated and those from the Untouchables just about literates. This system of selection is very intriguing. There seems to be a deep laid game behind it. Anyone who studies it carefully will find that it is designed to allow none but the Brahmins and the allied castes to form the main part of the ministry and to secure for them the support of a docile unintelligent crowd of non-Brahmins and Untouchables who by their intellectual attainments could never dream of becoming rivals of the minister-folk but would be content to follow the lead for no other consideration except that of having been raised to the status of members of the Legislatures. Mr Gandhi did not see this aspect of the case when he said that to be a minister the Untouchable aspiring for it must be a qualified person. Otherwise, he would have seen that if there were no qualified persons among the Untouchable Congressmen, it was because the Congress Parliamentary Board did not choose well-qualified candidates from the Untouchables.

If the present system of election continues, the Congress can always prevent educated Indians from becoming members of the Legislature, which is the stepping-stone for becoming a member of the cabinet. It is a very grave prospect and some steps will have to be taken to retrieve the position. In the meantime, it is enough to say that the scheme of selecting candidates adopted by the Congress dealt the Untouchables a severe blow by depriving them of Executive power under the cover of there being no qualified men to hold it which it created for itself by such clandestine and subterranean means.

The second misdeed of the Congress was to subject the Untouchable Congressmen to the rigours of party discipline. They were completely under the control of the Congress Party Executive. They could not ask a question which it did not like. They could not move a resolution which it did not permit. They could not bring in legislation to which it objected. They could not vote as they chose and could not speak what they felt. They were there as dumb, driven cattle. One of the objects of obtaining representation in the Legislature for the Untouchables is to enable them to ventilate their grievances and to obtain redress for their wrongs. The Congress successfully and effectively prevented this from happening.

To end this long and sad story, the Congress sucked the juice out of the Poona Pact and threw the rind in the face of the Untouchables.

Chapter 3

FREEDOM FROM THE GOVERNING CLASS

WHAT IS THE fundamental issue in the controversy between the Congress and the Untouchables? As I understand the matter, the fundamental issue is: Are the Untouchables a separate element in the national life of India or are they not?

This is the real issue in the controversy and it is on this issue that the Congress and the Untouchables have taken opposite sides. The answer of the Untouchables is yes. They say they are distinct and separate from the Hindus. The Congress, on the other hand, says 'No' and asserts that the Untouchables are a chip of the Hindu block. This is the attitude of the parties to the issue. The attitude of the British Government was made clear by Lord Linlithgow in his statements as Viceroy and Governor-General of India in which he declared in quite explicit terms that the Untouchables were a separate element in the national life of India. Many people who regard the issue of constitutional safeguards as the fundamental issue will feel surprised that I should regard as fundamental an issue so apparently different from what they regard as fundamental. Really speaking, there is no difference. It all depends upon what one regards as the proximate and what as ultimate. Others regard the question of constitutional safeguards as ultimate. I regard as proximate. What I have stated as fundamental, I regard as ultimate, from which the proximate follows, as the conclusion does from the premise in a logical syllogism. It may be as well for me to state why I have thought it necessary to make this difference. The evolution of the Indian Constitution appears to me to have established a sort of a logical syllogism. The major premise in the syllogism is that where there exists an element in the national life of India, which is definable as a separate and distinct element, it is entitled to constitutional safeguards. An element, making a claim for constitutional safeguards, must show that it is definable as separate and distinct from the rest. If it shows that it is separate and distinct, its right to constitutional safeguards is held admissible.

That is how the provisions for constitutional safeguards for Muslims, Indian Christians, Anglo-Indians, Europeans and Sikhs have come into being. It is true that the Constitution of India has not been framed in the light of principles. It has grown in a haphazard manner, more in answer to exigencies than in accordance with principles. Nevertheless, this silent postulate, if not a principle to which I have referred, seems to be working throughout. The right of a group to constitutional safeguards has come to be treated as consequential. It is deemed to follow automatically when the fundamental condition is satisfied, namely, that they do constitute a separate and a distinct element in the national life of India. In dealing with this controversy, one must deal with it as one is required to do with a syllogism. In a syllogism, both are fundamental, the conclusion as well as the premise, and to close the argument, it is not enough to deal with the conclusion and omit to examine the premise. Looking at the question from this angle, I think I ought not to close the case of the Untouchables with no more than a discussion of the constitutional safeguards. I feel that I ought to deal also with the premise, the ultimate, or the fundamental proposition, from which the constitutional safeguards seem to follow, if not as a matter of course, at least as a matter of precedent.

It will thus be seen that the decision I have taken to give a separate treatment to the ultimate as distinguished from the proximate proposition is not without justification. It also seems to be necessary to deal with it separately and substantially, because the Congress seems to be fully aware of the fact that this is the fundamental issue and knows that once it concedes that the Untouchables are a separate element, it cannot prevent them from succeeding in their claim for constitutional safeguards. If the Congress has come forward to contest this proposition, it is because it thinks that it is the first trench and if it fails to maintain it, it cannot save the situation.

It must be a matter of considerable surprise to those who know the conditions in India that the Congress should come forward to controvert what is incontrovertible, namely, that the Untouchables are separate from the Hindus. But, since the Congress has chosen to do so, I must deal with the issue as best as I can.

The grounds advanced by the Untouchables that they are separate from the Hindus are not difficult to comprehend. Nor do they require a long and an elaborate statement. The statement of their case can be fully covered by a simple question: In what sense are they Hindus? In the first place, the word 'Hindu' is used in various senses and one must know in what sense it is used before one can give a proper answer to the question. It is used in a territorial sense. Everyone who is an inhabitant of Hindustan is a Hindu: In that sense, it can certainly be claimed that the Untouchables are Hindus. But so are the Muslims, Christians, Sikhs, Jews, Parsis, etc. The second sense in which the word 'Hindu' is used is in a religious sense. Before one can draw any conclusion, it is necessary to separate the dogmas of Hinduism from the cults of Hinduism. Whether the Untouchables are Hindus in the religious sense of the word depends upon whether one adopts as his tests the dogmas or the cults. If the tests of Hinduism are the dogmas of caste and Untouchability, then every Untouchable would repudiate Hinduism and the assertion that he is a Hindu. If the test applied is the acceptance of a cult such as the worship of Rama, Krishna, Vishnu and Shiva and other gods and goddesses recognized by Hinduism, the Untouchables may be claimed to be Hindus. The Congress, as usual, maintains a body of agents from among the Untouchables to shout when need be that the Untouchables are Hindus and that they will die as Hindus. But even these paid agents will not agree to be counted as Hindus if they are asked to proclaim themselves as Hindus, if Hinduism means belief in caste and Untouchability.

One more point must be stressed. On the foregoing analysis, the Untouchable may be classed as a Hindu if the word Hindu is used in the religious but in the limited sense of a follower of a recognized cult. Even here, there is a necessity for giving a warning against concluding that the Hindu and the Untouchable have a common religion. The fact is that even as followers of recognized cults, they cannot be said to have a common religion. The exact and appropriate expression would be to say that they have a similar religion. A common religion means a common cycle of participation. Now, in the observances of the cults there is no such common cycle of participation. The Hindus and the

Untouchables practise their cults in segregation so that notwithstanding the similarity of their cults they remain as separate as two aliens do. Neither of these two senses of the word 'Hindu' can yield any result which can be of help in determining the political question, which alone can justify the discussion.

The only test which can be of use is its social sense as indicating a member of the Hindu Society. Can an Untouchable be held to be part of the Hindu Society? Is there any human tie that binds them to the rest of the Hindus? There is none. There is no *connubium*. There is no *commensalism*. There is not even the right to touch, much less to associate. Instead, the mere touch is enough to cause pollution to a Hindu. The whole tradition of the Hindus is to recognize the Untouchables as a separate element and insist upon it as a fact. The traditional terminology of the Hindus to distinguish Hindus and Untouchables furnishes the best evidence in favour of the contention of the Untouchables. According to this traditional terminology, Hindus are called Savarnas and the Untouchables are called Avarnas. It speaks of the Hindus as Chaturvarnikas and of the Untouchables as Panchamas. Such a terminology could not have come into existence if separation had not become so prominent and its observance so necessary as to require coining of special terms to give expression to the fact.

There is thus hardly any substance in the Congress argument that the Untouchables are Hindus and that they cannot, therefore, demand the same political rights as the Muslims and others can. While the argument from tradition is a good and valid argument to prove that the Untouchables are not Hindus, it may appear to some to be a weak one. I do not wish to leave the field without directly meeting the Congress argument. For this purpose, I will grant that the Untouchables are Hindus by religion. But the question is: Does it matter if they are Hindus? Can it come in the way of their being recognized as a separate element in the national life of India? It is difficult to understand how the mere fact that they might be called Hindus by religion in such a limited sense can be the basis of an argument that they are an integral part of the Hindu society.

Admitting for the sake of argument that they are Hindus by religion, can it mean anything more than what I have said, namely, that they worship the same gods and goddesses as the rest of the Hindus, they go to the same places of pilgrimage, hold the same supernatural beliefs and regard the same stones, trees, mountains as sacred as the rest of the Hindus do? Is this enough to conclude that the Untouchables and the Hindus are parts of one single community? If that be the logic behind the contention of the Congress, then what about the Belgians, Dutch, Norwegians, Swedes, Germans, French, Italians, Slavs, etc.? Are they not all Christians? Do they not all worship the same God? Do they not all accept Jesus as their Saviour? Have they not the same religious beliefs? Obviously, there is a complete religious unity between all of them in thought, worship and beliefs. Yet, who can dispute that the French, Germans, Italians and the rest are not a single community? Take another case, that of the Whites and the Negroes in the United States of America. They too have a common religion. Both are Christians. Can anyone say that the two on that account form a single community? Take a third case, that of the Indian Christians, Europeans and Anglo-Indians. They profess and follow the same religion. Yet it is admitted that they do not form one single Christian community.

Take the case of the Sikhs. There are Sikhs, Mazbi Sikhs and Ramdasia Sikhs. All profess Sikhism. But, it is accepted that they do not form one community. In the light of these illustrations, it is obvious that the argument of the Congress is full of fallacies.

The first fallacy of the Congress lies in its failure to realize that the fundamental issue for settling the question whether to grant or not to grant constitutional safeguards is union versus separation of a social group in the population. Religion is only a circumstance from which unity or separation may be inferred. The Congress does not seem to have understood that the Musalmans and the Indian Christians have been given separate political recognition not because they are Musalmans or Christians but fundamentally because they form, in fact, separate elements from the Hindus.

The second fallacy of the Congress lies in its attempt to prove that where there is a common religion, social union must be presumed. It is on the basis of this reasoning that the Congress hopes to win. Unfortunately for the Congress, it cannot. For, the facts are strongly against making a conclusive inference. If religion was a circumstance from which social union was made the only permissible inference, then the fact that the Italians, French, Germans and Slavs in Europe, the Negroes and the Whites in the USA and the Indian Christians, Europeans, Anglo-Indians in India do not form a single community although they all profess the same religion is enough to negative such a contention. The pity of the matter is that the Congress is so completely enamoured of its argument based on religion as a unifying factor, that it has failed to realize that there is no concomitance between the two and that there are cases where there is no separation although religions are separate, that there are cases where separation exists in spite of a common religion and what is worst, separation exists because religion prescribes it.

To give a quietus to the Congress argument, it may be desirable to give one illustration of each of these cases. Of the first case, the best and the easiest illustration I can think of is that of the Sikhs and the Hindus. They differ in religion. But, they are not socially separate. They dine together; they marry together; and they live together. In a Hindu family, one son may be a Sikh, anothera Hindu. Religious difference does not break the social nexus. Of the second, the case of the Italians, French, Germans in Europe and Whites and Negroes in America are as good illustrations as one would want. This happens where religion is a binding force but is not powerful enough to withstand other forces tending to divide such as the sentiment of race. Hindus and Hinduism are the best and perhaps the only illustrations of the third case, where separation is the effect of religion itself. That there can be such a case, Hindus at any rate need not require to be told. For, it is well-known that Hinduism preaches separation instead of union. To be a Hindu means not to mix, to be separate in everything. The language commonly used that Hinduism upholds caste and Untouchability perhaps disguises and conceals its genius. The real genius of Hinduism is to divide. This is beyond dispute. For, what do caste and Untouchability stand for? Obviously, for separation. For, caste is another name for separation and Untouchability typifies the extremist form of separation of community from community. It is also beyond dispute that caste and Untouchability are not innocuous dogmas to be compared with other dogmas relating to the condition of the soul after death. They are parts of the code of conduct which every Hindu is bound to observe during his life on earth. Caste and Untouchability, far from being mere dogmas, are among the foremost observances prescribed by Hinduism. It is not enough for a Hindu to believe in the dogmas of caste and Untouchability. He must also observe caste and Untouchability in the conduct of his daily life.

The separation, which Hinduism has brought about between the Hindus and the Untouchables by its dogma of Untouchability, is not a mere imaginary line of separation, such as the one which the Pope once drew in a quarrel between the Portuguese and their rivals for Colonial possessions; it is not like the colour line which has length but no breadth and which one may observe or one may not observe; it is not like the race line, which involves distinction but no discrimination.

It has both depth and width. Factually, the Hindus and the Untouchables are divided by a fence made of barbed wire. Notionally, it is cordon sanitaire which the Untouchables have never been allowed to cross and can never hope to cross.

To put the matter in general terms, Hinduism and social union are incompatible. By its very genius, Hinduism believes in social separation, which is another name for social disunity and even creates social separation. If Hindus wish to be one, they will have to discard Hinduism. They cannot be one without violating Hinduism. Hinduism is the greatest obstacle to Hindu Unity. Hinduism cannot create that longing to belong which is the basis of all social unity. On the contrary, Hinduism creates an eagerness to separate.

The Congress does not seem to realize that the argument it is using goes against itself. Far from supporting the Congress contention, it is the best and the most effective argument that can be advanced to prove the contention of the Untouchables. For, if any conclusion is to be drawn from the hypothesis that the Untouchables are Hindus, it is that Hinduism has always insisted both in principle and in practice that the Untouchables are not to be recognized a chip of the Hindu block but are to be treated as a separate element and segregated from the Hindus.

If, therefore, the Untouchables say that they are a separate element, nobody can accuse them of having invented a new theory for the sake of political advantages. They are merely pointing out what the facts are and how these facts are the heritage of Hinduism itself. The Congress cannot honestly and convincingly use Hinduism as an argument for refusing to recognize the Untouchables as a separate element. If it does, it is only because it is actuated by selfish motives. It knows that the recognition of the Untouchables as an element in the national life of India, as distinct and separate from the Hindus, must result in the apportionment of places in the Executive, the Legislature, and in the Public Services between the Untouchables and the Hindus, and thus limit the share of the Hindus. The Congress does not like that the Hindus should be deprived of the share of the Untouchables which the Hindus are in the habit of appropriating to themselves. That is the real reason why the Congress refuses to recognize that the Untouchables are a separate element in the national life of India.

The second argument of the Congress is that the political recognition of the Untouchables as a separate element in the national life of India should not be permitted on the ground that it will perpetuate the separation between the Untouchables and the Hindus.

This is hardly an argument worth consideration. It is the weakest of its kind and shows that the Congress has nothing better to advance. Besides contradicting its previous argument, it is entirely misconceived.

If there is a real separation between the Hindus and the Untouchables and if there is the danger of discrimination being practised by the Hindus against the Untouchables, then the Untouchables must receive political recognition, and must be given political safeguards to protect themselves against the tyranny of the Hindus. The possibility of a better future cannot be used as an argument to prevent the Untouchables from securing the means of protecting themselves against the tyranny of the present.

In the second place, this argument can be used only by those who believe in the social fusion of the Hindus and the Untouchables and are actively engaged in pursuing means and methods which will bring about such a fusion. Congressmen have often been heard to say that the problem of the Untouchables is social and political. But, the point is, are Congressmen sincere when they say that it is a social question?

Or, do they use it as an excuse with a view to avoid the consequences of having to share political power with the Untouchables? And, if they are sincere in holding that it is a social question, what proof is there of their sincerity in this matter? Have Congressmen sponsored social reform among Hindus? Have they carried on a crusade in favour of inter-dining and inter-marriages? What is the record of Congressmen in the field of social reform?

♦

It might be well to state what view the Untouchables took of the problem of the Untouchables. Until the advent of the British, the Untouchables were content to remain Untouchables. It was a destiny preordained by the Hindu God and enforced by the Hindu State. As such, there was no escape from it. Fortunately or unfortunately, the East India Company needed soldiers for their army in India and it could find none but the Untouchables. The East India Company's army consisted, at any rate, in the early part of its history, of the Untouchables, and although the Untouchables are now included among the non-martial classes and are, therefore, excluded from the army, it is with the help of an army composed of Untouchables that the British conquered India. In the army of the East India Company, there prevailed the system of compulsory education for Indian soldiers and their children both male and female. The education received by the Untouchables in the army while it was open to them gave them one advantage which they never had before. It gave them a new vision and a new value. They became conscious that the low esteem in which they had been held was not an inescapable destiny but was a stigma imposed on their personality by the cunning contrivances of the priest. They felt the shame of it as they had never done before and were determined to get rid of it. They too, in the beginning, thought their problem was social, and struggled along the social lines for its solution. This was quite natural. For, they saw that the outward marks of their social inferiority were prohibition of inter-dining and inter-marriage between the Untouchables and the Hindus. They naturally concluded that for the removal of their stigma what was necessary was to establish social intercourse with the Hindus on terms of equality which in its turn meant the abolition of rules against inter-dining and inter-marriage. In other words, first programme of action which the Untouchables launched out for their salvation after they became aware of their servile position was to bring about social equality among all those, who come within the fold of Hinduism by insisting upon the abolition of the caste system.

In this, the Untouchables found an ally in a section of the Hindus. Like the Untouchables, the Hindus also, by the contact with the British, had come to realize that their social system was very defective and was the parent of many social evils. They too desired to launch forth a movement of social reform. It began with Raja Ram Mohan Roy in Bengal and from there had spread all over India and ultimately culminated in the formation of the Indian Social Reform Conference with its slogan of Social Reform before Political Reform. The Untouchables followed the Social Reform Conference and stood behind it as a body and gave it their full support. As every one knows, the Social Reform Conference is dead and buried and forgotten. Who killed it? The Congress. The Congress with its slogans 'Politics First, Politics Last,' 'Politics by Each, Politics by All' regarded the Social Reform Conference as its rival. It denied the validity of the creed of the Conference that social reform was a necessary percursor of political reform. Under a constant and steady fire from the Congress platform and from individual Congress leaders, the Social Reform Conference was burnt down and reduced to ashes. When the Untouchables lost all hope of their salvation through social reform, they were forced to seek political means for protecting themselves. Now for Congressmen to turn round and say that the problem is social is nothing but hypocrisy.

It is wrong to say that the problem of the Untouchables is a social problem. For, it is quite unlike the problems of dowry, widow remarriage, age of consent, etc., which are illustrations of what are properly called social problems. Essentially, it is a problem of quite a different nature in as much as it is a problem of securing to a minority liberty and equality of opportunity at the hands of a hostile majority which believes in the denial of liberty and equal opportunity to the minority and conspires to enforce its policy on the minority. Viewed in this light, the problem of the Untouchables is fundamentally a political problem. Granting, however, for the sake of argument that it is a social problem, it is difficult to understand why political recognition of and political safeguards for the security of the Untouchables should retard their social unification with the Hindus if there is a genuine desire to set in motion processes which will bring about such a result.

Congressmen appear to be arguing with no definite conception in their mind. They don't seem to have a clear idea of the inter-relation between political and social factors. This is well-illustrated by its opposition to separate electorates and its preference to joint electorates. The process of reasoning is worth attention. In a joint electorate, the Hindu votes for an Untouchable and the Untouchable votes for the Hindu. This builds up social solidarity. In a separate electorate, the Hindu votes for a Hindu and an Untouchable votes for an Untouchable. This prevents social solidarity. This is not the point of view from which the Untouchables look at the question of electorates. Their point of view is which of the two will enable the Untouchables to get an Untouchable of their choice elected. But, I am interested in scrutinizing the Congress argument. I do not wish to enlarge upon and complicate the argument. The reasoning of the Congress appears to be correct. But, it is only a superficial view of the matter. These elections take place once in five years. It may well be asked how can social solidarity between the Hindus and the Untouchables be advanced by one day devoted to joint voting if for the rest of the five years they are leading severely separate lives. Similarly, it may well be asked how can one day devoted to separate voting in the course of five years make greater separation than what already exists or contrary wise how can one day in five years devoted to separate voting prevent those who wish to work for union from carrying out their purposes. To make it concrete, how can separate electorate for the Untouchables prevent inter-marriage or inter-dining being introduced between them and the Hindus? Only a congenital idiot will say that they can. It is, therefore, puerile to say that the political recognition of the Untouchables as a separate element and granting them constitutional safeguards will perpetuate separation between them and the Hindus, if the Hindus desire to put an end to it.

Most people believe that Untouchability is a religious system. That is true. But, it is a mistake to suppose that it is only a religious system. Untouchability is more than a religious system. It is also an economic system, which is worse than slavery. In slavery, the master at any rate had the responsibility to feed, clothe and house the slave and keep him in good condition lest the market value of the slave should decrease. But, in the system of Untouchability, the Hindu takes no responsibility for the maintenance of the Untouchable. As an economic system, it permits exploitation without obligation. Untouchability is not only a system of unmitigated economic exploitation, but it is also a system of uncontrolled economic exploitation. That is because there is no independent public opinion to condemn it and there is no impartial machinery of administration to restrain it. There is no appeal to public opinion, for, whatever public opinion there is it is the opinion of the Hindus who belong to the exploiting class and as such favour exploitation. There is no check from the police or the judiciary for the simple reason that they are all drawn from the Hindus, and take the side of the exploiters.

Those who believe that Untouchability will soon vanish do not seem to have paid attention to the economic advantages which it gives to the Hindus. The Untouchable cannot do anything to get rid of his Untouchability. It does not arise out of any personal fault on his part. Untouchability is an attitude of the Hindu. For Untouchability to vanish, it is the Hindu who must change. Will he change?

Has a Hindu any conscience? Is he ever known to have been fired with a righteous indignation against a moral wrong? Assuming he does change so much as to regard Untouchability a moral wrong, assuming he is awakened to the sense of putting himself right with God and Man, will he agree to give up the economic and social advantages which Untouchability gives? History, I am afraid, will not justify the conclusion that a Hindu has a quick conscience or if he has it is so active as to charge him with moral indignation and drive him to undertake a crusade to eradicate the wrong. History shows that where ethics and economics come in conflict victory is always with economics. Vested interests have never been known to have willingly divested themselves unless there was sufficient force to compel them. The Untouchables cannot hope to generate any compelling force. They are poor and they are scattered. They can be easily suppressed should they raise their head.

On this analysis, Swaraj would make Hindus more powerful and Untouchables more helpless and it is quite possible that having regard to the economic advantages which it gives to the Hindus, Swaraj, instead of putting an end to Untouchability, may extend its life. That Untouchability is vanishing is, therefore, only wishful thinking and a calculated untruth. It would be most stupid—if not criminal—to take it into account in considering the demands of the Untouchables for constitutional safeguards and ignore the hard facts of the present and their certainty to continue in the indefinite future.

To start with it is well to know who constitute the governing class in India. The governing class in India consists principally of the Brahmins. It is strange that the present-day Brahmins repudiate the allegation that they belong to the governing class though at one time they described themselves as Bhudevas (Gods on Earth). What can this volte-face be due to? Is it due to a guilty conscience born out of the realization that they have committed criminal breach of the trust imposed upon the intellectual sections in every community by the sacred law of humanity not to serve the interest of their own class but to safeguard the interest of all and, therefore, dare not stand before the bar of the world? Or, is it due to their sense of modesty? It is unnecessary to stop to speculate as to which is the truth.

That the Brahmins are a governing class is hardly open to question. There are two tests one could apply. First is the sentiment of the people and the second is the control of administration. I am sure there cannot be better and more decisive tests than these two. As to the first, there cannot be any doubt. Taking the attitude of the people, the person of the Brahmin is sacred. In ancient times, he could not be hanged no matter what offence he committed. As a sacred person, he had immunities and privileges which were denied to the servile class. He was entitled to first fruits. In Malabar, where the Sambandham marriage prevails, the servile classes such as the Nairs regard it an honour to have their females kept as mistresses by Brahmins. Even kings invited

Brahmins[12] to deflower their queens on primae noctis. There was a

---

[12]The traveller Ludovico Di Varthema who came to India in the middle of the 16th century and visited Malabar says:

'It is proper and at the same time a pleasant thing to know who these Brahmins are. You must know that they are the chief persons of the faith, as priests are among us. And, when the king takes a wife, he selects the most worthy and the most honoured of these Brahmins and makes him sleep the first night with his wife, in order that he may deflower her. Do not imagine that the Brahmin goes willingly to perform this operation. The king is obliged to pay him four hundred to five hundred ducats. The king only and no other person in Calicut adopts this practice.'—*Voyages of Varthema*, Hakluyat Society, Vol. I, p 141.

Other travellers tell that the practice was widespread. Hamilton in his account of the East Indies says:

'When the Samorin marries, he must not cohabit with his bride till the Nambourie (Nambudri) or chief priest, has enjoyed her, and if he pleases he may have three nights of her company, because the first fruits of her nuptials must be a holy oblation to the God she worships and some of the nobles are so complacent as to allow the clergy the same tribute; but the common people cannot have that compliment paid to them, but are forced to supply the priests places themselves.'— Vol. I, p 308.

Buchanan in his narrative refers to the practice in the following terms:

'The ladies of the Tamuri family are generally impregnated by Nambudries; although if they choose they may employ the higher ranks of Nairs; but the sacred character of the Nambudries always procures them a preference.'—Pinkerton's Voyages, Vol. VIII, p 734.

Mr C.A. Innes, J.C.S., Editor of the *Gazetteer of Malabar and Anjengo* issued wider the authority of the Government of Madras says:

'Another institution found amongst all the classes following the marukak-kattayam system, as well as amongst many of those who observe makkattayam, is that known as "Tali-tying wedding" which has been described as "the most peculiar, distinctive and unique" among Malayali marriage customs. Its essence is the tying of a tali (a small piece of gold or other metal, like a locket, on a string) on a girls neck before she attains the age of puberty. This is done by a man of the same or of a higher caste (the usages of different classes differ), and it is only after it has been done that the girl is at liberty to contract a sambandham. It seems to be generally considered that the ceremony was intended to confer on the tali-tier or manavalan (bridegroom) a right to cohabit with the girl; and by some the origin of the ceremony is found in the claim of the Bhu-devas or 'Earth-Gods', (that is the Brahmins), and on a lower plane of Kshatriyas or ruling classes, to the first-fruits of lower caste womanhood, a right akin to the mediaeval droit de seigneurie.'—Vol. I, p 101.

time when no person of the servile class could take his food without drinking the water in which the toes of the Brahmins were washed. Sir P.C. Ray once described how in his childhood, rows of children belonging to the servile classes used to stand for hours together in the morning on the roadside in Calcutta with cups of water in their hands waiting for a Brahmin to pass ready to wash his feet and take it to their parents waiting to sip it before taking their food. Under the British Government and by reason of its equalitarian jurisprudence, these rights, immunities and privileges of the Brahmins have ceased to exist. Nonetheless, the advantages they gave still remain and the Brahmin is still preeminent and sacred in the eyes of the servile classes and is still addressed by them as 'Swami' which means lord.

The second test gives an equally positive result. To take only the Madras Presidency by way of illustration. Consider Table 1. It shows the distribution of gazetted posts between the Brahmins and other communities in the year 1943.

Similar data from other provinces could also be adduced to support this conclusion. But, it is unnecessary to labour the point. Whether the Brahmins claim themselves to be members of the governing class or not, the facts that they control the administration and that their supremacy is accepted by the servile classes, are enough to establish the point.

History shows that the Brahmin has always had other classes as his allies to whom he was ready to accord the status of a governing class provided they were prepared to work with him in subordinate cooperation. In ancient and medieval times, he made such an alliance with the Kshatriyas or the warrior class and the two ruled the masses, indeed ground them down, the Brahmin with his pen and the Kshatriya with his sword. At present, the Brahmin has made an alliance with the Vaishya class called Banias. The shifting of this alliance from Kshatriya to Bania is natural. In these days of commerce, money is more important than sword. That is one reason for this change in party alignment. The second reason is the need for money to rim the political machine. Money can come only from the Bania. It is the Bania who is financing the Congress, largely because Mr Gandhi is a Bania and also because he [Bania] has realized that money invested in politics gives large dividends. Those who have any doubts in the matter might do well to read what Mr Gandhi told Mr Louis Fisher on 6 June 1942. Reports Fisher:[13]

'I said I had several questions to ask him about the Congress Party. Very highly placed Britishers, I recalled, had told me that Congress was in the hands of big business and that Gandhi was supported by the Bombay millowners who gave him as much money as he wanted. "What truth is there in these assertions," I asked.

"'Unfortunately, they are true," he declared simply, "Congress hasn't enough money to conduct its work. We thought in the beginning to collect four annas (about eight cents) from each member per year and operate on that. But it hasn't worked."

"'What proportion of the Congress budget," I asked, "is covered by rich Indians?"

"'Practically all of it," he stated; "In this ashram, for instance, we could live much more poorly than we do and spend less money. But we do not and the money comes from our rich friends."'

For this reason, it is impossible for the Brahmin to exclude the Bania from the position of a governing class. In fact, he has established not merely a working but a cordial alliance with the Bania. The result is that the governing class in India today is a Brahmin–Bania instead of Brahmin–Kshatriya combine as it used to be.

The existence of the governing class does not cover the whole story. What is significant is that the members of the governing class in India are quite conscious of the fact that they do belong to the governing class and that they alone are destined to rule. The late Mr Tilak could never forget that he was a Brahmin and belonged to the governing class. The same is reported to be the case about Pandit Jawaharlal Nehru and his sister Mrs Vijaya Laxmi Pandit. Nor is Mr Vallabhbhai Patel free from the feeling that he belongs to the governing class. Mr Tilak is held out as the father of the Swaraj movement. Pandit Nehru and Mr Vallabhbhai Patel are the leading members of the Congress High Command. Not only are they conscious of the fact that they

---

[13]Fischer, Louis, *A Week with Gandhi*, p 41, 1943.

belong to the governing class but some of them hold that the servile classes are a contemptible people, who must remain servile and who must never aspire to rule. Indeed, they have felt no shame and no remorse in giving public expression to such views. In 1918, when the non-Brahmins and the Backward Classes had started an agitation for separate representation in the Legislature, Mr Tilak, in a public meeting held in Sholapur, said he did not understand why the oil pressers, tobacco shopkeepers, washermen, etc.—that was his description of the non-Brahmins and the Backward Classes—should want to go into the Legislature. In his opinion, their business was to obey the laws and not to aspire for power to make laws. In 1942, Lord Linlithgow invited 52 important Indians representing different sections of the people to discuss what steps could be taken to make the Central Government more popular with a view to enlist the sympathy and cooperation of all Indians in war effort. Among those that were invited were members belonging to the Scheduled Castes. Mr Vallabhbhai Patel could not bear the idea that the Viceroy should have invited such a crowd of mean men. Soon after the event, Mr Vallabhbhai Patel made a speech in Ahmedabad and said:[14]

> 'The Viceroy sent for the leaders of the Hindu Mahasabha, he sent for the leaders of the Muslim League and he sent for Ghanchis (oil pressers), Mochis (cobblers) and the rest.'

Although Mr Vallabhbhai Patel in his malicious and stinging words referred only to Ghanchis and Mochis, his speech is indicative of the general contempt in which the governing class and the members of the Congress High Command hold the servile classes of this country. Further illustrations of this attitude of the governing class and the Congress High Command can be found from incidents that have taken place in the election campaigns. They are so relevant and so revealing that a special mention must be made of them.

Ever since 1919 when Mr Gandhi captured the Congress, Congressmen have looked upon the boycott of Legislature as one of the sanctions for making the British Government concede the demand

---

[14]Quoted by Sanjana in 'Sense and Nonsense in Politics'.

Table 1

Communities	Approximate Population in Lakhs	Percentage of Population	No. of Posts Held Out of Total No.		Non-Gazetted Posts			
			Gazetted Posts (2,200)	Percentage of Appointments held	Over Rs 100 Total No. 7,500		Over Rs 35 Total No. 20,782	
					No. held by	Percentage of Appointments held	No. held	Percentage of Appointments held
(1)	(2)	(3)	(4)	(5)	(6)	(7)	(8)	(9)
Brahmins	15	3	820	37	3,280	43.73	8,812	42.4
Christians	20	4	190	9	750	10	1,655	8.0
Muhammadana	37	7	150	7	497	6.63	1,624	7.8
Depressed Classes	70	14	25	1.5	39	.52	144	.69
Forward Non-Brahmins	113	22	620	27				
Non-Brahmins					2,543	33.9	8,440	40.6
Backward Classes	245	50	50	2				
Non-Asiatic and Anglo-Indians	—	—	—	—	372	5.0	83	.4
Others Communities	—	—	—	—	19	.5	24	.11

for Swaraj. Under this policy, every time there was an election in which the Congress decided not to take part, the Congress would not only refuse to put candidates on the Congress ticket but would carry on propaganda against any Hindu proposing to stand for election as an independent candidate. One need not quarrel over the merits of such a policy. But what were the means adopted by the Congress to prevent Hindus standing on an independent ticket? The means adopted were to make the legislatures objects of contempt. Accordingly, the Congress in various provinces started processions carrying placards saying 'Who will go in the Legislatures? Only barbers, cobblers, potters and sweepers.' In the processions one man would utter the question as part of the slogan and the whole crowd would repeat as answer the second part of the slogan. When Congressmen found that this was not enough to deter persons from standing for the elections, they decided to adopt sterner measures. Believing that respectable people would not be prepared to stand for election if they felt certain that they would have to sit with barbers, potters and sweepers, etc. in the legislatures, the Congress actually went to the extent of putting up candidates from these despised communities on the Congress ticket and got them elected. A few illustrations of this outrageous conduct of the Congress may be mentioned. In the 1920 election, the Congress elected a cobbler[15] in the Central Provinces Legislature. In the 1930 election, they elected in the Central Provinces two cobblers,[16] one milkman[17] and one barber[18] and in the Punjab one sweeper.[19] In 1934, the Congress elected a potter[20] to the Central Legislature. It might be said that this is old history. Let me correct such an impression by referring to what happened in 1943, in the Municipal Elections in Andheri—a suburb of Bombay. The Congress put up a barber to bring the Municipality in contempt.

What an enormity! The Sinn Fein in Ireland boycotted the

---

[15]Faguwa Rohidas
[16]Guru Gosain Agamdas and Balaraj Jaiswar
[17]Chunnu
[18]Arjunlal
[19]Bansi Lal Chaudhari
[20]Bhagat Chandi Mal Gola

British Parliament. But, did they make such hideous use of their own countrymen for affecting their purposes? The campaign of boycott of legislature which took place in 1930 is of particular interest. The elections to the Provincial Legislatures in 1930 in which these instances occurred coincided with Mr Gandhi's Salt Satyagraha campaign of 1930! I hope that the future (the official historian Dr Pattabhi Sitamayya has failed to do so) historian of Congress while recording how Mr Gandhi decided to serve notice on the Viceroy, Lord Irwin, presenting him with a list of demands to be conceded before a certain date and on failure by the Viceroy in this behalf, how Mr Gandhi decided to launch a campaign of civil disobedience, how Mr Gandhi elected an Englishman to carry his notice, how Mr Gandhi selected Salt Act as a target for attack, how he selected Dandi as a scene of battle, how he decided to put himself at the head of the campaign, how he marched out from his Ashram in Ahmedabad with all pomp and ceremony, how the women of Ahmedabad came out with Arthi and applied tilak (saffron mark) to his forehead wishing him victory, how Mr Gandhi assured them by saying that Gujarat alone will win Swaraj for India, how Mr Gandhi proclaimed his determination by saying that he will not return to Ahmedabad until he has won Swaraj, will not fail to record that while, on the one hand, Congressmen were engaged in fighting for Swaraj which they said they wanted to win in the name and for the masses, on the other hand, and in the very year they were committing the worst outrages upon the very masses by exhibiting them publicly as objects of contempt to be shunned and avoided.

Such is the mentality of the governing classes in India towards the servile classes.

◆

What is to be the fate of the servile classes of India under this governing class?

The Congress promises to do wonders for the servile classes—the Congress speaks of masses, it ought really to speak of them as the servile classes held in bondage by the governing classes—when Swaraj comes. It says that it would like to make revolutionary changes but it has no power to make them and it must wait for Swaraj. It is this glib talk which goes to deceive the gullible foreigner. Leaving aside the boast and bluster which lie behind the statement, one may ask what really can happen if India does become a sovereign and an independent state? One thing is certain. The governing class will not disappear by the magic wand of Swaraj. It will remain as it is and, having been freed from the incubus of British Imperialism, will acquire greater strength and vigour. It will capture power as the governing classes in every country do. In short, Swaraj will not be government by the people but it will be a government run by the governing class and in the absence of government by the people, government for the people will be what the governing class will choose to make of it.

What will the governing class do when India becomes a sovereign and an independent state? Some hope that they will undertake reform of tenancy laws, enlarge factory legislation, extend primary education, introduce prohibitor and train people to ply charklia, construct roads and canals, improve currency, regulate weights and measures, open dispensaries and undertake other measures to ameliorate the condition of the servile classes. No one from the servile class can be very enthusiastic about such a programme. In the first place, there is nothing very great in it. In the world of today, no governing class can omit to undertake reforms which are necessary to maintain society in a civilized state. Personally, I have grave doubts about the governing class in India coming forward to carry out even such a modest programme of social amelioration. Most people forget that what leads the Congress today to mouth such a programme is the desire to show that the Congress is better than the British bureaucracy. But once the bureaucracy is liquidated, will there be the same incentive to better the lot of the masses? I entertain very grave doubts on the point. Apart from this, is social amelioration the be all and end all of Swaraj? Speaking for the servile classes, I have no doubt that what they expect to happen in a sovereign and free India is a complete destruction of Brahminism as a philosophy of life and as a social order. If I may say so, the servile classes do not care for social amelioration. The want and poverty which has been their lot is nothing to them as compared to the insult and indignity which they have to bear as a result of the vicious social order. Not bread but honour is what they want. The question therefore is:

Will the governing classes in India, having captured the machinery of the State, undertake a programme for the reform of the social order as distinguished from a programme of social amelioration?

The statement by Congressmen that Congress can do wonders if only India was a sovereign and an independent State, supposing that it is an honest aspiration and not mere propaganda, proceeds on the assumption that for a man to do what he wants, nothing more is necessary than power. Such a belief is not only pitiable but is really a dangerous illusion. Those who are inclined to cherish such an illusion forget that there are serious limitations on sovereignty, no matter how absolute it is. None has described these limitations in more telling language than Dicey. In his law of the Constitution, he says:

> 'The actual exercise of authority by any sovereign whatever, and notably by Parliament, is bounded or controlled by two limitations. Of these, the one is an external, the other is an internal limitation.
>
> 'The external limit to the real power of a sovereign consists in the possibility or certainty that his subjects or a large number of them will disobey or resist his laws.
>
> 'This limitation exists even under the most despotic monarchies. A Roman Emperor, or a French King during the middle of the eighteenth century, was (as is the Russian Czar at the present day) in strictness a "sovereign" in the legal sense of that term. He had absolute legislative authority. Any law made by him was binding, and there was no power in the empire or kingdom which could annul such law... But it would be an error to suppose that the most absolute ruler who ever existed could inreality make or change every law at his pleasure...
>
> 'The authority, that is to say, even of a despot, depends upon the readiness of his subjects or of some portion of his subjects to obey his behests; and this readiness to obey must always be in reality limited. This is shown by the most notorious facts of history. None of the early Caesars could at their pleasure have subverted the worship of fundamental institutions of the Roman world... The Sultan could not abolish Mahommedanism. Louis the Fourteenth at the height of his power could revoke the Edict of Nantes, but he would have found it impossible to establish the supremacy of Protestantism, and for the

same reason which prevented James the Second from establishing the supremacy of Roman Catholicism… What is true of the power of a despot or of the authority of a constituent assembly is specially true of the sovereignty of Parliament; it is limited on every side by the possibility of popular resistance. Parliament might legally establish an Episcopal Church in Scotland; Parliament might legally tax the Colonies; Parliament might without any breach of law change the succession to the throne or abolish the monarchy; but everyone knows that in the present state of the world the British Parliament will do none of these things. In each case, widespread resistance would result from legislation which, though legally valid, is in fact beyond the stretch of Parliamentary power.

'The internal limit to the exercise of sovereignty arises from the nature of the sovereign power itself. Even a despot exercises his powers in accordance with his character, which is itself moulded by the circumstances under which he lives, including under that head the moral feelings of the time and the society to which he belongs. The Sultan could not, if he would, change the religion of the Mahommedan world, but if he could do so, it is in the very highest degree improbable that the head of Mahommedanism should wish to overthrow the religion of Mahomet; the internal check on the exercise of the Sultan's power is at least as strong as the external limitation. People sometimes ask the idle question: Why the Pope does not introduce this or that reform? The true answer is that a revolutionist is not the kind of man who becomes a Pope, and that the man who becomes a Pope has no wish to be a revolutionist…'

None can gainsay the truth of what Dicey has said. What the governing class may do depends not so much upon the degree of its sovereignty as upon what Dicey calls the external and internal limitations in sovereignty. Of these two, if the failure to do good arises out of the external limitations, nobody need blame the governing class. The fear of external limitations blocking progress need not cause much apprehension. For, it is the internal limitations of the governing class that have a greater determining force than the external limitations. Progress depends more upon internal limitations of the governing class than upon external limitations. What are the factors which determine these internal limitations? The internal limitations are born out of the outlook, traditions, vested interests and the social philosophy of the governing class. The purpose of this discussion is to warn the foreigner that before believing what the Congress proposes to do for the servile classes, he should make it a point to ask: What is the outlook of the governing class? What are its traditions? What is its social philosophy?

To take the Brahmins first. Historically, they have been the most inveterate enemy of the servile classes (Shudras and the Untouchables) who together constitute about 80 per cent of the total Hindu population. If the common man belonging to the servile classes in India is today so fallen, so degraded, so devoid of hope and ambition, it is entirely due to the Brahmins and their philosophy. The cardinal principles of this philosophy of Brahminism are five: (1) graded inequality between the different classes; (2) complete disarmament of the Shudras and the Untouchables; (3) complete prohibition of the education of the Shudras and the Untouchables; (4) ban on the Shudras and the Untouchables occupying places of power and authority; and (5) ban on the Shudras and the Untouchables acquiring property and complete subjugation and suppression of women. Inequality is the official doctrine of Brahminism and the suppression of the lower classes aspiring to equality has been looked upon by them and carried out by them, without remorse as their bounden duty. There are countries where education did not spread beyond a few. But, India is the only country where the intellectual class, namely, the Brahmins not only made education their monopoly but declared acquisition of education by the lower classes a crime punishable by cutting off of the tongue or by the pouring of molten lead in the ear of the offender. The Congress politicians complain that the British are ruling India by a wholesale disarmament of the people of India. But, they forget that disarmament of the Shudras and the Untouchables was the rule of law promulgated by the Brahmins.

Indeed, so strongly did the Brahmins believe in the disarmament of the Shudras and the Untouchables that when they revised the law to enable the Brahmins to arm themselves for the protection of their own privileges, they maintained the ban on the Shudras and the Untouchables as it was without lessening its rigour. If the large majority of people of India appear today to be thoroughly emasculated, spiritless, with no manliness, it is the result of the Brahminic policy of wholesale disarmament to which they have been subjected for the untold ages. There is no social evil and no social wrong to which the Brahmin does not give his support. Man's inhumanity to man, such as the feeling of caste, Untouchability, unapproachability and unseeability is a religion to him. It would, however, be a mistake to suppose that only the wrongs of man are a religion to him. For, the Brahmin has given his support to the worst wrongs that women have suffered from in any part of the world. Widows were burnt alive as sattees. The Brahmin gave his fullest support to Sattee, the burning alive of a widow. Widows were not allowed to remarry. The Brahmin upheld the doctrine. Girls were required to be married before eight and the husband had the right to consummate the marriage at any time thereafter, whether she had reached puberty or not did not matter. The Brahmin gave the doctrine his strongest support. The record of the Brahmins as law-givers for the Shudras, for the Untouchables and for women is the blackest as compared with the record of the intellectual classes in other parts of the world. For no intellectual class has prostituted its intelligence to invent a philosophy to keep his uneducated countrymen in a perpetual state of ignorance and poverty as the Brahmins have done in India.

Every Brahmin today believes in this philosophy of Brahminism propounded by his forefathers. He is an alien element in the Hindu Society. The Brahmin vis-a-vis Shudras and the Untouchables as foreign is the German is to the French, as the Jew is to the Gentile or as the white is to the Negro. There is a real gulf between him and the lower classes of Shudras and Untouchables. He is not only alien to them but he is also hostile to them. In relationship with them, there is no room for conscience and there is no call for justice.

The Bania is the worst parasitic class known to history. In him the vice of money-making is unredeemed by culture or conscience. He is like an undertaker who prospers when there is an epidemic. The only difference between the undertaker and the Bania is that the undertaker does not create an epidemic while the Bania does. He does not use his money for production. He uses it to create poverty and more poverty by lending money for unproductive purposes. He lives on interest and as he is told by his religion that money lending is the occupation prescribed to him by Manu, he looks upon it as both right and righteous. With the help and assistance of the Brahmin judge, who is ready to decree his suits, he is able to carry on his trade. Interest, interest on interest, he adds on and on, and thereby draws families perpetually into his net. Pay him as much as a debtor may, he is always in debt. With no conscience, there is no fraud, and no chicanery that he will not commit. His grip over the nation is complete. The whole of poor, starving, illiterate India is mortgaged to the Bania.

To sum up, the Brahmin enslaves the mind and the Bania enslaves the body. Between them, they divide the spoils which belong to the governing classes. Can anyone who realizes what the outlook, tradition and social philosophy of the governing class in India is believe that under the Congress regime, a sovereign and Independent India will be different from the India we have today?

If the Congress is honest and sincere in its professions as the champion and the guardian of the servile classes, the Congress may well be called upon to show what steps it took to destroy the power of the governing class. It is repeated from house-tops that the Congress swept the polls in the elections that took place in 1937. Overlooking the hyperbole, a question could legitimately be asked: It is true that the Congress won the victory but which is the class among the Indian people which carried the trophy? Unfortunately, no Indian publicist has as yet undertaken to compile an Indian counterpart of Dodd's Parliamentary Manual. Consequently, it is difficult to have precise particulars regarding the caste, occupation, education and social status of members of the legislature elected on the Congress ticket. The matter is so important that I thought of collecting the necessary information on these points relating to members of the Provincial Legislatures elected in 1937 on the Congress ticket. I did not succeed in getting precise information about every member. There are many whom I have had to leave as unclassified. But the information I have been able to gather throws a glaring light upon victory of the Congress and shows what it means to the people of India in terms of their freedom and their well-being.

Table 2 shows the proportion of Brahmins and non-Brahmins and the Scheduled Castes that were elected to the Provincial Legislative Assemblies on the Congress Ticket.

Table 2
Classification of Congress Members of Provincial Assemblies by castes

Province	Brahmins	Non-Brahmins	Scheduled Castes	Not Stated	Total
Assam	6	21	1	5	33
Bengal	15	27	6	6	54
Bihar	31	39	16	12	98
C.P.	28	35	7	—	70
Madras	38	90	26	5	159
Orissa	11	20	5	—	36
United Provinces	39	54	16	24	133

Those who do not know how small is the proportion of the Brahmins to the total population of Hindus may not be able to realize the representation which the Brahmins have secured in the Congress Election. But, those who know it will realize that in proportion to their numbers, the Brahmins have secured overwhelming representation.

What degree of representation did the Congress give to the propertied classes, such as Banias, businessmen and landlords? Table 3 shows how many Banias, businessmen and landlords were elected on the Congress ticket.

Here again the representation secured by the Banias, landlords and businessmen standing on the Congress ticket is overwhelming. Is there any doubt that the Congress instead of warring against the governing class actually helped the governing class to capture political power? There is one other feature of the Congress victory in the election which needs to be exposed. It relates to the composition of the Congress ministries.[21]

Tables 4 and 5 give an idea of the position of the Brahmins in the Congress ministries in provinces in which the Congress had obtained a majority.

In all the Hindu provinces, the Prime Ministers were Brahmins. In all Hindu provinces, if the non-Hindu ministers were excluded, the cabinets were wholly composed of Brahmins. This was particularly so in United Provinces, the province to which Pandit Jawaharlal Nehru belongs.

Is there any doubt that the Brahmins form the governing class in India? Is there any doubt that the Congress' fight for freedom is for the freedom of the governing class? Is there any doubt that the Congress is the governing class and the governing class is the Congress? Is there any doubt that when Swaraj came in 1937 in the form of provincial autonomy, the Congress shamelessly put the governing class in places of power and authority?

To be true to facts, it is an understatement to say that the Congress put the governing classes into places of power and authority. It did more than that. Here again, so strange has been the result that people will not believe what the Congress did unless they see the facts. The fact is that the Congress High Command in selecting a candidate had a definite policy, namely, in the case of Brahmins, to give preference to a candidate who had the highest educational qualifications and in the case of the non-Brahmins and the Scheduled Castes, to give preference to a candidate who had the lowest educational qualification. Let those who have any doubts in the matter consider the facts summarized in Table 6.

It is obvious that in the case of the Brahmins the relative proportion of graduates to non-graduates is far higher than what it is in the case of the non-Brahmins and the Scheduled Castes. The difference in terms of graduates and non-graduates does not really reveal the correct situation. To put it correctly, the Brahmin graduates were seasoned politicians of high repute while the non-Brahmin graduates were raw graduates with the career of second-class politicians to recommend them.

---

[21]Indian Information for 15 July 1939.

Table 3

Classification of the Congress Members of the Provincial Legislatures in terms of Occupation

Province	Lawyers	Medical Practitioners	Landlords	Businessmen	Private officials	Moneylenders	Nil	Not Stated	Total
Assam	16	2	2	1	—	—	3	9	33
Bengal	9	2	16	5	2	—	16	4	54
Bihar	14	4	56	6	3	—	1	14	98
Central Provinces	20	2	25	10	—	—	8	5	70
Madras	52	2	45	18	2	1	3	36	159
Orissa	3	1	17	4	4	1	1	—	36

Why did the Congress select the best-educated Brahmins as its candidates for election? Why did the Congress select the least-educated non-Brahmins and Scheduled Castes as its candidates for election? To this question, I can see only one answer. It was to prevent the non-Brahmins in the Congress from forming a ministry. The Congress seems to have deliberately preferred an uneducated non-Brahmin to an educated one because, from the point of view of the governing class, the uneducated non-Brahmin has two definite advantages over an educated non-Brahmin. In the first place, he is likely to be more grateful to the Congress High Command for having got him elected than an educated non-Brahmin is likely to be, and would not be ready to revolt against the Congress ministry, formed by the governing classes, by joining hands with the educated non-Brahmins in the Congress Party should the latter aspire to form a government of their own against the government of the governing classes. In the second place, if more undergraduates or more raw non-Brahmin graduates were selected, it was with the purpose to prevent the non-Brahmins in the Congress from forming a competent and alternative ministry to the detriment of the governing class. The non-Brahmins in the Congress do not know how the Congress has deceived them, and how in drawing them inside the Congress, the Congress was making a concealed attempt to permanently entrench the governing classes in places of power and authority.

There is a tragic side to the foreigner's view of Indian politics to which it is impossible not to make a reference. The foreigners who take interest in Indian politics fall into three groups. The first group is aware of the social cleavages which rend Indian politics, cleavages of majorities and minorities, Hindus and Untouchables and so on. Their main object is not to solve these cleavages by appropriate constitutional safeguards and to open the way to constitutional advancement of India but to use these cleavages to block constitutional progress. The second group of foreigners are those who pay no attention to the cleavages, who care a button what happens to the minorities and to the Untouchables. They are out to support the Congress demand and would fulfil it without bothering about safeguards. The third group consists of tourists who come 'to do' India and learn about its politics

Table 4

Composition of the Cabinets in the Congress Provinces*

Province	Total No. of cabinet Ministers	Total No. of Non-Hindu Ministers	Hindu Ministers in the Cabinet				Prime Minister
			Total	Brahmins	Non-Brahmins	Scheduled Castes	
Assam	8	3	5	?	?	Nil	Brahmin
Bihar	4	1	3	?	?	1	Brahmin
Bombay	7	2	5	3	2	Nil	Brahmin
Central Provinces	5	1	4	3	1	Nil	Brahmin
Madaras	9	2	7	3	3	1	Bralimin
Orissa	3	Nil	3	?	?	?	?
United Provinces	6	2	4	4	Nil	Nil	Brahmin

*This table represents the position as it stood in May 1939 and as reported in the Issue of July 15,1939 of the Indian Information. Question mark indicates inability to classify whether Brahmin or Non-Brahmin.

Table 5

Classification of Parliamentary Secretaries in Congress Provinces*

Province	Total No. of Parliamentary Secretaries	Total No. of Non-Hindu Parliamentary Secretaries	Hindu Parliamentary Secretaries			
			Total	Brahmins	Non-Brahmins	Scheduled Castes
Assam	Nil	Nil	Nil	Nil	Nil	Nil
Bihar	8	Nil	8	2	5	1
Bombay	6	Nil	6	1	5	Nil
Central Provinces	Nil	Nil	Nil	Nil	Nil	Nil
Madaras	8	1	7	3	4	1
Orissa	3	Nil	3	?	?	Nil
United Provinces	12	1	11	2	8	1

*Compiled from Indian Information Issue of July 15, 1939. Question mark indicates inability to classify whether Brahmin or non-Brahmin.

if possible overnight. All three are dangerous people. But, the third group is the most dangerous from the point of view of the ultimate interest of the Indian people.

That there should be foreigners of the tourist sort who cannot understand the intricacies of Indian politics and who, therefore, support the Congress on no other ground except that which Mr Pickwick gave to Sam Weller—to shout with the biggest crowd—is quite understandable. But, what annoys most is the attitude of the leaders of the British Labour Party, heads of radical and leftist groups in Europe and America, represented by men like Laski, Kingsley Martin, Brailsford and editors of journals like the *Nation* in America, and the *New Statesman* in England championing the cause of the oppressed and the suppressed people. How can these men support the Congress passes one's comprehension. Do they not know that the Congress means the governing class and that the governing class means the Congress: Do they not know that the governing class in India is a Brahmin–Bania combine? That are drawn in the Congress only to be camp followers with no say in the making of Congress policy? Do they not realize that for the reasons for which the Sultan could not abolish Islam or the Pope could not repudiate Catholicism, the governing class in India will not decree the destruction of Brahminism and that so long as the governing class remains what it is, Brahminism which preaches the supremacy of Brahmins and the allied castes and which recognizes the suppression and degradation of the Shudras and the Untouchables as the sacred duty of the State will continue to be the philosophy of the State even if India became free?

Do they not know that this governing class in India is not a part of the Indian people, is not only completely isolated from them, but believes in isolating itself, lest it should be contaminated by them, has implanted in its mind by reason of the Brahminic philosophy, motives and interests which are hostile to those who are outside its fold and, therefore, does not sympathize with the living forces operating in the servile masses whom it has trodden down, is not charged with their wants, their pains, their cravings, their desires, is inimical to their aspirations, does not favour any advance in their education, promotion to high office and disfavours every movement calculated to raise their

Table 6
Classification of Brahmin and Non-Brahmin Congress Partymen by Literacy

Provincial Assemblies	castes	Total	Graduates	Non-Graduates	Matriculates	Illiterates	Not Stated
Assam	Brahmin	6	5	1	–	–	–
	Non-Brahmin	21	15	2	–	1	9
Bengal	Brahmin	15	14	1	–	–	–
	Non-Brahmin	27	21	4	–	1	7
	Scheduled Castes	6	3	–	1	2	–
Bihar	Brahmin	31	11	5	8	4	3
	Non-Brahmin	39	23	4	3	8	13
	Scheduled Castes	–	1	1	4	10	–
Central Province	Brahmin	39	15	–	2	9	2
	Non-Brahmin	54	15	–	2	17	1
	Scheduled Castes	-	1	–	–	6	–
Madras	Brahmin	38	16	2	3	4	13
	Non-Brahmin	90	31	3	1	7	61
	Scheduled Castes	26	1	1	1	14	–
	Backward Class	-	1	–	–	–	–
Orissa	Brahmin	11	6	1	–	3	1
	Non-Brahmin	20	7	3	2	7	1
	Scheduled Castes	5	–	–	–	5	–

dignity and their self-respect? Do they not know that in the Swaraj of India is involved the fate of 60 millions of Untouchables? It would be impossible to say that the leaders of the British Labour Party, that Kingsley Martin, Brailsford and Laski, whose writings on liberty and democracy are a source of inspiration to all suppressed people, do not know these facts. Yet, if they refer to India, it is always to support the Congress. It is very, very seldom that they are found to discuss the problem of the Untouchables which ought to make the strongest appeal to all radicals and democrats. Their exclusive attention to Congress activities and their utter neglect of other elements in the national life of India shows how misguided they have been. One could well understand their support to the Congress if the Congress was fighting for political democracy. But is it? As every one knows, the Congress is only fighting for national liberty and is not interested in political democracy. The party in India who is fighting for political democracy is the party of the Untouchables who fear that this Congress fight for liberty, if it succeeds, will mean liberty to the strong and the powerful to suppress the weak and the downtrodden unless they are protected by constitutional safeguards. It is they who ought to receive the help of these radical leaders. But, the Untouchables have been waiting in vain for all these years even for a gesture of goodwill and support from them. These radicals and leftists in Europe and America have not even cared to know the forces behind the Congress. Ignorant or unmindful, one does not know, but the fact remains that these leftists and radical leaders have been giving blind and unquestioning support to the Congress which admittedly is run by capitalists, landlords, money lenders and reactionaries, only because the Congress calls its activities by the grandiloquent name of 'Fight for Freedom'. All battles for freedom are not on equal moral plane for the simple reason that the motives and purposes behind these battles of freedom are not always the same. To take only a few illustrations from English History, the Barons' Rebellion against John, which resulted in the Magna Charta, could be called a battle for freedom. But could any democrat in modern times give it the same support which he would give—say to the Levellers' Rebellion or to the Peasant's Revolt in English History, merely because it could logically be described as a battle for freedom?

To do so will be to respond to a false cry of freedom. Such crude conduct would have been forgivable, had it proceeded from groups not intelligent enough to make a distinction between freedom to live and freedom to oppress. But, it is quite inexcusable in radical and leftist groups led by Messrs. Laski, Kingsley Martin, Brailsford, Louis Fisher and other well-known champions of democracy.

When pressed to explain why they don't support Indian Parties which stand for true democracy, they are reported to meet the charge by a counter question. Are there any such parties in India? Insist that there are such parties and they turn round and say: If such parties exist, how is it the Press does not report their activities? When told that the Press is a Congress Press, they retort: How is it that the foreign correspondents of the English Papers do not report them? I have shown why nothing better can be expected from these foreign correspondents. The Foreign Press Agency in India is no better than the Indian Press. Indeed it cannot be better. There are in India what are called foreign correspondents. In a large majority of cases they are Indians. Only a very few are foreigners. The selection of Indians as foreign correspondents is so made that they are almost always from the Congress camp. The foreign correspondents who are foreigners fall into two groups. If they are Americans, they are just anti-British, and for that reason, pro-Congress. Any political party in India which is not madly anti-British does not interest them. Those who are not in the Congress will testify how hard it was for them to persuade the American War correspondents who trooped into this country in 1941–42, even to entertain the possibility of the Congress not being the only party, much less to induce them to interest themselves in other political parties. It took a long time before they recovered their sanity and, when they did, they either abused the Congress as an organization led by impossible men or just lost interest in Indian politics. They never got interested in other political parties in India and never cared to understand their point of view. The situation is no better in the case of foreign correspondents who are Britishers. They too are interested only in that kind of politics which is first and foremost anti-British. They are uninterested in those political parties in India whose foremost concern is to make a free India safe for democracy. The result is that the foreign Press provides the same kind of news about Indian politics as does the Indian Press. These reasons cannot be beyond the ken of these radicals. Correspondents or no correspondents, is it not the duty of radicals to keep in touch with their kindred in other parts of the world to encourage them, to help them and to see that true democracy lives everywhere? It is a most unfortunate thing that the radicals of England and America should have forgotten the class to whom they owe a duty to help and have become the publicity agents of Indian Tories who are just misusing the slogan of liberty to be fool and befog the world.

The sooner they get out of this fog created by the Congress and realize that democracy and self-government in India cannot be real unless freedom has become the assured possession of all, the better for them and the better for the people of India. But, if they persist in giving their blind support to the Congress on the basis of an empty slogan without examining its relation to facts and intentions, I for one will have no hesitation in saying that far from being the friends of India, they are a positive menace to the freedom of the Indian masses. It is a pity that they do not seem to distinguish the case of a tyrant who is held down and who pleads for liberty because he wants to regain his right to oppress and the case of an oppressed class seeking to be free from the oppression of the tyrant. In their hurry to bring freedom to India, they have no time to realize that by siding with the Congress what they are doing is not to make India safe for democracy but to free the tyrant to practise his tyrannies. Is it necessary to tell them that to support Congress is to let tyranny have freedom to enslave?

Chapter 4

THE PAKISTAN QUESTION

On 26 March 1940, Hindu India was startled to attention as it had
never been before. On that day, the Muslim League at its Lahore
Session passed the following resolution:

'1. While approving and endorsing the action taken by the Council
     and the Working Committee of the All India Muslim League
     as indicated in their resolutions dated the 27th of August, 17th
     and 18th of September and 22nd of October 1939 and 3rd of
     February 1940 on the constitutional issue, this Session of the All
     India Muslim League emphatically reiterates that the Scheme of
     Federation embodied in the Government of India Act, 1935, is
     totally unsuited to, and unworkable in the peculiar conditions of
     this country and is altogether unacceptable to Muslim India;

2.   It further records its emphatic view that while the declaration
     dated the 18th of October 1939 made by the Viceroy on behalf
     of His Majesty's government is reassuring in as far as it declares
     that the policy and plan on which the Government of India
     Act, 1935, is based will be reconsidered in consultation with
     the various parties, interests and communities in India, Muslim
     India will not be satisfied unless the whole constitutional plan
     is reconsidered de novo and that no revised plan would be
     acceptable to the Muslims, unless it is framed with their approval
     and consent;

3.   Resolved that it is the considered view of this Session of the
     All India Muslim League that no constitutional plan would be
     workable in this country or acceptable to the Muslims unless
     it is designated on the following basic principle, viz. that
     geographically contiguous units are demarcated into regions
     which should be so constituted with such territorial readjustments
     as may be necessary, that the areas in which the Muslims are

numerically in a majority as in the North-Western and Eastern Zones of India should be grouped to constitute "Independent States" in which the Constituent Units shall be autonomous and sovereign;

4. That adequate, effective and mandatory safeguards should be specifically provided in the constitution for minorities in these units and in the regions for the protection of their religious, cultural, economic, political, administrative and other rights, and interests in consultation with them; and in other parts of India where the Musalmans are in a minority, adequate, effective and mandatory safeguards shall be specifically provided in the constitution for them and other minorities for the protection of their religious, cultural, economic, political, administrative and other rights, and interests in consultation with them;

5. This Session further authorizes the Working Committee to frame a Scheme of Constitution in accordance with these basic principles, providing for the assumption finally by the respective regions of all powers such as defence, external affairs, communication, customs, and such other matters as may be necessary.'

What does this Resolution contemplate? A reference to paragraph 3 of the Resolution will show that the Resolution contemplates that the areas in which Muslims predominate shall be incorporated into independent States. In concrete terms, it means that the Punjab, the North-Western Frontier Province, Baluchistan and Sind in the North-West and Bengal in the East instead of remaining as the provinces of British India shall be incorporated as independent States outside of British India. This is the sum and substance of the Resolution of the Muslim League.

Does the Resolution contemplate that these Muslim provinces, after being incorporated into States, will remain each an independent sovereign State or will they be joined together into one constitution as members of a single State, federal or unitary? On this point, the Resolution is rather ambiguous, if not self-contradictory. It speaks of grouping the zones into 'Independent States in which the Constituent

Units shall be autonomous and sovereign.' The use of the term 'Constituent Units' indicates that what is contemplated is a Federation. If that is so, then, the use of the word 'sovereign' as an attribute of the Units is out of place. Federation of Units and sovereignty of Units are contradictions. It may be that what is contemplated is a confederation. It is, however, not very material for the moment whether these independent States are to form into a federation or a confederation. What is important is the basic demand, namely, that these areas are to be separated from India and formed into independent States.

The Resolution is so worded as to give the idea that the scheme adumbrated in it is a new one. But, there can be no doubt that the Resolution merely resuscitates a scheme which was put forth by Sir Mahomed Iqbal in his Presidential address to the Muslim League at its Annual Session held at Lucknow in December 1930. The scheme was not then adopted by the League. It was, however, taken up by one Mr Rehmat Ali who gave it the name, Pakistan, by which it is known. Mr Rehmat Ali, M.A., LL.B., founded the Pakistan Movement in 1933. He divided India into two, namely, Pakistan and Hindustan. His Pakistan included the Punjab, N.W.F. Province, Kashmir, Sind and Baluchistan. The rest to him was Hindustan. His idea was to have an 'independent and separate Pakistan' composed of five Muslim provinces in the North as an independent State. The proposal was circulated to the members of the Round Table Conference but never officially put forth. It seems an attempt was made privately to obtain the assent of the British Government, who, however, declined to consider it because they thought that this was a 'revival of the old Muslim Empire'.[22]

The League has only enlarged the original scheme of Pakistan. It has sought to create one more Muslim State in the east to include the Muslims in Bengal and Assam. Barring this, it expresses in its essence and general outline the scheme put forth by Sir Mahomed Iqbal and propagated by Mr Rehmat Ali. There is no name given to this new Muslim State in the East. This has made no difference in the theory and the issues involved in the ideology of Mr Rehmat Ali. The only

---

[22]Halide Edib, *Inside India*, p 355.

difficulty one feels is that the League, while enlarging the facets, has not christened the two Muslim States with short and sweet names as it might have been expected to do. That it did not do and we are left to carry on the discussion with two long jaw-breaking names of Muslim State in the west and Muslim State in the east. I propose to solve this difficulty by reserving the name Pakistan to express the ideology underlying the two-nation theory and its consequent effect, namely, partition, and by designating the two Muslim States in the North-West and North-East as Western Pakistan and Eastern Pakistan.

The scheme not only called Hindu India to attention but it shocked Hindu India. Now it is natural to ask, what is there that is new or shocking in this scheme?

That there are factors, administrative, linguistic or cultural, which are the predisposing causes behind these demands for separation, is a fact which is admitted and understood by all. Nobody minds these demands and many are prepared to concede them. But, the Hindus say that the Muslims are going beyond the idea of separation and questions, such as what has led them to take this course, why are they asking for partition, for the annulment of the common tie by a legal divorce between Pakistan and Hindustan, are being raised.

The answer is to be found in the declaration made by the Muslim League in its Resolution that the Muslims of India are a separate nation. It is this declaration by the Muslim League, which is both resented and ridiculed by the Hindus.

The Hindu resentment is quite natural. Whether India is a nation or not, has been the subject-matter of controversy between the Anglo-Indians and the Hindu politicians ever since the Indian National Congress was founded. The Anglo-Indians were never tired of proclaiming that India was not a nation, that 'Indians' was only another name for the people of India. In the words of one Anglo-Indian 'to know India was to forget that there is such a thing as India.' The Hindu politicians and patriots have been, on the other hand, equally persistent in their assertion that India is a nation. That the Anglo-Indians were right in their repudiation cannot be gainsaid. Even Dr Tagore, the national poet of Bengal, agrees with them. But, the Hindus have never yielded on the point even to Dr Tagore.

This was because of two reasons. Firstly, the Hindu felt ashamed to admit that India was not a nation. In a world where nationality and nationalism were deemed to be special virtues in a people, it was quite natural for the Hindus to feel, to use the language of Mr H.G. Wells, that it would be as improper for India to be without a nationality as it would be for a man to be without his clothes in a crowded assembly. Secondly, he had realized that nationality had a most intimate connection with the claim for self-government. He knew that by the end of the nineteenth century, it had become an accepted principle that the people, who constituted a nation, were entitled on that account to self-government and that any patriot who asked for self-government for his people had to prove that they were a nation. The Hindu for these reasons never stopped to examine whether India was or was not a nation in fact. He never cared to reason whether nationality was merely a question of calling a people a nation or was a question of the people being a nation. He knew one thing, namely, that if he was to succeed in his demand for self-government for India, he must maintain, even if he could not prove it, that India was a nation.

In this assertion, he was never contradicted by any Indian. The thesis was so agreeable that even serious Indian students of history came forward to write propagandist literature in support of it, no doubt out of patriotic motives. The Hindu social reformers, who knew that this was a dangerous delusion, could not openly contradict this thesis. For, anyone who questioned it was at once called a tool of the British bureaucracy and enemy of the country. The Hindu politician was able to propagate his view for a long time. His opponent, the Anglo-Indian, had ceased to reply to him. His propaganda had almost succeeded. When it was about to succeed comes this declaration of the Muslim League—this rift in the lute. Just because it does not come from the Anglo-Indian, it is a deadlier blow. It destroys the work which the Hindu politician has done for years. If the Muslims in India are a separate nation, then, of course, India is not a nation. This assertion cuts the whole ground from under the feet of the Hindu politicians. It is natural that they should feel annoyed at it and call it a stab in the back.

But, stab or no stab, the point is, can the Musalmans be said to constitute a nation? Everything else is beside the point. This raises the question: What is a nation? Tomes have been written on the subject. Those who are curious may go through them and study the different basic conceptions as well as the different aspects of it. It is, however, enough to know the core of the subject and that can be set down in a few words. Nationality is a social feeling. It is a feeling of a corporate sentiment of oneness which makes those who are charged with it feel that they are kith and kin. This national feeling is a double-edged feeling. It is at once a feeling of fellowship for one's own kith and kin and an anti-fellowship feeling for those who are not one's own kith and kin. It is a feeling of 'consciousness of kind' which on the one hand binds together those who have it, so strongly that it over-rides all differences arising out of economic conflicts or social gradations and, on the other, severs them from those who are not of their kind. It is a longing not to belong to any other group. This is the essence of what is called a nationality and national feeling.

Now apply this test to the Muslim claim. Is it or is it not a fact that the Muslims of India are an exclusive group? Is it not or is it not a fact that they have a consciousness of kind? Is it or is it not a fact that every Muslim is possessed by a longing to belong to his own group and not to any non-Muslim group?

If the answer to these questions is in the affirmative, then the controversy must end and the Muslim claim that they are a nation must be accepted without cavil.

What the Hindus must show is that notwithstanding some differences, there are enough affinities between Hindus and Musalmans to constitute them into one nation, or, to use plain language, which make Muslims and Hindus long to belong together.

Hindus, who disagree with the Muslim view that the Muslims are a separate nation by themselves, rely upon certain features of Indian social life which seem to form the bonds of integration between Muslim society and Hindu society.

In the first place, it is said that there is no difference of race between the Hindus and the Muslims. That the Punjabi Musalman and the Punjabi Hindu, the Uttar Pradesh [UP] Musalman and the Uttar Pradesh Hindu, the Bihar Musalman and the Bihar Hindu, the Bengal Musalman and the Bengal Hindu, the Madras Musalman and the Madras Hindu, and the Bombay Musalman and the Bombay Hindu are racially of one stock. Indeed there is more racial affinity between the Madras Musalman and the Madras Brahmin than there is between the Madras Brahmin and the Punjab Brahmin. In the second place, reliance is placed upon linguistic unity between Hindus and Muslims. It is said that the Musalmans have no common language of their own which can mark them off as a linguisticgroup separate from the Hindus. On the contrary, there is a complete linguistic unity between the two. In the Punjab, both Hindus and Muslims speak Punjabi. In Sind, both speak Sindhi. In Bengal, both speak Bengali. In Gujarat, both speak Gujarati. In Maharashtra, both speak Marathi. So is it in every province. It is only in towns that the Musalmans speak Urdu and the Hindus the language of the province. But outside, in the mofussil, there is complete linguistic unity between Hindus and Musalmans. Thirdly, it is pointed out that India is the land which the Hindus and Musalmans have now inhabited together for centuries. It is not exclusively the land of the Hindus, nor is it exclusively the land of the Mahomedans.

Reliance is placed not only upon racial unity but also upon pertain common features in the social and cultural life of the two communities. It is pointed out that the social life of many Muslim groups is honeycombed with Hindu customs. For instance, the Avans of the Punjab, though they are nearly all Muslims, retain Hindu names and keep their genealogies in the Brahmanic fashion. Hindu surnames are found among Muslims. For instance, the surname Chaudhari is a Hindu surname but is common among the Musalmans of UP and Northern India. In the matter of marriage, certain groups of Muslims are Muslims in name only. They either follow the Hindu form of the ceremony alone, or perform the ceremony first by the Hindu rites and then call the Kazi and have it performed in the Muslim form. In some sections of Muslims, the law applied is the Hindu law in the matter of marriage, guardianship and inheritance. Before the Shariat Act was passed, this was true even in the Punjab and the N.W.F.P. In the social sphere, the caste system is alleged to be as much a part of Muslim society as it is of Hindu society. In the religious sphere, it is pointed out that many Muslim pirs had Hindu disciples; and similarly some Hindu yogis have had Muslim chelas. Reliance is placed on instances of friendship between saints of the rival creeds. At Girot, in the Punjab, the tombs of two ascetics, Jamali Sultan and Diyal Bhawan, who lived in close amity during the early part of the nineteenth century, stand close to one another, and are reverenced by Hindus and Musalmans alike. Bawa Fathu, a Muslim saint, who lived about AD 1700 and whose tomb is at Ranital in the Kangra District, received the title of prophet by the blessing of a Hindu saint, Sodhi Guru Gulab Singh. On the other hand, Baba Shahana, a Hindu saint whose cult is observed in the Jang District, is said to have been the chela of a Muslim pir who changed the original name (Mihra) of his Hindu follower into Mir Shah.

All this, no doubt, is true. That a large majority of the Muslims belong to the same race as the Hindus is beyond question. That all Mahomedans do not speak a common tongue, that many speak the same language as the Hindus cannot be denied. That there are certain social customs which are common to both cannot be gainsaid. That certain religious rites and practices are common to both is also a matter of fact. But the question is: Can all this support the conclusion that the Hindus and the Mahomedans on account of them constitute one nation or these things have fostered in them a feeling that they long to belong to each other?

'What justification have the Musalmans of India for demanding the partition of India and the establishment of separate Muslim States? Why this insurrection? What grievances have they?'—ask the Hindus in a spirit of righteous indignation.

Anyone who knows history will not fail to realize that it has now been a well-established principle that nationalism is a sufficient justification for the creation of a national state. As the great historian Lord Acton points out:

'In the old European system, the rights of nationalities were neither recognized by Governments nor asserted by the people. The interest of the reigning families, not those of the nations, regulated the frontiers, and the administration was conducted generally without any reference to popular desires. Where all liberties were suppressed, the claims of national independence were necessarily ignored, and a princess, in the words of Fenelon, carried a monarchy in her wedding portion.'

Nationalities were at first listless. When they became conscious:

'They first rose against their conquerors in defence of their legitimate rulers. They refused to be governed by usurpers. Next came a time when they revolted because of the wrongs inflicted upon them by their rulers. The insurrections were provoked by particular grievances justified by definite complaints. Then came the French Revolution which effected a complete change. It taught the people to regard their wishes and wants as the supreme criterion of their right to do what they liked to do with themselves. It proclaimed the idea of the sovereignty of the people uncontrolled by the past and uncontrolled by the existing state. This text taught by the French Revolution became an accepted dogma of all liberal thinkers. Mill gave it his support. "One hardly knows," says Mill, "what any division of the human race should be free to do, if not to determine with which of the various collective bodies of human beings they choose to associate themselves. "'

He even went so far as to hold that:

'It is in general a necessary condition of free institutions that the boundaries of governments should coincide in the main with those of nationalities.'

Thus history shows that the theory of nationality is imbedded in the democratic theory of the sovereignty of the will of a people. This means that the demand by a nationality for a national state does not require to be supported by any list of grievances. The will of the people is enough to justify it.

But, if grievances must be cited in support of their claim, the Muslims say that they have them in plenty. They may be summed up in one sentence, that constitutional safeguards have failed to save them from the tyranny of the Hindu majority.

At the Round Table Conference, the Muslims presented their list of safeguards, which were formulated in the well-known fourteen points.

The Hindu representatives at the Round Table Conference would not consent to them. There was an impasse. The British Government intervened and gave what is known as 'the Communal decision'. By that decision, the Muslims got all their fourteen points. There was much bitterness amongst the Hindus against the Communal Award. But, the Congress did not take part in the hostility that was displayed by the Hindus generally towards it, although it did retain the right to describe it as anti-national and to get it changed with the consent of the Muslims. So careful was the Congress not to wound the feelings of the Muslims that when the Resolution was moved in the Central Assembly condemning the Communal Award, the Congress, though it did not bless it, remained neutral, neither opposing nor supporting it. The Mahomedans were well-justified in looking upon this Congress attitude as a friendly gesture.

The victory of the Congress at the polls in the provinces, where the Hindus are in a majority, did not disturb the tranquillity of the Musalmans. They felt they had nothing to fear from the Congress and the prospects were that the Congress and the Muslim League would work the constitution in partnership. But, two years and three months of the Congress government in the Hindu Provinces have completely disillusioned them and have made them the bitterest enemies of the Congress. The Deliverance Day celebration held on the 22 December 1939 shows the depth of their resentment. What is worse, their bitterness is not confined to the Congress. The Musalmans, who at the Round Table Conference joined in the demand for Swaraj, are today the most ruthless opponents of Swaraj.

What has the Congress done to annoy the Muslims so much? The Muslim League has asserted that under the Congress regime the Muslims were actually tyrannized and oppressed. Two committees appointed by the League are said to have investigated and reported on the matter. But apart from these matters which require to be examined by an impartial tribunal, there are undoubtedly two things which have produced the clash: (1) the refusal by the Congress to recognize the Muslim League as the only representative body of the Muslims, (2) the refusal by the Congress to form coalition ministries in the Congress provinces.

On the first question, both the Congress and the League are adamant. The Congress is prepared to accept the Muslim League as one of the many Muslim political organizations, such as the Ahrars, the National Muslims and the Jamiat-ul-Ulema. But it will not accept the Muslim League as the only representative body of the Muslims. The Muslim League, on the other hand, is not prepared to enter into any talk unless the Congress accepts it as the only representative body of the Musalmans of India. The Hindus stigmatize the claim of the League as an extravagant one and try to ridicule it. The Muslims may say that if the Hindus would only stop to inquire how treaties between nations are made, they would realize the stupidity of their view. It may be argued that when a nation proceeds to make a treaty with another nation, it recognizes the government of the latter as fully representing it. In no country does the government of the day represent the whole body of people. Everywhere it represents only a majority. But nations do not refuse to settle their disputes because the governments, which represent them, do not represent the whole people. It is enough if each government represents a majority of its citizens. This analogy, the Muslims may contend, must apply to the Congress–League quarrel on this issue. The League may not represent the whole body of the Muslims but if it represents a majority of them, the Congress should have no compunction to deal with it for the purpose of effecting a settlement of the Hindu–Muslim question. Of course, it is open to the government of a country not to recognize the government of another country where there is more than one body claiming to be the government. Similarly, the Congress may not recognize the League. It must, however, recognize either the National Muslims or the Ahrars or the Jamiat-ul-Ulema and fix the terms of settlement between the two communities. Of course, it must act with the full knowledge as to which is more likely to be repudiated by the Muslims—an agreement with the League or an agreement with the other Muslim parties. The Congress must deal with one or the other. To deal with neither is not only stupid but mischievous. This attitude of the Congress only serves to annoy the Muslims and to exasperate them. The Muslims rightly interpret this attitude of the Congress as an attempt to create divisions among them with a view to cause confusion in their ranks and weaken their front.

On the second issue, the Muslim demand has been that in the cabinets there shall be included Muslim ministers who have the confidence of the Muslim members in the Legislature. They expected that this demand of theirs would be met by the Congress if it came in power. But, they were sorely disappointed. With regard to this demand, the Congress took a legalistic attitude. The Congress agreed to include Muslims in their cabinets, provided they resigned from their parties, joined the Congress and signed the Congress pledge. This was resented by the Muslims on three grounds.

In the first place, they regarded it as a breach of faith. The Muslims say that this demand of theirs is in accordance with the spirit of the Constitution. At the Round Table Conference, it was agreed that the cabinets shall include representatives of the minority communities. The minorities insisted that a provision to that effect should be made a part of the statute. The Hindus, on the other hand, desired that the matter should be left to be regulated by convention. A via media was found. It was agreed that the provision should find a place in the Instrument of Instructions to the Governors of the provinces and an obligation should be imposed upon them to see that effect was given to the convention in the formation of the cabinets. The Musalmans did not insist upon making this provision a part of the statute because they depended upon the good faith of the Hindus. This agreement was broken by a party which had given the Muslims to understand that towards them its attitude would be not only correct but considerate.

In the second place, the Muslims felt that the Congress view was a perversion of the real scope of the convention. They rely upon the text of the clause[23] in the Instrument of Instructions and argue that

---

[23]'In making appointments to his Council of Ministers, our Governor shall use his best endeavours to select his Ministers in the following manner, that is to say, to appoint in consultation with the person who in his judgement is most likely to command a stable majority in the Legislature, those persons (including so far as practicable, members of important minority communities) who will best be in a position collectively to command the confidence of the Legislature. In so acting, he shall bear constantly in mind the need for fostering a sense of joint responsibility among his Ministers.'

the words 'member of a minority community' in it can have only one meaning, namely, a person having the confidence of the community. The position taken by the Congress is in direct contradiction with the meaning of this clause and is indeed a covert attempt to break all other parties in the country and to make the Congress the only political party in the country. The demand for signing the Congress pledge can have no other intention. This attempt to establish a totalitarian state may be welcome to the Hindus, but it meant the political death of the Muslims as a free people.

This resentment of the Muslims was considerably aggravated when they found the governors, on whom the obligation was imposed to see that effect was given to the convention, declining to act. Some governors declined, because they were helpless by reason of the fact that the Congress was the only majority party which could produce a stable government, that a Congress government was the only government possible and that there was no alternative to it except suspending the constitution. Other governors declined, because they became active supporters of the Congress government and showed their partisanship by praising the Congress or by wearing khadi [clothes] which is the official party dress of the Congress. Whatever be the reasons, the Muslims discovered that an important safeguard had failed to save them.

The Congress reply to these accusations by the Muslims is twofold. In the first place, they say that coalition cabinets are inconsistent with collective responsibility of the cabinets. This, the Musalmans refuse to accept as an honest plea. The English people were the first and the only people, who made it a principle of their system of government. But even there it has been abandoned since. The English Parliament debated[24] the issue and came to the conclusion that it was not so sacrosanct as it was once held and that a departure from it need not necessarily affect the efficiency or smooth working of the governmental machine. Secondly, as a matter of fact, there was no collective responsibility in the Congress government. It was a government by departments. Each

---

[24]See the announcement on 22 January 1932 by the British Prime Minister on the decision of the cabinet to agree to differ on the Tariff Question and the debate on it in the Parliament.

minister was independent of the other and the prime minister was just a minister. For the Congress to talk about collective responsibility was really impertinent. The plea was even dishonest, because it is a fact that in the provinces where the Congress was in a minority, they did form coalition ministries without asking the ministers from other parties to sign the Congress pledge. The Muslims are entitled to ask 'If coalition is bad, how can it be good in one place and bad in another?'

The second reply of the Congress is that even if they take Muslim ministers in their cabinet who have not the confidence of the majority of the Muslims, they have not failed to protect their interests. Indeed they have done every thing to advance the interests of the Muslims. This no doubt rests on the view Pope held of government when he said:

'For forms of government let fools contest; what is best administered is best.'

In making this reply, the Congress High Command seems to have misunderstood what the main contention of the Muslims and the minorities has been. Their quarrel is not on the issue whether the Congress has or has not done any good to the Muslims and the minorities. Their quarrel is on an issue which is totally different. Are the Hindus to be a ruling race and the Muslims and other minorities to be subject races under Swaraj? That is the issue involved in the demand for coalition ministries.

On that, the Muslims and other minorities have taken a definite stand. They are not prepared to accept the position of subject races.

That the ruling community has done good to the ruled is quite beside the point and is no answer to the contention of the minority communities that they refuse to be treated as a subject people. The British have done many good things in India for the Indians. They have improved their roads, constructed canals on more scientific principles, effected their transport by rail, carried their letters by penny post, flashed their messages by lightning, improved their currency, regulated their weights and measures, corrected their notions of geography, astronomy and medicine, and stopped their internal quarrels and effected some advancement in their material conditions. Because of these acts of good government, did anybody ask the Indian people to remain grateful to the British and give up their agitation for self-government? Or because of these acts of social uplift, did the Indians give up their protest against being treated as a subject race by the British? The Indians did nothing of the kind. They refused to be satisfied with these good deeds and continued to agitate for their right to rule themselves. This is as it should be. For, as was said by Curran, the Irish patriot, no man can be grateful at the cost of his self-respect, no woman can be grateful at the cost of her chastity and no nation can be grateful at the cost of its honour. To do otherwise is to show that one's philosophy of life is just what Carlyle called 'pig philosophy'. The Congress High Command does not seem to realize that the Muslims and other minorities care more for the recognition of their self-respect at the hand of the Congress than for mere good deeds on the part of the Congress. Men, who are conscious of their being, are not pigs who care only for fattening food. They have their pride which they will not yield even for gold. In short, 'life is more than the meat.'

It is no use saying that the Congress is not a Hindu body. A body which is Hindu in its composition is bound to reflect the Hindu mind and support Hindu aspirations. The only difference between the Congress and the Hindu Mahasabha is that the latter is crude in its utterances and brutal in its actions while the Congress is political and polite. Apart from this difference of fact, there is no other difference between the Congress and the Hindu Mahasabha.

Similarly, it is no use saying that the Congress does not recognize the distinction between the ruler and the ruled. If this is so, the Congress must prove its bonafides by showing its readiness to recognize the other communities as free and equal partners. What is the test of such recognition? It seems to me that there can be only one—namely, agreeing to share power with the effective representatives of the minority communities. Is the Congress prepared for it? Everyone knows the answer. The Congress is not prepared to share power with a member of a community who does not owe allegiance to the Congress. Allegiance to the Congress is a condition precedent to sharing power. It seems to be a rule with the Congress that if allegiance to the Congress is not forthcoming from a community, that community must be excluded from political power.

Exclusion from political power is the essence of the distinction between a ruling race and a subject race; and inasmuch as the Congress maintained this principle, it must be said that this distinction was enforced by the Congress while it was in the saddle. The Musalmans may well complain that they have already suffered enough and that this reduction to the position of a subject race is like the proverbial last straw. Their decline and fall in India began ever since the British occupation of the country. Every change, executive, administrative, or legal, introduced by the British; has inflicted a series of blows upon the Muslim community. The Muslim rulers of India had allowed the Hindus to retain their law in civil matters. But, they abrogated the Hindu Criminal law and made the Muslim Criminal law the law of the State, applicable to all Hindus as well as Muslims. The first thing the British did was to displace gradually the Muslim Criminal law by another of their making, until the process was finally completed by the enactment of Macaulay's Penal Code. This was the first blow to the prestige and position of the Muslim community in India. This was followed by the abridgement of the field of application of the Shariat or the Muslim Civil law. Its application was restricted to matters concerning personal relations, such as marriage and inheritance, and then only to the extent permitted by the British. Side by side came the abolition, in 1837, of Persian as the official language of the court and of general administration and the substitution of English and the vernaculars in place of Persian. Then came the abolition of the Qazis, who, during the Muslim rule, administered the Shariat. In their places, were appointed law officers and judges, who might be of any religion but who got the right of interpreting Muslim law and whose decisions became binding on Muslims. These were severe blows to the Muslims. As a result, the Muslims found their prestige gone, their laws replaced, their language shelved and their education shorn of its monetary value. Along with these came more palpable blows in the shape of annexation of Sind and Oudh and the Mutiny. The last, particularly, affected the higher classes of Muslims, who suffered enormously by the extensive confiscation of property inflicted upon them by the British, as a punishment for their suspected complicity in the Mutiny. By the end of the Mutiny, the Musalmans, high and low, were brought down by these series of events to the lowest depths of broken pride, black despair and general penury. Without prestige, without education and without resources, the Muslims were left to face the Hindus. The British, pledged the neutrality, were indifferent to the result of the struggle between the two communities. The result was that the Musalmans were completely worsted in the struggle. The British conquest of India brought about a complete political revolution in the relative position of the two communities. For six hundred years, the Musalmans had been the masters of the Hindus. The British occupation brought them down to the level of the Hindus. From masters to fellow subjects was degradation enough, but a change from the status of fellow subjects to that of subjects of the Hindus is really humiliation. Is it unnatural, ask the Muslims, if they seek an escape from so intolerable a position by the creation of separate national States, in which the Muslims can find a peaceful home and in which the conflicts between a ruling race and a subject race can find no place to plague their lives?

Before the Hindus complain of the destruction of the unity of India, let them make certain that the unity they are harping upon does exist. What unity is there between Pakistan and Hindustan?

Those Hindus, who maintain the affirmative, rely chiefly upon the fact that the areas which the Muslims want to be separated from India have always been a part of India. Historically this is, no doubt, true. This area was a part of India when Chandragupta was the ruler; it continued to be a part of India when Hsuan Tsang, the Chinese pilgrim, visited India in the AD seventh century. In his diary, Hsuan Tsang has recorded that India was divided into five divisions or to use his language, there were 'five Indies':[25] (1) Northern India, (2) Western India, (3) Central India, (4) Eastern India and (5) Southern India; and that these five divisions contained eighty kingdoms. According to Hsuan Tsang, Northern India comprised the Punjab proper, including Kashmir and the adjoining hill states with the whole of Eastern Afghanistan beyond the Indus, and the present Cis-Satlaj states to the west of

---

[25]Cunningham, Alexander, *Ancient Geography of India* (Ed. Majumdar), pp 13–14. The writers of the Puranas divided India into nine divisions.

the Sarasvati river. Thus, in Northern India there were included the districts of Kabul, Jallalabad, Peshawar, Ghazni and Bannu, which were all subject to the ruler of Kapisa, who was a Hindu Kshatriya and whose capital was most probably at Charikar, 27 miles from Kabul. In the Punjab proper, the hilly districts Taxila, Singhapura, Urasa, Punch and Rajaori, were subject to the Raja of Kashmir; while the whole of the plains, including Multan and Shorkot, were dependent on the ruler of Taki or Sangala, near Lahore. Such was the extent of the northern boundary of India at the time when Hsuan Tsang came on his pilgrimage.

But as Prof. Toynbee points out:

'We must be on our guard against "historical sentiment" that is against arguments taken from conditions which once existed or were supposed to exist, but which are no longer real at the present moment. They are most easily illustrated by extreme examples. Italian newspapers have described the annexation of Tripoli as recovering the soil of the Fatherland because it was once a province of the Roman Empire; and the entire region of Macedonia is claimed by Greek Chauvinists on the one hand, because it contains the site of Pella, the cradle of Alexander the Great in the fourth century B.C., and by Bulgarians on the other, because Ochrida, in the opposite corner, was the capital of the Bulgarian Tzardom in the tenth century A.D., though the drift of time has buried the tradition of the latter almost as deep as the achievements of the "Emathian Conqueror" on which the modern Greek nationalists insist so strongly.'

The same logic applies here. Here also arguments are taken from conditions which once existed but which are no longer real and which omit to take into consideration later facts which history has to record during practically one thousand years—after the return of Hsuan Tsang.

It is true that when Hsuan Tsang came, not only the Punjab but what is now Afghanistan was part of India and further, the people of the Punjab and Afghanistan were either Vedic or Buddhist by religion. But what has happened since Hsuan Tsang left India?

The most important thing that has happened is the invasion of India by the Muslim hordes from the north-west. The first Muslim invasion of India was by the Arabs who were led by Mahommad Bin Qasim. It took place in AD 711 and resulted in the conquest of Sind. This first Muslim invasion did not result in a permanent occupation of the country because the Caliphate of Baghdad, by whose order and command the invasion had taken place, was obliged by the middle of the AD ninth century to withdraw[26] its direct control from this distant province of Sind. Soon after this withdrawal, there began a series of terrible invasions by Muhammad of Ghazni in AD 1001, Muhammad died in AD 1030, but within the short span of thirty years he invaded India seventeen times. He was followed by Mahommad Ghori who began his career as an invader in 1173. He was killed in 1206. For thirty years Muhammad of Ghazni had ravaged India and for thirty years Mahommad Ghori harried the same country in the same way. Then followed the incursions of the Moghul hordes of Chenghiz Khan. They first came in 1221. They then only wintered on the border of India but did not enter it. Twenty years after, they marched on Lahore and sacked it. Of their inroads, the most terrible was under Taimur in 1398. Then comes on the scene a new invader in the person of Babar who invaded India in 1526. The invasions of India did not stop with that of Babar. There occurred two more invasions. In 1738 Nadir Shah's invading host swept over the Punjab like a flooded river 'furious as the ocean'. He was followed by Ahmadshah Abdalli who invaded India in 1761, smashed the forces of the Mahrattas at Panipat and crushed forever the attempt of the Hindus to gain the ground which they had lost to their Muslim invaders.

The methods adopted by the invaders have left behind them their aftermath. One aftermath is the bitterness between the Hindus and the Muslims which they have caused. This bitterness between the two is so deep-seated that a century of political life has neither succeeded in assuaging it, nor in making people forget it. As the invasions were accompanied with destruction of temples and forced conversions, with spoliation of property, with slaughter, enslavement and abasement of men, women and children, what wonder if the memory of these invasions has ever remained green, as a source

---

[26]Sind was reoccumed by Mahommed Ghori.

of pride to the Muslims and as a source of shame to the Hindus? But these things apart, this north-west corner of India has been a theatre in which a stern drama has been played. Muslim hordes, in wave after wave, have surged down into this area and from thence scattered themselves in spray over the rest of India. These reached the rest of India in thin currents. In time, they also receded from their farthest limits; while they lasted, they left a deep deposit of Islamic culture over the original Aryan culture in this north-west corner of India which has given it a totally different colour, both in religious and political outlook. The Muslim invaders, no doubt, came to India singing a hymn of hate against the Hindus. But, they did not merely sing their hymn of hate and go back burning a few temples on the way. That would have been a blessing. They were not content with so negative a result. They did a positive act, namely, to plant the seed of Islam. The growth of this plant is remarkable. It is not a summer sapling. It is as great and as strong as an oak. Its growth is the thickest in Northern India. The successive invasions have deposited their 'silt' more there than anywhere else, and have served as watering exercises of devoted gardeners. Its growth is so thick in Northern India that the remnants of Hindu and Buddhist culture are just shrubs. Even the Sikh axe could not fell this oak. Sikhs, no doubt, became the political masters of Northern India, but they did not gain back Northern India to that spiritual and cultural unity by which it was bound to the rest of India before Hsuan Tsang. The Sikhs coupled it back to India. Still, it remains like Alsace–Lorraine, politically detachable and spiritually alien so far as the rest of India is concerned. It is only an unimaginative person who could fail to take notice of these facts or insist in the face of them that Pakistan means breaking up into two what is one whole.

What is the unity the Hindu sees between Pakistan and Hindustan? If it is geographical unity, then that is no unity. Geographical unity is unity intended by nature. In building up a nationality on geographical unity, it must be remembered that it is a case where Nature proposes and Man disposes. If it is unity in external things, such as ways and habits of life, that is no unity. Such unity is the result of exposure to a common environment. If it is administrative unity, that again is no unity. The instance of Burma is in point. Arakan and Tenasserim were annexed in 1826 by the Treaty of Yendabu. Pegu and Martaban were annexed in 1852. Upper Burma was annexed in 1886. The administrative unity between India and Burma was forged in 1826. For over 110 years that administrative unity continued to exist. In 1937, the knot that tied the two together was cut asunder and nobody shed a tear over it. The unity between India and Burma was not less fundamental. If unity is to be of an abiding character, it must be founded on a sense of kinship, in the feeling of being kindred. In short, it must be spiritual. Judged in the light of these considerations, the unity between Pakistan and Hindustan is a myth. Indeed, there is more spiritual unity between Hindustan and Burma than there is between Pakistan and Hindustan. And if the Hindus did not object to the severance of Burma from India, it is difficult to understand how the Hindus can object to the severance of an area like Pakistan, which, to repeat, is politically detachable from, socially hostile and spiritually alien to the rest of India.

Does Pakistan solve the Communal Question, is a natural question which every Hindu is sure to ask. A correct answer to this question calls for a close analysis of what is involved in it. One must have a clear idea as to what is exactly meant, when the Hindus and Muslims speak of the Communal Question. Without it, it will not be possible to say whether Pakistan does or does not solve the Communal Question.

It is not generally known that the Communal Question, like the 'Forward Policy' for the frontier, has a 'greater' and a 'lesser' intent, and that in its lesser intent it means one thing, and in its greater intent it means quite a different thing.

To begin with the Communal Question in its 'lesser intent'. In its lesser intent, the Communal Question relates to the representation of the Hindus and the Muslims in the Legislatures. Used in this sense, the question involves the settlement of two distinct problems:

(1) The number of seats to be allotted to the Hindus and the Muslims in the different legislatures, and

(2) The nature of the electorates through which these seats are to be filled in.

The Muslims at the Round Table Conference claimed:

(1) That their representatives in all the Provincial as well as in the Central Legislatures should be elected by separate electorates;

(2) That they should be allowed to retain the weightage in representation given to Muslim minorities in those provinces in which they were a minority in the population, and that in addition, they should be given in those provinces where they were a majority such as the Punjab, Sind, North-West Frontier Province and Bengal, a guaranteed statutory majority of seats.

The Hindus from the beginning objected to both these Muslim demands. They insisted on joint electorates for Hindus and Muslims in all elections to all the Legislatures, Central and Provincial, and on population ratio of representation, for both minorities, Hindus and Muslims, wherever they may be, and raised the strongest objections to a majority of seats being guaranteed to any community by statute.

The Communal Award of His Majesty's government settled this dispute by the simple, rough and ready method of giving the Muslims all that they wanted, without caring for the Hindu opposition. The Award allowed the Muslims to retain weightage and separate electorates, and in addition, gave them the statutory majority of seats in those provinces where they were a majority in the population.

What is it in the Award that can be said to constitute a problem? Is there any force in the objections of the Hindus to the Communal Award of His Majesty's government? This question must be considered carefully to find out whether there is substance in the objections of the Hindus to the Award.

Firstly, as to their objection to the weightage to Muslim minorities in the matter of representation. Whatever may be the correct measure of allotting representation to minorities, the Hindus cannot very well object to the weightage given to Muslim minorities, because similar weightage has been given to the Hindus in those provinces in which they are a minority and where there is sufficient margin for weightage to be allowed. The treatment of the Hindu minorities in Sind and the North-West Frontier Province is a case in point.

Secondly, as to their objection to a statutory majority. That again does not appear to be well-founded. A system of guaranteed representation may be wrong and vicious and quite unjustifiable on theoretical and philosophical grounds. But considered in the light of circumstances, such as those obtaining in India, the system of statutory majority appears to be inevitable. Once it is granted that the representation to be given to a minority must not reduce the majority to minority, that very provision creates, as a mere counterpart, a system of statutory majority to the majority community. For, fixing the seats of the minority involves the fixation of the seats of the majority. There is, therefore, no escape from the system of statutory majority, once it is conceded that the minority is not entitled to representation which would convert a majority into a minority. There is, therefore, no great force in the objections of the Hindus to a statutory majority of the Muslims in the Punjab, the North-West Frontier Province, Sind and Bengal. For, even in the provinces where the Hindus are in a majority and the Muslims are in minority, the Hindus have got a statutory majority over the Muslims. At any rate, there is a parity of position and to that extent there can be said to be no ground for complaint.

This does not mean that because the objections set forth by the Hindus have no substance, there are no real grounds for opposing the Communal Award. There does exist a substantial ground of objection to the Communal Award, although it does not appear to have been made the basis of attack by the Hindus.

This objection may be formulated in order to bring out its point in the following manner. The Muslim minorities in the Hindu provinces insisted on separate electorates. The Communal Award gives them the right to determine that issue. This is really what it comes to when one remembers the usual position taken, viz., that the Muslim minorities could not be deprived of their separate electorates without their consent, and the majority community of the Hindus has been made to abide by their determination. The Hindu minorities in Muslim provinces insisted that there should be joint electorates. Instead of conceding their claim, the Communal Award forced upon them the system of separate electorates to which they objected. If in the Hindu provinces, the Muslim minorities are allowed the right of self-determination in the matter of electorates, the question arises: Why are not the Hindu minorities in the Muslim provinces given the right of self-determination in the matter of their electorates? What is the answer to this question? And, if there is no answer, there is undoubtedly a deep-seated inequity in the Communal Award of His Majesty's government, which calls for redress.

It is no answer that the Hindus also have a statutory majority based on separate electorates[27] in those provinces where the Musalmans are in a minority. A little scrutiny will show that there is no parity of position in these two cases. The separate electorates for the Hindu majorities in the Hindu Provinces are not a matter of their choice. It is a consequence resulting from the determination of the Muslim minorities who claimed to have separate electorates for themselves. A minority in one set of circumstances may think that separate electorates would be a better method of self-protection and may have no fear of creating against itself and by its own action a statutory majority based on separate electorates for the opposing community. Another minority or, for the matter of that, the same minority in a different set of circumstances, would not like to create by its own action and against itself a statutory majority based upon separate electorates and may, therefore, prefer joint electorates to separate electorates as a better method of self-protection. Obviously the guiding principle, which would influence a minority, would be: Is the majority likely to use its majority in a communal manner and purely for communal purposes? If it felt certain that the majority community is likely to use its communal majority for communal ends, it may well choose joint electorates, because it would be the only method by which it would hope to take away the communal cement of the statutory majority by influencing the elections of the representatives of the majority community in the Legislatures. On the other hand, a majority community may not have the necessary

---

[27] It is perhaps not quite correct to speak of a Hindu electorate. The Electorate is a general electorate consisting of all those who are not included in any separate electorate. But as the majority in the general electorate consists of Hindus, it is called a Hindu electorate.

communal cement, which alone would enable it to use its communal majority for communal ends, in which case a minority, having no fear from the resulting statutory majority and separate electorates for the majority community, may well choose separate electorates for itself. To put it concretely, the Muslim minorities in choosing separate electorates are not afraid of the separate electorates and the statutory majority of the Hindus, because they feel sure that by reason of their deep-seated differences of caste and race the Hindus will never be able to use their majorities against the Muslims. On the other hand, the Hindu minorities in the Muslim provinces have no doubt that, by reason of their social solidarity, the Muslims will use their statutory majority to set into operation a 'Resolute Muslim Government', after the plan proposed by Lord Salisbury for Ireland as a substitute for Home Rule; with this difference, that Salisbury's Resolute Government was to last for twenty years only, while the Muslim Resolute Government was to last as long as the Communal Award stood. The situations, therefore, are not alike. The statutory majority of the Hindus based on separate electorates is the result of the choice made by the Muslim minority. The statutory majority of the Muslims based on separate electorates is something which is not the result of the choice of the Hindu minority. In one case, the government of the Muslim minority by a Hindu communal majority is the result of the consent of the Muslim minority. In the other case, the government of the Hindu minority by the Muslim majority is not the result of the consent of the Hindu minority, but is imposed upon it by the might of the British Government.

To sum up this discussion of the Communal Award, it may be said that, as a solution of the Communal Question in its 'lesser intent', there is no inequity in the Award on the ground that it gives weightage to the Muslim minorities in the Hindu provinces. For it gives weightage also to Hindu minorities in Muslim provinces. Similarly, it may be said that there is no inequity in the Award, on the ground that it gives a statutory majority to the Muslims in Muslim provinces in which they are a majority. If there is any, the statutory limitation put upon the Muslim number of seats, also gives to the Hindus in Hindu provinces a statutory majority. But the same cannot be said of the Award in the matter of the electorates. The Communal Award is iniquitous inasmuch as it accords unequal treatment to the Hindu and Muslim minorities in the matter of electorates. It grants the Muslim minorities in the Hindu provinces the right of self-determination in the matter of electorates, but it does not grant the same right to the Hindu minorities in the Muslim provinces. In the Hindu provinces, the Muslim minority is allowed to choose the kind of electorates it wants and the Hindu majority is not permitted to have any say in the matter. But in the Muslim provinces, it is the Muslim majority which is allowed to choose the kind of electorates it prefers and the Hindu minority is not permitted to have any say in the matter. Thus, the Muslims in the Muslim provinces having been given both statutory majority and separate electorates, the Communal Award must be said to impose upon the Hindu minorities Muslim rule, which they can neither alter nor influence.

This is what constitutes the fundamental wrong in the Communal Award. That this is a grave wrong must be admitted. For it offends against certain political principles, which have now become axiomatic. First is, not to trust anyone with unlimited political power. As has been well said:

'If in any state there is a body of men who possess unlimited political power, those over whom they rule can never be free. For, the one assured result of historical investigation is the lesson that uncontrolled power is invariably poisonous to those who possess it. They are always tempted to impose their canon of good upon others, and in the end, they assume that the good of the community depends upon the continuance of their power. Liberty always demands a limitation of political authority…'

The second principle is that, as a king has no divine right to rule, so also a majority has no divine right to rule. Majority rule is tolerated only because it is for a limited period and subject to the right to have it changed, and secondly because it is a rule of a political majority, i.e., majority which has submitted itself to the suffrage of a minority and not a communal majority. If such is the limited scope of authority permissible to a political majority over a political minority, how can a minority of one community be placed under the perpetual subjection of a majority of another community? To allow a majority of one community to rule a minority of another community without requiring the majority to submit itself to the suffrage of the minority, especially when the minority demands it, is to enact a perversion of democratic principles and to show a callous disregard for the safety and security of the Hindu minorities.

◆

To turn to the Communal Question in its 'greater intent'. What is it that the Hindus say is a problem? In its greater intent the Communal Question relates to the deliberate creation of Muslim provinces. At the time of the Lucknow Pact, the Muslims only raised the Communal Question in its lesser intent. At the Round Table Conference, the Muslims put forth, for the first time, the plan covered by the Communal Question in its greater intent. Before the Act of 1935, there were a majority of provinces in which the Hindus were in a majority and the Muslims in a minority. There were only three provinces in which the Muslims were in a majority and the Hindus in a minority. They were the Punjab, Bengal and the North-West Frontier Province. Of these, the Muslim majority in the North-West Frontier Province was not effective, because there was no responsible government in that province, the Montagu–Chemsford Scheme of Political Reforms not being extended to it. So, for all practical purposes, there were only two provinces—the Punjab and Bengal—wherein the Muslims were in majority and the Hindus in minority. The Muslims desired that the number of Muslim provinces should be increased. With this object in view, they demanded that Sind should be separated from the Bombay Presidency and created into a new self-governing province, and that the North-West Frontier Province, which was already a separate province, should be raised to the status of a self-governing province. Apart from other considerations, from a purely financial point of view, it was not possible to concede this demand. Neither Sind nor the North-West Frontier Province were financially self-supporting. But in order to satisfy the Muslim demand, the British Government went to the length of accepting the responsibility of giving an annual subvention to Sind[28] and North-West Frontier Province[29] from the Central Revenues, so as to bring about a budgetary equilibrium in their finances and make them financially self-supporting.

These four provinces with Muslims in majority and Hindus in minority, now functioning as autonomous and self-governing provinces, were certainly not created for administrative convenience, nor for purposes of architectural symmetry—the Hindu provinces poised against the Muslim provinces. It is also true that the scheme of Muslim provinces was not a matter of satisfying Muslim pride which demanded Hindu minorities under Muslim majorities to compensate the humiliation of having Muslim minorities under Hindu majorities. What was then, the motive underlying this scheme of Muslim provinces? The Hindus say that the motive for the Muslim insistence, both on statutory majority and separate electorates, was to enable the Muslims in the Muslim provinces to mobilize and make Muslim power effective in its exclusive form and to the fullest extent possible. Asked what could be the purpose of having the Muslim political power mobilized in this fashion, the Hindus answer that it was done to place in the hands of the Muslims of the Muslim provinces an effective weapon to tyrannize their Hindu minorities, in case the Muslim minorities in the Hindu Provinces were tyrannized by their Hindu majorities. The scheme thus became a system of protection, in which blast was to be met by counter-blast, terror by terror and tyranny by tyranny. The plan is undoubtedly, a dreadful one, involving the maintenance of justice and peace by retaliation, and providing an opportunity for the punishment of an innocent minority, Hindus in Muslim provinces and Muslims in Hindu provinces, for the sins of their co-religionists in other provinces. It is a scheme of communal peace through a system of communal hostages.

That the Muslims were aware from the very start, that the system of communal provinces was capable of being worked in this manner, is clear from the speech made by Maulana Abul Kalam Azad as President

---

[28]Sind gets an annual subvention of Rs 105,00,000.
[29]North-West Frontier Province gets an annual subvention of Rs 100,00,000.

of the Muslim League Session held in Calcutta in 1927. In that speech the Maulana declared:

'…That by the Lucknow Pact they had sold away their interests. The Delhi proposals of March last opened the door for the first time to the recognition of the real rights of Musalmans in India. The separate electorates granted by the Pact of 1916 only ensured Muslim representation, but what was vital for the existence of the community was the recognition of its numerical strength. Delhi opened the way to the creation of such a state of affairs as would guarantee to them in the future of India a proper share. Their existing small majority in Bengal and the Punjab was only a census figure, but the Delhi proposals gave them for the first time five provinces of which no less than three (Sind, the Frontier Province and Baluchistan) contained a real overwhelming Muslim majority. If the Muslims did not recognize this great step they were not fit to live. There would now be nine Hindu provinces against five Muslim provinces, and whatever treatment Hindus accorded in the nine provinces, Muslims would accord the same treatment to Hindus in the five provinces. Was not this a great gain? Was not a new weapon gained for the assertion of Muslim rights?'

That those in charge of these Muslim provinces know the advantage of the scheme, and do not hesitate to put it to the use for which it was intended, is clear from the speeches made not long ago by Mr Fazl-ul-Huq, as prime minister of Bengal.

That this scheme of Communal Provinces, which constitutes the Communal Question in its larger intent, can be used as an engine of communal tyranny, there can be no doubt. The system of hostages, which is the essence of the scheme of communal provinces, supported by separate electorates, is indeed insupportable on any ground. If this is the underlying motive of the demand for the creation of more Muslim provinces, the system resulting from it is undoubtedly a vicious system.

This analysis leaves no doubt that the communal statutory majority based on separate communal electorates and the communal provinces, especially constituted to enable the statutory majority to tyrannize the minority, are the two evils which compose what is called the 'Communal Problem'.

For the existence of this problem the Hindus hold the Muslims responsible and the Muslims hold the Hindus responsible. The Hindus accuse the Muslims of contumacy. The Muslims accuse Hindus of meanness. Both, however, forget that the communal problem exists not because the Muslims are extravagant and insolent in their demands and the Hindus are mean and grudging in their concessions. It exists and will exist wherever a hostile majority is brought face to face against a hostile minority. Controversies relating to separate versus joint electorates, controversies relating to population ratio versus weightage, are all inherent in a situation where a minority is pitted against a majority. The best solution of the communal problem is not to have two communities facing each other, one a majority and the other a minority, welded in the steel-frame of a single government.

How far does Pakistan approximate to the solution of the Communal Question?

The answer to this question is quite obvious. If the scheme of Pakistan is to follow the present boundaries of the provinces in the North-West and in Bengal, certainly it does not eradicate the evils which lie at the heart of the Communal Question. It retains the very elements which give rise to it, namely, the pitting of a minority against a majority. The rule of the Hindu minorities by the Muslim majorities and the rule of the Muslim minorities by the Hindu majorities are the crying evils of the present situation.

This very evil will reproduce itself in Pakistan, if the provinces marked out for it are incorporated into it as they are, i.e., with boundaries drawn as at present. Besides this, the evil which gives rise to the Communal Question in its larger intent, will not only remain as it is but will assume a new malignity. Under the existing system, the power centered in the communal provinces to do mischief to their hostages is limited by the power which the Central government has over the Provincial governments. At present, the hostages are at least within the pale of a Central government which is Hindu in its composition and which has power to interfere for their protection. But, when Pakistan becomes a Muslim State with full sovereignty over internal and external affairs, it would be free from the control of the Central government. The Hindu minorities will have no recourse to an outside authority with overriding powers, to interfere on their behalf and curb this power of mischief, as under the scheme, no such overriding authority is permitted to exist. So, the position of the Hindus in Pakistan may easily become similar to the position of the Armenians under the Turks or of the Jews in Tsarist Russia or in Nazi Germany. Such a scheme would be intolerable and the Hindus may well say that they cannot agree to Pakistan and leave their co-religionist as a helpless prey to the fanaticism of a Muslim National State.

This, of course, is a very frank statement of the consequences which will flow from giving effect to the scheme of Pakistan. But care must be taken to locate the source of these consequences. Do they flow from the scheme of Pakistan itself or do they flow from particular boundaries that may be fixed for it? If the evils flow from the scheme itself, i.e., if they are inherent in it, it is unnecessary for any Hindu to waste his time in considering it. He will be justified in summarily dismissing it. On the other hand, if the evils are the result of the boundaries, the question of Pakistan reduces itself to a mere question of changing the boundaries.

A study of the question amply supports the view that the evils of Pakistan are not inherent in it. If any evil results follow from it they will have to be attributed to its boundaries. This becomes clear if one studies the distribution of population. The reasons why these evils will be reproduced within Western and Eastern Pakistan is because, with the present boundaries, they do not become single ethnic states. They remain mixed states, composed of a Muslim majority and a Hindu minority as before. The evils are the evils which are inseparable from a mixed state. If Pakistan is made a single unified ethnic state, the evils will automatically vanish. There will be no question of separate electorates within Pakistan, because in such a homogeneous Pakistan, there will be no majorities to rule and no minorities to be protected. Similarly, there will be no majority of one community to hold, in its possession, a minority of an opposing community.

The question, therefore, is one of demarcation of boundaries and reduces itself to this: Is it possible for the boundaries of Pakistan to be so fixed, that instead of producing a mixed state composed of majorities and minorities, with all the evils attendant upon it, Pakistan will be an ethnic state composed of one homogeneous community, namely Muslims? The answer is that in a large part of the area affected by the project of the League, a homogeneous state can be created by shifting merely the boundaries, and in the rest, homogeneity can be produced by shifting only the population.

Chapter 5

THE COMMON FATE

THE SOCIAL EVILS which characterize the Hindu Society have been well-known. The publication of *Mother India* by Miss Mayo gave these evils the widest publicity. But while *Mother India* served the purpose of exposing the evils and calling their authors at the bar of the world to answer for their sins, it created the unfortunate impression throughout the world that while the Hindus were grovelling in the mud of these social evils and were conservative, the Muslims in India were free from them, and as compared to the Hindus, were a progressive people. That such an impression should prevail is surprising to those who know the Muslim Society in India at close quarters.

One may well ask if there is any social evil which is found among the Hindus and is not found among the Muslims.

Take child marriage. The secretary of the Anti-Child-Marriage Committee, constituted by the All India Women's Conference, published a bulletin which gives the extent of the evil of child marriage in the different communities in the country. The figures, which were taken from the Census Report of 1931, are as follows:

Married Females Aged 0–15 per 1,000 Females of that Age

	Hindus	Muslims	Jains	Sikhs	Christians
1881	208	153	189	170-	33
1891	193	141	172	143	37
1901	186	131	164	101	38
1911	184	123	130	88	39
1921	170	111	117	72	32
1931	199	186	125	80	43

Can the position among the Musalmans, so far as child marriage goes, be considered better than the position among the Hindus?

Take the position of women. It is insisted by Muslims that the legal rights given to Muslim women ensure them a greater measure of independence than allowed to other Eastern women—for example, Hindu women—and are in excess of the rights given to women in some Western countries. Reliance is placed on some of the provisions of the Muslim law.

Firstly, it is said the Muslim law does not fix any age for marriage, and recognizes the right of a girl to marry any time. Further, except where the marriage is celebrated by the father or the grandfather, a Muslim girl, if given in marriage in childhood, has the power to repudiate her marriage on attaining puberty.

Secondly, it is held out that marriage among the Musalmans is a contract. Being a contract, the husband has a right to divorce his wife, and the Muslim law has provided ample safeguards for the wife which, if availed of, would place the Muslim wife on the same footing as the husband in the matter of divorce. For it is claimed that the wife under the Muslim law can, at the time of the marriage, or even thereafter in some cases, enter into a contract by which she may, under certain circumstances, obtain a divorce.

Thirdly, the Mahomedan law requires that a wife can claim from her husband, by way of consideration for the surrender of her person, a sum of money or other property—known as her 'dower'. The dower may be fixed even after marriage, and if no amount is fixed, the wife is entitled to proper dower. The amount of dower is usually split into two parts, one is called 'prompt', which is payable on demand, and the other 'deferred', which is payable on dissolution of marriage by death or divorce. Her claim for dower will be treated as a debt against the husband's estate. She has complete dominion over her dower, which is intended to give her economic independence. She can remit it, or she can appropriate the income of it as she pleases.

Granting all these provisions of law in her favour, the Muslim woman is the most helpless person in the world. To quote an Egyptian Muslim leader:

'Islam has set its seal of inferiority upon her, and given the sanction of religion to social customs which have deprived her of the full opportunity for self-expression and development of personality.'

No Muslim girl has the courage to repudiate her marriage, although it may be open to her on the ground that she was a child and that it was brought about by persons other than her parents. No Muslim wife will think it proper to have a clause entered into her marriage contract reserving her the right to divorce. In that event, her fate is 'once married, always married'. She cannot escape the marriage tie, however irksome it may be. While she cannot repudiate the marriage, the husband can always do it, without having to show any cause. Utter the word 'talak' and observe continence for three weeks, and the woman is cast away. The only restraint on his caprice is the obligation to pay dower. If the dower has already been remitted, his right to divorce is a matter of his sweet will.

This latitude in the matter of divorce destroys that sense of security which is so fundamental for a full, free and happy life for a woman. This insecurity of life to which a Muslim woman is exposed, is greatly augmented by the right of polygamy and concubinage, which the Muslim law gives to the husband.

Mahomedan law allows a Muslim to marry four wives at a time. It is not unoften said that this is an improvement over the Hindu law, which places no restriction on the number of wives a Hindu can have at any given time. But it is forgotten that in addition to the four legal wives, the Muslim law permits a Mahomedan to cohabit with his female slaves. In the case of female slaves, nothing is said as to the number. They are allowed to him without any restriction whatever and without any obligation to marry them.

No words can adequately express the great and many evils of polygamy and concubinage, and especially as a source of misery to a Muslim woman. It is true that because polygamy and concubinage are sanctioned, one must not suppose they are indulged in by the generality of Muslims; still the fact remains that they are privileges which are easy for a Muslim to abuse to the misery and unhappiness of his wife.

Mr John J. Pool, no enemy of Islam, observes:[30]

'This latitude in the mailer of divorce is very greatly taken advantage of by some Mohamedans. Stobart, commenting on this subject in his book *Islam & Its Founder*, says: "Some Mohamodans make a habit of continually changing their wives. We read of young men who have had twenty and thirty wives, a new one every three months: and thus it comes about that women are liable to be indefinitely transferred from one man to another, obliged to accept a husband and a home whenever they can find one, or in case of destitution, to which divorce may have driven them, to resort to other more degrading means of living. Thus, while keeping the strict letter of the law, and possessing only one or certainly not more than four wives, unscrupulous characters may yet by divorce obtain in a lifetime as many wives as they please."

'In another way also a Mohammedan may really have more than four wives, and yet keep within the law. This is by means of living with concubines, which the Koran expressly permits. In that sura which allows four wives, the words are added, "of the slaves which ye shall have acquired". Then in the 70th sura, it is revealed that it is no sin to live with slaves. The very words are: "The slaves which their right hands possess, as to them they shall be blameless." At the present day, as in days past, in multitudes of Mohamedan homes, slaves are found; as Muir says, in his *Life of Mahomet*, "so long as this unlimited permission of living with their female slaves continues, it cannot be expected that there will be any hearty attempt to put a stop to slavery in Mohamedan countries." Thus the Koran, in this matter of slavery, is the enemy of the mankind. And women, as usual, are the greater sufferers.'

Take the caste system. Islam speaks of brotherhood. Everybody infers that Islam must be free from slavery and caste. Regarding slavery, nothing needs to be said. It stands abolished now by law. But while it existed, much of its support was derived from Islam and Islamic countries. While the prescriptions by the Prophet regarding the just and humane treatment of slaves contained in the Koran are praiseworthy, there is nothing whatever in Islam that lends support to the abolition

---

[30]Pool, John J., *Studies in Mahommedanism*, pp 34–35.

of this curse. As Sir W. Muir has well said:[31]

> '...rather, while lightening, he riveted the fetter... There is no obligation on a Muslim to release his slaves...'

But if slavery has gone, caste among Musalmans has remained. As an illustration, one may take the conditions prevalent among the Bengal Muslims. The Superintendent of the Census for 1901 for the Province of Bengal records the following interesting facts regarding the Muslims of Bengal:

> 'The conventional division of the Mahomedans into four tribes— Sheikh, Saiad, Moghul and Pathan—has very little application to this Province (Bengal). The Mahomedans themselves recognize two main social divisions, (1) Ashraf or Sharaf and (2) Ajlaf. Ashraf means "noble" and includes all undoubted descendants of foreigners and converts from high caste Hindus. All other Mahomedans including the occupational groups and all converts of lower ranks, are known by the contemptuous terms, "Ajlaf", "wretches" or mean people: they are also called Kamina or Itar, "base" or Rasil, a corruption of Rizal, worthless. In some places, a third class, called "Arzal" or lowest of all, is added. With them no other Mahomedan would associate, and they are forbidden to enter the mosque to use the public burial ground.'

Within these groups there are castes with social precedence of exactly the same nature as one finds among the Hindus.

I. Ashraf or better class Mahomedans.

(1) Saiads
(2) Sheikhs
(3) Pathans
(4) Moghul
(5) Mallik
(6) Mirza

II. Ajlaf or lower class Mahomedans.

---

[31]Muir, William, *The Koran, its Composition and Teaching and the Testimony It Bears to the Holy Scriptures*, p 58.

(1) Cultivating Sheikhs, and others who were originally Hindus but who do not belong to any functional group, and have not gained admittance to the Ashraf Community, e.g. Pirali and Thakrai.

(2) Darzi, Jolaha, Fakir and Rangrez.

(3) Barhi, Bhalhiara, Chik, Churihar, Dai, Dhawa, Dhunia, Gaddi, Kalal, Kasai, Kula Kunjara, Laheri, Mahifarosh, Mallah, Naliya and Nikari.

(4) Abdal, Bako, Bediya, Bhat, Chamba, Dafali, Dhobi, Hajjam, Mucho, Nagarchi, Nat, Panwaria and Madaria, Tuntia.

III. Arzal or degraded class.

(1) Bhanar, Halalkhor, Hijra, Kasbi, Lalbegi, Maugta, Mehtar.

The Census Superintendent mentions another feature of the Muslim social system, namely, the prevalence of the panchayat system. He states:

'The authority of the panchayat extends to social as well as trade matters and…marriage with people of other communities is one of the offences of which the governing body takes cognizance. The result is that these groups are often as strictly endogamous as Hindu castes. The prohibition on inter-marriage extends to higher as well as to lower castes, and a Dhuma, for example, may marry no one but a Dhuma. If this rule is transgressed, the offender is at once hauled up before the panchayat and ejected ignominiously from his community. A member of one such group cannot ordinarily gain admission to another, and he retains the designation of the community in which he was born even if he abandons its distinctive occupation and takes to other means of livelihood…thousands of Jolahas are butchers, yet they are still known as Jolahas.'

Similar facts from other provinces of India could be gathered from their respective Census Reports, and those who are curious may refer to them. But the facts for Bengal are enough to show that the Mahomedans observe not only caste but also Untouchability.

There can, thus, be no manner of doubt that the Muslim Society in India is afflicted by the same social evils as afflict the Hindu Society. Indeed, the Muslims have all the social evils of the Hindus and something more. That something more is the compulsory system of purdah for Muslim women.

As a consequence of the purdah system, a segregation of the Muslim women is brought about. The ladies are not expected to visit the outer rooms, verandahs, or gardens; their quarters are in the backyard. All of them, young and old, are confined in the same room. No male servant can work in their presence. A woman is allowed to see only her sons, brothers, father, uncles and husband, or any other near relation who may be admitted to a position of trust. She cannot go even to the mosque to pray, and must wear burqa (veil) whenever she has to go out. These burqa women walking in the streets is one of the most hideous sights one can witness in India. Such seclusion cannot but have its deteriorating effects upon the physical constitution of Muslim women. They are usually victims to anaemia, tuberculosis, and pyorrhoea. Their bodies are deformed, with their backs bent, bones protruded, hands and feet crooked. Ribs, joints and nearly all their bones ache. Heart palpitation is very often present in them. The result of this pelvic deformity is untimely death at the time of delivery. Purdah deprives Muslim women of mental and moral nourishment. Being deprived of healthy social life, the process of moral degeneration must and does set in. Being completely secluded from the outer world, they engage their minds in petty family quarrels, with the result that they become narrow and restricted in their outlook.

They lag behind their sisters from other communities, cannot take part in any outdoor activity and are weighed down by a slavish mentality and an inferiority complex. They have no desire for knowledge, because they are taught not to be interested in anything outside the four walls of the house. Purdah women in particular become helpless, timid and unfit for any fight in life. Considering the large number of purdah women among Muslims in India, one can easily understand the vastness and seriousness of the problem of purdah.

The physical and intellectual effects of purdah are nothing as compared with its effects on morals. The origin of purdah lies, of course, in the deep-rooted suspicion of sexual appetites in both sexes and the purpose is to check them by segregating the sexes.

But far from achieving the purpose, purdah has adversely affected the morals of Muslim men. Owing to purdah, a Muslim has no contact with any woman outside those who belong to his own household. Even with them, his contact extends only to occasional conversation. For a male there is no company of, and no commingling with, the females, except those who are children or aged. This isolation of the males from females is sure to produce bad effects on the morals of men. It requires no psychoanalyst to say that a social system which cuts off all contact between the two sexes produces an unhealthy tendency towards sexual excesses and unnatural and other morbid habits and ways.

The evil consequences of purdah are not confined to the Muslim community only. It is responsible for the social segregation of Hindus from Muslims which is the bane of public life in India. This argument may appear far-fetched, and one is inclined to attribute this segregation to the unsociability of the Hindus rather than to purdah among the Muslims. But the Hindus are right when they say that it is not possible to establish social contact between Hindus and Muslims, because such contact can only mean contact between women from one side and men from the other.

Not that purdah and the evils consequent thereon are not to be found among certain sections of the Hindus in certain parts of the country. But the point of distinction is that among the Muslims, purdah has a religious sanctity which it has not with the Hindus. Purdah has deeper roots among the Muslims than it has among the Hindus, and can only be removed by facing the inevitable conflict between religious injunctions and social needs. The problem of purdah is a real problem with the Muslims—apart from its origin—which it is not with the Hindus. Of any attempt by the Muslims to do away with it, there is no evidence.

There is thus a stagnation not only in the social life but also in the political life of the Muslim community of India. The Muslims have no interest in politics as such. Their predominant interest is religion. This can be easily seen by the terms and conditions that a Muslim constituency makes for its support to a candidate fighting for a seat. The Muslim constituency does not care to examine the programme of the candidate. All that the constituency wants from the candidate is that he should agree to replace the old lamps of the masjid by supplying new ones at his cost, to provide a new carpet for the masjid because the old one is torn, or to repair the masjid because it has become dilapidated. In some places, a Muslim constituency is quite satisfied if the candidate agrees to give a sumptuous feast, and in other[s] if he agrees to buy votes for so much apiece. With the Muslims, election is a mere matter of money, and is very seldom a matter of social programme of general improvement. Muslim politics takes no note of purely secular categories of life, namely, the differences between rich and poor, capital and labour, landlord and tenant, priest and layman, reason and superstition. Muslim politics is essentially clerical and recognizes only one difference, namely, that existing between Hindus and Muslims. None of the secular categories of life have any place in the politics of the Muslim community; and if they do find a place—and they must, because they are irrepressible—they are subordinated to one and the only governing principle of the Muslim political universe, namely, religion.

◆

The existence of these evils among the Muslims is distressing enough. But, far more distressing is the fact that there is no organized movement of social reform among the Musalmans of India on a scale sufficient to bring about their eradication. The Hindus have their social evils. But, there is this relieving feature about them—namely, that some of them are conscious of their existence, and a few of them are actively agitating for their removal. The Muslims, on the other hand, do not realize that they are evils, and consequently do not agitate for their removal. Indeed, they oppose any change in their existing practices. It is noteworthy that the Muslims opposed the Child-Marriage Bill brought in the Central Assembly in 1930, whereby the age for marriage of a girl was raised to fourteen and of a boy to eighteen, on the ground that it was opposed to the Muslim canon law. Not only did they oppose the bill at every stage, but that when it became law they started a campaign of civil disobedience against that Act. Fortunately, the civil disobedience campaign of the Muslims against the Act did not swell and was submerged in the Congress Civil Disobedience campaign which synchronized with it. But, the campaign only proves how strongly the Muslims are opposed to social reform.

The question may be asked, why are the Muslims opposed to social reform?

The usual answer given is that the Muslims all over the world are an unprogressive people. This view, no doubt, accords with the facts of history. After the first spurts of their activity, the scale of which was undoubtedly stupendous, leading to the foundations of vast empires— the Muslims suddenly fell into a strange condition of torpor, from which they never seem to have become awake. The cause assigned for this torpor by those who have made a study of their condition, is said to be the fundamental assumption made by all Muslims that Islam is a world religion, suitable for all people, for all times and for all conditions. It has been contended that:

'The Musalman, remaining faithful to his religion, has not progressed; he has remained stationary in a world of swiftly moving modern forces. It is, indeed, one of the salient features of Islam that it immobilizes in their native barbarism, the races whom it enslaves. It is fixed in a crystallization, inert and impenetrable. It is unchangeable; and political, social or economic changes have no repercussion upon it.

'Having been taught that outside Islam there can be no safety; outside its law no truth and outside its spiritual message there is no happiness, the Muslim has become incapable of conceiving any other condition than his own, any other mode of thought than the Islamic thought. He firmly believes that he has arrived at an unequalled pitch of perfection; that he is the sole possessor of true faith, of the true doctrine, the true wisdom; that he alone is in possession of the truth—no relative truth subject to revision, but absolute truth.

'The religious law of the Muslims has had the effect of imparting to the very diverse individuals of whom the world is composed, a unity of thought, of feeling, of ideas, of judgement.'

It is urged that this uniformity is deadening and is not merely imparted to the Muslims, but is imposed upon them by a spirit of intolerance which is unknown anywhere outside the Muslim world for its severity and its violence and which is directed towards the suppression of all rational thinking which is in conflict with the teachings of Islam. As Renan observes:[32]

'Islam is a close union of the spiritual and the temporal; it is the reign of a dogma, it is the heaviest chain that humanity has ever borne... Islam has its beauties as a religion; but, to the human reason, Islamism has only been injurious. The minds that it has shut from the light were, no doubt, already closed in their own internal limits; but it has persecuted free thought, I shall not say more violently than other religions, but more effectually. It has made of the countries that it has conquered a closed field to the rational culture of the mind. What is, in fact, essentially distinctive of the Musalman is his hatred of science, his persuasion that research is useless, frivolous, almost impious—the natural sciences, because they are attempts at rivalry with God; the historical sciences, because they apply to times anterior to Islam, they may revive ancient heresies...'

Renan concludes by saying:

'Islam, in treating science as an enemy, is only consistent, but it is a dangerous thing to be consistent. To its own misfortune, Islam has been successful. By slaying science, it has slain itself; and is condemned in the world to a complete inferiority.'

This answer, though obvious, cannot be the true answer. If it were the true answer, how are we to account for the stir and ferment that is going on in all Muslim countries outside India, where the spirit of inquiry, the spirit of change and the desire to reform are noticeable in every walk of life? Indeed, the social reforms which have, taken place in Turkey have been of the most revolutionary character. If Islam has not come in the way of the Muslims of these countries, why should it come in the way of the Muslims of India? There must be some special reason for the social and political stagnation of the Muslim community in India.

What can that special reason be? It seems to me that the reason for the absence of the spirit of change in the Indian Musalman is to

---

[32]Renan, Ernest, 'Nationality and Other Essays'.

be sought in the peculiar position he occupies in India: He is placed in a social environment which is predominantly Hindu. That Hindu environment is always silently but surely encroaching upon him. He feels that it is de-musalmanizing him. As a protection against this gradual weaning away, he is led to insist on preserving everything that is Islamic without caring to examine whether it is helpful or harmful to his society. Secondly, the Muslims in India are placed in a political environment which is also predominantly Hindu. He feels that he will be suppressed and that political suppression will make the Muslims a depressed class. It is this consciousness that he has to save himself from being submerged by the Hindus socially and politically, which to my mind is the primary cause why the Indian Muslims as compared with their fellows outside are backward in the matter of social reform. Their energies are directed to maintaining a constant struggle against the Hindus for seats and posts, in which there is no time, no thought and no room for questions relating to social reform. And if there is any, it is all overweighed and suppressed by the desire, generated by pressure of communal tension, to close the ranks and offer a united front to the menace of the Hindus and Hinduism by maintaining their socio-religious unity at any cost.

The same is the explanation of the political stagnation in the Muslim community of India. Muslim politicians do not recognize secular categories of life as the basis of their politics because to them it means the weakening of the community in its fight against the Hindus. The poor Muslims will not join the poor Hindus to get justice from the rich. Muslim tenants will not join Hindu tenants to prevent the tyranny of the landlord. Muslim labourers will not join Hindu labourers in the fight of labour against capital. Why? The answer is simple. The poor Muslim sees that if he joins in the fight of the poor against the rich, he may be fighting against a rich Muslim. The Muslim tenant feels that if he joins in the campaign against the landlord, he may have to fight against a Muslim landlord. A Muslim labourer feels that if he joins in the onslaught of labour against capital, he will be injuring a Muslim mill-owner. He is conscious that any injury to a rich Muslim, to a Muslim landlord or to a Muslim mill-owner, is a disservice to the Muslim community, for it is thereby weakened in its struggle against the Hindu community.

How Muslim politics has become perverted is shown by the attitude of the Muslim leaders to the political reforms in the Indian states. The Muslims and their leaders carried on a great agitation for the introduction of representative government in the Hindu state of Kashmir. The same Muslims and their leaders are deadly opposed to the introduction of representative governments in other Muslim States. The reason for this strange attitude is quite simple. In all matters, the determining question with the Muslims is how it will affect the Muslims vis-a-vis the Hindus. If representative government can help the Muslims, they will demand it, and fight for it. In the state of Kashmir, the ruler is a Hindu, but the majority of the subjects are Muslims. The Muslims fought for representative government in Kashmir, because representative government in Kashmir meant the transfer of power from a Hindu king to the Muslim masses. In other Muslim States, the ruler is a Muslim but the majority of his subjects are Hindus. In such States, representative government means the transfer of power from a Muslim ruler to the Hindu masses, and that is why the Muslims support the introduction of representative government in one case and oppose it in the other. The dominating consideration with the Muslims is not democracy. The dominating consideration is how democracy with majority rule will affect the Muslims in their struggle against the Hindus. Will it strengthen them; or will it weaken them? If democracy weakens them, they will not have democracy. They will prefer the rotten state to continue in the Muslim States, rather than weaken the Muslim ruler in his hold upon his Hindu subjects.

The political and social stagnation in the Muslim community can be explained by one and only one reason. The Muslims think that the Hindus and Muslims must perpetually struggle; the Hindus to establish their dominance over the Muslims, and the Muslims to establish their historical position as the ruling community—that in this struggle the strong will win, and to ensure strength they must suppress or put in cold storage everything which causes dissension in their ranks.

If the Muslims in other countries have undertaken the task of reforming their society and the Muslims of India have refused to do so, it is because the former are free from communal and political clashes with rival communities, while the latter are not.

It is not that this blind spirit of conservatism which does not recognize the need of repair to the social structure has taken hold of the Muslims only. It has taken hold of the Hindus also. The Hindus at one time did recognize that without social efficiency no permanent progress in other fields of activity was possible; that owing to the mischief wrought by evil customs, Hindu society was not in a state of efficiency; and that ceaseless efforts must be made to eradicate these evils. It was due to the recognition of this fact that the birth of the National Congress was accompanied by the foundation of the Social Conference. While the Congress was concerned with defining the weak points in the political organization of the country, the Social Conference was engaged in removing the weak points in the social organization of the Hindu Society. For some time, the Congress and the Conference worked as two wings of one common body, and held their annual sessions in the same pandal. But, soon the two wings developed into two parties, a Political Reform Party and a Social Reform Party, between whom raged fierce controversy. The Political Reform Party supported the National Congress, and the Social Reform Party supported the Social Conference. The two bodies became two hostile camps. The point at issue was whether social reform should precede political reform. For a decade, the forces were evenly balanced, and the battle was fought without victory to either side. It was, however, evident that the fortunes of the Social Conference were ebbing fast. The gentlemen who presided over the sessions of the Social Conference lamented that the majority of the educated Hindus were for political advancement and indifferent to social reform, and that while the number of those who attended the Congress was very large and the number who did not attend but who sympathized with it even larger, the number of those who attended the Social Conference was very much smaller. This indifference, this thinning of its ranks, was soon followed by active hostility from the politicians, like the late Mr Tilak. In course of time, the party in favour of political reform won and the Social Conference vanished and was forgotten.[33] With it also vanished from the Hindu Society the urge for social reform. Under the leadership of Mr Gandhi, the Hindu society, if it did not become a political mad-house, certainly became mad after politics. Non-cooperation, Civil Disobedience and the cry for Swaraj took the place which social reform once had in the minds of the Hindus. In the din and dust of political agitation, the Hindus do not even know that there are any evils to be remedied. Those who are conscious of it, do not believe that social reform is as important as political reform, and when forced to admit its importance argue that there can be no social reform unless political power is first achieved. They are so eager to possess political power that they are impatient even of propaganda in favour of social reform, as it means so much time and energy deducted from political propaganda. A correspondent of Mr Gandhi put the point of view of the nationalists very appropriately, if bluntly, when he wrote[34] to Mr Gandhi, saying:

> 'Don't you think that it is impossible to achieve any great reform without winning political power? The present economic structure has got to be tackled. No reconstruction is possible without political reconstruction and I am afraid all this talk of polished and unpolished rice, balanced diet and so on and so forth is mere moonshine.'

The Social Reform Party, led by Ranade, died, leaving the field to the Congress. There has grown up among the Hindus another party which is also a rival to the Congress. It is the Hindu Mahasabha. One would expect from its name that it was a body for bringing about the reform of Hindu society. But it is not. Its rivalry with the Congress has nothing to do with the issue of social reform versus political reform. Its quarrel with the Congress has its origin in the pro-Muslim policy of the Congress. It is organized for the protection of Hindu rights against Muslim encroachment. Its plan is to organize the Hindus for offering a united front to the Muslims. As a body organized to protect Hindu rights, it is all the time engaged in keeping

---

[33]For a more detailed statement see my tract in *Annihilation of caste.*
[34]*Harijan,* 1 January 1936.

an eye on political movements, on seats and posts. It cannot spare any thought for social reform. As a body keen on bringing about a united front of all Hindus, it cannot afford to create dissensions among its elements, which would be the case if it undertook to bring about social reforms. For the sake of the consolidation of the Hindu rank and file, the Hindu Mahasabha is ready to suffer all social evils to remain as they are. For the sake of consolidation of the Hindus, it is prepared to welcome the Federation as devised by the Act of 1935, in spite of its many iniquities and defects. For the same purpose, the Hindu Mahasabha favours the retention of the Indian States, with their administration as it is. 'Hands off the Hindu States' has been the battle-cry of its President. This attitude is stranger than that of the Muslims. Representative government in Hindu States cannot do harm to the Hindus. Why then should the President of the Hindu Mahasabha oppose it? Probably because it helps the Muslims, whom he cannot tolerate.

How long will this menace last? It is sure to last as long as the Hindus and Muslims are required to live as members of one country under the mantle of a single constitution. For, it is the fear of the single constitution with the possibility of the shifting of the balance— for nothing can keep the balance at the point originally fixed by the constitution—which makes the Hindus a menace to the Muslims and the Muslims a menace to the Hindus. If this is so, Pakistan is the obvious remedy. It certainly removes the chief condition which makes for the menace. Pakistan liberates both the Hindus and the Muslims from the fear of enslavement of arid encroachment against each other. It removes, by providing a separate constitution for each, Pakistan and Hindustan, the very basis which leads to this perpetual struggle for keeping a balance of power in the day-to-day life, and frees them to take in hand those vital matters of urgent social importance which they are now forced to put aside in cold storage, and improve the lives of their people, which after all is the main object of this fight for Swaraj.

Without some such arrangement, the Hindus and the Muslims will act and react as though they were two nations, one fearing to be conquered by the other. Preparations for aggression will always have precedence over social reform, so that the social stagnation which has set in must continue. This is quite natural, and no one need be surprised at it. For, as Bernard Shaw pointed out:

> 'A conquered nation is like a man with cancer; he can think of nothing else. A healthy nation is as unconscious of its nationality as a healthy man of his bones. But if you break a nation's nationality, it will think of nothing else but getting it set again. It will listen to no reformer, to no philosopher, to no preacher until the demand of the nationalist is granted. It will attend to no business, however vital, except the business of unification and liberation.'

Unless there is unification of the Muslims who wish to separate from the Hindus, and unless there is liberation of each from the fear of domination by the other, there can be no doubt that this malaise of social stagnation will not be set right.

Even a superficial observer cannot fail to notice that a spirit of aggression underlies the Hindu attitude towards the Muslim and the Muslim attitude towards the Hindu. The Hindu's spirit of aggression is a new phase which he has just begun to cultivate. The Muslim's spirit of aggression is his native endowment, and is ancient as compared with that of the Hindu. It is not that the Hindu, if given time, will not pick up and overtake the Muslim. But as matters stand today, the Muslim in this exhibition of the spirit of aggression leaves the Hindu far behind.

Enough has been said about the social aggression of the Muslims in the chapter dealing with communal riots. It is necessary to speak briefly of the political aggression of the Muslims. For, this political aggression has created a malaise which cannot be overlooked.

Three things are noticeable about this political aggression of the Muslims.

First is the ever-growing catalogue of the Muslim's political demands. Their origin goes back to the year 1892.

In 1885, the Indian National Congress was founded. It began with a demand for good government, as distinguished from self-government. In response to this demand, the British Government felt the necessity of altering the nature of the Legislative Councils, Provincial and Central, established under the Act of 1861. In that nascent stage of Congress agitation, the British Government did not feel called upon to make them fully popular. It thought it enough to give them a popular colouring. Accordingly, the British Parliament passed in 1892 what is called the Indian Councils Act. This Act is memorable for two things. It was in this Act of 1892 that the British Government for the first time accepted the semblance of the principle of popular representation as the basis for the constitution of the Legislatures in India. It was not a principle of election. It was a principle of nomination, only it was qualified by the requirement that before nomination a person must be selected by important public bodies such as municipalities, district boards, universities, and the associations of merchants, etc. Secondly, it was in the legislatures that were constituted under this Act that the principle of separate representation for Musalmans was for the first time introduced in the political constitution of India.

The introduction of this principle is shrouded in mystery. It is a mystery because it was introduced so silently and so stealthily. The principle of separate representation does not find a place in the Act. The Act says nothing about it. It was in the directions—but not in the Act—issued to those charged with the duty of framing regulations as to the classes and interests to whom representation was to be given that the Muslims were named as a class to be provided for.

It is a mystery as to who was responsible for its introduction. This scheme of separate representation was not the result of any demand put forth by any organized Muslim association. In whom did it then originate? It is suggested[35] that it originated with the Viceroy, Lord Dufferin, who, as far back as the year 1888, when dealing with the question of representation in the Legislative Councils, emphasized the necessity that in India representation will have to be, not in the way representation is secured in England, but representation by interests. Curiosity leads to a further question, namely, what could have led Lord Dufferin to propose such a plan? It is suggested[36] that the idea was

---

[35]See the speech of Sir Mahomad Shaifin the Minorities Sub-committee of the first R.T.C. (Indian Edition), p 57.
[36]See the speech of Raja Narendranath, Ibid., p 65.

to wean[37] away the Musalmans from the Congress, which had already been started three years before. Be that as it may, it is certain that it is by this Act that separate representation for Muslims became, for the first time, a feature of the Indian Constitution. It should, however, be noted that neither the Act nor the Regulations conferred any right of selection upon the Muslim community, nor did the Act give the Muslim community a right to claim a fixed number of seats. All that it did was to give the Muslims the right to separate representation.

Though, to start with, the suggestion of separate representation came from the British, the Muslims did not fail to appreciate the social value of separate political rights; with the result that when in 1909 the Muslims came to know that the next step in the reform of the Legislative Councils was contemplated, they waited of their own accord in deputation[38] upon the Viceroy, Lord Minto, and placed before him the following demands:

(i) Communal representation in accordance with their numerical strength, social position and local influence on district and municipal boards.

(ii) An assurance of Muhammadan representation on the governing bodies of universities.

(iii) Communal representation on provincial councils, election being by special electoral colleges composed of Muhammadan landlords, lawyers, merchants, and representatives of other important interests, university graduates of a certain standing and members of district and municipal boards.

(iv) The number of Muhammadan representatives in the Imperial Legislative Council should not depend on their numerical strength, and Muhammadans should never be in an ineffective minority. They should be elected as far as possible (as opposed

---

[37]The Musalmans had already been told by Sir Sayad Ahmad not to join the Congress in the two speeches, one delivered at Lucknow on 28 December 1887, and the other at Meerut on 16 March 1988. Mr Mahomed Ali in his presidential address speaks of them as historic speeches.

[38]Mr Mahomed Ali in his speech as the President of the Congress said that this deputation was a 'command performance'.

to being nominated), election being by special Muhammadan colleges composed of landowners, lawyers, merchants, members of provincial councils, fellows of universities, etc.

These demands were granted and given effect to in the Act of 1909. Under this Act, the Muhammadans were given (1) the right to elect their representatives, (2) the right to elect their representatives by separate electorates, (3) the right to vote in the general electorates as well, and (4) the right to weightage in representation.

The second thing that is noticeable among the Muslims is the spirit of exploiting the weaknesses of the Hindus. If the Hindus object to anything, the Muslim policy seems to be to insist upon it and give it up only when the Hindus show themselves ready to offer a price for it by giving the Muslims some other concessions. As an illustration of this, one can refer to the question of separate and joint electorates. The Hindus have been to my mind utterly foolish in fighting over joint electorates especially in provinces in which the Muslims are in a minority. Joint electorates can never suffice for a basis for nationalism. Nationalism is not a matter of political nexus or cash nexus, for the simple reason that union cannot be the result of calculation of mere externals. Where two communities live a life which is exclusive and self-enclosed for five years, they will not be one, because, they are made to come together on one day in five years for the purposes of voting in an election. Joint electorates may produce the enslavement of the minor community by the major community: but by themselves they cannot produce nationalism. Be that as it may, because the Hindus have been insisting upon joint electorates, the Muslims have been insisting upon separate electorates. That this insistence is a matter of bargain only can be seen from Mr Jinnah's 14 Points and the resolution[39] passed in the Calcutta session of the All India Muslim League held on 30 December 1927. Therein, it was stipulated that only when the Hindus agreed to the separation of Sind and to the raising of the N.W.F.P. to the status of a self-governing province, the Musalmans would consent to

---

[39]For the resolution and the speech of Mr Barkat Ali thereon, see the Indian Quarterly Register, 1927, Vol. II, pp 447–48.

give up separate electorates.[40] The Musalmans evidently did not regard separate electorates as vital. They regarded them as a good quid pro quo for obtaining their other claims.

Another illustration of this spirit of exploitation is furnished by the Muslim insistence upon cow-slaughter and the stoppage of music before mosques. Islamic law does not insist upon the slaughter of the cow for sacrificial purposes and no Musalman, when he goes to Haj, sacrifices the cow in Mecca or Medina. But, in India, they will not be content with the sacrifice of any other animal. Music may be played before a mosque in all Muslim countries without any objection. Even in Afghanistan, which is not a secularized country, no objection is taken to music before a mosque. But, in India, the Musalmans must insist upon its stoppage for no other reason except that the Hindus claim a right to it.

The third thing that is noticeable is the adoption by the Muslims of the gangster's method in politics. The riots are a sufficient indication that gangsterism has become a settled part of their strategy in politics. They seem to be consciously and deliberately imitating the Sudeten Germans in the means employed by them against the Czechs.[41] So long as the Muslims were the aggressors, the Hindus were passive, and in the conflict they suffered more than the Muslims did. But, this is no longer true. The Hindus have learned to retaliate and no longer feel any compunction in knifing a Musalman. This spirit of retaliation bids fair to produce the ugly spectacle of gangsterism against gangsterism.

How to meet this problem must exercise the minds of all concerned. There are the simple-minded Hindu Mahasabha patriots who believe that the Hindus have only to make up their minds to wipe the Musalmans and they will be brought to their senses. On the other hand, there are the Congress Hindu Nationalists whose policy is to tolerate and appease the Musalmans by political and other concessions, because they believe that they cannot reach their cherished goal of

---

[40]The unfortunate thing for the Hindus is that they did not get joint electorates although the Musalmans got the concessions.

[41]In the Karachi session of the All India Muslim League, both Mr Jinnah and Sir Abdulah Haroon compared the Muslims of India to the 'Sudeten' of the Muslim world and [as] capable of doing what the Sudelen Germans did to Czechoslovakia.

independence unless the Musalmans back their demand. The Hindu Mahasabha plan is no way to unify. On the contrary, it is a sure block to progress. The slogan of the Hindu Mahasabha President— 'Hindustan for Hindus'—is not merely arrogant but is arrant nonsense. The question, however, is: Is the Congress way the right way? It seems to me that the Congress has failed to realize two things. The first thing which the Congress has failed to realize is that there is a difference between appeasement and settlement, and that the difference is an essential one. Appeasement means buying off the aggressor by conniving at his acts of murder, rape, arson and loot against innocent persons who happen for the moment to be the victims of his displeasure. On the other hand, settlement means laying down the bounds which neither party to it can transgress. Appeasement sets no limits to the demands and aspirations of the aggressor.

Settlement does. The second thing the Congress has failed to realize is that the policy of concession has increased Muslim aggressiveness, and what is worse, Muslims interpret these concessions as a sign of defeatism on the part of the Hindus and the absence of the will to resist. This policy of appeasement will involve the Hindus in the same fearful situation in which the Allies found themselves as a result of the policy of appeasement which they adopted towards Hitler. This is another malaise, no less acute than the malaise of social stagnation. Appeasement will surely aggravate it. The only remedy for it is a settlement. If Pakistan is a settlement, it is a proposition worth consideration. As a settlement, it will do away with this constant need of appeasement and ought to be welcomed by all those who prefer the peace and tranquillity of a settlement to the insecurity due to the growing political appetite shown by the Muslims in their dealings with the Hindus.

Suppose an Indian was asked, what is the highest destiny you wish for your country, what would be his answer? The question is important, and the answer cannot but be instructive.

There can be no doubt that other things being equal, a 100 per cent Indian, proud of his country, would say, 'An integral and independent India is my ideal of India's destiny.' It will be equally true to say that unless this destiny was accepted by both Hindus as well as Muslims, the ideal can only convey a pious wish, and can never take a concrete form. Is it only a pious wish of some, or is it a goal to be pursued by all?

So far as profession of political aims goes, all parties seem to be in agreement, inasmuch as all of them have declared that the goal of India's political evolution is independence. The Congress was the first to announce that its aim was to achieve political independence for India. In its Madras session, held in December 1927, the creed of the Congress was defined in a special resolution to the effect that the goal of the Indian people[42] was complete national independence. The Hindu Mahasabha until 1932 was content to have Responsible Government as the goal of India's political evolution. It made no change in its political creed till 1937 when in its session held at Ahmedabad it declared that the Hindu Mahasabha believed in 'Poorna Swaraj', i.e., absolute independence for India. The Muslim League declared its political creed in 1912 to be the establishment of Responsible Government in India. In 1937, it made a similar advance by changing its creed from Responsible Government to independence and thereby brought itself in line with the Congress and the Hindu Mahasabha.

The independence defined by the three political bodies means freedom from British Imperialism. But, an agreement on freedom from the yoke of British Imperialism is not enough. There must be an agreement upon maintaining an Independent India. For this, there must be an agreement that India shall not only be free and independent of the British but that her freedom and independence shall be maintained as against any other foreign power. Indeed, the obligation to maintain her freedom is more important than merely winning freedom from the British. But, on this more important obligation there does not seem to be the same unanimity. At any rate, the attitude of the Muslims on this point has not been very assuring. It is obvious from the numerous

---

[42]The creed of the Congress was not changed at Madras. It was changed at the Lahore session of the Congress by a resolution passed on 31 December 1929. In the Madras session, only a resolution in favour of independence was passed. In the Calcutta session of the Congress, held in December 1928, both Mr Gandhi and the President of the Congress declared themselves willing to accept dominion status if it was offered by the British Government by midnight of 31 December 1929.

utterances of Muslim leaders that they do not accept the obligation to maintain India's freedom.

◆

Summing up the whole discussion, it appears that an integral India is incompatible with an Independent India or even with India as a dominion. On the footing that India is to be one integral whole there is a frustration of all her hopes of freedom writ large on her future. There is frustration, if the national destiny is conceived in terms of independence, because the Hindus will not follow that path. They have reason not to follow it. They fear that way lies in the establishment of the domination of the Muslims over the Hindus. The Hindus see that the Muslim move for independence is not innocent.

It is to be used only to bring the Hindus out of the protecting shield of the British Empire in the open and then by alliance with the neighbouring Muslim countries and by their aid subjugate them. For the Muslims, independence is not the end. It is only a means to establish Muslim Raj. There is frustration if the national destiny is conceived of in terms of dominion status because the Muslims will not agree to abide by it. They fear that under dominion status, the Hindus will establish Hindu Raj over them by taking benefit of the principle of one man one vote and one vote one value, and that however much the benefit of the principle is curtailed by weightage to Muslims, the result cannot fail to be a government of the Hindus, by the Hindus and, therefore, for the Hindus. Complete frustration of her destiny, therefore, seems to be the fate of India if it is insisted that India shall remain as one integral whole.

It is a question to be considered whether integral India is an ideal worth fighting for. In the first place, even if India remained as one integral whole it will never be an organic whole. India may in name continue to be known as one country, but in reality it will be two separate countries—Pakistan and Hindustan—joined together by a forced and artificial union. This will be specially so under the stress of the two-nation theory. As it is, the idea of unity has had little hold on the Indian world of fact and reality, little charm for the common Indian, Hindu or Muslim, whose vision is bounded by the valley in which he lives. But it did appeal to the imaginative and unsophisticated minds on both sides. The two-nation theory will not leave room even for the growth of that sentimental desire for unity. The spread of that virus of dualism in the body politic must some day create a mentality which is sure to call for a life and death struggle for the dissolution of this forced union. If by reason of some superior force, the dissolution does not take place, one thing is sure to happen to India—namely, that this continued union will go on sapping her vitality, loosening its cohesion, weakening its hold on the love and faith of her people and preventing the use, if not retarding the growth, of its moral and material resources. India will be an anaemic and sickly state, ineffective, a living corpse, dead though not buried.

The second disadvantage of this forced union will be the necessity for finding a basis for Hindu–Muslim settlement. How difficult it is to reach a settlement no one needs to be told. Short of dividing India into Pakistan and Hindustan what more can be offered—without injury to the other interests in the country—than what has already been conceded with a view to bring about a settlement, it is difficult to conceive. But, whatever the difficulties, it cannot be gainsaid that if this forced union continues, there can be no political advance for India unless it is accompanied by communal settlement. Indeed, a communal settlement—rather an international settlement for now and hereafter the Hindus and the Muslims must be treated as two nations—will remain under this scheme of forced union, a condition precedent for every inch of political progress.

There will be a third disadvantage of this forced political union. It cannot eliminate the presence of a third party. In the first place, the constitution, if one comes in existence, will be a federation of mutually suspicious and unfriendly states. They will of their own accord want the presence of a third party to appeal to in cases of dispute. For, their suspicious and unfriendly relationship towards each other will come in the way of the two nations ever reaching satisfaction by the method of negotiation. India will not have in future even that unity of opposition to the British which used to gladden the hearts of so many in the past. For, the two nations will be more opposed to each other than before, ever to become united against the British. In the second place, the basis of the constitution will be the settlement between the Hindus and the Muslims, and for the successful working of such a constitution, the presence of a third party, and be it noted, with sufficient armed force, will be necessary to see that the settlement is not broken.

All this, of course, means the frustration of the political destiny, which both Hindus and Muslims profess to cherish and the early consummation of which they so devoutly wish… What else, however, can be expected if two warring nations are locked in the bosom of one country and one constitution?

Compare with this dark vista, the vista that opens out if India is divided into Pakistan and Hindustan. The partition opens the way to a fulfilment of the destiny each may fix for itself. Muslims will be free to choose for their Pakistan independence or dominion status, whatever they think good for themselves. Hindus will be free to choose for their Hindustan independence or dominion status, whatever they may think wise for their condition. The Muslims will be freed from the nightmare of Hindu Raj. Thus the path of political progress becomes smooth for both. The fear of the object being frustrated gives place to the hope of fulfilment. Communal settlement must remain a necessary condition precedent, if India, as one integral whole desires to make any political advance. But, Pakistan and Hindustan are free from the rigorous trammels of such a condition precedent, and even if a communal settlement with minorities remained to be a condition precedent it will not be difficult to fulfil. The path of each is cleared of this obstacle. There is another advantage of Pakistan which must be mentioned. It is generally admitted that there does exist a kind of antagonism between Hindus and Muslims which if not dissolved will prove ruinous to the peace and progress of India. But, it is not realized that the mischief is caused not so much by the existence of mutual antagonism as by the existence of a common theatre for its display. It is the common theatre which calls this antagonism into action. It cannot but be so. When the two are called to participate in acts of common concern what else can happen except a display of that antagonism which is inherent in them? Now the scheme of Pakistan has this advantage, namely, that it leaves no theatre for the play of that social antagonism which is the cause of disaffection among the Hindus and the Muslims. There is no fear of Hindustan and Pakistan suffering from that disturbance of peace and tranquillity which has torn and shattered India for so many years. Last, but by no means least, is the elimination of the necessity of a third party to maintain peace. Freed from the trammels, which one imposes upon the other by reason of this forced union, Pakistan and Hindustan can each grow into a strong stable State with no fear of disruption from within. As two separate entities, they can reach their respective destinies which, as parts of one whole they never can.

Those who want an integral India must note what Mr Mahomed Ali as President of the Congress in 1923 said. Speaking about the unity among Indians, Mr Mahomed Ali said:

'Unless some new force other than the misleading unity of opposition unites this vast continent of India, it will remain a geographical misnomer.'

Is there any new force which remains to be harnessed? All other forces having failed, the Congress, after it became the government of the day, saw a new force in the plan of mass contact. It was intended to produce political unity between Hindus and Muslim masses by ignoring or circumventing the leaders of the Muslims. In its essence, it was the plan of the British Conservative Party to buy Labour with 'Tory gold'. The plan was as mischievous as it was futile. The Congress forgot that there are things so precious that no owner, who knows their value, will part with and any attempt to cheat him to part with them is sure to cause resentment and bitterness. Political power is the most precious thing in the life of a community especially if its position is constantly being challenged and the community is required to maintain it by meeting the challenge. Political power is the only means by which it can sustain its position. To attempt to make it part with it by false propaganda, by misrepresentation or by the lure of office or of gold is equivalent to disarming the community, to silencing its guns and to making it ineffective and servile. It may be a way of producing unity. But, the way is despicable for it means suppressing the opposition by a false and unfair method. It cannot produce any unity. It can only create exasperation, bitterness and hostility.[43] This is precisely what the mass contact plan of the Congress did. For, there can be no doubt that this mad plan of mass contact has had a great deal to do with the emergence of Pakistan.

It might be said that it was unfortunate that mass contact was conceived and employed as a political lever and that it might have been used as a force for social unity with greater success. But, could it have succeeded in breaking the social wall which divides the Hindus and the Muslims? It cannot but be matter of the deepest regret to every Indian that there is no social tie to draw them together. There is no inter-dining and no inter-marriage between the two. Can they be introduced? Their festivals are different. Can the Hindus be induced to adopt them or join in them? Their religious notions are not only divergent but repugnant to each other so that on a religious platform, the entry of the one means the exit of the other. Their cultures are different; their literatures and their histories are different. They are not only different, but so distasteful to each other, that they are sure to cause aversion and nausea. Can anyone make them drink from the same fount of these perennial sources of life? No common meeting ground exists. None can be cultivated. There is not even sufficient physical contact, let alone their sharing a common cultural and emotional

---

[43]So sober a person as Sir Abdul Rahim, in his presidential address to the session of the Muslim League held in Aligarh on 30 December 1925, gave expression to this bitterness caused by Hindu tactics wherein he 'deplored the attacks on the Muslim community in the form of Shuddhi, Sangathan and Hindu Mahasabha movements and activities led by politicians like Lala Lajpal Rai and Swami Shradhanand' and said, 'Some of the Hindu leaders had spoken publicly of driving out Muslims from India as Spaniards expelled Moors from Spain. Musalmans would be loo big a mouthful for their Hindu friends to swallow. Thanks to the artificial conditions under which they lived they had to admit that Hindus were in a position of great advantage and even the English had learned to dread their venomous propaganda. Hindus were equally adept in the art of belittling in every way possible the best Musalmans in public positions excepting only those who had subscribed to the Hindu political creed. They had in fact by their provocative and aggressive conduct made it clearer than ever to Muslims that the latter could not entrust their fate to Hindus and must adopt every possible measure of self-defence.'—All India Register, 1925, Vol. II, p 356.

life. They do not live together. Hindus and Muslims live in separate worlds of their own. Hindus live in villages and Muslims in towns in those provinces where the Hindus are in a majority. Muslims live in villages and Hindus in towns in those provinces where the Muslims are in a majority. Wherever they live, they live apart. Every town, every village has its Hindu quarters and Muslim quarters, which are quite separate from each other. There is no common continuous cycle of participation. They meet to trade or they meet to murder. They do not meet to befriend one another. When there is no call to trade or when there is no call to murder, they cease to meet. When there is peace, the Hindu quarters and the Muslim quarters appear like two alien settlements. The moment war is declared, the settlements become armed camps. The periods of peace and the periods of war are brief. But, the interval is one of continuous tension. What can mass contact do against such barriers? It cannot even get over on the other side of the barrier, much less can it produce organic unity.

Chapter 6

DEBUNKING PAKISTAN

THINKING OF THE Hindu alternative to Pakistan, the scheme that at once comes to one's mind is the one put forth by the late Lala Hardayal in 1925. It was published in the form of a statement which appeared in the *Pratap* of Lahore. In this statement, which he called his political testament, Lala Hardayal said:

> 'I declare that the future of the Hindu race, of Hindustan and of the Punjab, rests on these four pillars: (1) Hindu Sangathan, (2) Hindu Raj, (3) Shuddhi of Moslems, and (4) Conquest and Shuddhi of Afghanistan and the Frontiers. So long as the Hindu nation does not accomplish these four things, the safety of our children and great-grandchildren will be ever in danger, and the safety of the Hindu race will be impossible. The Hindu race has but one history, and its institutions are homogeneous. But the Musalmans and Christians are far removed from the confines of Hindustan, for their religions are alien and they love Persian, Arab and European institutions. Thus, just as one removes foreign matter from the eye, Shuddhi must be made of these two religions. Afghanistan and the hilly regions of the frontier were formerly part of India, but are at present under the domination of Islam… Just as there is Hindu religion in Nepal, so there must be Hindu institutions in Afghanistan and the frontier territory; otherwise it is useless to win Swaraj. For mountain tribes are always warlike and hungry. If they become our enemies, the age of Nadir Shah and Zaman Shah will begin anew. At present English officers are protecting the frontiers; but it cannot always be… If Hindus want to protect themselves, they must conquer Afghanistan and the frontiers and convert all the mountain tribes.'

I do not know how many Hindus would come forward to give their support to this scheme of Lala Hardayal as an alternative to Pakistan.[44]

---

[44]'Through Indian Eyes', *Times of India*, 25 July 1925.

In the first place, Hindu religion is not a proselytizing religion. Maulana Mahomed Ali was quite right when, in the course of his address as President of the Congress, he said:

'Now, this has been my complaint for a long lime against Hinduism, and on one occasion, lecturing at Allahabad in 1907, I had pointed out the contrast between Musalmans and Hindus, by saying that the worst that can be said of a Muslim was that he had a tasteless mess which he called a dish fit for kings, and wanted all to share it with him, thrusting it down the throats of such as did not relish it and would rather not have it, while his Hindu brother, who prided himself on his cookery, retired into the privacy of his kitchen and greedily devoured all that he had cooked, without permitting even the shadow of his brother to fall on his food, or sparing even a crumb for him. This was said not altogether in levity; and in fact, I once asked Mahatma Gandhi to justify this feature of his faith to me.'

What answer the Mahatma gave to his question, Mr Mahomed Ali did not disclose. The fact is that however much the Hindus may wish, Hindu religion cannot become a missionary religion like Islam or Christianity. It is not that the Hindu religion was never a missionary religion. On the contrary, it was once a missionary religion—indeed could not but have been a missionary religion, otherwise it is difficult to explain how it could have spread over an area so vast as the Indian continent.[45] But once a missionary religion, Hinduism perforce ceased to be a missionary religion after the time when the Hindu society developed its system of castes. For caste is incompatible with conversion. To be able to convert a stranger to its religion, it is not enough for a community to offer its creed. It must be in a position to admit the convert to its social life and to absorb and assimilate him among its kindred. It is not possible for the Hindu society to satisfy this prerequisite of effective conversion. There is nothing to prevent a Hindu, with a missionary zeal, to proceed to convert an alien to the Hindu

---

[45]On the question whether the Hindu religion was a missionary religion and if it was, why it ceased to be so, see my essay on 'caste and Conversion' in the Annual Number of the *Telugu Samachar* for 1926.

faith. But before he converts the alien, he is bound to be confronted with the question: What is to be the caste of the convert? According to the Hindus, for a person to belong to a caste he must be born in it. A convert is not born in a caste and, therefore, he belongs to no caste. This is also an important question. More than political or religious, man is a social animal. He may not have, need not have, religion; he may not have, need not have, politics. He must have society; he cannot do without society. For a Hindu to be without caste is to be without society. Where there is no society for the convert, how can there be any conversion? So long as Hindu society is fragmented in autonomous and autogenic castes, Hindu religion cannot be a missionary religion. The conversion of the Afghans and the frontier tribes to Hinduism is, therefore, an idle dream.

In the second place, Lala Hardayal's scheme must call for financial resources, the immensity of which it is hardly possible to compute. Who can furnish the funds necessary for the conversion of the Afghans and the frontier tribesmen to Hinduism? The Hindus, having ceased to convert others to their faith for a long time, have also lost the zeal for conversion. Want of zeal is bound to affect the question of finances. Further, Hindu society being moulded in the cast of the Chaturvarna, wealth has, from very ancient times, been most unevenly distributed. It is only the Baniya who is the heir to wealth and property among the Hindus. There are, of course, the landlords who are the creation of foreign invaders or native rebels, but they are not as numerous as the Baniya. The Baniya is money-made and his pursuits are solely for private gain. He knows no other use of money except to hold it and to transmit it to his descendants. Spread of religion or acquisition and promotion of culture do not interest him. Even decent living has no place in his budget. This has been his tradition for ages. If money is excepted, he is not much above the brute in the conception and manner of life. Only one new service, on the expenditure side, has found a place in his budget. That service is politics. This happened since the entry of Mr Gandhi as a political leader. That new service is the support of Gandhian politics. Here again, the reason is not love of politics. The reason is to make private gain out of public affairs. What hope is there that such men will spend money on such a bootless cause as the spread of Hindu religion among the Afghans and frontier tribes?

Thirdly, there is the question of facilities for conversion that may be available in Afghanistan. Lala Hardayal evidently thought that it is possible to say in Afghanistan, with the same impunity as in Turkey, that the Koran is wrong or out of date. Only one year before the publication of his political testament by Lala Hardayal, i.e., in 1924, one Niamatulla—a follower of Mirza Ghulam Ahamed of Quadiyan—who claimed to be the messiah and Mahdi and a prophet of a sort—was stoned to death[46] at Kabul by the order of the highest ecclesiastical tribunal of Afghanistan. The crime of this man was, as reported by a Khilafat paper, that he was professing and preaching ideas and beliefs, inconsistent with Islam and Shariat. This man, says the same paper, was stoned to death according to the agreeing judgements of the first Shariat (canon) Court, the Central Appellate Court and the Ulema and Divines of the final Appellate Committee of the Ministry of Justice. In the light of these difficulties, the scheme must be said to be wild in its conception and is sure to prove ruinous in its execution. It is adventurous in character and is too fantastic to appeal to any reasonable man except perhaps some fanatical Arya Samajists of the Punjab.

The stand taken by Hindu Mahasabha has been defined by Mr V.D. Savarkar, the President of the Sabha, in his presidential addresses at the annual sessions of the Sabha. As defined by him, the Hindu Mahasabha is against Pakistan and proposes to resist it by all means. What these means are we do not know. If they are force, coercion and resistance, they are only negative alternatives and Mr Savarkar and the Hindu Mahasabha alone can say how far these means will succeed.

It would, however, not be fair to Mr Savarkar to say that he has only a negative attitude towards the claim put forth by the Muslims of India. He has put forth his positive proposals in reply to them.

To understand his positive proposals, one must grasp some of his basic conceptions. Mr Savarkar lays great stress on a proper understanding of the terms, Hinduism, Hindutva and Hindudom.

---

[46]'Through Indian Eyes', *Times of India*, 25 July 1925.

He says:[47]

> 'In expounding the ideology of the Hindu movement, it is absolutely necessary to have a correct grasp of the meaning attached to these three terms. From the word "Hindu" has been coined the word "Hinduism" in English. It means the schools or system of religion the Hindus follow. The second word "Hindutva" is far more comprehensive and refers not only to the religious aspects of the Hindu people as the word "Hinduism" does but comprehend even their cultural, linguistic, social and political aspects as well. It is more or less akin to "Hindu Polity" and its nearly exact translation would be "Hinduness". The third word "Hindudom" means the Hindu people spoken of collectively. It is a collective name for the Hindu World, just as Islam denotes the Moslem World.'

Mr Savarkar takes it as a gross misrepresentation to say that the Hindu Mahasabha is a religious body. In refutation of this misrepresentation, Mr Savarkar says:[48]

> 'It has come to my notice that a very large section of the English-educated Hindus hold back from joining the Hindu Mahasabha…under the erroneous idea that it is an exclusively religious organization—something like a Christian Mission. Nothing could be far from truth. The Hindu Mahasabha is not a Hindu Mission. It leaves religious questions regarding theism, monotheism, pantheism or even atheism to be discussed and determined by the different Hindu schools of religious persuasions. It is not a Hindu Dharma Mahasabha, but a Hindu National Mahasabha. Consequently, by its very constitution it is debarred to associate itself exclusively as a partisan with any particular religious school or sect even within the Hindu fold. As a national Hindu body it will of course propagate and defend the National Hindu Church comprising each and all religions of Hindusthani origin against any non-Hindu attack or encroachment. But the sphere of its activity is far more comprehensive than that of an exclusively religious body. The Hindu Mahasabha

---

[47]Speech at the Calcutta Session of the Hindu Mahasabha held in December 1939, p 14.
[48]Ibid., p 25.

identifies itself with the National life of Hindudom in all its entirety, in all its social, economic, cultural and above all political aspects and is pledged to protect and promote all that contributes to the freedom, strength and glory of the Hindu nation; and as an indispensable means to that end to attain Purna Swarajya, absolute political Independence of Hindusthan by all legitimate and proper means.'

Such is the scheme of Mr Savarkar and the Hindu Mahasabha. As must have been noticed, the scheme has some disturbing features.

One is the categorical assertion that the Hindus are a nation by themselves. This, of course, means that the Muslims are a separate nation by themselves. That this is his view, Mr Savarkar does not leave to be inferred. He insists upon it in no uncertain terms and with the most absolute emphasis he is capable of. Speaking at the Hindu Mahasabha Session held at Ahmedabad in 1937, Mr Savarkar said:

'Several infantile politicians commit the serious mistake in supposing that India is already welded into a harmonious nation, or that it could be welded thus for the mere wish to do so. These our well-meaning but unthinking friends take their dreams for realities. That is why they are impatient of communal tangles and attribute them to communal organizations. But the solid fact is that the so-called communal questions are but a legacy handed down to us by centuries of a cultural, religious and national antagonism between the Hindus and the Muslims. When the time is ripe you can solve them; but you cannot suppress them by merely refusing recognition of them. It is safer to diagnose and treat deep-seated disease than to ignore it. Let us bravely face unpleasant facts as they are. India cannot be assumed today to be a unitarian and homogeneous nation, but on the contrary these are two nations in the main, the Hindus and the Muslims in India.'

Strange as it may appear, Mr Savarkar and Mr Jinnah, instead of being opposed to each other on the one nation versus two nations issue, are in complete agreement about it. Both agree, not only agree but insist, that there are two nations in India—one the Muslim nation and the other the Hindu nation. They differ only as regards the terms and conditions on which the two nations should live. Mr Jinnah says India should be cut up into two, Pakistan and Hindustan, the Muslim nation to occupy Pakistan and the Hindu nation to occupy Hindustan. Mr Savarkar on the other hand insists that, although there are two nations in India, India shall not be divided into two parts, one for Muslims and the other for the Hindus; that the two nations shall dwell in one country and shall live under the mantle of one single constitution; that the constitution shall be such that the Hindu nation will be enabled to occupy a predominant position that is due to it and the Muslim nation made to live in the position of subordinate cooperation with the Hindu nation. In the struggle for political power between the two nations, the rule of the game which Mr Savarkar prescribes is to be one man one vote, be the man Hindu or Muslim. In his scheme a Muslim is to have no advantage which a Hindu does not have. Minority is to be no justification for privilege and majority is to be no ground for penalty. The State will guarantee the Muslims any defined measure of political power in the form of Muslim religion and Muslim culture. But the State will not guarantee secured seats in the Legislature or in the Administration and, if such guarantee is insisted upon by the Muslims,[49] such guaranteed quota is not to exceed their proportion to the general population. Thus by confiscating its weightages, Mr Savarkar would even strip the Muslim nation of all the political privileges it has secured so far.

This alternative of Mr Savarkar to Pakistan has about it a frankness, boldness and definiteness which distinguishes it from the irregularity, vagueness and indefiniteness which characterizes the Congress declarations about minority rights. Mr Savarkar's scheme has at least the merit of telling the Muslims, thus far and no further. The Muslims know where they are with regard to the Hindu Mahasabha. On the other hand, with the Congress the Musalmans find themselves nowhere because the Congress has been treating the Muslims and the minority question as a game in diplomacy, if not in duplicity.

At the same time, it must be said that Mr Savarkar's attitude is illogical, if not queer. Mr Savarkar admits that the Muslims are a separate nation. He concedes that they have a right to cultural

---

[49]See his manifesto dated 23 March 1919.

autonomy. He allows them to have a national flag. Yet he opposes the demand of the Muslim nation for a separate national home. If he claims a national home for the Hindu nation, how can he refuse the claim of the Muslim nation for a national home?

It would not have been a matter of much concern if inconsistency was the only fault of Mr Savarkar. But Mr Savarkar in advocating his scheme is really creating a most dangerous situation for the safety and security of India. History records two ways as being open to a major nation to deal with a minor nation when they are citizens of the same country and are subject to the same constitution. One way is to destroy the nationality of the minor nation and to assimilate and absorb it into the major nation, so as to make one nation out of two. This is done by denying to the minor nation any right to language, religion or culture and by seeking to enforce upon it the language, religion and culture of the major nation. The other way is to divide the country and to allow the minor nation a separate, autonomous and sovereign existence, independent of the major nation. Both these ways were tried in Austria and Turkey, the second after the failure of the first.

Mr Savarkar adopts neither of these two ways. He does not propose to suppress the Muslim nation. On the contrary, he is nursing and feeding it by allowing it to retain its religion, language and culture elements which go to sustain the soul of a nation. At the same time, he does not consent to divide the country so as to allow the two nations to become separate, autonomous states, each sovereign in its own territory. He wants the Hindus and the Muslims to live as two separate nations in one country, each maintaining its own religion, language and culture. One can understand and even appreciate the wisdom of the theory of suppression of the minor nation by the major nation because the ultimate aim is to bring into being one nation. But one cannot follow what advantage a theory has which says that there must ever be two nations but that there shall be no divorce between them. One can justify this attitude only if the two nations were to live as partners in friendly intercourse with mutual respect and accord. But that is not to be, because Mr Savarkar will not allow the Muslim nation to be co-equal in authority with the Hindu nation. He wants the Hindu nation to be the dominant nation and the Muslim nation to be the servient nation. Why Mr Savarkar, after sowing this seed of enmity between the Hindu nation and the Muslim nation, should want that they should live under one constitution and occupy one country, is difficult to explain.

Mr Savarkar is quite unconcerned about the Muslim reaction to his scheme. He formulates his scheme and throws it in the face of the Muslims with the covering letter 'take it or leave it'. He is not perturbed by the Muslim refusal to join in the struggle for Swaraj. He is quite conscious of the strength of the Hindus and the Hindu Mahasabha and proposes to carry on the struggle in the confident hope that, alone and unaided, the Hindus will be able to wrest Swaraj from the British. Mr Savarkar is quite prepared to say to the Musalmans:

> 'If you come, with you, if you don't, without you; and if you oppose, in spite of you—the Hindus will continue to fight for their national freedom as best as they can.'

Not so Mr Gandhi. At the very commencement of his career as a political leader of India when Mr Gandhi startled the people of India by his promise to win Swaraj within six months, Mr Gandhi said that he could perform the miracle only if certain conditions were fulfilled. One of these conditions was the achievement of Hindu–Muslim unity. Mr Gandhi is never tired of saying that there is no Swaraj without Hindu–Muslim unity. Mr Gandhi did not merely make this slogan the currency of Indian politics but he has strenuously worked to bring it about. Mr Gandhi, it may be said, began his carrier as a political leader of India with the manifesto dated 2 March 1919 declaring his intention to 1919 declaring his intention to launch Satyagraha against the Rowlatt Act and asking those who desired to join him to sign the Satyagraha pledge. That campaign of Satyagraha was a short-lived campaign and was suspended by Mr Gandhi on 18 April 1919. As a part of his programme Mr Gandhi had fixed the 6th March 1919 to be observed all over India as a day of protest against the Rowlatt Act. Mass meetings were to be held on that day and Mr Gandhi had prescribed that the masses attending the meetings should take a vow in the following terms:

'With God as witness, we Hindus and Mahomedans declare that we shall behave towards one another as children of the same parents, that we shall have no differences, that the sorrows of each shall be the sorrows of the other and that each shall help the other in removing them. We shall respect each other's religion and religious feelings and shall not stand in the way of our respective religious practices. We shall always refrain from violence to each other in the name of religion.'

There was nothing in the campaign of Satyagraha against the Rowlatt Act which could have led to any clash between the Hindus and Muslims. Yet Mr Gandhi asked his followers to take the vow. This shows how insistent he was from the very beginning upon Hindu–Muslim unity.

The Mahomedans started the Khilafat movement in 1919. The objective of the movement was twofold; to preserve the Khilafat and to maintain the integrity of the Turkish Empire. Both these objectives were unsupportable. The Khilafat could not be saved simply because the Turks, in whose interest this agitation was carried on, did not want the Sultan. They wanted a republic and it was quite unjustifiable to compel the Turks to keep Turkey a monarchy when they wanted to convert it into a republic. It was not open to insist upon the integrity of the Turkish Empire because it meant the perpetual subjection of the different nationalities to the Turkish rule and particularly of the Arabs, especially when it was agreed on all hands that the doctrine of self-determination should be made the basis of the peace settlement.

The movement was started by the Mahomedans. It was taken up by Mr Gandhi with a tenacity and faith which must have surprised many Mahomedans themselves. There were many people who doubted the ethical basis of the Khilafat movement and tried to dissuade Mr Gandhi from taking any part in a movement the ethical basis of which was so questionable. But Mr Gandhi had so completely persuaded himself of the justice of the Khilafat agitation that he refused to yield to their advice. Time and again he argued that the cause was just and it was his duty to join it. The position taken up by him may be summed up in his own words.[50]

---

[50] *Young India,* 2 June 1920.

'(1) In my opinion, the Turkish claim is not only not immoral and unjust, but it is highly equitable, only because Turkey wants to retain what is her own. And the Mahomedan manifesto has definitely declared that whatever guarantee may be necessary to be taken for the protection of the non-Muslim and non-Turkish races/should be taken so as to give the Christians theirs and the Arabs their self-government under the Turkish suzerainty;

(2) I do not believe the Turk to be weak, incapable or cruel. He is certainly disorganized and probably without good generalship. The argument of weakness, incapacity and cruelly one often hears quoted in connection with those from whom power is sought to be taken away. About the alleged massacres a proper commission has been asked for, but never granted. And in any case security can be taken against oppression;

(3) I have already stated that, if I were not interested in the Indian Mahomedans, I would not interest myself in the welfare of the Turks any more than I am in that of the Austrians or the Poles. But I am bound as an Indian to share the sufferings and trials of fellow-Indians. If I deem the Mahomedan to be my brother, it is my duty to help him in his hour of peril to the best of my ability, if his cause commends itself to me as just;

(4) The fourth refers to the extent Hindus should join hands with the Mahomedans. It is, therefore, a matter of feeling and opinion. It is expedient to suffer for my Mahomedan brother to the utmost in a just cause and I should, therefore, travel with him along the whole road so long as the means employed by him are as honourable as his end. I cannot regulate the Mahomedan feeling. I must accept his statement that the Khilafat is with him a religious question in the sense that it binds him to reach the goal even at the cost of his own life.'

Mr Gandhi not only agreed with the Muslims in the Khilafat cause but acted as their guide and their friend. The part played by Mr Gandhi in the Khilafat agitation and the connection between the Khilafat agitation and the Non-cooperation Movement has become obscure by the reason of the fact that most people believed that it was the

Congress which initiated the Non-cooperation Movement and it was done as a means for winning Swaraj. That such a view should prevail is quite understandable because most people content themselves with noting the connection between the Non-cooperation Movement and the special session of the Congress held at Calcutta on 7th and 8th September 1920. But anyone, who cares to go behind September 1920 and examine the situation as it then stood, will find that this view is not true. The truth is that the Non-cooperation has its origin in the Khilafat agitation and not in the Congress Movement for Swaraj: that it was started by the Khilafatists to help Turkey and adopted by the Congress only to help the Khilafatists; that Swaraj was not its primary object, but its primary object was Khilafat and that Swaraj was added as a secondary object to induce the Hindus to join it will be evident from the following facts.

The Hindus say they have an alternative to Pakistan. Have the Muslims also an alternative to Pakistan? The Hindus say yes, the Muslims say no. The Hindus believe that the Muslim proposal for Pakistan is only a bargaining manoeuvre put forth with the object of making additions to the communal gains already secured under the Communal Award. The Muslims repudiate the suggestion. They say there is no equivalent to Pakistan and, therefore, they will have Pakistan and nothing but Pakistan. It does seem that the Musalmans are devoted to Pakistan and are determined to have nothing else, and that the Hindus in hoping for an alternative are merely indulging in wishful thinking. But assuming that the Hindus are shrewd enough in divining what the Muslim game is, will the Hindus be ready to welcome the Muslim alternative to Pakistan? The answer to the question must, of course, depend upon what the Muslim alternative is.

What is the Muslim alternative to Pakistan? No one knows. The Muslims, if they have any, have not disclosed it and perhaps will not disclose it till the day when the rival parties meet to revise and settle the terms on which the Hindus and the Muslims are to associate with each other in the future. To be forewarned is to be forearmed. It is, therefore, necessary for the Hindus to have some idea of the possible Muslim alternative to enable them to meet the shock of it; for the alternative cannot be better than the Communal Award and is sure to be many degrees worse.

In the absence of the exact alternative proposal one can only make a guess. Now one man's guess is as good as that of another, and the party concerned has to choose on which of these he will rely. Among the likely guesses, my guess is that the Muslims will put forth as their alternative some such proposal as the following:

That the future constitution of India shall provide:

(i)   That the Muslims shall have 50 per cent representation in the Legislature, Central as well as Provincial, through separate electorates.

(ii)   That 50 per cent of the Executive in the Centre as well as in the Provinces shall consist of Muslims.

(iii)   That in the Civil Service, 50 per cent of the posts shall be assigned for the Muslims.

(iv)   That in the Fighting Forces, the Muslim proportion shall be one half, both in the ranks and in the higher grades.

(v)   That Muslims shall have 50 per cent representation in all public bodies, such as councils and commissions, created for public purposes.

(vi)   That Muslims shall have 50 per cent representation in all international organizations in which India will participate.

(ii)   That if the Prime Minister be a Hindu, the Deputy Prime Minister shall be a Muslim.

(viii)   That if the Commander-in-Chief be a Hindu, the Deputy Commander-in-Chief shall be a Muslim.

(ix)   That no changes in the Provincial boundaries shall be made except with the consent of 66 per cent of the Muslim members of the Legislature.

(x)   That no action or treaty against a Muslim country shall be valid unless the consent of 66 per cent of the Muslim members of the Legislature is obtained.

(ix)   That no law affecting the culture or religion or religious usage of Muslims shall be made except with the consent of 66 per cent of the Muslim members of the Legislature.

(ix)   That the national language for India shall be Urdu.

(ix) That no law prohibiting or restricting the slaughter of cows or the propagation of and conversion to Islam shall be valid unless it is passed with the consent of 66 per cent of the Muslim members of the Legislature.

(x) That no change in the constitution shall be valid unless the majority required for effecting such changes also includes a 66 per cent majority of the Muslim members of the Legislature.

This guess of mine is not the result of imagination let loose. It is not the result of a desire to frighten the Hindus into an unwilling and hasty acceptance of Pakistan. If I may say so, it is really an intelligent anticipation based upon available data coming from Muslim quarters.

An indication of what the Muslim alternative is likely to be, is obtainable from the nature of the Constitutional Reforms which are contemplated for the Dominions of His Exalted Highness the Nizam of Hyderabad.

The Hyderabad scheme of Reforms is a novel scheme. It rejects the scheme of communal representation obtaining in British India. In its place is substituted what is called Functional Representation i.e., representation by classes and by professions. The composition of the Legislature, which is to consist of 70 members, is to be as follows:

Elected			Nominated		
Agriculture		12	Illkas		8
Patidar	8		Sarf-i-Khas	2	
Tenants	4		Paigahs	3	
Women		1			
Graduates		1	Peshkari	1	
University		1			
Jagirdars		2	Salar Jung	1	
Maashdars		1			
Legal		2	Samasthans	1	
Western	1		Officials		18
			Rural Arts and Crafts		1

Oriental	1		Backward Classes		1
Teaching		1	Minor Unrepresented Classes		3
Commerce		1	Others		6
Industries		2			
Banking		2			
Indigenous	1				
Cooperative and	1				
Joint Stock					
Organized Labour		1			
Harijan		1			
District Municipalities		1			
City Muncipality		1			
Rural Boards		1			
Total		33	Total		37

Whether the scheme of functional representation will promote better harmony between the various classes and sections than communal representation does is more than doubtful. In addition to perpetuating existing social and religious divisions, it may quite easily intensify class struggle by emphasizing class consciousness. The scheme appears innocuous, but its real character will come out when every class will demand representation in proportion to its numbers. Be that as it may, functional representation is not the most significant feature of the Hyderabad scheme of Reforms. The most significant feature of the scheme is the proposed division of seats between Hindus and Musalmans in the new Hyderabad Legislature. Under the scheme as approved by H.E.H. the Nizam, communal representation is not altogether banished. It is retained along with functional representation. It is to operate through joint electorates. But there is to be equal representation for 'the two majority communities' on every[51] elective

---

[51]Beside the Central Legislature there are to be constituted under the scheme of Reforms other popular bodies such as Panchayats, Rural Boards, Municipalities

body including the legislature, and no candidate can succeed unless he secures 40 per cent, of the votes polled by—members of his community. This principle of equal representation to Hindus and Muslims irrespective of their numbers[52] is not only to apply to every elective body but it is to apply to both elected as well as nominated members of the body.

In justification of this theory of equal representation it is stated that:

'The importance of the Muslim community in the state, by virtue of its historical position and its status in the body politic, is so obvious that it cannot be reduced to the status of a minority in the Assembly.'

Quite recently there have appeared in the press the proposals formulated by one Mr Mir Akbar Ali Khan calling himself the leader of the Nationalist Party, as a means of settling the Hindu–Muslim problem in British India. They are as follows:

(1) The future Constitution of India must rest upon the broad foundation of adequate military defence of the country and upon making the people reasonably military-minded. The Hindus must have the same military-mindedness as the Muslims.

(2) The present moment offers a supreme opportunity for the two communities to ask for the defence of India being made over to them. The Indian Army must consist of an equal number of Hindus and Muslims and no regiment should be on a communal, as distinguished from regional, basis.

(3) The Governments in the provinces and at the Centre should be wholly National Governments composed of men who are reasonably military-minded. Hindu and Muslim ministers should be equal in number in the Central as well as all Provincial cabinets; other important minorities might wherever necessary

and Town Committees.

[52]The distribution of population of Hyderabad State (excluding Berar) is, according to the Census of 1931, as follows:

Hindus	Untouchables	Muslims	Christians	Others	Total
96,99,615	24,73,230	15,34,666	1,51,382	5,77.255	1,44,36,148

be given special representation. This scheme will function most satisfactorily with joint electorates, but in the present temper of the country separate electorates might be continued. The Hindu ministers must be elected by the Hindu members of the legislature and the Muslim ministers by the Muslim members.

(4) The cabinet is to be removable only on an express vote of no-confidence, against the cabinet as a whole, passed by a majority of 2/3rd of the whole House which majority must be of Hindus and Muslims taken separately.

(5) The religion, language, script and personal law of each community should be safeguarded by a paramount constitutional check enabling the majority of members representing that community in the legislature to place a veto on any legislative or other measure affecting it. A similar veto must be provided against any measure designed or calculated to affect adversely the economic well-being of any community.

(6) An adequate communal representation in the services must be agreed to as a practical measure of justice in administration and in the distribution patronage.

If the proposals put forth by a Muslim leader of the Nationalist Party in Hyderabad State is an indication of the direction in which the mind of the Muslims in British India is running, then, the guess I have made as to what is likely to be the alternative to Pakistan derives additional support.

Hindus who will not yield to the demand of the Muslims for the division of India into Pakistan and Hindustan, and would insist upon maintaining the geographical unity of India without counting the cost, will do well to study the fate that has befallen other countries which, like India, harboured many nations and sought to harmonize them.

It is not necessary to review the history of all such countries. It is enough to recount here the story of two, Turkey and Czechoslovakia.

What is the lesson to be drawn from the story of these two countries?

There is some difference as to how the matters should be put. Mr Sydney Brooks would say that the cause of these wars of disruption is nationalism, which according to him is the enemy of the universal peace.

Mr Norman Angell, on the other hand, would say it is not nationalism but the threat to nationalism which is the cause. To Mr Robertson, nationalism is an irrational instinct, if not a positive hallucination, and the sooner humanity got rid of it the better for all.

In whatever way the matter is put and howsoever ardently one may wish for the elimination of nationalism, the lesson to be drawn is quite clear: that nationalism is a fact which can neither be eluded nor denied. Whether one calls it an irrational instinct or positive hallucination, the fact remains that it is a potent force which has a dynamic power to disrupt empires. Whether nationalism is the cause or the threat to nationalism is the cause, is a difference of emphasis only. The real thing is to recognize, as does Mr Toynbee, that 'Nationalism is strong enough to produce war in spite of us. It has terribly proved itself to be no outworn creed, but a vital force to be reckoned with.' As was pointed out by him, 'The right reading of nationalism has become an affair of life and death.' It was not only so for Europe. It was so for Turkey. It was so for Czechoslovakia. And what was a question of life and death to them could not but be one of life and death to India. Prof. Toynbee pleaded, as was done before him by Guizot, for the recognition of nationality as the necessary foundation of European peace. Could India ignore to recognize this plea? If she does, she will be acting at her peril. That nationalism is a disruptive force is not the only lesson to be learnt from the history of these two countries. Their experience embodies much else of equal, if not of greater, significance. What that is, will be evident if certain facts are recalled to memory.

The Turks were by no means as illiberal as they are painted. They allowed their minorities a large measure of autonomy. The Turks had gone far towards solving the problem of how people of different communities with different social heritages are to live together in harmony when they are geographically intermingled. The Ottoman Empire had accorded, as a matter of course, to the non-Muslim and non-Turkish communities within its frontiers, a degree of territorial as well as cultural autonomy which had never been dreamt of in the political philosophy of the West. Ought not the Christian subjects to have been satisfied with this? Say what one may, the nationalism of Christian minorities was not satisfied with this local autonomy. It fought for complete freedom, and in that fight, Turkey was slit open.

The Turks were bound to the Arabs by the tie of religion. The religious tie of Islam is the strongest known to humanity. No social confederacy can claim to rival the Islamic brotherhood in point of solidarity. Add to this the fact that while the Turks treated his Christian subjects as his inferior, he acknowledged the Arab as his equal. All non-Muslims were excluded from the Ottoman army. But the Arab soldiers and officers served side by side with Turks and Kurds. The Arab officer class, educated in Turkish school, served in military and civil capacities on the same terms as the Turks. There was no derogating distinction between the Turk and the Arab, and there was nothing to prevent the Arab from rising to the highest rank in the Ottoman services. Not only politically but even socially, the Arab was treated as his equal by the Turk; and Arabs married Turkish wives, and Turks married Arab wives. Ought not the Arabs to have been satisfied with this Islamic brotherhood of Arabs and Turks based on fraternity, liberty and equality? Say what one may, the Arabs were not satisfied. Arab nationalism broke the bonds of Islam and fought against his fellow Muslim, the Turk, for its independence. It won, but Turkey was completely dismantled.

As to Czechoslovakia, she began with the recognition that both the Czechs and the Slovaks were one people. Within a few years, the Slovaks claimed to be a separate nation. They would not even admit that they were a branch of the same stock as the Czechs. Their nationalism compelled the Czechs to recognize the fact that they were a distinct people. The Czechs sought to pacify the nationalism of the Slovaks by drawing a hyphen as a mark indicating distinctness. In place of Czechoslovakia they agreed to have Czecho–Slovakia. But, even with the hyphen, the Slovak nationalism remained discontented. The act of autonomy was both a hyphen separating them from the Czechs, as well as a link joining them with the Czechs.

The hyphen as making separation was welcome to the Slovaks, but as making a link with the Czechs was very irksome to them. The Slovaks accepted the autonomy with its hyphen with great relief, and promised to be content and loyal to the state. But, evidently, this was only a matter of strategy. They did not accept it as an ultimate end. They accepted it because they thought that they could use it as a vantage ground for destroying the hyphen, which was their main aim, and convert autonomy into independence. The nationalism of the Slovaks was not content with a hyphen. It wanted a bar in place of the hyphen. Immediately the hyphen was introduced, they began their battle to replace the hyphen between the Czechs and the Slovaks by a bar. They did not care what means they should employ. Their nationalism was so wrong-headed and so intense that when they failed they did not hesitate to call the aid of the Germans.

Thus a deeper study of the disruption of Turkey and Czechoslovakia shows that neither local autonomy nor the bond of religion is sufficient to withstand the force of nationalism, once it is set on the go.

This is a lesson which the Hindus will do well to grasp. They should ask themselves: If the Greek, Balkan and Arab nationalism has blown up the Turkish State, and if Slovak nationalism has caused the dismantling of Czechoslovakia, what is there to prevent. Muslim nationalism from disrupting the Indian State? If experience of other countries teaches that this is the inevitable consequence of pent-up nationalism, why not profit by their experience, and avoid the catastrophe, by agreeing to divide India into Pakistan and Hindustan? Let the Hindus take the warning that if they refuse to divide India into two before they launch on their career as a free people, they will be sailing in those shoal waters in which Turkey, Czechoslovakia and many others have foundered. If they wish to avoid shipwreck in mid-ocean, they must lighten the draught by throwing overboard all superfluous cargo. They will ease the course of their voyage considerably if they—to use the language of Prof. Toynbee—reconcile themselves to making jetsam of less cherished and more combustible cargo.

Will the Hindus really lose if they agree to divide India into two, Pakistan and Hindustan?

With regard to Czechoslovakia, it is instructive to note the real feelings of its government on the loss of their territory caused by the Munich Pact. They were well-expressed by the Prime Minister of Czechoslovakia in his message to the people of Czechoslovakia. In it he said:[53]

---

[53]Henderson, Alexander, *Eye-witness in Czecho–slovakia*, 1939, pp 229–30.

'Citizens and soldiers, I am living through the hardest hour of my life; I am carrying out the most painful task, in comparison with which death would be easy. But precisely because I have fought and because I know under what conditions a war is won, must tell you frankly…that the forces opposed to us at this moment compel us to recognize their superior strength and to act accordingly…

'In Munich, four European Great Powers met and decided to demand of us the acceptance of new frontiers, according to which the German areas of our State would be taken away. We had the choice between desperate and hopeless defence, which would have meant the sacrifice not only of the adult generation but also of women and children, and the acceptance of conditions which in their ruthlessness, and because they were imposed by pressure without war, have no parallel in history. We desired to make a contribution to peace; we would gladly have made it. But not by any means in the way it has been forced upon us.

'But we were abandoned, and were alone… Deeply moved, all your leaders considered, together with the army and the President of the Republic, all the possibilities which remained. *They recognized that in choosing between narrower frontiers and the death of the nation it was their sacred duty to save the life of our people, so that we may not emerge weakened from these terrible times, and so that we may remain certain that our nation will gather itself together again, as it has done so often in the past. Let us all see that our State re-establishes itself soundly within its new frontiers, and that its population is assured of a new life of peace and fruitful labour.* With your help we shall succeed. We rely upon you, and you have confidence in us.'

It is evident that the Czechs refused to be led by the force of historic sentiment. They were ready to have narrower frontiers and a smaller Czechoslovakia (rather than consent) to the ultimate destruction of their people.

With regard to Turkey, the prevalent view was the one that was expressed in 1853 by the Czar Nicholas I, during a conversation with British Ambassador in St. Petersburg in which he said , 'We have on our hand a sick man—a very sick man… He may suddenly die upon our hands.' From that day, the imminent decease of Turkey, the sick man of Europe, was awaited by all his neighbours. The shedding of the territories was considered as the convulsions of a dying man who is alleged to have breathed his last by affixing his signature to the Treaty of Severs.

Is this really a correct view to take of Turkey in the process of dissolution? It is instructive to note the comments of Arnold Toynbee on this view. Referring to the Czar's description of Turkey as the sick man who may suddenly die, he says:[54]

'In this second and more sensational part of his diagnosis Czar Nicholas went astray because he did not understand the nature of the symptoms. If a person totally ignorant of natural history stumbled upon a snake in course of shedding its skin, he would pronounce dogmatically that the creature could not possibly recover. He could point out that when a man (or other mammal) has the misfortune to lose his skin, he is never known to survive. Yet while it is perfectly true that the leopard cannot change his spots nor the Ethiopian his skin, a wider study would have informed our amateur naturalist that a snake can do both and does both habitually. Doubtless, even for the snake, the process is awkward and uncomfortable. He becomes temporarily torpid, and in this condition he is dangerously at the mercy of his enemies. Yet, if he escapes the kites and crows until his metamorphosis is complete, he not only recovers his health but renews his youth with the replacement of his mortal coils. This is the recent experience of the Turk, and "moulting snake" is [a] better simile than sick man for a description of his distemper.'

In this view, the loss of her possessions by Turkey is the removal of an anomalous excrescence, and the gain of a new skin. Turkey is certainly homogeneous, and has no fear of any disruption from within.

The Muslim areas are an anomalous excrescence on Hindustan, and Hindustan is an anomalous excrescence on them. Tied together, they will make India the sick man of Asia. Welded together, they will make India a heterogeneous unit. If Pakistan has the demerit of cutting away parts of India, it has also the merit of introducing harmony in place of conflict.

---

[54]Toynbee, Arnold, *Turkey: A Past and a Future,* 1917, p 141.

Severed into two, each becomes a more homogeneous unit. The homogeneity of the two areas is obvious enough. Each has a cultural unity. Each has a religious unity. Pakistan has a linguistic unity. If there is no such unity in Hindustan, it is possible to have it without any controversy as to whether the common language should be Hindustani, Hindi or Urdu. Separated, each can become a strong and well-knit state. India needs a strong Central government. But it cannot have it so long as Pakistan remains a part of India. Compare the structure of the Federal government as embodied in the Government of India Act, 1935, and it will be found that the Central government as constituted under it is an effete ramshackle thing with very little life in it. As has already been pointed out, this weakening of the Central government is brought about by the desire to placate the Muslim provinces who wish to be independent of the authority of the Central government on the ground that the Central government is bound to be predominantly Hindu in character and composition. When Pakistan comes into being, these considerations can have no force. Hindustan can then have a strong Central government and a homogeneous population, which are necessary elements for the stability of the state, and neither of which will be secured unless there is severance of Pakistan from Hindustan.

With all that has gone before, the sceptic, the nationalist, the conservative and the old-world Indian will not fail to ask 'Must there be Pakistan?' No one can make light of such an attitude. For, the problem of Pakistan is indeed very grave, and it must be admitted that the question is not only a relevant and fair one to be put to the Muslims and to their protagonists, but it is also important. Its importance lies in the fact that the limitations on the case for Pakistan are so considerable in their force that they can never be easily brushed aside. A mere statement of these limitations should be enough to make one feel the force they have. It is writ large on the very face of them. That being so, the burden of proof on the Muslims for establishing an imperative need in favour of Pakistan is very heavy. Indeed, the issue of Pakistan or to put it plainly of partitioning India, is of such a grave character that the Muslims will not only have to discharge this burden of proof but they will have to adduce evidence of such a character as to satisfy the conscience of an international tribunal before they can win their case. Let us see how the case for Pakistan stands in the light of these limitations.

Must there be Pakistan because a good part of the Muslim population of India happens to be concentrated in certain defined areas which can be easily severed from the rest of India? Muslim population is admittedly concentrated in certain well-defined areas, and it may be that these areas are severable. But, what of that? In considering this question one must never lose sight of the fundamental fact that nature has made India one single geographical unit. Indians are, of course, quarrelling and no one can prophesy when they will stop quarrelling. But, granting the fact, what does it establish? Only that Indians are a quarrelsome people. It does not destroy the fact that India is a single geographical unit.

Her unity is as ancient as Nature. Within this geographic unit and covering the whole of it there has been a cultural unity from time immemorial. This cultural unity has defied political and racial divisions. And at any rate for the last hundred and fifty years all institutions—cultural, political, economic, legal and administrative—have been working on a single, uniform spring of action. In any discussion of Pakistan the fact cannot be lost sight of, namely, that the starting point, if not the governing factor, is the fundamental unity of India. For, it is necessary to grasp the fact that there are really two cases of partition which must be clearly distinguished. There is a case in which the starting point is a pre-existing state of separation so that partition is only a dissolution of parts which were once separate and which were subsequently joined together. This case is quite different from another in which the starting point at all times is a state of unity. Consequently, partition in such a case is the severance of a territory which has been one single whole into separate parts. Where the starting point is not unity of territory, i.e., where there was disunity before there was unity, partition—which is only a return to the original—may not give a mental shock. But, in India, the starting point is unity. Why destroy its unity now, simply because some Muslims are dissatisfied? Why tear it when the unit is one single whole from historical times?

Must there be Pakistan because there is communal antagonism between the Hindus and the Muslims? That the communal antagonism exists nobody can deny. The question, however, is whether the antagonism is such that there is no will to live together in one country and under one constitution? Surely that will to live together was not absent till 1937. During the formulation of the provisions of the Government of India Act, 1935, both Hindus and Musalmans accepted the view that they must live together under one constitution and in one country and participated in the discussions that preceded the passing of the Act. And what was the state of communal feeling in India between—say 1920 and 1935? As has been recorded in the preceding pages, the history of India from 1920 up to 1935 has been one long tale of communal conflict in which the loss of life and loss of property had reached a most shameful limit. Never was the communal situation so acute as it was between this period of fifteen years preceding the passing of the Government of India Act, 1935, and yet this long tale of antagonism did not prevent the Hindus and the Musalmans from agreeing to live in a single country and under a single constitution. Why make so much of communal antagonism now?

Must there be Pakistan because the Muslims have lost faith in the Congress majority? As reasons for the loss of faith Muslims cite some instances of tyranny and oppression practised by the Hindus and connived at by the Congress ministries during the two years and three months the Congress was in office. Unfortunately, Mr Jinnah did not persist in his demand for a Royal Commission to inquire into these grievances. If he had done it, we could have known what truth there was in these complaints. A perusal of these instances, as given in the reports[55] of the Muslim League Committees, leaves upon the reader the impression that although there may be some truth in the allegations there is a great deal which is pure exaggeration. The Congress ministries concerned have issued statements repudiating the charges. It may be that the Congress during the two years and three months that it was

[55]On this point, see Report of the Inquiry Committee appointed by the All India Muslim League to inquire into Muslim grievances in Congress provinces, popularly known as Pirpur Report. Also, Report of the Bihar Provincial Muslim League to inquire into some grievances of Muslims in Bihar, and the Press Note issued by the Information Officer, Government of Bihar, replying to some of the allegations contained in these reports, published in *Amrita Bazar Patrika*, 13 March 1939.

in office did not show statesmanship, did not inspire confidence in the minorities, nay, tried to suppress them. But can it be a reason for partitioning India? Is it not possible to hope that the voters who supported the Congress last time will grow wiser and not support the Congress? Or, may it not be that if the Congress returns to office, it will profit by the mistakes it has made, revise its mischievous policy, and thereby allay the fear created by its past conduct?

Must there be Pakistan because the Musalmans are a nation? It is a pity that Mr Jinnah should have become a votary and champion of Muslim nationalism at a time when the whole world is decrying against the evils of nationalism and is seeking refuge in some kind of international organization. Mr Jinnah is so obsessed with his new-found faith in Muslim nationalism that he is not prepared to see that there is a distinction between a society, parts of which are disintegrated, and a society, parts of which have become only loose, which no sane man can ignore. When a society is disintegrating—and the two-nation theory is a positive disintegration of society and country—it is evidence of the fact that there do not exist what Carlyle calls 'organic filaments'—i.e., the vital forces which work to bind together the parts that are cut asunder. In such cases, disintegration can only be regretted. It cannot be prevented. Where, however, such organic filaments do exist, it is a crime to overlook them and deliberately force the disintegration of society and country as the Muslims seem to be doing. If the Musalmans want to be a different nation, it is not because they have been, but because they want to be. There is much in the Musalmans which, if they wish, can roll them into a nation. But isn't there enough that is common to both Hindus and Musalmans, which if developed, is capable of moulding them into one people? Nobody can deny that there are many modes, manners, rites and customs which are common to both. Nobody can deny that there are rites, customs and usages based on religion which do divide Hindus and Musalmans. The question is, which of these should be emphasized. If the emphasis is laid on things that are common, there need be no two nations in India. If the emphasis is laid on points of difference, it will no doubt give rise to two nations. The view that seems to guide Mr Jinnah is that Indians are only a people, and that they can never be a nation. This follows the line of British writers who make it a point of speaking of Indians as the people of India, and avoid speaking of the Indian nation. Granted Indians are not a nation, that they are only a people. What of that? History records that before the rise of nations as great corporate personalities, there were only peoples. There is nothing to be ashamed [of] if Indians are no more than a people. Nor is there any cause for despair that the people of India—if they wish—will not become one nation. For, as Disraeli said, a nation is a work of art and a work of time. If the Hindus and Musalmans agree to emphasize the things that bind them and forget those that separate them, there is no reason why in course of time they should not grow into a nation. It may be that their nationalism may not be quite so integrated as that of the French or the Germans. But, they can easily produce a common state of mind on common questions, which is the sum total which the spirit of nationalism helps to produce and for which it is so much prized. Is it right for the Muslim League to emphasize only differences, and ignore altogether the forces that bind? Let it not be forgotten that if two nations come into being it will not be because it is predestined. It will be the result of deliberate design.

Must there be Pakistan because otherwise Swaraj will be a Hindu Raj? The Musalmans are so easily carried away by this cry that it is necessary to expose the fallacies underlying it.

In the first place, is the Muslim objection to Hindu Raj a conscientious objection, or is it a political objection? If it is a conscientious objection, all one can say is that it is a very strange sort of conscience. There are really millions of Musalmans in India who are living under unbridled and uncontrolled Hindu Raj of Hindu Princes and no objection to it has been raised by the Muslims or the Muslim League. The Muslims had once a conscientious objection to the British Raj. Today, not only have they no objection to it, but they are the greatest supporters of it. That there should be no objection to British Raj or to undiluted Hindu Raj of a Hindu Prince, but that there should be objection to Swaraj for British India on the ground that it is Hindu Raj, as though it was not subjected to checks and balances, is an attitude whose logic it is difficult to follow.

The political objections to Hindu Raj rest on various grounds. The first ground is that Hindu society is not a democratic society. True, it is not. It may not be right to ask whether the Muslims have taken any part in the various movements for reforming Hindu society, as distinguished from proselytizing. But, it is right to ask if the Musalmans are the only sufferers from the evils that admittedly result from the undemocratic character of Hindu society. Are not the millions of Shudras and non-Brahmins, or millions of the Untouchables, suffering the worst consequences of the undemocratic character of Hindu society? Who benefits from education, from public service and from political reforms, except the Hindu governing class—composed of the higher castes of the Hindus—which form[s] not even 10 per cent, of the total Hindu population? Has not the governing class of the Hindus, which controls Hindu politics, shown more regard for safeguarding the rights and interests of the Musalmans than they have for safeguarding the rights and interests of the Shudras and the Untouchables? Is not Mr Gandhi, who is determined to oppose any political concession to the Untouchables, ready to sign a blank cheque in favour of the Muslims? Indeed, the Hindu governing class seems to be far more ready to share power with the Muslims than it is to share power with the Shudras and the Untouchables. Surely, the Muslims have the least ground to complain of the undemocratic character of Hindu society.

Another ground on which the Muslim objection to Hindu Raj rests is that the Hindus are a majority community and the Musalmans are a minority community. True. But, is India the only country where such a situation exists? Let us compare the conditions in India with the conditions in Canada, South Africa and Switzerland. First, take the distribution of population. In Canada,[56] out of a total population of 10,376,786, only 2,927,990 are French. In South Africa,[57] the Dutch number 1,120,770 and the English are only 783,071. In Switzerland,[58] out of the total population of 4,066,400, the Germans are 2,924,313, the French 831,097, and the Italians 242,034.

This shows that the smaller nationalities have no fear of being placed

---

[56]*Canada Year Book*, 1936.
[57]*South Africa Year Book*, 1941.
[58]*Statesman's Year Book*, 1941.

under the Raj of a major community. Such a notion seems to be quite foreign to them. Why is this so? Is it because there is no possibility of the major nationality establishing its supremacy in those centres of power and authority, namely the Legislature and in the Executive? Quite the contrary. Unfortunately, no figures are available to show the actual extent of representation which the different major and minor nationalities have in Switzerland, Canada and South Africa. That is because there is no communal reservation of seats such as is found in India. Each community is left to win in a general contest what number of seats it can. But, it is quite easy to work out the probable number of seats which each nationality can obtain on the basis of the ratio of its population to the total seats in the Legislature. Proceeding on this basis, what do we find? In Switzerland, the total representatives in the Lower House is 187. Out of them the, German population has a possibility of winning 138, French 42 and Italians only 7 seats. In South Africa, out of the total of 153, there is a possibility of the English gaining 62, and the Dutch 94 seats. In Canada, the total is 245—of these, the French[59] have only 65.

On this basis, it is quite clear that in all these countries there is a possibility of the major nationality establishing its supremacy over the minor nationalities. Indeed, one may go so far as to say that speaking de jure and as a mere matter of form, in Canada the French are living under the British Raj, the English in South Africa under the Dutch Raj, and the Italians and French in Switzerland under the German Raj. But what is the position de facto? Have Frenchmen in Canada raised a cry that they will not live under British Raj? Have Englishmen in South Africa raised a cry that they will not live under Dutch Raj? Have the French and Italians in Switzerland any objection to living under the German Raj? Why should then the Muslims raise this cry of Hindu Raj?

Is it proposed that the Hindu Raj should be the rule of a naked communal majority? Are not the Musalmans granted safeguards against the possible tyranny of the Hindu majority? Are not the safeguards given to the Musalmans of India wider and better than the safeguards

---

[59]That is, for the province of Quebec.

which have been given to the French in Canada, to the English in South Africa and to the French and the Italians in Switzerland? To take only one item from the list of safeguards, haven't the Musalmans got an enormous degree of weightage in representation in the Legislature? Is weightage known in Canada, South Africa or Switzerland? And, what is the effect of this weightage to Muslims? Is it not to reduce the Hindu majority in the Legislature? What is the degree of reduction? Confining ourselves to British India and taking account only of the representation granted to the territorial constituencies, Hindu and Muslim, in the Lower House in the Central Legislature under the Government of India Act, 1935, it is clear that out of a total of 187, the Hindus have 105 seats and the Muslims have 82 seats. Given these figures, one is forced to ask, where is [any cause for] the fear of the Hindu Raj?

If [the] Hindu Raj does become a fact, it will, no doubt, be the greatest calamity for this country. No matter what the Hindus say, Hinduism is a menace to liberty, equality and fraternity. On that account it is incompatible with democracy. Hindu Raj must be prevented at any cost. But, is Pakistan the true remedy against it?

What makes communal Raj possible is a marked disproportion in the relative strength of the various communities living in a country. As pointed out above, this disproportion is not more marked in India than it is in Canada, South Africa and Switzerland. Nonetheless there is no British Raj in Canada, no Dutch Raj in South Africa, and no German Raj in Switzerland. How have the French, the English and the Italians succeeded in preventing the Raj of the majority community being established in their country? Surely not by partition. What is their method? Their method is to put a ban on communal parties in politics. No community in Canada, South Africa or Switzerland ever thinks of starting a separate communal party. What is important to note is that it is the minority nations which have taken the lead in opposing the formation of a communal party. For, they know that if they form a communal political party the major community will also form a communal party and the majority community will thereby find it easy to establish its communal Raj. It is a vicious method of self-protection. It is because the minority nations are fully aware how they will be hoisted on their own petard that they have opposed the formation of communal political parties.

◆

Among the many problems to which the partition of India into Pakistan and Hindustan must give rise will be the following three problems:

(1) The problem of the allocation of the financial assets and liabilities of the present Government of India.
(2) The problem of the delimitation of the areas.
(3) The problem of the transfer of population from Pakistan to Hindustan and vice versa.

Of these problems, the first is consequential (contingent), in the sense that it would be worthwhile to consider it only when the partition of India has been agreed to by the parties concerned. The two other problems stand on a different footing. They are conditions precedent to Pakistan in the sense that there are many people who will not make up their mind on Pakistan unless they are satisfied that some reasonable and just solution of them is possible. I will, therefore, confine myself to the consideration only of the last two problems of Pakistan.

On the question of the boundaries of Pakistan, we have had so far no clear and authoritative statement from the Muslim League. In fact, it is one of the complaints made by the Hindus that while Mr Jinnah has been carrying on a whirlwind campaign in favour of Pakistan, which has resulted in fouling the political atmosphere in the country, Mr Jinnah has not thought fit to inform his critics of the details regarding the boundaries of his proposed Pakistan. Mr Jinnah's argument has all along been that any discussion regarding the boundaries of Pakistan is premature and that the boundaries of Pakistan will be a matter for discussion when the principle of Pakistan has been admitted. It may be a good rhetorical answer, but it certainly does not help those who wish to apply their mind without taking sides to offer whatever help they can to bring about a peaceful solution of this problem. Mr Jinnah seems to be under the impression that if a person is committed to the principle of Pakistan, he will be bound to accept Mr Jinnah's plan of Pakistan. There cannot be a greater mistake than this. A person may accept the principle of Pakistan, which only means the partition of India. But, it is difficult to understand how the acceptance of this principle can commit him to Mr Jinnah's plan of Pakistan. Indeed, if no plan of Pakistan is satisfactory to him, he will be quite free to oppose any form of Pakistan, although he may be in favour of the principle of Pakistan. The plan of Pakistan and the principle of Pakistan are, therefore, two quite distinct propositions. There is nothing wrong in this view. By way of illustration, it may be said that the principle of self-determination is like an explosive substance. One may agree in principle to its use when the necessity and urgency of the occasion is proved. But, no one can consent to the use of the dynamite without first knowing the area that is intended to be blown up. If the dynamite is going to blow up the whole structure or if it is not possible to localize its application to a particular part, he may well refuse to apply the dynamite and prefer to use some other means of solving the problem. Specifications of boundary lines seem, therefore, to be an essential preliminary for working out in concrete shape the principle of Pakistan. Equally essential it is for a bona fide protagonist of Pakistan not to hide from the public the necessary particulars of the scheme of Pakistan. Such contumacy and obstinacy as [that] shown by Mr Jinnah in refusing to declare the boundaries of his Pakistan is unforgivable in a statesman. Nevertheless, those who are interested in solving the question of Pakistan need not wait to resolve the problems of Pakistan until Mr Jinnah condescends to give full details. Only, one has to carry on the argument on the basis of certain assumptions. In this discussion, I will assume that what the Muslim League desires is that the boundaries of the Western Pakistan should be the present boundaries of the Provinces of the North-West Frontier, the Punjab, Sind and Baluchistan, and that the boundaries of Eastern Pakistan should be the boundaries of the present province of Bengal with a few districts of Assam thrown in.

The question for consideration, therefore, is: Is this a just claim? The claim is said to be founded on the principle of self-determination. To be able to assess the justice of this claim, it is necessary to have a clear understanding of the scope and limitations of the principle of self-determination. Unfortunately, there seems to be a complete lack of such an understanding. It is, therefore, necessary to begin with the question: What is the de facto and de jure connotation of this principle of self-determination? The term self-determination has become current since the last few years. But, it describes something which is much older. The idea underlying self-determination has developed along two different lines. During the nineteenth century, self-determination meant the right to establish a form of government in accordance with the wishes of the people. Secondly, self-determination has meant the right to obtain national independence from an alien race irrespective of the form of government. The agitation for Pakistan has reference to self-determination in its second aspect.

Confining the discussion to this aspect of Pakistan, it seems to me essential that the following points regarding the issue of self-determination should be borne in mind.

In the first place, self-determination must be by the people. This point is too simple even to need mention. But, it has become necessary to emphasize it. Both the Muslim League and the Hindu Mahasabha seem to be playing fast and loose with the idea of self-determination. An area is claimed by the Muslim League for inclusion in Pakistan because the people of the area are Muslims. An area is also claimed for being included in Pakistan because the ruler of the area is a Muslim, though the majority of the people of that area are non-Muslims. The Muslim League is claiming the benefit of self-determination in India. At the same time, the League is opposed to self-determination being applied to Palestine. The League claims Kashmir as a Muslim State because the majority of a people are Muslims, and also Hyderabad because the ruler is Muslim. In like manner, the Hindu Mahasabha claims an area to be included in Hindustan because the people of the area are non-Muslims. It also comes forward to claim an area to be a part of Hindustan because the ruler is a Hindu though the majority of the people are Muslims. Such strange and conflicting claims are entirely due to the fact that either the parties to Pakistan, namely, the Hindus and the Muslims, do not understand what self-determination means, or are busy in perverting the principle of self-determination to enable them to justify themselves in carrying out the organized territorial loot in which they now seem to be engaged. India will be thrown into a state of utter confusion whenever the question of reorganization of its territories comes up for consideration, if people have no exact notions as to what self-determination involves and have not the honesty to stand by the principle and take the consequences whatever they be. It is, therefore, well to emphasize what might be regarded as too simple to require mention, namely, that self-determination is a determination by the people and by nobody else.

The second point to note is the degree of imperative character with which the principle of self-determination can be said to be invested. As has been said by Mr O' Connor:[60]

'The doctrine of self-determination is not a universal principle at all. The most that can be said about it is that generally speaking, it is a sound working rule, founded upon justice, making for harmony and peace and for the development of people in their own fashion, which, again generally speaking, is the best fashion. But, it must yield to circumstances, of which size and geographical situation are some of the most important. Whether the rule should prevail against the circumstances or the circumstances against the rule can be determined only by the application of one's common sense or sense of justice, or, as a Benthamite would prefer to put it, by reference to the greatest good of the greatest number—all these three, if properly understood, are really different methods of expressing the same thing. In solving a particular case, very great difficulties may arise. There are facts one way and facts another way. Facts of one kind may make a special appeal to some minds, little or none to others. The problem may be of the kind that is called imponderable, that is to say, no definite conclusion that will be accepted by the generality of the mankind may be possible. There are cases in which it is no more possible to say that a nation is right in its claim to interfere with the self-determination of another nation than that it is to say that it is wrong. It is a matter of opinion, upon which honest and impartial minds may differ.'

There are two reasons why this must be so. Firstly, nationality is not such a sacrosanct and absolute principle as to give it the character of a

---

[60]O' Connor, *History of Ireland*, Vol. II.

categorical imperative, overriding every other consideration. Secondly, separation is not quite so essential for the maintenance and preservation of a distinct nationality.

There is a third point to be borne in mind in connection with the issue of self-determination. Self-determination for a nationality may take the form of cultural independence or may take the form of territorial independence. Which form it can take must depend upon the territorial layout of the population. If a nationality lives in easily severable and contiguous areas, other things being equal, a case can be made out for territorial independence. But, where owing to an inextricable intermingling the nationalities are so mixed up that the areas they occupy are not easily severable, then all that they can be entitled to is cultural independence. Territorial separation in a case like this is an impossibility. They are doomed to live together. The only other alternative they have is to migrate.

Having defined the scope and limitations of the idea of self-determination, we can now proceed to deal with the question of [the] boundaries of Pakistan. How does the claim of the Muslim League for the present boundary to remain the boundaries of Pakistan stand in the light of these considerations? The answer to this question seems to me quite clear. The geographical layout seems to decide the issue. No special pleading of any kind is required. In the case of the North-West Frontier Province, Baluchistan and Sind, the Hindus and the Muslims are intermixed. In these provinces, a case for territorial separation for the Hindus seems to be impossible. They must remain content with cultural independence and such political safeguards as may be devised for their safety. The case of the Punjab and Bengal stands on a different footing. A glance at the map shows that the layout of the population of the Hindus and the Muslims in these two provinces is totally different from what one finds in the other three provinces. The non-Muslims in the Punjab and Bengal are not found living in small islands in the midst of and surrounded by a vast Muslim population spread over the entire surface as is the case with the North-West Frontier Province, Baluchistan and Sind. In Bengal and the Punjab, the Hindus occupy two different areas contiguous and severable. In these circumstances, there is no reason for conceding what the Muslim

League seems to demand, namely, that the present boundaries of the Punjab and Bengal shall continue to be the boundaries of Western Pakistan and Eastern Pakistan.

Two conclusions necessarily follow from the foregoing discussion. One is that the non-Muslims of the Punjab and Bengal have a case for exclusion from Pakistan by territorial severance of the areas they occupy. The other is that the non-Muslims of North-West Frontier Province, Baluchistan and Sind have no case for exclusion and are only entitled to cultural independence and political safeguards. To put the same thing in a different way it may be said that the Muslim League claim for demanding that the boundaries of Sind, North-West Frontier and Baluchistan shall remain as they are cannot be opposed. But, that in the case of the Punjab and Bengal such a claim is untenable and that the non-Muslims of these provinces, if they desire, can claim that the territory they occupy should be excluded by a redrawing of the boundaries of these two provinces.

There are two sides to the question of Pakistan, the Hindu side and the Muslim side. This cannot be avoided. Unfortunately, however, the attitude of both is far from rational. Both are deeply embedded in sentiment. The layers of this sentiment are so thick that reason at present finds it extremely difficult to penetrate. Whether these opposing sentiments will wither away or they will thicken, time and circumstances alone can tell. How long Indians will have to wait for the melting of the snow no one can prophesy. But, one thing is certain, that until this snow melts, freedom will have to be put in cold storage. I am sure there must be many millions of thinking Indians who are dead opposed to this indefinite postponement of Indian freedom till an ideal and a permanent solution of Pakistan is found. I am one of them. I am one of those who hold that if Pakistan is a problem and not a pose, there is no escape and a solution must be found for it. I am one of those who believe that what is inevitable must be faced. There is no use burying one's head in the sand, and refusing to take notice of what is happening round about because the sound of it hurts one's sentiments. I am also one of those who believe that one must, if one can, be ready with a solution long before the hour of decision arrives. It is wise to build a bridge if one knows that one will be forced to cross the river.

The principal problem of Pakistan is: Who can decide whether there shall or shall not be Pakistan? I have thought over the subject for the last three years, and I have come to some conclusions as to the proper answer to this question. These conclusions I would like to share with others interested in the solution of the problem so that they may be further explored. To give clarity to my conclusions, I have thought that it would serve the purpose better if I were to put them in the form of an Act of Parliament. The following is the draft of the Act which embodies my conclusions.

Government of India (Preliminary Provisions) Act

Be it enacted by the King's most Excellent Majesty, by and with the advice and consent of the Lords Spiritual and Temporal, and Commons, in this present Parliament assembled, and by the authority of the same as follows:

I. (1) *If within six months from the date appointed in this behalf a majority of the Muslim members of the Legislatures of the Provinces of the North-West Frontier, the Punjab, Sind and Bengal pass a resolution that the predominantly Muslim areas be separated from British India, His Majesty shall cause a poll to be taken on that question of the Muslim and the non-Muslim electors of these Provinces and of Baluchistan in accordance with the provisions of this Act.*

(2) *The question shall be submitted to the electors in these Provinces in the following form:*
  (i) *Are you in favour of separation from British India?*
  (ii) *Are you against separation?*

(3) *Tire poll of Muslim and non-Muslim electors shall be taken separately.*

II. (1) *If on a result of the poll, a majority of Muslim electors are found to be in favour of separation and a majority of non-Muslim electors against separation, His Majesty shall by proclamation appoint a Boundary Commission for the purpose of preparing a list of such districts and areas in these Provinces in which a* majority of inhabitants are Muslims. Such districts and areas shall be called Scheduled Districts.

(2) The Scheduled Districts shall be collectively designated as Pakistan and the rest of British India as Hindustan. The Scheduled Districts lying in the North-west shall be called the State of Western Pakistan and those lying in the North-east shall be called Eastern Pakistan.

III. (1) After the findings of the Boundary Commission have become final either by agreement or the award of an Arbitrator, His Majesty shall cause another poll to be taken of the electors of the Scheduled Districts.

(2) The following shall be the form of the questions submitted to the electors:

(i) Are you in favour of separation forthwith?

(ii) Are you against separation forthwith?

IV. (1) If the majority is in favour of separation forthwith, it shall be lawful for His Majesty to make arrangements for the framing of two separate constitutions, one for Pakistan and the other for Hindustan.

(2) The New States of Pakistan and Hindustan shall commence to function as separate States on the day appointed by His Majesty by proclamation issued in that behalf.

(3) If the majority are against separation forthwith, it shall be lawful for His Majesty to make arrangements for the framing of a single constitution for British India as a whole.

V. No motion for the separation of Pakistan if the poll under the last preceding section has been against separation forthwith, and no motion for incorporation of Pakistan into Hindustan if the poll under the last preceding section has been in favour of separation forthwith, shall be entertained until ten years have elapsed from the date appointed by His Majesty for putting into effect the new constitution for British India or the two separate constitutions for Pakistan and Hindustan.

VI. (1) In the event of two separate constitutions coming into existence under Section Four, it shall be lawful for His Majesty to establish as soon as may be after the appointed day, a Council of India *with a view to the eventual establishment of a constitution for the whole of British India, and to bringing about harmonious action between the Legislatures and Governments of Pakistan and Hindustan, and to the promotion of mutual intercourse and uniformity in relation to matters affecting the whole of British India, and to providing for the administration of services which the two parliaments mutually agree should be administered uniformly throughout the whole of British India, or which by virtue of this Act are to be so administered.*

(2) *Subject as hereinafter provided, the Council of India shall consist of a President nominated in accordance with instructions from His Majesty and forty other persons, of whom twenty shall be members representing Pakistan and twenty shall be members representing Hindustan.*

(3) *The members of the Council of India shall be elected in each case by the members of the Lower Houses of the Parliament of Pakistan or Hindustan.*

(4) *The election of members of the Council of India shall be the first business of the Legislatures of Pakistan and Hindustan.*

(5) *A member of the Council shall, on ceasing to be a member of that House of the Legislature of Pakistan or Hindustan by which he was elected a member of the Council, cease to be a member of the Council: provided that, on the dissolution of the Legislature of Pakistan or Hindustan, the persons who are members of the Council shall continue to hold office as members of the Council until a new election has taken place and shall then retire unless re-elected.*

(6) *The President of the Council shall preside at each meeting of the Council at which he is present, and shall be entitled to vote in case of an equality of votes, but not otherwise.*

(7) *The first meeting of the Council shall be held at such time and place as may be appointed by the President.*

(8) *The Council may act notwithstanding a deficiency in their number, and the quorum of the Council shall be fifteen.*

(9) *Subject as aforesaid, the Council may regulate their own procedure, including the delegation of powers to committees.*

(10) The constitution of the Council of India may from *time to time be varied by identical Acts passed by the Legislature of Pakistan and the Legislature of Hindustan, and the Acts may provide for all or any of the members of the Council of India being elected by parliamentary electors, and determine the constituencies by which the several elective members are to be returned and the number of the members to be returned by the several constituencies and the method of election.*

VII. (1) *The Legislatures of Pakistan and Hindustan may, by identical Acts, delegate to the Council of India any of the powers of the Legislatures and Government of Pakistan and Hindustan, and such Acts may determine the manner in which the powers so delegated are to be exercisable by the Council.*

(2) *The powers of making laws with respect to railways and waterways shall, as from the day appointed for the operation of the new constitution, become the powers of the Council of India and not of Pakistan or Hindustan: provided that nothing in tins subsection shall prevent the Legislature of Pakistan or Hindustan making laws authorizing the construction, extension, or improvement of railways and waterways where the works to be constructed are situated wholly in Pakistan or Hindustan as the case may be.*

(3) *The Council may consider any questions which may appear in any way to bear on the welfare of both Pakistan and Hindustan, and may, by resolution, make suggestions in relation thereto as they may think proper, but suggestions so made shall have no legislative effect.*

(4) *It shall be lawful for the Council of India to make recommendations to the Legislatures of Pakistan and Hindustan as to the advisability of passing identical Acts delegating to the Council of India the administration of any All India subject, with a view to avoiding the necessity of administering them separately in Pakistan or Hindustan.*

(5) *It shall be lawful for either Legislature at any time by Act to deprive the delegation to the Council of India of any powers which are in pursuance of such identical Acts as aforesaid for*

the time being delegated to the Council and thereupon the powers in question shall cease to be exercisable by the Council of India and shall become exercisable in parts of British India within their respective jurisdictions by the Legislatures and Governments of Pakistan and Hindustan, and the Council shall take such steps as may be necessary to carry out the transfer, including adjustments of any funds in their hands or at their disposal.

VIII. (1) If at the end of ten years after [the] coming into operation of a constitution for British India as prescribed by Section IV-(3) a petition is presented to His Majesty by a majority of the Muslim members representing the Scheduled Districts in the Provincial and Central Legislatures, demanding a poll to be taken with regard to the separation of Pakistan from Hindustan, His Majesty shall cause a poll to be taken.

(2) The following shall be the form of the questions submitted to the electors:

(i) Are you in favour of [the] separation of Pakistan from Hindustan?

(i) Are you against the separation of Pakistan from Hindustan?

IX. If the result of the poll is in favour of separation, it shall he lawful for His Majesty to declare by an Order-in-Council that from a day appointed in that behalf, Pakistan shall cease to be a part of British India, and [to] dissolve the Council of India.

X. (1) Where two constitutions have come into existence under circumstances mentioned in Section IV, it shall be lawful for His Majesty to declare by an Order-in-Council that Pakistan shall cease to be a separate State and shall form part of Hindustan. Provided that no such order shall be made until ten years have elapsed from the commencement of the separate constitution for Pakistan. Provided also that no such declaration shall be made unless the Popular Legislatures of Pakistan and Hindustan have passed Constituent Acts as are provided for in Section X-(2).

(2) The popular Legislatures of Pakistan and Hindustan may, by identical Acts agreed to by an absolute majority of members at the third reading (hereinafter referred to as Constituent

Acts), establish, in lieu of the Council of India, a Legislature for United India, and may determine the number of members thereof, and the manner in which the members are to be appointed or elected, and the constituencies for which the several elective members are to be returned, and the number of members to be returned by the several constituencies, and the method of appointment or election, and the relations of the two Houses (if provided for) to one another.

XI. (1) On the date of the union of Pakistan and Hindustan, the Council of India shall cease to exist, and there shall be transferred to the Legislature and Government of India all powers then exercisable by the Council of India.

(2) There shall also be transferred to the Legislature and Government of British India all the powers and duties of the Legislatures and Government of Pakistan and Hindustan, including all powers as to taxation, and those Legislatures and Government shall cease to exist.

XII. (1) A poll under this Act shall be taken by ballot in the same manner so far as possible as a poll of electors for the election of a member to serve in a Legislature, and His Majesty may make rules adopting the election laws for the purpose of the taking of the poll.

(2) An elector shall not vote more than once at the poll, although registered in more than one place.

(3) Elector means every adult male and female residing in the provinces of North-West Frontier, the Punjab, Sind, and Bengal, and in Baluchistan.

XIII. This Act may be called the Indian Constitution (Preliminary Provisions) Act, 194 .

These are some of the possibilities I see. These possibilities should in my judgement be kept open for time and circumstances to have their effect. It seems to me to be wrong to say to the Musalmans, if you want to remain as part of India then you can never go out, or if you want to go then you can never come back. I have in my scheme kept the door open, and have provided for both the possibilities in the Act:

(1) for union after a separation of ten years, (2) for separation for ten years and union thereafter. I personally prefer the second alternative, although I have no strong views either way. It would be much better that the Musalmans should have the experience of Pakistan. A union after an experience of Pakistan is bound to be stable and lasting. In case Pakistan comes into existence forthwith, it seems to me necessary that the separation should not altogether be a severance, sharp and complete. It is necessary to maintain live contact between Pakistan and Hindustan, so as to prevent any estrangement growing up and preventing the chances of reunion. A Council of India is accordingly provided for in the Act. It cannot be mistaken for a federation. It is not even a confederation. Its purpose is to do nothing more than to serve as a coupling to link Pakistan to Hindustan until they are united under a single constitution.

Chapter 7

HISTORICITY OF THE SHUDRAS

EVERYBODY KNOWS THAT the Shudras formed the fourth 'varna' of the Indo–Aryan society. But very few have cared to inquire who were these Shudras and how they came to be the fourth varna. That such an enquiry is of first-rate importance is beyond question. For, it is worth knowing how the Shudras came to occupy the fourth place, whether it was the result of evolution or it was brought about by revolution.

Any attempt to discover who the Shudras were and how they came to be the fourth varna must begin with the origin of the Chaturvarnya in the Indo–Aryan society. A study of the Chaturvarnya must in its turn start with a study of the ninetieth Hymn of the Tenth Mandala of the Rig Veda—a Hymn, which is known by the famous name of Purusha Sukta.

What does the Hymn say? It says:[61]

'1. Purusha has a thousand heads, a thousand eyes, a thousand feet. On every side enveloping the earth he overpassed [it] by a space of ten fingers.

2. Purusha himself is this whole [universe], whatever has been and whatever shall be. He is the Lord of immortality, since [or when] by food he expands.

3. Such is his greatness, and Purusha is superior to this. All existences are a quarter to him; and three-fourths of him are that which is immortal in the sky.

4. With three-quarters, Purusha mounted upwards. A quarter of him was again produced here. He was then diffused everywhere over things which eat and things which do not eat.

5. From him was born Viraj, and from Viraj, Purusha. When born, he extended beyond the earth, both behind and before.

---

[61]Muir's Original Sanskrit Texts, Vol. I, p 9.

6. When the gods performed a sacrifice with Purusha as the oblation, the spring was its butter, the summer its fuel, and the autumn its (accompanying) offering.

7. This victim, Purusha, born in the beginning, they immolated on the sacrificial grass. With him the gods, the Sadhyas, and the rishis sacrificed.

8. From that universal sacrifice were provided curds and butter. It formed those aerial (creatures) and animals both wild and tame.

9. From that universal sacrifice sprang the rik and sarnan verses, the metres and the yajus.

10. From it sprang horses, and all animals with two rows of teeth; kine sprang from it; from it goats and sheep.

11. When (the gods) divided Purusha, into how many parts did they cut him up? What was his mouth? What arms (had he)? What (two objects) are said (to have been) his thighs and feet?

12. The Brahmin was his mouth, the Rajanya was made his arms; the being called the Vaishya, he was his thighs; the Shudra sprang from his feet.

13. The moon sprang from his soul (manas), the sun from the eye, Indra and Agni from his mouth and Vayu from his breath.

14. From his navel arose the air, from his head the sky, from his feet the earth, from his ear the (four) quarters; in this manner (the gods) formed the worlds.

15. When the gods, performing sacrifices, bound Purusha as a victim, there were seven sticks (stuck up) for it (around the fire), and thrice seven pieces of fuel were made.

16. With sacrifices the gods performed the sacrifice. These were the earliest rites. These great powers have sought the sky, where are the former Sadhyas, gods.'

The Purusha Sukta is a theory of the origin of the Universe. In other words, it is a cosmogony. No nation which has reached an advanced degree of thought has failed to develop some sort of cosmogony. The Egyptians had a cosmogony somewhat analogous with that set out in the Purusha Sukta. According to it,[62] it was god Khnumu,

---

[62]Encyclopaedia of religion and Ethics, Vol. IV, p 145.

the shaper, who shaped living things on the potter's wheel, 'created all that is, he formed all that exists, he is the father of fathers, the mother of mothers...he fashioned men, he made the gods, he was the father from the beginning...he is the creator of the heaven, the earth, the underworld, the water, the mountains...he formed a male and a female of all birds, fishes, wild beasts, cattle and of all worms.' A very similar cosmogony is found in Chapter I of the Genesis in the Old Testament.

Cosmogonies have never been more than matters of academic interest and have served no other purpose than to satisfy the curiosity of the student and to help to amuse children. This may be true of some parts of the Purusha Sukta. But it certainly cannot be true of the whole of it. That is because all verses of the Purusha Sukta are not of the same importance and do not have the same significance. Verses 11 and 12 fall in one category and the rest of the verses fall in another category. Verses other than 11 and 12 may be regarded as of academic interest. Nobody relies upon them. No Hindu even remembers them. But it is quite different with regard to verses 11 and 12. Prima facie these verses do no more than explain how the four classes, namely: (1) Brahmins or priests, (2) Kshatriyas or soldiers, (3) Vaishyas or traders, and (4) Shudras or menials, arose from the body of the Creator. But the fact is that these verses are not understood as being merely explanatory of a cosmic phenomenon. It would be a grave mistake to suppose that they were regarded by the Indo–Aryans as an innocent piece of a poet's idle imagination. They are treated as containing a mandatory injunction from the Creator to the effect that society must be constituted on the basis of four classes mentioned in the Sukta. Such a construction of the verses in question may not be warranted by their language. But there is no doubt that according to tradition this is how the verses are construed, and it would indeed be difficult to say that this traditional construction is not in consonance with the intention of the author of the Sukta. Verses 11 and 12 of the Purusha Sukta are, therefore, not a mere cosmogony. They contain a divine injunction prescribing a particular form of the constitution of society.

The constitution of society prescribed by the Purusha Sukta is known as Chaturvarnya. As a divine injunction, it naturally became the ideal of the Indo–Aryan society. This ideal of Chaturvarnya was the mould in which the life of the Indo–Aryan community in its early or liquid state was cast. It is this mould which gave the Indo–Aryan community its peculiar shape and structure.

This reverence, which the Indo–Aryan society had for this ideal mould of Chaturvarnya, is not only beyond question, but it is also beyond description. Its influence on the Indo–Aryan society has been profound and indelible. The social order prescribed by the Purusha Sukta has never been questioned by anyone except Buddha. Even Buddha was not able to shake it, for the simple reason that both after the fall of Buddhism and even during the period of Buddhism, there were enough law-givers, who made it their business not only to defend the ideal of the Purusha Sukta but to propagate it and to elaborate it.

To take a few illustrations of this propaganda in support of the Purusha Sukta, reference may be made to the Apastamba Dharma Sutra and the Vasishtha Dharma Sutra. The Apastamba Dharma Sutra states:

'There are four castes—Brahmins, Kshatriyas, Vaishyas and Shudras.

Among these, each preceding (caste) is superior by birth to the one following.[63]

For all these excepting Shudras and those who have committed bad actions are ordained (1) the initiation (Upanayana or the wearing of the sacred thread), (2) the study of the Veda and (3) the kindling of the sacred fire (i.e., the right to perform sacrifice).'[64]

This is repeated by Vasishtha Dharma Sutra which says:

'There are four castes (varnas), Brahmins, Kshatriyas, Vaishyas and Shudras. Three castes, Brahmins, Kshatriyas and Vaishyas (are called) twice-born. Their first birth is from their mother; the second from the investiture with the sacred girdle. In that (second birth) the Savitri is the mother, but the teacher is said to be the father.'

They call the teacher father, because he gives instruction in the

---

[63]Prasna I, Patala I, Khanda I, Sutras 4–5.
[64]Prasna I, Patala I, Khanda I, Sutra 6.

Vedas.[65] The four castes are distinguished by their origin and by particular sacraments.

There is also the following passage of the Veda: 'The Brahmin was his mouth, the Kshatriya formed his arms, the Vaishya his thighs; the Shudra was born from his feet.'

It has been declared in the following passage that a Shudra shall not receive the sacraments.

Many other law-givers have in a parrot-like manner repeated the theme of the Purusha Sukta and have reiterated its sanctity. It is unnecessary to repeat their version of it. All those, who had raised any opposition to the sanctity of the ideal set out in the Purusha Sukta, were finally laid low by Manu, the architect of the Hindu society. For Manu did two things. In the first place, he enunciated afresh the ideal of the Purusha Sukta as a part of divine injunction. He said:

'For the prosperity of the worlds, he (the creator) from his mouth, arms, thighs and feet created the Brahmin, Kshatriya and Vaishya and the Shudra.[66]

The Brahmin, Kshatriya (and) Vaishya (constitute) the three twice-born castes; but the fourth, the shudra, has only one birth.'[67]

In this he was no doubt merely following his predecessors. But he went a step further and enunciated another proposition in which he said:

'Veda is the only and ultimate sanction for Dharma.'[68]

Bearing in mind that the Purusha Sukta is a part of the Veda, it cannot be difficult to realize that Manu invested the social ideal of Chaturvarnya contained in the Purusha Sukta with a degree of divinity and infallibility which it did not have before.

A critical examination of the Purusha Sukta, therefore, becomes very essential.

It is claimed by the Hindus that the Purusha Sukta is unique.

---

[65]Chapter 11, Verses 1–4.
[66]Manu, Chapter I, Verse 31.
[67]Ibid, Chapter X, Verse 4.
[68]Manu, Chapter 11, Verse 6.

This is no doubt a tall claim for an idea which came to birth when the mind of man was primitive and was without the rich endowment of varied thought available in modern times. But there need not be much difficulty in admitting this claim provided it is understood in what respect the Purusha Sukta is unique.

The principal ground for regarding the Purusha Sukta as unique is that the ideal of social organization, namely, the ideal of Chaturvarnya which it upholds, is unique. Is this a sufficient ground for holding the Purusha Sukta as unique? The Purusha Sukta would really have been unique if it had preached a classless society as an ideal form of society. But what does the Purusha Sukta do? It preaches a class-composed society as its ideal. Can this be regarded as unique? Only a nationalist and a patriot can give an affirmative answer to this question. The existence of classes has been the de facto condition of every society, which is not altogether primitive. It is a normal state of society all over the world where society is in a comparatively advanced state. Looking at it from this point of view, what uniqueness can there be in the Purusha Sukta, when it does no more than recognize the sort of class composition that existed in the Indo–Aryan society?

Notwithstanding this, the Purusha Sukta must be admitted to be unique, though for quite different reasons. The unfortunate part of the matter is that many people do not know the true reasons why the Purusha Sukta should be regarded as unique. But, once the true reasons are known, people will not only have no hesitation in accepting that the Purusha Sukta is a unique production of the human intellect but will perhaps be shocked to know what an extraordinary production of human ingenuity it is.

What are the features of the social ideal of the Purusha Sukta, which give it the hall mark of being unique? Though the existence of classes is the de facto condition of every society, nevertheless no society has converted this de facto state of affairs into a de jure connotation of an ideal society. The scheme of the Purusha Sukta is the only instance in which the real is elevated to the dignity of an ideal. This is the first unique feature of the scheme set forth in the Purusha Sukta. Secondly, no community has given the de facto state of class composition a legal effect by accepting it as a dejure connotation of an ideal society. The case of the Greeks is a case in point. Class composition was put forth as an ideal social structure by no less an advocate than Plato. But the Greeks never thought of making it real by giving it the sanction of law. The Purusha Sukta is the only instance in which an attempt was made to give reality to the ideal by invoking the sanction of law. Thirdly, no society has accepted that the class composition is an ideal. At the most, they have accepted it as being natural. The Purusha Sukta goes further. It not only regards class composition as natural and ideal, but also regards it as sacred and divine. Fourthly, the number of the classes has never been a matter of dogma in any society known to history. The Romans had two classes. The Egyptians thought three were enough. The Indo–Iranians also had no more than three classes: (1) The Athravans (priests) (2) Rathaeshtar (warriors) and (3) the Vastrya-fshuyat (peasantry). The scheme of the Purusha Sukta makes the division of society into four classes a matter of dogma.

According to it, there can be neither more nor less. Fifthly, every society leaves a class to find its place vis-a-vis other classes according to its importance in society as may be determined by the forces operating from time to time. No society has an official gradation laid down, fixed and permanent, with an ascending scale of reverence and a descending scale of contempt. The scheme of the Purusha Sukta is unique, inasmuch as it fixes a permanent warrant of precedence among the different classes, which neither time nor circumstances can alter. The warrant of precedence is based on the principle of graded inequality among the four classes, whereby it recognizes the Brahmin to be above all, the Kshatriya below the Brahmin but above the Vaishya and the Shudra, the Vaishya below the Kshatriya but above the Shudra and the Shudra below all.

These are the real reasons why the Purusha Sukta is unique. But the Purusha Sukta is not merely unique, it is also extraordinary. It is extraordinary because it is so full of riddles. Few seem to be aware of these riddles. But anyone who cares to inquire will learn how real in their nature and how strange in their complexion these riddles are. The cosmogony set out in the Purusha Sukta is not the only cosmogony one comes across in the Rig Veda. There is another cosmogony which is expounded in the 72nd Hymn of the Tenth Mandala of the Rig

Veda. It reads as follows:[69]

1. Let us proclaim with a clear voice of the generation of the gods (the divine company), who, when their praises are recited, look (favourably on the worshipper) in this latter age.

2. Brahmanaspati filled these (generations of the gods) with breath as a blacksmith (his bellows); in the first age of the gods the existent was born of the non-existent.

3. In the first age of the gods the existent was born of the non-existent; after that the quarters (of the horizon) were born, and after them the upward-growing (trees).

4. The earth was born from the upward growing (tree), the quarters were born from the earth; Daksha was born from Aditi and afterwards Aditi from Daksha.

5. Aditi, who was thy daughter, Daksha, was born; after her, the gods were born, adorable, freed from the bonds of death.

6. When, gods, you abode in this pool well-arranged, then a pungent dust went forth from you as if you were dancing.

7. When, gods, you filled the worlds (with your radiance) as clouds (fill the earth with rain) then you brought forth the sun hidden in the ocean.

8. Eight sons (there were) of Aditi who were born from her body; she approached the gods with seven, she sent forth Martanda on high.

9. With seven sons Aditi went to a former generation, but she bore Martanda for the birth and death (of human beings).

The two cosmologies are fundamentally different in principle as well as in detail. The former explains creation ex nihilo 'being was born of non-being'. The latter ascribes creation to a being which it calls Purusha. Why in one and the same book two such opposite cosmologies should have come to be propounded? Why did the author of the Purusha Sukta think it necessary to posit a Purusha and make all creation emanate from him?

Anyone who reads the Purusha Sukta will find that it starts with

---

[69]Wilson's, Rig Veda, Vol. VI, p 129.

the creation of donkeyes, horses, goats, etc., but does not say anything about the creation of man. At a point when it would have been natural to speak of the creation of man, it breaks off the chain and proceeds to explain the origin of the classes in the Aryan society. Indeed, the Purusha Sukta appears to make the explaining of the four classes of the Aryan society to be its primary concern. In doing this, the Purusha Sukta stands in complete contrast not only with other theologies but with the other parts of the Rig Veda also.

No theology has made it its purpose to explain the origin of classes in society. Chapter I of the Genesis in the Old Testament, which can be said to be analogous in intention and purpose to the Purusha Sukta, does nothing more than explain how man was created. It is not that social classes did not exist in the old Jewish society. Social classes existed in all societies. The Indo–Aryans were no exception. Nevertheless, no theology has ever thought it necessary to explain how classses arise. Why then did the Purusha Sukta make the explanation of the origin of the social classes its primary concern?

The Purusha Sukta is not the only place in the Rig Veda where a discussion of the origin of creation occurs. There are other places in the Rig Veda where the same subject is referred to. In this connection, one may refer to the following passage in the Rig Veda which reads as follows:

Rig Veda, i.96.2: 'By the first nivid, by the wisdom of Ayu, he (Agni) created these children of men; by his gleaming light the earth and the waters, the gods sustained Agni the giver of the riches.'

In this, there is no reference at all to the separate creation of classes, though there is no doubt that even at the time of the Rig Veda, the Indo–Aryan society had become differentiated into classes; yet the above passage in the Rig Veda ignores the classes and refers to the creation of men only. Why did the Purusha Sukta think it necessary to go further and speak of the origin of the classes?

The Purusha Sukta contradicts the Rig Veda in another respect. The Rig Veda propounds a secular theory regarding the origin of the

Indo–Aryans as will be seen from the following texts:[70]

(1) Rig Veda, i.80:16: 'Prayers and hymns were formerly congregated in that Indra, in the ceremony which Atharvan, father Manu, and Dadhyanch celebrated.'

(2) Rig Veda, i.114.2: 'Whatever prosperity or succour father Manu obtained by sacrifice, may we gain all that under thy guidance, Rudra.'

(3) Rig Veda, ii.33.13: 'Those pure remedies of yours, O Maruts, those which are most auspicious, ye vigorous gods, those which are beneficent, those which our father Manu chose, those and the blessing and succour of Rudra, I desire.'

(4) Rig Veda, viii.52.1: 'The ancient friend hath been equipped with the powers of the mighty (gods). Father Manu has prepared hymns to him, as portals of access to the gods.'

(5) Rig Veda, iii.3.6: 'Agni, together with the gods, and the children (jantubhih) of Manush, celebrating a multiform sacrifice with hymns.'

(6) Rig Veda, iv. 37.1: 'Ye gods, Vajas, and Ribhukshana, come to our sacrifice by the path travelled by the gods, that ye, pleasing deities, may institute a sacrifice among these people of Manush (Manusho vikshu) on auspicious days.'

(7) Rig Veda, vi.14.2 : 'The people of Manush praise in the sacrifice Agni the invoker.'

From these texts it is beyond question that the rishis who were the authors of the hymns of the Rig Veda regarded Manu as the progenitor of the Indo–Aryans. This theory about Manu being the progenitor of the Indo–Aryans had such deep foundation that it was carried forward by the Brahmanas as well as the Puranas. It is propounded in the Aitareya Brahmana[71] in the Vishnu Purana[72] and the Matsya Purana.[73] It is true that they have made Brahma the progenitor of

---

[70]Muir, Vol. I.

[71]Quoted by Muir, Vol. I, p 108.

[72]Quoted by Muir, Vol. I, pp 105–107.

[73]Quoted by Muir, Vol. I, pp 110–112.

Manu; but the Rig Veda theory of Manu being the progenitor has been accepted and maintained by them.[74] Why does the Purusha Sukta make no mention of Manu?

This is strange because the author of the Purush Sukta seems to be aware of the fact that Manu Svayambhuva is called Viraj and Viraj is called Adi Purusha, since he too speaks of Virajo adhi Purushah in verse five of the Sukta.

There is a third point in which the Purush Sukta has gone beyond the Rig Veda. The Vedic Aryans were sufficiently advanced in their civilization to give rise to division of labour. Different persons among the Vedic Aryans followed different occupations. That they were conscious of it is evidenced by the following verse:

> Rig Veda, i.113.6: 'That some may go in pursuit of power, some in pursuit of fame, some in pursuit of wealth, some in pursuit of work, Ushas has awakened people so that each may go in pursuit of his special and different way of earning his livelihood.'

This is as far as the Rig Veda had gone. The Purusha Sukta goes beyond. It follows up the notion of division of labour and converts the scheme of division of work into a scheme of division of workers into fixed and permanent occupational categories. Why does the Purush Sukta commit itself to such a perversity?

There is another point in which the Purusha Sukta departs from the Rig Veda. It is not that the Rig Veda speaks only of man. It speaks also of the Indo–Aryan nation. This nation was made up of the five

---

[74]There is, however, a great deal of confusion when one comes to details. The Vishnu Purana says that Brahma divided his person into hoo parts: with the one half he became a male, with the other half a female. The female was called Satarupa who by incessantly practising austere fervour of a highly arduous description acquired for herself as a husband a male called Manu Svayambhuva. There is no suggestion in the Vishnu Purana of incest by Brahma with his daughter. The Aitareya Brahmana and the Matsya Purana on the other hand speak of Brahma having begotten Manu by committing incest with his daughter Satarupa; the Matsya Purana adds that Manu by his austerity obtained a beautiful wife named Ananta. According to the Ramayana (see Muir, I, p 117) Manu was not a male but a female and was a daughter of Daksha Prajapali and the wife of Kasyapa.

tribes, which had become assimilated into one common Indo–Aryan people. The following hymns refer to these five tribes as moulded into a nation:[75]

(1) Rig Veda, vi.11.4: 'Agni, whom, abounding in oblations, the five tribes, bringing offerings, honour with prostrations, as if he were a man.'

(2) Rig Veda, vii.15.2: 'The wise and youthful master of the house (Agni) who has taken up his abode among the five tribes in every house.'

There is some difference of opinion as to who these five tribes are. Yaska in his Nirukta says that it denotes Gandharvas, Pitris, Devas, Asuras and Rakshasas. Aupamanyava says that it denotes the four varnas and the Nishadas. Both these explanations seem to be absurd. Firstly, because the five tribes are praised collectively as in the following hymns:[76]

(1) Rig Veda, ii.2.10: 'May our glory shine aloft among the five tribes, like the heaven unsurpassable.'

(2) Rig Veda, vi.46.7: 'Indra, whatever force or vigour exists in the tribe of Nashusa or whatever glory belongs to the five races bring (for us).'

Such laudatory statements could not have been made if the five tribes included the Shudras. Besides, the word used is not varnas. The word used is Janah. That it refer to the five tribes and not to the four varnas and Nishadas is quite clear from the following verse of the Rig Veda:[77]

Rig Veda, i. 108.8: 'If, Indra and Agni, ye are abiding among the Yadus, Turvasas, Druhyus, Anus, Purus, come hither, vigorous heroes from all quarters, and drink the Soma which has been poured out.'

That these five tribes had been moulded into one Aryan people is clear from the Atharva Veda (iii.24.2) which says:

'These five regions, the five tribes springings from Manu.'

---

[75]Muir, Vol. I.
[76]Ibid.
[77]Ibid.

A sense of unity and a consciousness of kind can alone explain why the Rishis of the Rig Vedic hymns came to refer to the five tribes in such a manner. The questions are: why did the Purusha Sukta not recognize this unity of the five tribes and give a mythic explanation of their origin? Why instead did it recognize the communal divisions within the tribes? Why did the Purusha Sukta regard communalism more important than nationalism?

These are some of the riddles of the Purusha Sukta, which come to light when one compares it with the Rig Veda. There are others, which emerge when one proceeds to examine the Purusha Sukta from a sociological point of view.

Ideals as norms are good and are necessary. Neither a society nor an individual can do without a norm. But a norm must change with changes in time and circumstances. No norm can be permanently fixed. There must always be room for revaluation of the values of our norm. The possibility of revaluing values remains open only when the institution is not invested with sacredness. Sacredness prevents revaluation of its values. Once sacred, always sacred. The Purusha Sukta makes the Chaturvarnya a sacred institution, a divine ordination. Why did the Purusha Sukta make a particular form of social order so sacred as to be beyond criticism and beyond change? Why did it want to make it a permanent ideal beyond change and even beyond criticism? This is the first riddle of the Purusha Sukta which strikes a student of sociology.

In propounding the doctrine of Chaturvarnya, the Purush Sukta plays a double game. It proceeds first to raise the real, namely, the existence of the four classes in the Indo–Aryan society, to the status of an ideal. This is a deception because the ideal is in no way different from facts as they exist. After raising the real to the status of the ideal, it proceeds to make a show of giving effect to what it regards as an ideal. This again is a deception because the ideal already exists in fact.

This attempt of the Purusha Sukta to idealize the real and to realize the ideal, is a kind of political jugglery, the like of which, I am sure, is not to be found in any other book of religion. What else is it if not a fraud and a deception? To idealize the real, which more often than not is full of inequities, is a very selfish thing to do. Only when a person finds a personal advantage in things as they are that he tries to idealize the real. To proceed to make such an ideal real is nothing short of criminal. It means perpetuating inequity on the ground that whatever is once settled is settled for all times. Such a view is opposed to all morality. No society with a social conscience has ever accepted it. On the contrary, whatever progress in improving the terms of associated life between individuals and classes has been made in the course of history is due entirely to the recognition of the ethical doctrine that what is wrongly settled is never settled and must be resettled. The principle underlying the Purush Sukta is, therefore, criminal in intent and anti-social in its results. For, it aims to perpetuate an illegal gain obtained by one class and an unjust wrong inflicted upon another. What can be the motive behind this jugglery of the Purusha Sukta? This is the second riddle.

The last and the greatest of all these riddles, which emerge out of a sociological scrutiny of the Purusha Sukta, is the one relating to the position of the Shudra. The Purusha Sukta concerns itself with the origin of the classes, and says they were created by God—a doctrine which no theology has thought it wise to propound. This in itself is a strange thing. But what is astonishing is the plan of equating different classes to different parts of the body of the Creator. The equation of the different classes to different parts of the body is not a matter of accident. It is deliberate. The idea behind this plan seems to be to discover a formula which will solve two problems, one of fixing the functions of the four classes and the other of fixing the gradation of the four classes after a preconceived plan. The formula of equating different classes to the different parts of the body of the Creator has this advantage. The part fixes the gradation of the class and the gradation in its turn fixes the function of the class. The Brahmin is equated to the mouth of the Creator. Mouth being the noblest part of the anatomy, the Brahmin becomes the noblest of the four classes. As he is the noblest in the scale, he is given the noblest function, that of custodian of knowledge and learning. The Kshatriya is equated to the arms of the Creator. Among the limbs of a person, arms are next below the mouth. Consequently, the Kshatriya is given an order of precedence next below the Brahmin and is given a function which is second only to knowledge, namely, fighting. The Vaishya is equated to the thighs of the Creator. In the gradation of limbs the thighs are next below the arms. Consequently, the Vaishya is given an order of precedence next below the Kshatriya and is assigned a function of industry and trade which in name and fame ranks, or rather did rank in ancient times, below that of a warrior. The Shudra is equated to the feet of the Creator. The feet form the lowest and the most ignoble part of the human frame. Accordingly, the Shudra is placed last in the social order and is given the filthiest function, namely, to serve as a menial.

Why did the Purusha Sukta choose such a method of illustrating the creation of the four classes? Why did it equate the Shudras to the feet? Why did it not take some other illustration to show how the four classes were created. It is not that Purusha is the only stock simile used to explain creation. Compare the explanation of the origin of the Vedas contained in the Chandogya Upanishad. It says:[78]

'Prajapati infused warmth into the worlds, and from them so heated he drew forth their essences, viz., Agni (fire) from the earth, Vayu (wind) from the air, and Surya (the sun) from the sky. He infused warmth into these three deities, and from them so heated he drew forth their essences,—from Agni the rich verses, from Vayu the yajush verses and from Surya the saman verses. He then infused heat into this triple science, and from it so heated he drew forth its essences—from rich verses the syllable bhuh, from yajus verses bhuvah, and from Saman verses svar.'

Here is an explanation of the origin of the Vedas from different deities. So far as the Indo–Aryans are concerned, there was no dearth of them. There were thirty crores of them. An explanation of the origin of the four varnas from four gods would have maintained equality of dignity by birth of all the four classes. Why did the Purusha Sukta not adopt this line of explanation?

◆

---

[78]Muir, Vol. III. p 5.

Has the Brahminic literature any explanation to offer which can account for the origin of the Shudras? There is no doubt that the Brahminic literature is full of legends regarding creation which touch upon the creation of the universe, of man and of the different varnas. Whether or not they furnish any clue to discover the origin of the Shudras, there can be no doubt that all such theories should find a place in a book which is concerned with the problem of the Shudras if for no other reason than that of assembling all material relating to the Shudras in one place and making their story complete. It would be better to take each piece of the Brahminic literature separately, and note what contribution it has to make to the subject.

To begin with the Vedas. As to the Rig Veda, the legend about creation to be found in its Sukta known as the Purusha Sukta has already been set out in the previous chapter. It now remains to take note of the legends contained in the other Vedas.

There are two recensions of the Yajur Veda: (1) the White Yajur Veda and (2) the Black Yajur Veda. To take the White Yajur Veda first. The Vajasaneyi Samhita of the White Yajur Veda sponsors two theories. One is a mere reproduction of the Purusha Sukta of the Rig Veda with this difference that it has twenty-two verses, while the original as it occurs in the Rig Veda has only sixteen verses. The six additional verses in the White Yajur Veda read as follows:

17. Brought forth from the waters and from the essence of the earth, he was produced by Vishvakarman in the beginning. Tvashta gives him form; that is the Universe of Purusha on all sides in the beginning.

18. I know this great Purusha, of the colour of the sun, beyond darkness. Only by knowing him does one go beyond death; there is no other path for going.

19. Prajapati moves in the interior of the womb; though unborn, he is born in many forms. Wise men see his source; wise men desire the place of the Marichis.

20. He who shines for the gods, he who is the priest of the gods, he who was born before the gods—salutation to that shining offspring of Brahma.

21. The gods, generating the shining offspring of Brahma, said in the beginning: 'That Brahmin who knows thus—the gods will be under his control.'

22. Sri and Laxmi are his wives; the day and night his sides; the Stars his ornament; the Ashwins his bright face. Grant me my desires; grant me that; grant me everything.

The second explanation contained in the Vajasaneyi Samhita is quite different from the Purusha Sukta. It reads as follows:[79]

V.S., xiv: 'He lauded with one. Living beings were formed. He lauded with three: the brahman was created; Brahmanaspati was the ruler. He lauded with five: existing things were created; bhutanampati was the ruler. He lauded with seven: the seven rishis were created: Dhatri was the ruler. He lauded with nine: the Fathers were created: Aditi was the ruler. He lauded with eleven: the seasons were created: the Artavas were the rulers. He lauded with thirteen: the months were created: the year was the ruler. He lauded with fifteen: the Kshatra (the Kshatriya) was created: Indra was the ruler. He lauded with seventeen: animals were created: Brihaspati was the ruler. He lauded with nineteen: the Shudra and the Arya (Vaishya) were created: day and night were the rulers. He lauded with twenty-one: animals with undivided hoofs were created: Varuna was the ruler. He lauded with twenty-three: small animals were created: Pushan was the ruler. He lauded with twenty-five: wild animals were created: Vayu was the ruler (compare R.V., x.90.8). He lauded with twenty-seven: heaven and earth separated: Vasus, Rudras and Adityas separated after them: they were the rulers. He lauded with thirty-one: living beings were created: the first and second halves of the month were the rulers. He lauded with thirty one: existing things were tranquillized: Prajapati Parameshthin was the ruler.'

Now to turn to the Black Yajur Veda. The Taittriya Samhita of the Black Yajur Veda gives altogether five explanations. The one at iv. 3,10 is the same as has been put forth by the Vajasaneyi Samhita of the White Yajur Veda at (xiv.28) and which has been reproduced earlier. Of the

---

[79]Muir, Vol. I.

rest those which narrate the origin of the Shudra are set out below:[80]

T.S., ii.4.13.1: 'The gods were afraid of the Rajanya when he was in the womb. They bound him with bonds when he was in the womb. Consequently, this Rajanya is born bound. If he were born unbound he would go on slaying his enemies. In regard to whatever Rajanya, if one desires that he should be born unbound, and should go on slaying his enemies, let him offer for him this Aindra-Barhaspatya oblation. A Rajanya has the character of Indra, and a Brahmin is Brihaspati. It is through the Brahmin that anyone releases the Rajanya from his bond. The golden bond, a gift, manifestly releases from the bond that fetters him.'

T.S., vii. 1.1.4: 'Prajapati desired, "may I propagate". He formed the Trivrit (stoma) from his mouth. After it were produced the deity Agni, the metre Gayatri, the Saman (called) Rathantara, of men the Brahmin, of beasts the goats. Hence they are the chief (mukhyah) because they were created from the mouth (mukliatah). From (his) breast, from his arms, he formed the Panchadasa (stoma). After it were created the god, the indra, the Trishtubh metre, the Saman (called) Brihat, of men the Rajanya, of beasts the sheep. Hence they are vigorous, because they were created from vigour. From (his) middle he formed the Saptadasa (stoma). After it were created the gods (called) the Vishvedevas, the Jagati metre, the Saman called the Vairupa, of men the Vaishya, of beasts kine. Hence they are to be eaten, because they were created from the receptacle of food. Wherefore they are more numerous than others, for the most numerous deities were created after (the Saptadasa). From his foot he formed the Ekavimsa (Stoma). After it were created the Anushtubh metre, the saman called vairaja, of men the Shudra, of beasts the horse. Hence these two, both the horse and the Shudra, are transporters of (other) creatures. Hence (too) the Shudra is incapacitated for sacrifice, because no deities were created after (the Ekavimsa). Hence (too) these two subsist by their feet, for they were created from the foot.

Coming to the Atharva Veda, there are altogether four explanations. One of these is the same as the Purusha Sukta of the Rig Veda. It

---

[80]Muir, Vol. I.

occurs at xix.6. The others are as stated below:[81]

(1) A.V., iv.6.1: 'The Brahmin was born the first with ten heads and ten faces. He first drank the soma; he made poison powerless.'
(2) A.V., xv.8.I: 'He (the Vratya) became filled with passion, thence sprang the Rajanya.'
(3) A.V., xv.9.1: 'Let the king to whose house the Vratya who knows this, comes as a guest, cause him to be respected as superior to himself. So doing he does no injury to his royal rank, or to his realm. From him arose the Brahman (Brahmin) and the Kshattra (Kshatriya). They said "Into whom shall we enter," etc.'

To proceed to the Brahmanas. The Satapatha Brahmana contains six explanations. There are two which concern themselves with the creation of the varnas. Of the two, the one which speaks of the origin of the Shudras is given below:

S.B.[1] xiv.4.2.23: 'Brahma (here, according to the commentator, existing in the form of Agni and representing the Brahmin caste) was formerly this (universe), one only. Being one, it did not develop. It energetically created an excellent form, the Kshattra, viz., those among the gods who are powers (Kshattrani), Indra, Varuna, Soma, Rudra, Parjanya, Yama, Mrityu, Isana. Hence, nothing is superior to the Kshatra. Therefore, the Brahmin sits below the Kshatriya at the Rajasuya sacrifice; he confers that glory on the Kshattra (the royal power). This, the Brahma, is the source of the Kshattra. Hence although the king attains supremacy, he at the end resorts to the Brahmin as his source. Whoever destroys him (the Brahmin) destroys his own source. He becomes most miserable, as one who has injured a superior. He did not develop. He created the Vis, viz., those classes of gods who are designated by troops, Vasus, Rudras, Adityas, Visvedevas, Maruts. He did not develop. He created the Shudra class Pushan. This earth is Pushan; for she nourishes all that exists. He did not develop. He energetically created an excellent form, Justice (Dharma). This is the ruler (Kshattra) of the ruler (Kshattra), namely, Justice. Hence nothing, is superior to Justice. Therefore, the

---

[81]Muir, Vol. I.

weaker seeks (to overcome) the stronger by Justice, as by a king. This justice is truth. In consequence they say of a man who speaks truth, "he speaks justice". For this is both of these. This is the Brahma, Kshattra, Vis and Shudra. Through Agni it became Brahma among the gods, the Brahmin among men, through the (divine) Kshatriya a (human) Kshatriya, through the (divine) Vaishya a (human) Vaishya, through the (divine) Shudra a (human) Shudra. Wherefore it is in Agni among the gods and in a Brahmin among men that they seek after an abode.'

The Taittriya Brahmana is responsible for the following explanation:[82]

(1) T.B. i.2.6.7: 'The Brahmin caste is sprung from the gods; the Shudras from the Asuras.'
(2) T.B., iii. 2.3.9: 'This Shudra has sprung from non-existence.'

♦

Here is a complete collection of all the Brahminic speculations on the origin of the four classes and of the Shudras. The ancient Brahmins were evidently conscious of the fact that the origin of the four classes was an unusual and uncommon social phenomenon and that the place of the Shudra in it was very unnatural and that this called for some explanation. Otherwise, it would be impossible to account for these innumerable attempts to explain the origin of the Chaturvarnya and of the Shudra.

But what is one to say of these explanations? The variety of them is simply bewildering. Some allege that Purusha was the origin of the four varnas, and some attribute their origin to Brahma, some to Prajapati and some to Vratya. The same source gives differing explanations. The White Yajur Veda has two explanations, one in terms of Purusha, the other in terms of Prajapati. The Black Yajur Veda has three explanations to offer. Two are in terms of Prajapati, the third in terms of Brahmin. The Atharva Veda has four explanations, one in terms of Purusha, second in terms of Brahmin, third in terms of Vratya and fourth quite different from the first three. Even when the theory is the same, the details are not the same. Some explanations such as those in terms

---

[82]Muir, Vol. I.

of Prajapti, or Brahma are theological. Others in terms of Manu or Kasyapa are in humanistic terms. It is imagination running riot. There is in them neither history nor sense. Prof. Max Müller commenting on the Brahmanas has said:

'The Brahmanas represent no doubt a most interesting phase in the history of the Indian mind, but judged by themselves, as literary productions, they are most disappointing. No one would have supposed that at so early a period, and in so primitive a state of society, there could have risen up a literature which for pedantry and downright absurdity can hardly be matched anywhere. There is no lack of striking thoughts, of bold expressions, of sound reasoning, and curious traditions in these collections. But these are only like the fragments of a torso, like precious gems set in brass and lead. The general character of these works is marked by shallow and insipid grandiloquence, by priestly conceit, and antiquarian pedantry. It is most important to the historian that he should know how soon the fresh and healthy growth of a nation can be blighted by priestcraft and superstition. It is most important that we should know that nations are liable to these epidemics in their youth as well as in their dotage. These works deserve to be studied as the physician studies the twaddle of idiots, and the raving of madmen.'[83]

On reading these Brahminic speculations on the origin of the four varnas and particularly of the Shudras, one is very much reminded of these words of Prof. Max Müller. All these speculations are really the twaddles of idiots and ravings of madmen and as such they are of no use to the student of history who is in search of a natural explanation of a human problem.

◆

Who were the Shudras if they were not a non-Aryan aboriginal race? This question must now be faced. The theory I venture to advance may be stated in the following three propositions:

(1) The Shudras were Aryans.
(2) The Shudras belonged to the Kshatriya class.

---

[83]Müller, Max, Ancient Sanskrit Literature (Panini Office edition), p 200.

(3) The Shudras were so important a class of Kshatriyas that some of the most eminent and powerful kings of the ancient Aryan communities were Shudras.

This thesis regarding the origin of the Shudras is a startling if not a revolutionary thesis. So startling it is that not many people will be ready to accept it, even though there may be enough evidence to support it. My obligation is to produce the evidence, leaving the people to judge its worth.

The primary piece of evidence on which this thesis rests is a passage which occurs in Verses 38–40 of Chapter 60 of the Shanti Parvan of the Mahabharata. It reads as follows:

'It has been heard by us that in the days of old a Shudra of the name of Paijavana gave a Dakshina (in his own sacrifice) consisting of a hundred thousand Purnapatras according to the ordinance called Aindragni.'

The important statements contained in this passage are three: (1) that Paijavana was a Shudra; (2) that this Shudra Paijavana performed sacrifices; and (3) the Brahmins performed sacrifices for him and accepted Dakshina from him.

The passage quoted above is taken from Mr Roy's edition of the Mahabharata. The first thing is to ascertain whether the text is accurate or whether there are any variant readings. As regards the authenticity of his text, this is what Mr Roy says:[84]

'As far as my edition is concerned, it is substantially based on that of Royal Asiatic Society of Bengal, published about forty-five years ago under the superintendence of a few learned Pandits of Bengal, aided, as I believe, by an English Orientalist of repute. Manuscripts had been procured from all parts of India (the South unexcepted) and these were carefully collated. Although edited with such care, I have not, however, slavishly followed the Society's edition. I have compared it carefully with the Maharajah of Burdwan's text in the Bengalee character which was edited with still greater care. About 18 manuscripts procured from different parts of India (the South not excepted) were carefully collated

---

[84]Quoted in Sukthankar Memorial Edition, Vol. I, pp 43–44.

by the Burdwan Pandits before they admitted a single sloka as genuine.'

Prof. Sukthankar, the erudite editor of the critical edition of the Mahabharata, after examining many editions of the Mahabharata, concluded by saying that:[85]

'The editio princeps (Calcutta, 1856) remains the best edition of the Vulgate, after the lapse of nearly a century.'

Although the authenticity of Mr Roy's edition of the Mahabharata cannot be doubted, it would not be unreasonable if critics were to say that they would like to know what other manuscript support there is behind this text, which is made the basis of this new theory of the origin of the Shudras. In undertaking such an inquiry, it is necessary to point to two considerations. One[86] is that there is no such thing as a Mahabharata manuscript in the sense of complete sets of manuscripts covering all the eighteen Parvans. Each Parvan is treated as a separate unit with the result that the number of copies of the different Parvans to be found differ by a vast margin. Consequently, the number of manuscripts to be taken as a basis for deciding which is the correct text must vary with each Parvan.

The second[87] consideration to which attention must be drawn is the fact that the text of the Mahabharata has been handed down in two divergent forms: a Northern and a Southern recension, texts, typical of the Aryavrata and the Dakshinapatha.

It is obvious that an examination of manuscript support must be based upon collation from a fair number of manuscripts and a fair distribution of the manuscripts between the Northern and the Southern recensions. Bearing these considerations in mind, the results of the collation[1] of the text of Shloka 38 of the 60th chapter of the Shanti Parvan of the Mahabharata with which we are primarily concerned from different manuscripts is presented below:

1. शूद्रः पैजवनो नाम   (K)S

---

[85]Quoted in Sukthankar Memorial Edition, Vol. I, p 131.

[86]Sukthankar, op. cit., p 14.

[87]Ibid, pp 9–42.

Shudrah Piajavano nama

2. शूद्र: पैलवनो नाम   (M/1: M/2)S
Shudrah Pailavano nama

3. शूद्र: यैलननो नाम   (M/3 : M/4)S
Shudrah Piajavano nama

4. शूद्र: यैजननो नाम   (F)
Shudrah Yaijanano nama

5. शूद्रोऽपि: यजने नाम   (L)
Shudropi Yajane nama

6. शूद्र: पौंजलक नाम   (TC)S
Shudrah Paunjalka nama

7. शूद्धो वैभवनो नाम   (G)N
Shuddho Vaibhavano nama

8. पुरा वैजवनो नाम   (A, D/2)
Pura Vaijavano nama

9. पुरा वैजननो नाम   (M)N
Pura Vaijanano nama

Here is the result of the collation of nine manuscripts. Are nine manuscripts enough for constituting a text which has a number of variant readings? It is true that the number of manuscripts taken for the critical edition of the different Parvans of the Mahabharata exceeds nine. For the entire Mahabharata, the minimum number of manuscripts taken for constituting the text is only ten.[88] It cannot, therefore, be contended that nine is an insufficient number. The nine manuscripts fall into two geographical divisions: Northern and Southern. MI, M2, M3, M4 and TC belong to the Southern recession. A, M, G, D2 belong to the Northern recession. The selections of the manuscripts, therefore, satisfy the two tests which experts have laid down.

A scrutiny of the readings shows that:

(1) There is a variation in the description of Paijavana;
(2) There is a variation in the name of Paijavana;
(3) Of the nine texts, six agree in describing him as a Shudra. One

---

[88]Sokthankar, Vol. I, p 14.

describes him as Shuddha and two, instead of speaking of the class to which he belonged, refer to the time when he lived and use the word 'Pura';

(4) With regard to the name, there is no agreement between any two of the nine manuscripts. Each gives a different reading.

Given this result, the question is: What is the real text? Taking first the texts relating to the name, it is obvious that this is not a matter in which the question of meaning is involved. It does not raise any questions such as interpretation versus emendation or of giving preference to a reading which suggests how other readings might have arisen. The question is: Which is the correct name and which readings are scriptural blunders committed by the scribes? There seems to be no doubt that the correct text is Paijavana. It is supported by both the recessions, Southern as well as Northern. For Vaijavano in No. 8 is the same as Paijavano. All the rest are variations which are due to the ignorance of the scribes in not being able to read the original copy correctly and then trying to constitute the text in their own way.

Turning to the description of Paijavana, the change from Shudrah to Pura, it must be granted, is not accidental. It appears to be deliberate. Why this change has occurred it is difficult to say categorically. Two things appear to be quite clear. In the first place, the change appears to be quite natural. In the second place, the change does not militate against the conclusion that Paijavana was a Shudra. The above conclusion will be obvious if the context, in which verses 38–40 occur, is borne in mind. The context will be clear from the following verses which precede them:

'The Shudra should never abandon his master whatever the nature or degree of the distress into which the latter may fall. If the master loses his wealth, he should with excessive zeal be supported by the Shudra servant. A Shudra cannot have any wealth that is his own. Whatever he possesses belongs to his master. Sacrifice has been laid down as a duty of the three other orders. It has been ordained for the Shudra also, O! Bharata. A Shudra, however, is not competent to utter swaha and svadha or any other mantra. For this reason, the Shudra, without observing the vows laid down in the Vedas, should worship the gods in minor sacrifices called Pakayajnas. The gift called Pumapatra is declared to be the Dakshina of such sacrifices.'

Taking the verses 38 to 40 in the context of these verses preceding them, it becomes clear that the whole passage deals with the Shudra. The story of Paijavana is a mere illustration. Against this background, it is unnecessary to repeat the word 'Shudra' before Paijavana. This explains why the word Shudra does not occur before Paijavana in the two manuscripts. As to the reason for the use of the word pura in place of Shudra, it must be remembered that the case of Paijavana had occurred in very ancient times. It was, therefore, quite natural for the scribe to feel that it was desirable to put this fact in express terms. The writer being aware that there was no necessity for describing Paijavana as Shudra since that was made clear from the context, it was not necessary to emphasize it. On the other hand, knowing that Paijavana had lived in very ancient times and that that fact was not made very clear from the context, the writer thought it more appropriate to add the word Pura which was necessary and omit the word Shudrah which having regard to the context was unnecessary.

If this explanation is well-founded, we may take it as well-established that the person referred to in the passage in the Shanti Parvan of the Mahabharata is Paijavana and that this Paijavana was a Shudra.

The next question that falls due for consideration is the identification of Paijavana. Who is this Paijavana?

Yaska's Nirukta seems to give us a clue. In Nirukta ii.24 Yaska says:[89]

'The seer Vishvamitra was the purohita of Sudas, the son of Pijavana. Vishvamitra, friend of all. All, moving together. Sudas a bountiful giver. Paijavana, son of Pijavana. Again Pi-javana one whose speed is enviable or whose gait is inimitable.'

From Yaska's Nirukta we get two very important facts: (1) Paijavana means son of Pijavana, and (2) the person who is the son of Paijavana is Sudas. With the help of Yaska, we are able to answer the question: who is Paijavana referred to in the passage in the Shanti Parvan of

[89]Sarup, Lakshman, *The Nighantu and Nirukta*, pp 35–36.

the Mahabharata? The answer is that Paijavana is simply another name for Sudas.

The next question is: who is this Sudas and what do we know about him? A search in the Brahminic literature discloses three persons with the name Sudas. One Sudas is mentioned in the Rig Veda. His family particulars are given in the following stanzas of the Rig Veda:[90]

1. Rig Veda, vii.18.21: 'Parashara, the destroyer of hundreds (of Rakshasas), and Vasishtha, they who, devoted to thee, have glorified thee in every dwelling, neglect not the friendship of thee (their) benefactor; therefore prosperous days dawn upon the pious.'

2. Rig Veda, vii. 18.22: 'Praising the liberality of Sudas, the grandson of Devavata, the son of Paijavana, the donor of two hundred cows, and of two chariots with two wives, I, worthy (of the gift), circumambulate thee, Agni, like the ministrant priest in the chamber (of sacrifice).'

3. Rig Veda, vii.18.23: 'Four (horses), having golden trappings, going steadily on a difficult road, celebrated on the earth, the excellent and acceptable gifts (made) to me by Sudas, the son of Pijavana; bear me as a son (to obtain) food and progeny.'

4. Rig Veda, vii. 18.24: 'The seven worlds praise (Sudas) as if he were Indra; him whose fame (spreads) through the spacious heaven and earth; who, munificent, has distributed (wealth) on every eminent person, and (for whom) the flowing (rivers) have destroyed Yudhyamadhi in war.'

5. Rig Veda, vii.18.25: 'Maruts, leaders (of rites), attend upon this (prince) as you did upon Divodasa, the father of Sudas; favour the prayers of the devout son of Pijavana, and may his strength be unimpaired, undecaying.'

The two others are mentioned by the Vishnu Purana. One Sudas is mentioned in Chapter IV as the descendant of Sagara. The genealogical tree connecting this Sudas with Sagara is as follows:[91]

---

[90]Wilson's Rig Veda, Vol. IV (Poona Reprint), p 146.
[91]Wilson's Vishnu Purana, pp 377–380.

'Sumati, the daughter of Kasyapa, and Kesirri, the daughter of Raja Vidarbha, were the two wives of Sagara. Being without progeny, the king solicited the aid of the sage Aurva with great earnestness, and the Muni pronounced this boon, that one wife should bear one son, the upholder of his race, and the other should give birth to sixty thousand sons; and he left it to them to make their election. Kesini chose to have the single son; Sumati the multitude; and it came to pass in a short time that the former bore Asamanjas, a prince through whom the dynesty continued; and the daughter of Vinata (Sumati) had sixty thousand sons. The son of Asamanjas was Ansumat. The son of Ansumat was Dilipa; his son was Bhagiratha, who brought Ganga down to earth, whence she is called Bhagirathi. The son of Bhagiratha was Sruta; his son was Nabhaga; his son was Ambarisha; his son was Sindhudvipa; his son was Ayutashva; his son was Rituparna, the friend of Nala, skilled profoundly in dice. The son of Rituparna was Sarvakama; his son was Sudasa; his son was Saudasa, named also Mitrasaha.'

Another Sudas is mentioned in Chapter XIX as a descendant of Puru. The genealogical tree connecting this Sudas with Puru is as follows:

'The son of Puru was Janamejaya; his son was Prachinvat; his son was Pravira, his son was Manasyu; his son was Bhayada; his son was Sudhumna; his son was Bahugava; his son was Samyati; his son was Bhamyati; his son was Raudrashva, who had ten sons, Riteyu, Kaksheyu, Sthandileyu, Ghriteyu, Jaleyu, Sthaleyu, Dhaneyu, Vaneyu, and Vrateyu. The son of Riteyu was Rantinara whose sons were Tansu. Aprtiratha, and Dhruva. The son of the second of these was Kanva, and his son was Medhatithi, from whom the Kanvayana Brahmins are descended. Anila was the son of Tansu, and he had four sons, of whom Dushyanta was the elder. The son of Dushyanta was the emperor Bharata…

'Bharata had by different wives nine sons, but they were put to death by their own mothers, because Bharata remarked that they bore no resemblance to him, and the women were afraid that he would, therefore, desert them. The birth of his sons being thus unavailing, Bharata sacrificed to the Maruts, and they gave him Bharadvaja, the son of Brihaspati by Mamata the wife of Utathya. 'He was also termed

Vitatha, in allusion to the unprofitable (vitatha) birth of the sons of Bharata. The son of Vitatha was Bhavanmanyu; his sons were many, and amongst them the chief were Brihatkshatra, Mahavirya, Nara and Garga. The son of Nara was Sankriti; his sons were Ruchiradhi and Rantideva. The son of Garga was Sini; and their descendants called Gargyas and Sainyas, although Kshatriyas by birth, became Brahmins. The son of Mahavirya was Urukshaya, who had three sons, Trayyaruna, Pushkarin and Kapi, the last of whom became a Brahmin. The son of Brihatkshatra was Suhotra, whose son was Hastin, who founded the city of Hastinapur. The sons of Hastin were Ajamidha, Dvimidha and Purumidha. One son of Ajamidha was Kanva, whose son was Medhatithi, his other son was Brihadishu, whose son was Brihadvasu; his son was Brihatkarman: his son was Jayadratha, his son was Vishvajit, his son was Senajit, whose sons were Ruchirashva, Kasya, Dridhadhanush, and Vasahanu. The son of Ruchirashva was Prithusena: his son was Para; his son was Nipa; he had a hundred sons, of whom Samara, the principal, was the ruler of Kampilya. Samara had three sons, Para, Sampara, Sadashva. The son of Para was Prithu; his son was Sukriti; his son was Vibhratra; his son was Anuha, who married Kritvi, the daughter of Shuka (the son of Vyasa), and had by her Brahmadatta; his son was Vishvaksena; his son was Udaksena; and his son was Bhallata. The son of Dvimidha was Yavinara; his son was Dhritimat; his son was Satyadhriti; his son was Dridhanemi; his son was Suparshya, his son was Sumati; his son was Sannatimat; his son was Krita, to whom Hiranyanabha taught the philosophy of the Yoga, and he compiled twenty-four Samhitas (or compendia) for the use of the eastern Brahmins, who study the Sama Veda. The son of Krita was Ugrayudha, by whose prowess the Nipa race of Kshatriyas was destroyed; his son was Kshemya; his son was Suvira; his son was Nripanjaya; his son was Bahuratha. These were all called Pauravas. 'Ajamidha had a wife called Nilini, and by her he had a son named Nila: his son was Santi; his son was Susanti; his son was Purujanu; his son was Chakshu; his son was Haryashva, who had five sons: Mudgala, Srinjaya, Brihadishu, Pravira, and Kampilya. Their father said, "These my five (pancha) sons are able (alam) to protect the countries"; and hence they were termed the

Panchalas. From Mudgala descended the Maudgalya Brahmins; he had also a son named Bahvashva, who had two children, twins, a son and daughter, Divodasa and Ahalya. 'The son of Divodasa was Mitrayu; his son was Chyavana; his son was Sudasa; his son was Saudasa, also called Sahadeva; his son was Somaka; he had a hundred sons, of whom Jantu was the eldest, and Prishata the youngest. The son of Prishata was Drupada; his son was Dhrishtadyumna; his son was Dhrishtaketu. 'Another son of Ajamidha was named Riksha; his son was Samvarana; his son was Kuru, who gave his name to the holy district Kurukshetra; his sons were Sudhanush, Parikshit, and many others. The son of Sudhanush was Suhotra; his son was Chyavana; his son was Kritaka; his son was Uparichara the Vasu, who had seven children: Brihadratha, Pratyagra, Kushamba, Mavella, Matsya, and others. The son of Brihadratha was Kusagra; his son was Rishabha; his son was Pushpavat; his son was Satyadhrita; his son was Sudhanvan; and his son was Jantu. Brihadratha had another son, who being born in two parts, which were put together (sandhita) by a female fiend named Jara, he was denominated Jarasandha; his son was Sahadeva; his son was Somapi; his son was Srutasravas, These were kings of Magadha.'

The immediate ancestry of the three Sudasas is put below in parallel columns to facilitate the settlement of the question whether they are one or three different persons:

From the table [below], two things are as clear as daylight. First is that neither Sudas mentioned in the Vishnu Purana has anything to do with the Sudas mentioned in the Rig Veda. The second point which is clear is that if the Paijavana mentioned in the Mahabharata can be identified with anybody who lived in ancient times, it can only be with Sudas mentioned in Rig Veda, who was called Paijavana because he was the son of Pijavana, which was another name of Divodasa.[92]

---

[92]Some difficulty is felt about the genealogy of this Sudas in the Rig Veda, which is sought to be got over by identifying Devavata with Divodasa. This difficulty has mainly arisen because of the different texts of Stanzas 22, 23 and 25 which nobody seems to have cared to collect properly. Chitrava Shastri's edition of Rig Veda has Pijavana throughout. Satavalekar's edition has Paijavana throughout.

Status in Rig Veda			Sudas in Vishnu Purana	
VII, 18:22	*VII, 18:23*	*VII, 18:25*	*In the Sagar Family*	*In the Puru Family*
Devavata | Pijavana | Sudas	Pijavana | Sudas	Divodasa = Pijavana | Sudas	Rituparna | Sarvakama Sudas Saudasa = Mitrasaha	Bahvashva | Divodasa | Mitrayu | Chyavana | Sudas | Saudasa | Somaka

Fortunately, for me, my conclusion is the same as that of Prof. Weber. In commenting upon the passage in the Shanti Parvan of the Mahabharata on which my thesis is based, Prof. Weber[1] says:

'Here the remarkable tradition is recorded that Paijavana, i.e., Sudas, who was so famous for his sacrifices and who is celebrated in the Rig Veda as the patron of Vishvamitra and enemy of Vasishtha, was a Shudra.'

Prof. Weber unfortunately did not realize the full significance of this passage. This is another matter. It is enough for my purpose to find that he too thinks that the Paijavana of the Mahabharata is no other than Sudas of the Rig Veda.

◆

Wilson has Paijavana in 22 and 23 and Pijavana in 25. Wilson's text seems to be accurate. For, even Yaska has noticed the existence of the name Paijavana in his Nirukta which he endeavours to explain. If Wilson's text in 25 is taken as correct, no difficulty can arise. Pijavana would then appear to be another name of Divodasa and Paijavana would be another name of Sudas.

That there were from the very beginning four varnas in the Indo–Aryan society is a view which is universally accepted by all classes of Hindus, and also by European scholars. If the thesis advanced in the last chapter, namely, that the Shudras were Kshatriyas, is accepted, then it follows that this theory is wrong and that there was a time when there were only three varnas in the Indo–Aryan society, viz Brahmins, Kshatriyas and Vaishyas. Thus, the thesis, while it solves one problem, at the same time creates another. Whether anybody else sees the importance of this problem or not, I do. Indeed, I am aware of the fact that unless I succeed in proving that there were originally only three varnas, my thesis that the Shudras were Kshatriyas may not be said to be proved beyond the shadow of a doubt.

While it is unfortunate that I should have landed on a thesis, which, while holding out a promise of solving the problem, creates another, I feel fortunate in having strong and cogent evidence to show that there were originally only three varnas among the Indo–Aryans.

The first piece of evidence I rely upon is that of the Rig Veda itself. There are some scholars who maintain that the varna system did not exist in the age of the Rig Veda. This statement is based on the view that the Purusha Sukta is an interpolation which has taken place long after the Rig Veda was closed. Even accepting that the Purusha Sukta is a later interpolation, it is not possible to accept the statement that the varna system did not exist in the time of the Rig Veda. Such a system is in open conflict with the text of the Rig Veda. For, the Rig Veda, apart from the Purusha Sukta, does mention Brahmins, Kshatriyas and Vaishyas not once but many times. The Brahmins are mentioned as a separate varna fifteen times, Kshatriyas nine times. What is important is that the Rig Veda does not mention Shudra as a separate varna. If Shudras were a separate varna, there is no reason why the Rig Veda should not have mentioned them. The true conclusion to be drawn from the Rig Veda is not that the varna system did not exist, but that there were only three varnas and that Shudras were not regarded as a fourth and a separate varna.

The second piece of evidence I rely on is the testimony of the two Brahmanas, the Satapatha and the Taittiriya. Both speak of the creation of three varnas only. They do not speak of the creation of the Shudras as a separate varna.

The Satapatha Brahmana says:[93]

> II. 1.4.11: '(Uttering), "bhuh", Prajapati generated this earth, (uttering) "bhuvah", he generated the air, and (utering) "svah", he generated the sky. This universe is coextensive with these worlds. (The fire) is placed with the whole. Saying "bhuh", Prajapali generated the Brahmin; saying "bhuvah", he generated the Kshattra; (and saying) "svah", he generated the Vis. The fire is placed with the whole. (Saying) "bhuh", Prajapati generated himself; (saying) "bhuvah", he generated offspring; saying "svah", he generated animals. This world is so much as self, offspring, and animals. (The fire) is placed with the whole.'

The Taittiriya Brahmana says:[94]

> III. 12.9.2: 'This entire (universe) has been created by Brahma. Men say that the Vaishya class was produced from rich verses. They say that the Yajur Veda is the womb from which the Kshattriya was born. The Sama Veda is the source from which the Brahmins sprang. This word the ancients declared to the ancients.'

Here is my evidence. It consists of an inference from the Rig Veda and two statements from two Brahmanas which in point of authority are co-equal with the Vedas. For both are Shruti, both say in definite and precise terms that there were only three varnas. Both agree that the Shudras did not form a separate and a distinct varna, much less the fourth varna. There cannot, therefore, be better evidence in support of my contention that there were originally only three varnas, that the Shudras were only a part of the second varna.

Such is my evidence. On the other side, there is, of course, the evidence contained in the Purusha Sukta of the Rig Veda, which maintains that there were four varnas from the very beginning. The question now is: Which of the two should be accepted as the correct? How is this question to be decided? It cannot be decided by applying the rules of Mimamsa. If we did apply it, we will have to admit that

---

[93]Muir, Vol. I.
[94]Ibid.

both the statements, one in the Purusha Sukta that there were four varnas and the statement in the two Brahmanas that there were three varnas, are true. This is an absurd position. We must decide this matter in the light of the canons of historical criticism, such as sequence of time and intrinsic criticism, etc. The main question is whether the Purusha Sukta is a later composition added to the original Rig Veda. The question has been dealt with on the basis of the language of the Sukta as compared with the language of the rest of the Rig Veda. That it is a late production is the opinion of all scholars. This is what Colebrooke says:[95]

'That remarkable hymn (the Purusha Sukta) is in language, metre, and style, very different from the rest of the prayers with which it is associated. It has a decidedly more modern tone; and must have been composed after the Sanskrit language had been refined, and its grammar and rhythm perfected. The internal evidence which it furnishes serves to demonstrate the important fact that the compilation of the Vedas, in their present arrangement, took place after the Sanskrit tongue had advanced from the rustic and irregular dialect in which the multitude of hymns and prayers of the Veda was composed, to the polished and sonorous language in which the mythological poems, sacred and profane (puranas and kavyas), have been written.'

In the opinion of Prof. Max Müller:[96]

'There can be little doubt, for instance, that the 90th hymn of the 10th book…is modern both in its character and in its diction. It is full of allusions to the sacrificial ceremonials, it uses technically philosophical terms, it mentions the three seasons in the order of Vasanta, spring, Grishma, summer and Sharad, autumn; it contains the only passage in the Rig Veda where the four castes are enumerated. The evidence of language for the modern date of this composition is equally strong. Grishma, for instance, the name for the hot season, does not occur in any other hymn of the Rig Veda; and Vasanta also, the name of spring does not belong to the earliest vocabulary of the Vedic poets. It occurs

---

[95]Muir, Vol. I.
[96]Muir, Vol. I.

but once more in the Rig Veda (x. 161.4), in a passage where the three seasons are mentioned in the order of Sharad, autumn; Hemanta, winter; and Vasanta, spring.'

Prof. Weber observes:[97]

'That the Purusha Sukta, considered as a hymn of the Rig Veda, is among the latest portions of that collection, is clearly perceptible from its contents. The fact, that the Sama Samhita has not adopted any verse from it, is not without importance (compare what I have remarked in my Academical Prelections). The Naigeya school, indeed, appears (although it is not quite certain) to have extracted the first five verses in the seventh prapathaka of the first Archika, which is peculiar to it.'

This is one line of argument. There is also another line of argument which also helps us to determine whether the Purusha Sukta is an earlier or later production. For this, it is necessary to find out how many Samhitas of the Vedas have adopted the Purusha Sukta.

Examining the different Vedas and the Samhitas, the position is as follows:

'The Sama Veda produces only 5 verses from the Purusha Sukta. As to the White Yajur Veda, the Vajasaneyi Samhita includes it, but the difference between the two is great. The Purusha Sukta, as it stands in the Rig Veda, has only sixteen verses. But, the Purusha Sukta in the Vajasaneyi Samhita has twenty-two verses. Of the Black Yajur Veda, there are three Samhitas available at present. But none of the three Samhitas, the Taittiriya, the Katha and the Maitrayani, gives any place to the Purusha Sukta. The Atharva Veda is the only Veda which contains a more or less exact reproduction of the Purusha Sukta of the Rig Veda.'

The text of the Purusha Sukta, as it occurs in the different Vedas, is not uniform. The six additional verses of the Vajasaneyi Samhita are special to it and are not to be found in the text as it occurs in the Rig Veda, the Sama Veda or the Atharva Veda. There is another difference which relates to verse 16. The 16th verse of the Rig Veda is to be found neither in the Atharva Veda nor in the Sama Veda

---

[97] Ibid.

nor in the Yajur Veda. Similarly, the 16th verse of the Atharva Veda is to be found neither in the Rig Veda nor in the Yajur Veda. Of the fifteen verses, which are common to the three Vedas, their texts are not identical. Nor is the order in which the verses stand in the three Vedas the same as may be seen from the following table:

Yajur Veda	Rig Veda	Sama Veda	Atharva Veda
1	1	3	1
2	2	5	4
3	3	6	3
4	4	4	2
5	5	7	9
6	8	*	10
7	9	*	11
8	10	*	14
9	7	*	13
10	11	*	12
11	12	*	5
12	13	*	6
13	14	*	7
14	6	*	8
15	15	*	15
16	16	*	16
17	*	*	*
18		*	*
19	*	*	*
20	*	*	*
21	*	*	*
22	*	*	*

The point is that if the Purusha Sukta had been an old, hoary text, sanctified by ancient tradition, could the other Vedas have taken such a liberty with it? Could they have changed it and chopped it as they have done?

The place of the Purusha Sukta in the hymns of the different Vedas is also very significant. In the Rig Veda, it occurs in the miscellaneous part, and in the Atharva Veda, it occurs in what is known as the supplementary part. If it was the earliest composition of the Rig Veda, why should it have been placed in such inconsequential collection? What do these points suggest? They suggest that:

(1) If the Purusha Sukta was not incorporated in the Taittiriya, Kathaka and Maitrayani Samhitas of the Black Yajur Veda, it follows that the Purusha Sukta was added to the Rig Veda after the Taittiriya Samhita, the Kathaka Samhita, the Maitrayani Samhita of the Black Yajur Veda.

(2) That it had to be put in the miscellaneous and supplementary portions of the Vedas shows that it was composed at a later stage.

(3) That the freedom which the authors of the different Samhitas took in adding, omitting and recording the verses shows that they did not regard it as an ancient hymn, which they were bound to reproduce in its exact original form.

These points go a long way in furnishing corroborative evidence in support of the views held by Prof. Max Müller and others that the Purusha Sukta is a later interpolation.

◆

What is the technique which the Brahmins employed to bring about the degradation of the Shudras from the rank of the second to the rank of the fourth varna?

The discussion has so far centred round two questions as to whether or not the Shudras were originally a part of the second or Kshatriya varna and whether or not the Brahmins had not received sufficient provocation to degrade the Shudras. It is now necessary to deal with the question, which is logically next in order of sequence. What is the technique of degradation employed by the Brahmins?

My answer to the question is that the technique employed by the Brahmins for this purpose was to refuse to perform the Upanayana of the Shudras. I have no doubt that it is by this technique that the

Brahmins accomplished their end and thereby wreaked their vengeance upon the Shudras.

It is perhaps necessary to explain what Upanayana means and what importance it had in the Indo–Aryan society. The best way to give an idea of Upanayana is to give a description of the ceremony.

As a rite, Upanayana was originally a very simple ceremony. The boy came to the teacher with a samidh (a grass blade) in his hand and told the teacher that he desired to become a Brahmachari (i.e a student) and begged the teacher to allow him to stay with him for purposes of study. At a later date it became a very elaborate ceremony. How elaborate it had become may be realized from the following description of Upanayana in the Ashvalayana Grihya Sutra:

'Let him initiate the boy who is decked, whose hair (on the head) is shaved (and arranged), who wears a new garment or an antelope skin if a Brahmin, rum skin if a Kshatriya, a goat's skin if a Vaishya; if they put on garments they should put on dyed ones, reddish-yellow, red and yellow (for a Brahmin, Kshatriya, Vaishya respectively); they should have girdles and staffs (as described above). While the boy takes hold of (the hand of) his teacher, the latter offers (a homa of clarified butter oblations) in the fire (as described above), and seats himself to the north of the fire with his face turned to the east, while the other one (the boy) stations himself in front (of the teacher) with his face turned to the west. The teacher then fills the folded hands of both himself and of the boy with water and with the verse "we choose that of Savitri" (Rg.V. 82.1) the teacher drops down the water in his own folded hands on to the water in the folded hands of the boy; having thus poured the water, he should seize with his own hand the boy's hand together with the thumb (of the boy) with the formula by the urge (or order) of the god Savitri, with the arms of the two Ashvins, with the hands of Pushan, I seize thy hand, oh so, and so, with the words "Savitri has seized thy hand, oh so and so" a second time (the teacher seizes the boy's hand) with the words "Agni is thy teacher oh so and so" a third time. The teacher should cause the boy to look at the sun, while the teacher repeats "God Savitri, this is thy brahmachari, protect him, may he not die" and (the teacher should further) say: "Whose brahmachari art thou? Thou art the brahmachari of Prana. Who does initiate thee and whom (does he initiate)? I give thee to Ka (to Prajapati)." With the half verse (Rg. III.8.4) "the young man well attired and dressed, come hither" he (the teacher) should cause him to turn round to the right and with his two hands placed over (the boy's) shoulders he should touch the place of the boy's heart repeating the latter half (of Rg. III. 8.4). Having wiped the ground round the fire, the brahmachari should put (on the fire) a fuel stick silently, since it is known (from sruti) "what belongs to Prajapati is silently done," and the brahmachari belongs to Prajapati. Some do this (offering of a fuel stick) with a mantra to Agni: "I Have brought a fuel stick, to the great Jatavedas;by the fuel stick mayst thou increase, Oh agni, and may we (increase) through brahman (prayer or spiritual lore), svaha." Having put the fuel stick (on the fire) and having touched the fire, he (the student) thrice wipes off his face with the words "I anoint myself with lustre," it is known (from sruti) for he does anoint himself with lustre. "May Agni bestow on me, insight, offspring and lustre; on me may Indra bestow insight, offspring and vigour (Indriya); on me may the sun bestow insight, offspring and radiance; what thy lustre is, Oh Agni, may I thereby become lustrous; what thy strength is, Agni, may I thereby become strong; what thy consuming power is, Agni, may I thereby acquire consuming power." Having waited upon (worshipped) Agni with these formulae, (the student) should bend his knees, embrace (the teachers feet) and say to him "recite, Sir, recite, Sir, the Savitri." Seizing the student's hands with the upper garment (of the student) and his own hands, the teacher recites the Savitri first pada by pada, then hemistich by hemistich (and lastly) the whole verse. He (the teacher) should make him (the student) recite (the Savitiri) as much as he is able. On the place of the student's heart the teacher lays his hand with the fingers upturned with the formula "I place thy heart unto duty to me, may thy mind follow my mind; may you attend on my words single-minded; may Brihaspati appoint thee unto me." Having tied the girdle round him (the boy) and having given him the staff, the teacher should instruct him in the observances of a brahmachari with the words "a brahmachari art thou, sip water, do service, do not sleep by day, depending (completely) on the teacher learn the Veda." He (the student) should beg (food) in the evening and the morning; he should put a fuel stick (on fire) in the evening and morning. That (which he has received by begging) he should announce to the teacher; he should not sit down (but should be standing) the rest of the day.'

The Upanayana ends with the teaching by the Acharya to the boy of the Vedic Mantra known as the Gayatri Mantra. Why the Gayatri Mantra is regarded as so essential as to require the ceremony of Upanayana before it is taught it is difficult to say.

From this description of the Upanayana ceremony two things are clear. First is that the purpose of Upanayana was to initiate a person in the study of the Vedas which commenced with the teaching of Gayatri Mantra by the Acharya to the Brahmachari. The second thing that is clear is that certain articles were regarded as very essential for the Upanayana ceremony. They are (1) two garments: one for the lower part of the body technically called Vasa and the other for the upper part of the body called Uttariya, (2) Danda or wooden staff, (3) Mekhala or a girdle of grass tied across the waist.

Any one who compares this description of Upanayana as it was performed in ancient times with the details of the ceremony as performed in later days is bound to be surprised at the absence of any mention of thread called Yajnopavita to be worn by the Brahmachari as a part of his Upanayana. The centre of the modern ceremony of Upanayana is the wearing of this thread and the whole purpose of the Upanayana has come to be the wearing of this Yajnopavita. So important a part this Yajnopavita has come to play that most elaborate rules have come to be framed about its manufacture and its use.

The Yajnopavita should have three threads, each thread to be of nine strands well twisted. One tantu (strand) stands for one devata (deity).

The Yajnopavita should reach as far as the navel, should not reach beyond the navel, nor should it be above the chest.

A person could wear more than one Yajnopavita.

A man must always wear Yajnopavita. If he took his meals without wearing the Yajnopavita, or answers the call of nature without having the Yajnopavita placed on the right ear, he had to undergo prayascitta, viz., to bathe, to mutter prayers and fast.

Wearing of another's Yajnopavita along with several other things (such as shoes, ornament, garland and kamandalu) is forbidden.

Three ways of wearing the Yajnopavita are recognized: (1)nivita, (2) pracinavita, and (3)upavita. When the cord is carried over the neck, both shoulders and the chest and is held with both the thumbs (of the two hands) lower than the region of the heart and above the navel, it is called nivita. Suspending the cord over the left shoulder in such a way that it hangs down on his right side, it becomes upavita. Suspending it on his right shoulder in such a way that it hangs down on his left side, it becomes pracinavita.

How did this Yajnopavita come in? Mr Tilak offers an explanation which is worth quoting. Mr Tilak says:

> 'Orion or Mrigashiras is called Prajapati in the Vedic works, otherwise called Yajna. A belt or girdle of cloth round the waist of Orion or Yajna will therefore be naturally named after him as Yajnopavita, the upavita or the cloth of yajna.'

The term, however, now denotes the sacred thread of the Brahmins, and it may naturally be asked whether it owes its character, if not the origin, to the belt of Orion. I think it does on the following grounds:

> 'The word yajnopavita is derived by all native scholars from Yajna + Upavita; but there is a difference of opinion as to whether we should understand the compound to mean an upavita for yajna i.e., for sacrificial purposes, or, whether it is the "upavita of Yajnas". The former is not incorrect, but authority is in favour of the latter. Thus the Prayoga-writers quote a smriti to the effect that "the High Soul is termed Yajna by the hotris, this is his upavita; therefore it is yajna-upavita." A mantra, which is recited on the occasion of wearing the sacred thread means, "I bind you with the upavita of yajna, while the first half of the general formula with which a Brahmin always puts on his sacred thread is as follows:

यज्ञोपवीतं परमंपवित्रं प्रजापतेर्यत्सहजं पुरस्तात्

The Mantra is not to be found in any of the existing Samhitas, but is given in the Brahmopanishad and by Baudhayana. This verse is strikingly similar to the verse quoted above from the Haoma Yesht. It

says, "yajnopavita is high and sacred; it was born with Prajapati, of old."
The word purastat corresponds with paurvanim in the Avesta verse and
thus decides the question raised by Dr Haug, while sahaja, born with
the limbs of Prajapati, conveys the same meaning as mainyutastem. The
coincidence between these verses cannot be accidental, and it appears
to me that the sacred thread must be derived from the belt of Orion.
Upavita, from ve to weave, literally means a piece of cloth and not a
thread. It appears, therefore, that a cloth worn round the waist was
the primitive form of yajnopavita, and that the idea of sacredness was
introduced by the theory that it was to be a symbolic representation of
Prajapati's waistcloth or belt.'

This explanation by Mr Tilak is no doubt very interesting. But it does
not help to explain some of the difficulties. It does not explain the
relation of the Yajnopavita to the two garments the Uttariya, and
the vasa, which are necessary for a person to wear while undergoing
Upanayana. Was the Yajnopavita in addition to the two garments? If
so, how is it that there is no mention of it in the early description of
the ceremony of the Upanayana? It does not explain another difficulty.
If that thread is a substitute for the cloth, how is it that the wearing
of the cloth is retained in the Upanayana?

There seems to be another explanation. I offer it for what it is
worth. According to it, the wearing of the thread had to do with the
adoption of the gotra. Its object was to tie oneself to a particular gotra.
It had nothing to do with the Upanayana as such, the object of which
was to initiate a person in the study of the Vedas. It is not sufficiently
realized that under the Ancient Aryan law, a son did not naturally
inherit the gotra of his father. The father had to perform a special
ceremony to give his gotra to his son. It is only when this ceremony
was performed that the son became the same gotra as the father. In
this connection, reference may be made to two rules observed by the
Indo–Aryan society. One is the rule of impurities. The other is the
rule of adoption. With regard to the rule of impurity, brought about
by death, the days of impurity vary with the kinship with the dead. If
the kinship is very close, the days of impurity are greater than those
in the case where the kinship is less close. The impurities attached to

the death of a boy who has not been invested with the thread are very meagre, not extending for more than a few days. With regard to the rule of adoption, it lays down that a boy who was invested with the thread was not eligible for adoption. What is the idea behind these rules? The idea seems to be quite clear. The impurities are nominal because there being no thread, the boy had not formally entered into the gotra of his father. Adoption me us entering into the gotra of the adoptive father. Once the thread ceremony had taken place, the boy had already and irrevocably entered another gotra.

There was no room for adoption left. Both these rules show that the thread ceremony was connected with gotra and not with Upanayana.

The view that the thread has connection with gotra seems to receive support from Jain literature. Shloka 87 of the fourth Parvan of the Padmapurana by Acharya Ravishena reads as follows:

> 'Bhagwan! You have told us the origin of Kshatriya, Vaishya and Shudra. I am anxious to know the origin of those who wear the thread in their neck.'

The words 'those who wear the thread in the neck' are very important. There is no doubt that it is a description of the Brahmins. From this it is clear that there was a time when the Brahmins alone wore the thread and no other class did. Read with the fact that the gotra relationship was confined only to the Brahmins, it is clear that the thread ceremony was connected with bringing the boy into—actually tying him up to—the gotra of his father, and had nothing to do with Upanayana which was connected with the initiation in the teaching of the Vedas.

If this is true, then the thread ceremony and the Upanayana ceremony had different purposes to serve. At some later date, the two merged into one. The reason for this merger appears to be very natural. The Upanayana without the thread ceremony involved the danger of the Acharya taking the boy in his gotra. It was to avoid the danger that the father of the boy performed the thread ceremony before handing him over to the Acharya. This is the probable reason why the two ceremonies came to be performed simultaneously.

Be that as it may, Upanayana means the teaching of the Veda by the Vedic Brahmin.

Chapter 8

THE LIBERATION

So much for the Brahminic view of the origin of the Shudra. Turning to the Brahminic view of the civil status of the Shudra, what strikes one is the long list of disabilities, accompanied by a most dire system of pains and penalties to which, the Shudra is subjected by the Brahminic law-givers.

The disabilities and penalties of the Shudra found in the Samhitas and the Brahmanas were few, as may be seen from the following extracts:

I. According to the Kathaka Samhita (xxxi.2) and the Maitrayani Samhita (iv.l.3;i.8.3)
    'A shudra should not be allowed to milk the cow whose milk is used for Agnihotra.'
II. The Satapatlia Brahmana (iii.1.1.10), the Maitrayani Samhita (vii.1.1.6) and also the Panchavimsa Brahmana (vi.1.11) say:
    'The Shudra must not be spoken to when performing a sacrifice and a Shudra must not be present when a sacrifice is being performed.'
III. The Satapatlia Brahmana (xiv.1.31) and the Katliaka Samhita (xi. lO) further provide that:
    'The Shudra must not be admitted to Soma drink.'
IV. The Aitareya Braivmana (vii.29.4) and the Pandiavimsa Bralimana (vi.1.11) reached the culminating point when they say:
    'Shudra is a servant of another (and cannot be anything else).'

But what in the beginning was a cloud no bigger than a man's hand, seems to have developed into a storm, which has literally overwhelmed the Shudras. For, as will be seen from the extracts given from later penal legislation by the Sutrakaras like Apastamba, Baudhayana, etc. and the Smritikaras like Manu and others, the growth of the disabilities of the Shudras has been at a maddening speed and to an extent which is quite unthinkable.

The disabilities are so deadening that it would be impossible to believe them unless one sees them in cold print. They are, however, so numerous that it is impossible to present them in their fullness. To enable those, who do not know them, to have some idea of these disabilities, I have assembled below in one place illustrative statements by the different Sutrakaras and Smritikaras relating to the disabilities of the Shudras scattered in their law Books.

◆

Such were the laws made against the Shudras by the Brahminic law-givers. The gist of them may be summarized under the following heads:

(1) That the Shudra was to take the last place in the social order.
(2) That the Shudra was impure and, therefore, no sacred act should be done within his sight and within his hearing.
(3) That the Shudra is not to be respected in the same way as the other classes.
(4) That the life of a Shudra is of no value and anybody may kill him without having to pay compensation and if at all of small value as compared with that of the Brahmin, Kshatriya and Vaishya.
(5) That the Shudra must not acquire knowledge and it is a sin and a crime to give him education.
(6) That a Shudra must not acquire property. A Brahmin can take his property at his pleasure.
(7) That a Shudra cannot hold office under the State.
(8) That the duty and salvation of the Shudra lies in his serving the higher classes.
(9) That the higher classes must not inter-marry with the Shudra. They can, however, keep a Shudra woman as a concubine. But if the Shudra touches a woman of the higher classes, he will be liable to dire punishment.
(10) That the Shudra is born in servility and must be kept in servility forever.

Anyone who reads this summary will be struck by two considerations.

He will be struck by the consideration that Shudra alone has been selected by the Brahminic law-givers as a victim for their law-making authority. The wonder must be all the greater when it is recalled that in the ancient Brahminic literature the oppressed class in the ancient Indo–Aryan society was the Vaishya and not the Shudra. In this connection a reference may be made to the Aitareya Brahmana. The Aitareya Brahmana in telling the story of King Vishvantara and the Shyaparna Brahmins refers to the sacrificial drink to which the different classes are entitled. In the course of the story, it speaks of the Vaishya in the following terms:

> 'Next, if (the priest brings) curds, that is the Vaishya's draught, with it thou shall satisfy the Vaishyas. One like a Vaishya shall be born in thy line, one who is tributary to another, who is to be used (lit. eaten) by another, and who may be oppressed at will.'

The question is: Why was the Vaishya let off and why the fury directed towards the Shudras?

He will also be struck by the close connection of the disabilities of the Shudra with the privileges of the Brahmin. The Shudra is below the Traivarnikas and is contrasted with the Traivarnikas. That being so, one would expect all the Traivarnikas to have the same rights against the Shudras. But what are the facts? The facts are that the Kshatriyas and Vaishyas have no rights worth speaking of against the Shudras. The only Traivarnika who has special rights and privileges is the Brahmin. For instance, if the Shudra is guilty of an offence against the Brahmin, the Brahmin has the privilege of demanding a higher punishment than what a Kshatriya or a Vaishya could. A Brahmin could take the property of the Shudra without being guilty of an offence if he needed it for the purpose of performing a sacrifice. A Shudra should not accumulate property because he thereby hurts the Brahmin. A Brahmin should not live in a country where the king is a Shudra. Why is this so? Had the Brahmin any cause to regard the Shudra as his special enemy?

There is one other consideration more important than these. It is, what does the average Brahmin think of these disabilities of the Shudras? That they are extraordinary in their conception and shameful in their nature will be admitted by all. Will the Brahmin admit it? It would not be unnatural if this catalogue of disabilities may not make any impression upon him. In the first place, by long habit and usage, his moral sense has become so dulled that he has ceased to bother about the how and why of these disabilities of the Shudras. In the second place, those of them who are conscious of them feel that similar disabilities have been imposed on particular classes in other countries and there is, therefore, nothing extraordinary nor shameful in the disabilities of the Shudras. It is the second attitude that needs to be exposed.

This attitude is a very facile one and is cherished because it helps to save reputation and slave conscience. It is, however, no use leaving things as they are. It is absolutely essential to show that these disabilities have no parallel anywhere in the world. It is impossible to compare the Brahminic law with every other legal system on the point of rights and disabilities. A comparison of the Brahminic law with the Roman law ought to suffice.

It will be well to begin this comparison by noting the classes which under the Roman law had rights and those which suffered from disabilities. The Roman jurists divided men into five categories: (1) Patricians and Plebians; (2) Freemen and Slaves; (3) Citizens and Foreigners; (4) Persons who were sui juris and persons who were alieni juris; and (5) Chirstians and Pagans.

Under the Roman law, persons who were privileged were: (1) Patricians; (2) Freemen; (3) Citizens; (4) Sui juris; and (5) Christians. As compared to these, persons who suffered disabilities under the Roman law were: (1) the Plebians; (2) Slaves; (3) Foreigners; (4) Persons who were alieni juris; and (5) Pagans.

A Freeman, who was a citizen under the Roman law, possessed civil rights as well as political rights. The civil rights of a citizen comprised rights of *connubium* and *commercium*. In virtue of the connubium, the citizen could contract a valid marriage according to the jus civile, and acquire the rights resulting from it, and particularly the paternal power and the civil relationship called agnation, which was absolutely necessary to enable him in law to succeed to the property of persons who died intestate. In virtue of the commercium he could acquire and dispose of property of all kinds, according to the forms and with the peculiar privileges of the Roman law. The political rights of the Roman citizen included jus suffragii and jus honorum, the right to vote in public elections and the right to hold office.

The slave differed from the Freeman in as much as he was owned by the master and as such had no capacity to acquire rights.

Foreigners, who were called Peregrine, were not citizens and had none of the political or civil rights which went with citizenship. A foreigner could obtain no protection unless he was under the protection of a citizen.

The alieni juris differed from sui juris inasmuch as the former were subject to the authority of another person, while the latter were free from it. This authority was variously called (1)Potestas, (2)Manus and (3) Mancipium, though they had the same effect. Potestas under the Roman law fell into two classes. Persons subject to Potestas were (1)slaves, (2)children, (3)wife in Manus, (4)debtor assigned to the creditor by the court, and (5)a hired gladiator. Potestas gave to one in whom it was vested rights to exclusive possession of those to whom it extended and to vindicate any wrong done to them by anyone else.

The correlative disabilities which persons alieni juris suffered as a result of being subject to Potestas were: (1)they were not free, (2)they could not acquire property, and (3)they could not directly vindicate any wrong or injury done to them.

The disabilities of the Pagans began with the advent of Christianity. Originally, when all the Romans followed the same Pagan worship, religion could occasion no difference in the enjoyment of civil rights. Under the Christian Emperors, heretics and apostates as well as Pagans and Jews were subjected to vexatious restrictions, particularly as regards their capacity to succeed to property and to act as witnesses. Only orthodox Christians who recognized the decisions of the four oecumenical councils had the full enjoyment of civil rights.

This survey of rights and disabilities of the Roman law may well give comfort to Hindus that the Brahminic law was not the only law which was guilty of putting certain classes under disabilities, although the disabilities imposed by the Roman law have nothing of the cruelty which characterises the disabilities imposed by the Brahminic law. But when one compares the principles of the Roman law with those of the Brahminic law underlying these disabilities, the baseness of the Brahminic law becomes apparent.

Let us first ask: What was the basis of rights and disabilities under the Roman law? Even a superficial student of Roman law knows that they were based upon (1)*Caput* and (2)*Existimatio.*

Caput meant the civil status of a person. Civil status among the Romans had reference chiefly to three things: liberty, citizenship and family. The status libertatis consisted of being a freeman and not a slave. If a freeman was also a Roman citizen, he enjoyed the status civitatis. Upon this quality depended not only the enjoyment of political rights, but the capacity of participating in the jus civile. Finally, the status familice consisted in a citizen belonging to a particular family, and being capable of enjoying certain rights in which the members of that family, in their quality of agnates, could alone take part.

If an existing status came to be lost or changed, the person suffered what was called a capitis diminutio, which extinguished either entirely or to some extent his former legal capacity. There were three changes of state or condition attended with different consequences, called maxima, media and minima. The greatest involves the loss of liberty, citizenship, and family; and this happened when a Roman citizen was taken prisoner in war, or condemned to slavery for his crimes. But a citizen who was captured by the enemy, on returning from captivity, was restored to all his civil rights jure postliminii.

The next change of status consisted of the loss of citizenship and family rights, without any forfeiture of personal liberty; and this occurred when a citizen became a member of another state. He was then forbidden the use of fire and water, so as to be forced to quit the Roman territory, or was sentenced to deportation under the empire.

Finally, when a person ceased to belong to a particular family, without losing his liberty or citizenship, he was said to suffer the least change of state, as for instance, where one sui juris came under the power of another by arrogation, or a son who had been under the patria potestas was legally emancipated by his father.

Citizenship was acquired first by birth. In a lawful marriage, the child followed the condition of the father, and became a citizen, if the father was so at the time of conception. If the child was not the issue of justoe nuptioe, it followed the condition of the mother at the time of its birth. Secondly, by manumission, according to the formalities prescribed by law, the slave of a Roman citizen became a citizen. This rule was modified by the laws Elia Sentia and Junia Norbana, according to which, in certain cases, the freedman acquired only the status of a foreigner, peregrinus dedititius or of a Latin, Latinus Junianus, Justinian restored the ancient principle, according to which every slave, regularly enfranchised, became in full right a Roman citizen. Thirdly, the right of citizenship was often granted as a favour, either to a whole community or to an individual, by the people or the senate during the republic, and by the reigning prince during the empire; and this was equivalent to what the moderns call naturalization.

Citizenship was lost—firstly, by the loss of liberty—as, for instance, when a Roman became a prisoner of war; secondly, by renouncing the character of Roman citizen, which took place when anyone was admitted a citizen of another state; thirdly, by a sentence of deportation or exile, as a punishment for crime.

The civil status of a person under the Roman law may or may not be civis optimo jure. Civis optimo jure included not only capacity for civil rights but also capacity for political rights such as jus suffragii et honorum, i.e., the right to vote and the capacity to hold a public office. Capacity for political rights depended upon existimatio. Existimatio means reputation in the eye of the law. A Roman citizen may have caput as well as existimatio. On the other hand, a Roman may have caput but may not have existimatio. Whoever had caput as well as existimatio had civil rights as well as political rights. Whoever had caput but had no existimatio could claim civil rights only. He could not claim political rights.

A parson's existimatio was lost in two ways. It was lost by loss of freedom or by conviction for an offence. If a person lost his freedom, his existimatio was completely extinguished. Loss of existimatio by conviction for offence varied according to the gravity of the offence. If the offence was serious, the diminution of his existimatio was called infamia. If the offence was less grave, it was called turpitudo. Infamia resulted in the extinguishment of existimatio. Under the Roman law, a defendant, in addition to ordinary damages, was subjected to infamia. Condemnation for theft, robbery, injuria or fraud entailed infamy. So a partner, a mandatarius, a depositarius, tutor, a mortgagee (in contractus fiducioe) if condemned for wilful breach of duty, was held to be infamous.

The consequence of infamia was exclusion from political rights, not merely from office (honours), but even from the right to vote in elections (suffragium).

From this brief survey of the basis of rights and disabilities in Roman law, it will be clear that the basis was the same for all. They did not differ from community to community. Rights and disabilities according to Roman law were regulated by general considerations, such as caput and existimatio. Whoever had caput and existimatio had rights. Whoever lost his caput and his existimatio suffered disabilities. What is the position under the Brahminic law? There again, it is quite clear that rights and disabilities were not based on general uniform considerations. They were based on communal considerations. All rights for the first three varnas and all disabilities for the Shudras was the principle on which the Brahminic law was based.

The protagonists of Brahminic laws may urge that this comparison is too favourable to Roman law and that the statement that Roman law did not distribute rights and liabilities on communal basis is not true. This may be conceded. For so far as the relation between the Patricians and Plebians was concerned, the distribution of rights and liabilities was communal. But in this connection, the following facts must be noted.

In the first place, it must be noted that Plebians were not slaves. They were Freemen inasmuch as they enjoyed jus commercii or the right to acquire, hold and transfer property. Their disabilities consisted in the denial of political and social rights. In the second place, it must be noted that their disabilities were not permanent. There were two social disabilities from which they suffered. One arose from the interdict on inter-marriage between them and the Patricians imposed by the Twelve Tables. This disability was removed in 445 BC by the passing of the Canulenian law which legalized inter-marriage between

Particians and Plebians. The other disability was their ineligibility to hold the office of Pontiffs and Augurs in the Public Temples of Rome. This disability was removed by the Ogulnian law passed in 300 BC.

As to the political disabilities of the Plebians, they had secured the right to vote in popular assemblies (jus suffragii) under the Constitution of Servius Tullius the Sixth King of Rome. The political disabilities which had remained unredressed were those which related to the holding of office. This too was removed in course of time after the Republic was established in 509 BC. The first step taken in this direction was the appointment of Plebian Tribunes in 494 BC; the Questorship was opened to them, formally in 421 BC; actually in 409 BC; the Consulship in 367 BC; the curuleaedileship in 366 BC; the dictatorship in 356 BC; the Censorship in 351 BC; and the Praetorshipin 336 BC. The Hortensian law enacted in 287 BC marked a complete triumph for the Plebians. By that law the resolutions of the assembly of the tribes were to be directly and without modification, control or delay, binding upon the whole of the Roman people.

This marks a complete political fusion of Patricians and Plebians on terms of equality.

Not only were the Plebians placed on the same footing as to political capacity and social status with the Patricians but the road to nobility was also thrown open to them. In Roman society, birth and fortune were the two great sources of rank and personal distinction. But in addition to this, the office of Curule Magistracy was also a source of ennoblement to the holder thereof. Every citizen, whether Patrician or Plebian, who won his way to a Curule Magistracy, from that Aedile upwards, acquired personal distinction, which was transmitted to his descendants, who formed a class called Nobiles, or men known, to distinguish them from the ignobiles, or people who were not known. As the office was thrown open to the Plebians, many Plebians had become nobles and had even surpassed the Patricians in point of nobility.

It may be that the Roman law did recognize communal distinction in distributing rights and disabilities. The point is that the disabilities of the Plebians were not regarded as permanent. Although they existed, they were in course of time removed. That being so, the protagonists of Brahminic law cannot merely take solace in having found a parallel in the Roman law but have to answer why the Brahminic law did not abolish the distinction between the Traivarnikas and the Shudras as the Roman law did by equating the Plebians with the Patricians? One can, therefore, contend that the Roman law of rights and disabilities was not communal while the Brahminic law was.

This is not the only difference between the Roman law and the Brahminic law. There are two others. One is equality before law in criminal matters. The Roman law may not have recognized equality in matters of civil and political rights. But in matters of criminal law, it made no distinction between one citizen and another, not even between Patrician and Plebian. The same offence the same punishment, no matter who the complainant and who the accused was. Once an offence was proved, the punishment was the same. What do the Dharma Sutras and the Smritis do? They follow an entirely different principle. For the same offence, the punishment varies according to the community of the accused and the community of the complainant. If the complainant is a Shudra and the accused belonged to any one of the three classes, the punishment is less than what it would be if the relations were reversed. On the other hand, if the complainant was Traivarnika and the accused a Shudra, the punishment is far heavier than in the first case. This is another barbarity which distinguishes the Brahminic law from the Roman law.

The next feature of the Roman law which distinguishes it from the Brahminic law is most noteworthy. It relates to the extinction of disabilities. Two points need be borne in mind. First is that the disabilities under the Roman law were only contingent. So long as certain conditions lasted, they gave rise to certain disabilities. The moment the conditions changed, the disabilities vanished and a step in the direction of equality before law was taken. The second point is that the Roman law never attempted to fix the conditions forever and thereby perpetuate the disabilities. On the other hand, it was always ready to remove the conditions to which these disabilities were attached as is evident in the case of the Plebians, the Slaves, the Foreigners and the Pagans.

If these two points about the disabilities under the Roman law are borne in mind, one can at once see what michief the Dharma Sutras and the Smritis have done in imposing the disabilities upon the Shudras. The imposition of disabilities would not have been so atrocious if the disabilities were dependent upon conditions and if the disabled had the freedom to outgrow those conditions. But what the Brahminic law does is not merely to impose disabilities but it tries to fix the conditions by making, an act which amounts to a breach of those conditions to be a crime involving dire punishment. Thus, the Brahminic law not only seeks to impose disabilities but it endeavours to make them permanent. One illustration will suffice. A Shudra is not entitled to perform Vedic sacrifices as he is not able to repeat the Vedic Mantras. Nobody would quarrel with such a disability. But the Dharma Sutras do not stop here. They go further and say that it will be a crime for a Shudra to study the Vedas or hear it being pronounced and if he does commit such a crime his tongue should be cut or molten lead should be poured into his ear. Can anything be more barbarous than preventing a man to grow out of his disability? What is the explanation of these disabilities? Why did the Brahminic law-givers take such a cruel attitude towards the Shudras? The Brahminic law books merely state the disabilities. They say that the Shudras have no right to Upanayana. They say that the Shudras shall hold no office. They say that the Shudras shall not have property. But they do not say why. The whole thing is arbitrary. The disabilities of the Shudra have no relation to his personal conduct. It is not the result of infamy. The Shudra is punished just because he was a Shudra. This is a mystery which requires to be solved. As the Brahminic law books do not help us to solve it, it is necessary to look for explanation elsewhere.

To me this Chaturvarnya with its old labels is utterly repellent, and my whole being rebels against it. But I do not wish to rest my objection to Chaturvarnya on mere grounds of sentiments. There are more solid grounds on which I rely for my opposition to it. A close examination of this ideal has convinced me that as a system of social organization, Chaturvarnya is impracticable, is harmful, and has turned out to be a miserable failure.[98] From a practical point of view, the system of Chaturvarnya raises several difficulties which its protagonists [advocates] do not seem to have taken into account. The principle underlying caste is fundamentally different from the principle underlying Chaturvarnya.[99] Not only are they fundamentally different, but they are also fundamentally opposed.

The former [Chaturvarnya] is based on worth. How are you going to compel people who have acquired a higher status based on birth, without reference to their worth, to vacate that status? How are you going to compel people to recognize the status due to a man, in accordance with his worth, who is occupying a lower status based on his birth? For this, you must first break up the caste system, in order to be able to establish the Chaturvarnya system. How are you going to reduce the four thousand castes, based on birth, to the four varnas, based on worth? This is the first difficulty which the protagonists of the Chaturvarnya must grapple with.

There is a second difficulty which the protagonists of Chaturvarnya must grapple with, if they wish to make the establishment of Chaturvarnya a success.[100] Chaturvarnya pre-supposes that you can classify people into four definite classes. Is this possible?[101] In this respect, the ideal of Chaturvarnya has, as you will see, a close affinity to the Platonic ideal. To Plato, men fell by nature into three classes. In some individuals, he believed,[102] mere appetites dominated. He assigned them to the labouring and trading classes. Others revealed to him that over and above appetites, they had a courageous disposition. He classed them as defenders in war and guardians of internal peace.

---

[98]The lines at the beginning of 16.1 till '…a miserable failure' figure under Section XV of AoC 1936. The lines that follow from here (beginning, 'From a practical…') till the first sentence of 16.3 (ending, '…chaturvarnya a success.') have been added in the 1937 edition.

[99]This is given as 'varna' in AoC 1936 and 1937; Ambedkar changes it to 'chaturvarnya' in 1944.

[100]In AoC 1936, Section 16 begins here, with the sentence: 'The practicability of the chaturvarnya presupposes two things. It presupposes…'

[101]This question does not appear in AoC 1936.

[102]Phrase added in 1937.

Others showed a capacity to grasp the universal reason underlying things. He made them the law-givers of the people.

The criticism to which Plato's Republic is subject, is also the criticism which must apply to the system of Chaturvarnya, insofar as it proceeds upon the possibility of an accurate classification of men into four distinct classes.[103] The chief criticism against Plato is that his idea of lumping individuals into a few sharply-marked-off classes is a very superficial view of man and his powers. Plato had no perception of the uniqueness of every individual, of his incommensurability with others, of each individual as forming a class of his own. He had no recognition of the infinite diversity of active tendencies, and the combination of tendencies of which an individual is capable. To him, there were types of faculties or powers in the individual constitution.

All this is demonstrably wrong. Modem science has shown that the lumping together of individuals into a few sharply marked-off classes is a superficial view of man, not worthy of serious consideration. Consequently, the utilization of the qualities of individuals is

---

[103]Plato's *The Republic*, addressing the question of justice, deduces that the human soul has three parts: the 'logical', thinking part; the 'spirited' part, by which we develop anger and get into a temper; and the 'appetitive' part, by which we experience hunger, thirst, eroticism, love for moneymaking and other such desires. The book also categorizes men into three classes based on which part of their soul masks the others: the 'guardians' are persons in whom the logical part dominates, in the 'auxiliaries' spirit dominates, and the 'producers' are people who have let their appetite dominate. The guardians must rule, the auxiliaries must help in running the guardians' writ, and the producers must work. (See also: Note 161 on the guna-karma theory.) Ambedkar disagrees with Plato on many levels. He is not convinced that there are only three qualities on the basis of which a soul can be divided. He believes that the multitude of human characteristics is so complex that it is impossible to identify and categorize them. He also points out that different characteristics become more or less important in the same person at different times. His criticism is also what was later popularized as the problem of the 'one-dimensional man' by Herbert Marcuse (1964/1991). From his experience of caste, Ambedkar's critique is that in such an arrangement where most of the power is vested with the guardians and the remaining with the auxiliaries (the 'twice-born' Brahmins, Kshatriyas and Vaishyas in the caste context), there is no mechanism to ensure that they will not oppress the producers (Shudras and Untouchables).

incompatible with their stratification by classes, since the qualities of individuals are so variable. Chaturvarnya must fail for the very reason for which Plato's Republic must fail—namely, that it is not possible to pigeonhole men, according as they belong to one class[104] or the other. That it is impossible to accurately classify people into four definite classes, is proved by the fact that the original four classes have now become four thousand castes.

There is a third difficulty in the way of the establishment of the system of Chaturvarnya. How are you going to maintain the system of Chaturvarnya, supposing it was established? One[105] important requirement for the successful working of Chaturvarnya is the maintenance[106] of the penal system which could maintain it by its sanction. The system of Chaturvarnya must perpetually face the problem of the transgressor. Unless there is a penalty attached to the act of transgression, men will not keep to their respective classes. The whole system will break down, being contrary to human nature. Chaturvarnya cannot subsist by its own inherent goodness. It must be enforced by law.

That without penal sanction the ideal of Chaturvarnya cannot be realized, is proved by the story in the Ramayana of Rama killing Shambuka.[107] Some people seem to blame Rama because he wantonly

---

[104]In AoC 1936, this merely reads as 'not possible to pigeon men into holes'. In 1937, Ambedkar amends this to 'not possible to pigeon men into holes according as he belongs to one class or the other'. The subsequent lines, beginning 'That it is impossible...' till '... it was established?' in 16.6 are absent in AoC 1936.

[105]This sentence begins with 'Another' in AoC 1936; perhaps changed in the light of new sentences added in 1937.

[106]The word used is 'existence' in AoC 1936.

[107]The story of Shambuka is told in the seventh book, Uttarakanda, of the Valmiki Ramayana. Shambuka wants to achieve a higher status than the suras (devtas, gods) through meditation and austerities. On discovering that Shambuka, a Shudra, was indeed meditating, Rama promptly beheads him to restore varnasharma dharma. The story has been used by the Dravidian movement and in anticaste literature to ridicule the idea of Rama as the embodiment of perfection. Kuvempu (Kuppalli Venkatappa Puttappa) (1904–94), a Jnanpith-winning Kannada author wrote Sudra Tapasvi (1944), a novel based on Shambuka's life. Sikhamani, a contemporary Telugu Dalit poet, writes: 'The sword that severed/ Shambuka's head could remain/

and without reason killed Shambuka. But to blame Rama for killing Shambuka is to misunderstand the whole situation. Ram Raj was a Raj based on Chaturvarnya. As a king, Rama was bound to maintain Chaturvarnya. It was his duty therefore to kill Shambuka, the Shudra who had transgressed his class and wanted to be a Brahmin. This is the reason why Rama killed Shambuka. But this also shows that penal sanction is necessary for the maintenance of Chaturvarnya. Not only penal sanction is necessary, but the penalty of death is necessary. That is why Rama did not inflict on Shambuka a lesser punishment. That is why the Manusmriti[108] prescribes such heavy sentences as cutting

---

sharp and safe for centuries./ It has just changed hands/ and no longer recognises you./ No Manu to save you now!' See 'Steel Nibs are Sprouting...' in Satyanarayana and Tharu (2013, 554).

[108]The Manusmriti represents itself as the dharma that Brahma declares to Manu, 'the first Man', and is passed on by him to Bhrigu, one of the ten 'great sages'. The text is believed to have attained its present form around the second century CE. Ambedkar writes in another, posthumously published work, Revolution and Counter-Revolution in Ancient India (BAWS 5, 273): 'Pushyamitra Sunga and his successors could not have tolerated these exaggerated claims of the Brahmins unless they themselves were Brahmins interested in the establishment of Brahmanism. Indeed it is quite possible that the Manusmriti was composed at the command of Pushyamitra Brahman king (185–149 BC) himself, and forms the book of the philosophy of Brahmanism.' In another work, The Untouchables: Who Were They and Why they Became Untouchable, Ambedkar (BAWS 9, 373) says: 'After taking all facts into consideration Prof Buhler has fixed a date which appears to strike the truth. According to Buhler, the Manusmriti, in the shape in which it exists now, came into existence in the Second Century AD.' A contemporary scholar, J.L. Brockington (1996, 92) arrives at a similar conclusion. Many editions of the Manusmriti have been published in Sanskrit since its first edition in 1813. The first translation was Institutes of Hindu law, or, The ordinances of Menu [sic], according to the gloss of Culluca: comprising the Indian system of duties, religious and civil: verbally translated from the original Sanscrit: with a preface, by Sir William Jones (1796). One of the best-known translations is George Buhler's Laws of Manu (1886/2004), which contains an exhaustive introduction and extracts from seven commentaries. In her modern translation, Wendy Doniger states that no work in the tradition of Western scholarship compares with the fame and sustained authority exercised across centuries by the Manusmriti. See Doniger and Smith (1991, xviii–xix). As C.J. Fuller (2003, 484) notes, British administrators depended on Dharmashastras such as the Manusmriti to develop a legal system

off the tongue, or pouring of molten lead in the ears, of the Shudra who recites or hears the Veda.[109] The supporters of Chaturvarnya must give an assurance that they could successfully classify men, and that they could induce modern society in the twentieth century to re-forge the penal sanctions of the Manusmriti.

The protagonists of Chaturvarnya do not seem to have considered what is to happen to women in their system. Are they also to be divided into four classes, Brahmin, Kshatriya, Vaishya and Shudra? Or are they to be allowed to take the status of their husbands? If the status of the woman is to be the consequence of marriage, what becomes of the underlying principle of Chaturvarnya—namely, that the status of a person should be based upon the worth of that person? If they are to be classified according to their worth, is their classification to be nominal or real?

If it is to be nominal, then it is useless; and then the protagonists of Chaturvarnya must admit that their system does not apply to women. If it is real, are the protagonists of Chaturvarnya prepared to follow the logical consequences of applying it to women? They must be

---

for India, thus subjecting the Hindu population as a whole to a Brahminical legal code. For the most authoritative, exhaustively annotated edition (1,131 pages) of the Manusmriti, see Patrick Olivelle (2005).

[109]Such verses do not figure in the Manusmriti. Buhler's edition, which Ambedkar may have possibly accessed, offers two verses that come close to the import. 'A once-born man (a Shudra), who insults a twice-born man with gross invective, shall have his tongue cut out; for he is of low origin' (8.270; 1886/2004, 211). And: 'If he arrogantly teaches Brahmins their duty, the king shall cause hot oil to be poured into his mouth and into his ears' (8.272; 2004, 211). For Ambedkar's extended discussion of the Manusmriti, see the annotated edition of 'Castes in India' in Rege (2013, 77–108). Ambedkar seems to be citing these punishments from chapter 12 of Gautama Dharma Sutra (600 BCE to 300 BCE, predating the Manusmriti) which he also cites in his posthumous work, Philosophy of Hinduism (BAWS 3). Buhler's translation (1898, 239) of Gautama Dharma Sutra talks of similar punishments for the Shudra: '4. Now if a Shudra listens intentionally to (a recitation of) the Veda, his ears shall be filled with (molten) tin or lac. 5. If he recites (Vedic texts), his tongue shall be cut out. 6. If he remembers them, his body shall be split in twain. 7. If he assumes a position equal (to that of twice-born men) in sitting, in lying down, in conversation or on the road, he shall undergo (corporal) punishment.'

prepared to have women priests and women soldiers. Hindu society has grown accustomed to women teachers and women barristers. It may grow accustomed to women brewers and women butchers. But he would be a bold person who would say that it will allow women priests and women soldiers. But that will be the logical outcome of applying Chaturvarnya to women. Given these difficulties, I think no one except a congenital idiot could hope for and believe in a successful regeneration of the Chaturvarnya.

There is no doubt, in my opinion, that unless you change your social order you can achieve little by way of progress. You cannot mobilize the community either for defence or for offence. You cannot build anything on the foundations of caste. You cannot build up a nation, you cannot build up a morality. Anything that you will build on the foundations of caste will crack, and will never be a whole.

The only question that remains to be considered is—*How to bring about the reform of the Hindu social order? How to abolish caste?*[110] This is a question of supreme importance. There is a view that in the reform of caste, the first step to take is to abolish sub-castes. This view is based upon the supposition that there is a greater similarity in manners and status between sub-castes than there is between castes. I think this is an erroneous supposition. The Brahmins of Northern and Central India are socially of lower grade, as compared with the Brahmins of the Deccan and Southern India. The former are only cooks and water-carriers, while the latter occupy a high social position. On the other hand, in Northern India, the Vaishyas and Kayasthas are intellectually and socially on a par with the Brahmins of the Deccan and Southern India.

Again, in the matter of food there is no similarity between the Brahmins of the Deccan and Southern India, who are vegetarians, and the Brahmins of Kashmir and Bengal, who are non-vegetarians. On the other hand, the Brahmins of the Deccan and Southern India have more in common so far as food is concerned with such non-Brahmins as the Gujaratis, Marwaris, Banias, and Jains.

There is no doubt that from the standpoint of making the

---

[110]These questions are given in bold in AoC 1936.

transition[111] from one caste to another easy, the fusion of the Kayasthas of Northern India and the other Non-Brahmins of Southern India with the Non-Brahmins of the Deccan and the Dravidian[112] country is more practicable than the fusion of the Brahmins of the South with the Brahmins of the North. But assuming that the fusion of sub-castes is possible, what guarantee is there that the abolition of subcastes will necessarily lead to the abolition of castes? On the contrary, it may happen that the process may stop with the abolition of sub-castes. In that case, the abolition of sub-castes will only help to strengthen the castes, and make them more powerful and therefore more mischievous. This remedy is therefore neither practicable nor effective, and may easily prove to be a wrong remedy.

Another plan of action for the abolition of caste is to begin with inter-caste dinners. This also, in my opinion, is an inadequate remedy. There are many castes which allow inter-dining. But it is a common experience that inter-dining has not succeeded in killing the spirit of caste and the consciousness of caste. I am convinced that the real remedy is inter-marriage. Fusion of blood can alone create the feeling of being kith and kin, and unless this feeling of kinship, of being marriage. Fusion of blood can alone create the feeling of being kith and kin, and unless this feeling of kinship, of being kindred, becomes paramount, the separatist feeling—the feeling of being aliens—created by caste will not vanish. Among the Hindus, inter-marriage must necessarily be a factor of greater force in social life than it need be in the life of the non-Hindus. Where society is already well-knit by other ties, marriage is an ordinary incident of life. But where society is cut asunder, marriage as a binding force becomes a matter of urgent necessity. *The real remedy for breaking caste is inter-marriage. Nothing else will serve as the solvent of caste.*

Your Jat-Pat-Todak Mandal has adopted this line of attack. It is a direct and frontal attack, and I congratulate you upon a correct diagnosis, and more upon your having shown the courage to tell the Hindus what is really wrong with them. Political tyranny is nothing

---

[111]'Transit' in AoC 1936 and subsequent editions.
[112]'Dravid' in all previous editions.

compared to social tyranny, and a reformer who defies society is a much more courageous man than a politician who defies the government. You are right in holding that caste will cease to be an operative force only when inter-dining and inter-marriage have become matters of common course. You have located the source of the disease.

But is your prescription the right prescription for the disease? Ask yourselves this question: why is it that a large majority of Hindus do not inter-dine and do not inter-marry? Why is it that your cause is not popular?

There can be only one answer to this question, and it is that inter-dining and inter-marriage are repugnant to the beliefs and dogmas which the Hindus regard as sacred. Caste is not a physical object like a wall of bricks or a line of barbed wire which prevents the Hindus from commingling and which has, therefore, to be pulled down. Caste is a notion, it is a state of the mind. The destruction of caste does not therefore mean the destruction of a physical barrier. It means a *notional* change.

Caste may be bad. Caste may lead to conduct so gross as to be called man's inhumanity to man. All the same, it must be recognized that the Hindus observe caste not because they are inhuman or wrong-headed. They observe caste because they are deeply religious. People are not wrong in observing caste. In my view, what is wrong is their religion, which has inculcated this notion of caste. If this is correct, then obviously the enemy you must grapple with is not the people who observe caste, but the Shastras which teach them this religion of caste. Criticizing and ridiculing people for not inter-dining or inter-marrying, or occasionally holding inter-caste dinners and celebrating inter-caste marriages, is a futile method of achieving the desired end. The real remedy is to destroy the belief in the sanctity of the Shastras.

How do you expect to succeed, if you allow the Shastras to continue to mould the beliefs and opinions of the people? Not to question the authority of the Shastras—to permit the people to believe in their sanctity and their sanctions, and then to blame the people and to criticize them for their acts as being irrational and inhuman—is an incongruous way of carrying on social reform. Reformers working for the removal of Untouchability, including Mahatma Gandhi, do not seem to realize that the acts of the people are merely the results of their beliefs inculcated in their minds by the Shastras, and that people will not change their conduct until they cease to believe in the sanctity of the Shastras on which their conduct is founded.

No wonder that such efforts have not produced any results. You also seem to be erring in the same way as the reformers working in the cause of removing Untouchability. To agitate for and to organise inter-caste dinners and inter-caste marriages is like forced feeding brought about by artificial means. Make every man and woman free from the thraldom of the Shastras, cleanse their minds of the pernicious notions founded on the Shastras, and he or she will inter-dine and inter-marry, without your telling him or her to do so.

Chapter 9

CRITIQUE OF GANDHI

THE MAHATMA SEES great virtue in a Brahmin remaining a Brahmin all his life. Leaving aside the fact that there are many Brahmins who do not like to remain Brahmins all their lives, what can we say about those Brahmins who have clung to their ancestral calling of priesthood? Do they do so from any faith in the virtue of the principle of ancestral calling, or do they do so from motives of filthy lucre? The Mahatma does not seem to concern himself with such queries. He is satisfied that these are 'real Brahmins who are living on alms freely given to them, and giving freely what they have of spiritual treasures.' This is how a hereditary Brahmin priest appears to the Mahatma—a carrier of spiritual treasures.

But another portrait of the hereditary Brahmin can also be drawn. A Brahmin can be a priest to Vishnu—the god of love. He can be a priest to Shankar—the god of destruction. He can be a priest at Buddha Gaya[113] worshipping Buddha—the greatest teacher of mankind, who

---

[113]Buddha Gaya or Bodh Gaya is the most sacred site in Buddhism, revered as the place where Buddha attained enlightenment. The temple complex has for long been controlled by Brahmin mahants (priests). The Bodhgaya Temple Act, passed two years after India's independence, provides for a chairman and a committee of eight members, four Buddhist and four Hindu, 'to manage and control the temple land and the properties appertaining thereto.' Section 3(3) of the Act provides that 'the District Magistrate of Gaya shall be the ex-officio Chairman of the Committee: provided that the State Government shall nominate a Hindu as Chairman of the Committee for the period during which the district Magistrate of Gaya is non-Hindu.' For the uncanny resemblance this state of affairs has with the Conflict of Orders in ancient Rome, especially with the history of the process of appointment of consuls and tribunes, and the role of the Oracle at Delphi, see Note 27 at 2.20 and Note 36 at 3.5 of AoC. An amendment to allow non-Hindu chairmen in the committee was passed only in August 2013 by the Bihar Assembly.

taught the noblest doctrine of love. He also can be a priest to Kali, the goddess who must have a daily sacrifice of an animal to satisfy her thirst for blood. He will be a priest of the temple of Rama—the Kshatriya god! He will also be a priest of the temple of Parshuram, the god who took on an avatar to destroy the Kshatriyas! He can be a priest to Brahma, the creator of the world. He can be a priest to a pir,[114] whose god Allah will not brook the claim of Brahma to share his spiritual dominion over the world! No one can say that this is a picture which is not true to life.

If this is a true picture, one does not know what to say of this capacity to bear loyalties to gods and goddesses whose attributes are so antagonistic that no honest man can be a devotee to all of them. The Hindus rely upon this extraordinary phenomenon as evidence of the greatest virtue of their religion—namely, its catholicity, its spirit of toleration. As against this facile view, it can be urged that what is toleration and catholicity may be really nothing more creditable than indifference or flaccid latitudinarianism. These two attitudes are hard to distinguish in their outer seeming. But they are so vitally unlike in their real quality that no one who examines them closely can mistake one for the other.

---

[114]A pir, meaning elder or saint, is the spiritual guide to the followers of Sufism, the mystic branch of Islam. Sufis are organized into orders around a master who helps his disciples along the path of surrendering the ego in the worship of god. When Ambedkar says a Brahmin can be a priest to a pir, he is referring to the adaptability of the Brahmin which helps him survive any challenge. Elaborating on this in a sharper way in his critique of the Congress and Gandhi, he says (BAWS 9, 195): 'I am quite aware that there are some protagonists of Hinduism who say that Hinduism is a very adaptable religion, that it can adjust itself to everything and absorb anything. I do not think many people would regard such a capacity in a religion as a virtue to be proud of just as no one would think highly of a child because it has developed the capacity to eat dung, and digest it. But that is another matter. It is quite true that Hinduism can adjust itself. The best example of its adjustability is the literary production called Allahupanishad which the Brahmins of the time of Akbar produced to give a place to his Din-e-llahi within Hinduism and to recognize it as the Seventh system of Hindu philosophy.' For an understanding of Sufism, see the classic work of Annemarie Schimmel (1975) and the more recent work of Tanvir Anjum (2011).

That a man is ready to render homage to many gods and goddesses may be cited as evidence of his tolerant spirit. But can it not also be evidence of an insincerity born of a desire to serve the times? I am sure that this toleration is merely insincerity. If this view is well-founded, one may ask, what spiritual treasure can there be within a person who is ready to be a priest and a devotee to any deity which it serves his purpose to worship and to adore? Not only must such a person be deemed to be bankrupt of all spiritual treasures, but for him to practise so elevating a profession as that of a priest simply because it is ancestral—without faith, without belief, merely as a mechanical process handed down from father to son—is not a conservation of virtue; it is really the prostitution of a noble profession which is no other than the service of religion.

Why does the Mahatma cling to the theory of everyone following his or her ancestral calling? He gives his reasons nowhere. But there must be some reason, although he does not care to avow it. Years ago, writing on 'caste versus Class' in his *Young India*,[115] he argued that the caste system was better than a class system on the ground that caste was the best possible adjustment for social stability. If that be the reason

---

[115] *Young India*, a weekly in English, was founded and published from Bombay since 1915 by Indulal Yagnik, along with Jamnadas Dwarkadas and Shankerlal Banker. Yagnik also brought out Navajivan, a monthly in Gujarati. In 1919, Yagnik requested Gandhi, who had returned from South Africa, to take over as editor of *Young India* and *Navajivan*. Under Gandhi's editorship, *Young India* appeared since 7 May 1919 as a biweekly and from 7 September 1919 as a weekly from Sabarmati Ashram, Ahmedabad (Rajmohan Gandhi, 2007, 211). Gandhi published *Young India* till he founded the Harijan in 1932. Ambedkar here is referring to Gandhi's piece dated 29 December 1920, where he argues why caste is better than class: 'The beauty of the caste system is that it does not base itself upon distinctions of wealth-possessions. Money, as history has proved, is the greatest disruptive force in the world. Even the sacredness of family ties is not safe against the pollution of wealth, says Shankaracharya. Caste is but an extension of the principle of the family. Both are governed by blood and heredity… caste does not connote superiority or inferiority. It simply recognizes different outlooks and corresponding modes of life. But it is no use denying the fact that a sort of hierarchy has been evolved in the caste system, but it cannot be called the creation of the Brahmins.' (CWMG 22, 154–5)

why the Mahatma clings to the theory of everyone following his or her ancestral calling, then he is clinging to a false view of social life.

Everybody wants social stability, and some adjustment must be made in the relationship between individuals and classes in order that stability may be had. But two things, I am sure, nobody wants. One thing nobody wants is a static relationship, something that is unalterable, something that is fixed for all times. Stability is wanted, but not at the cost of change when change is imperative. The second thing nobody wants is mere adjustment. Adjustment is wanted, but not at the sacrifice of social justice.

Can it be said that the adjustment of social relationships on the basis of caste—i.e., on the basis of each to his hereditary calling—avoids these two evils? I am convinced that it does not. Far from being the best possible adjustment, I have no doubt that it is of the worst possible kind, inasmuch as it offends against both the canons of social adjustment—namely, fluidity and equity.

Some might think that the Mahatma has made much progress, inasmuch as he now only believes in varna and does not believe in caste. It is true that there was a time when the Mahatma was a full-blooded and a blue-blooded sanatani Hindu.[116] He believed in the

---

[116]Gandhi on his being a sanatani: 'The friend next asked me for a definition of a sanatani Hindu and said: 'Could a sanatani Hindu Brahmin inter-dine with a Hindu non-Brahmin although the latter may be a non-vegetarian?'' My definition of a sanatani Brahmin is: He who believes in the fundamental principles of Hinduism is a sanatani Hindu. And the fundamental principles of Hinduism are absolute belief in truth (satya) and ahimsa (non-violence).' Reported in *The Hindu*, 23 March 1925, from a speech in Madras at the height of the non-Brahmin Movement in the Madras Presidency. In another speech in Calcutta, around the same time, Gandhi says: 'Let the sanatani Hindus understand from me who claims to be a sanatani Hindu. I do not ask you to inter-dine with anybody; I do not ask you to exchange your daughters with the Untouchables or with anybody, but I do ask you to remove this curse [of Untouchability] so that you may not put him beyond the pale of service.' From *Amrita Bazar Patrika*, 2 May 1925. Anil Nauriya, however, makes the case (2006, 1835) that Gandhi's views on varna changed in the mid-1940s and that he came to denounce varnashrama: 'Gandhi incrementally unfurled a critique of the fourfold varna order, taking the concept of such an order in the end, by the mid-1940s, to vanishing point.' On such

Vedas, the Upanishads, the puranas, and all that goes by the name of Hindu scriptures; and therefore, in avatars and rebirth. He believed in caste and defended it with the vigour of the orthodox.[117]

He condemned the cry for inter-dining, inter-drinking, and inter-marrying, and argued that restraints about inter-dining to a great extent 'helped the cultivation of will-power and the conservation of a certain social virtue.'[118]

It is good that he has repudiated this sanctimonious nonsense and admitted that caste 'is harmful both to spiritual and national growth', and maybe his son's marriage outside his caste has had something to do with this change of view. But has the Mahatma really progressed? What is the nature of the varna for which the Mahatma stands? Is it the Vedic conception as commonly understood and preached by Swami Dayanand Saraswati and his followers, the Arya Samajists? The essence of the Vedic conception of varna is the pursuit of a calling which is appropriate to one's natural aptitude. The essence of the Mahatma's conception of varna is the pursuit of one's ancestral calling, irrespective of natural aptitude.

What is the difference between caste and varna, as understood by the Mahatma? I find none. As defined by the Mahatma varna becomes merely a different name for caste, for the simple reason that

exercises in 'cherry picking', see Roy's introduction to this volume.

[117]David Hardiman writes (2004, 126) that during the South African years, Gandhi 'had appeared to have little time for the caste system. He had been expelled from his own Baniya sub-caste for travelling overseas—considered a 'polluting' act at that time—and had never sought to gain readmission to the caste. In 1909, he condemned the caste system and caste tyranny. On his return to India he adopted a much softer line on the question. He denied that the caste system had harmed India, arguing that it was no more than a form of labour division, similar to occupational divisions all over the world. It was in fact superior to class divisions, 'which were based on wealth primarily'. He also believed that reform could be brought about through caste organizations.'

[118]Ambedkar is once again citing Gandhi from his *Young India* piece of 29 December 1920: 'Inter-dining has never been known to promote brotherhood in any special sense. But the restraints about inter-dining have to a great extent helped the cultivation of will-power and the conservation of certain social virtues' (CWMG 22, 156).

it is the same in essence—namely, pursuit of one's ancestral calling. Far from making progress, the Mahatma has suffered retrogression. By putting this interpretation upon the Vedic conception of varna, he has really made ridiculous what was sublime. While I reject the Vedic varnavyavastha for reasons given in the speech, I must admit that the Vedic theory of varna as interpreted by Swami Dayanand and some others is a sensible and an inoffensive thing. It did not admit birth as a determining factor in fixing the place of an individual in society. It only recognized worth.

The Mahatma's view of varna not only makes nonsense of the Vedic varna, but it makes it an abominable thing. Varna and caste are two very different concepts. Varna is based on the principle of each according to his worth, while caste is based on the principle of each according to his birth. The two are as distinct as chalk is from cheese. In fact, there is an antithesis between the two. If the Mahatma believes, as he does, in everyone following his or her ancestral calling, then most certainly he is advocating the caste system, and in calling it the varna system he is not only guilty of terminological inexactitude, but he is causing confusion worse confounded.

I am sure that all his confusion is due to the fact that the Mahatma has no definite and clear conception as to what is varna and what is caste, and as to the necessity of either for the conservation of Hinduism. He has said—and one hopes that he will not find some mystic reason to change his view—that caste is not the essence of Hinduism. Does he regard varna as the essence of Hinduism? One cannot as yet give any categorical answer.

Readers of his article on 'Dr Ambedkar's Indictment' will answer 'No'. In that article he does not say that the dogma of varna is an essential part of the creed of Hinduism. Far from making varna the essence of Hinduism, he says 'the essence of Hinduism is contained in its enunciation of one and only God as truth and its bold acceptance of ahimsa as the law of the human family.'

But readers of his article in reply to Mr Sant Ram will say 'Yes'. In that article he says 'How can a Muslim remain one if he rejects the Quran, or a Christian remain Christian if he rejects the Bible? If caste and varna are convertible terms, and if varna is an integral part of the shastras which define Hinduism, I do not know how a person who rejects caste, i.e., varna, can call himself a Hindu.' Why this prevarication? Why does the Mahatma hedge? Whom does he want to please? Has the saint failed to sense the truth? Or does the politician stand in the way of the saint?

The real reason why the Mahatma is suffering from this confusion is probably to be traced to two sources. The first is the temperament of the Mahatma. He has in almost everything the simplicity of the child, with the child's capacity for self-deception. Like a child, he can believe in anything he wants to believe in. We must therefore wait till such time as it pleases the Mahatma to abandon his faith in varna, as it has pleased him to abandon his faith in caste.

The second source of confusion is the double role which the Mahatma wants to play—of a Mahatma and a politician. As a Mahatma, he may be trying to spiritualize politics. Whether he has succeeded in it or not, politics have certainly commercialized him. A politician must know that society cannot bear the whole truth, and that he must not speak the whole truth; if he is speaking the whole truth it is bad for his politics. The reason why the Mahatma is always supporting caste and varna is because he is afraid that if he opposed them he would lose his place in politics. Whatever may be the source of this confusion the Mahatma must be told that he is deceiving himself, and also deceiving the people, by preaching caste under the name of varna.

The Mahatma says that the standards I have applied to test Hindus and Hinduism are too severe, and that judged by those standards every known living faith will probably fail. The complaint that my standards are high may be true. But the question is not whether they are high or whether they are low. The question is whether they are the right standards to apply. A people and their religion must be judged by social standards based on social ethics. No other standard would have any meaning, if religion is held to be a necessary good for the well-being of the people.

Now, I maintain that the standards I have applied to test Hindus and Hinduism are the most appropriate standards, and that I know of none that are better. The conclusion that every known religion would fail if tested by my standards may be true. But this fact should not give the Mahatma as the champion of Hindus and Hinduism a ground for comfort, any more than the existence of one madman should give comfort to another madman, or the existence of one criminal should give comfort to another criminal.

I would like to assure the Mahatma that it is not the mere failure of the Hindus and Hinduism which has produced in me the feelings of disgust and contempt with which I am charged. I realize that the world is a very imperfect world, and anyone who wants to live in it must bear with its imperfections.

But while I am prepared to bear with the imperfections and shortcomings of the society in which I may be destined to labour, I feel I should not consent to live in a society which cherishes wrong ideals, or a society which, having right ideals, will not consent to bring its social life into conformity with those ideals. If I am disgusted with Hindus and Hinduism, it is because I am convinced that they cherish wrong ideals and live a wrong social life. My quarrel with Hindus and Hinduism is not over the imperfections of their social conduct. It is much more fundamental. It is over their ideals.

Hindu society seems to me to stand in need of a moral regeneration which it is dangerous to postpone. And the question is, who can determine and control this moral regeneration? Obviously, only those who have undergone an intellectual regeneration and those who are honest enough to have the courage of their convictions born of intellectual emancipation. Judged by this standard, the Hindu leaders who count are, in my opinion, quite unfit for the task. It is impossible to say that they have undergone the preliminary intellectual regeneration. If they had undergone an intellectual regeneration, they would neither delude themselves in the simple way of the untaught multitude, nor would they take advantage of the primitive ignorance of others as one sees them doing.

Notwithstanding the crumbling state of Hindu society, these leaders will nevertheless unblushingly appeal to ideals of the past which have in every way ceased to have any connection with the present—ideals which, however suitable they might have been in the days of their origin, have now become a warning rather than a guide. They still have a mystic respect for the earlier forms which makes them disinclined—nay, opposed—to any examination of the foundations of their society.

The Hindu masses are of course incredibly heedless in the formation of their beliefs. But so are the Hindu leaders. And what is worse is that these Hindu leaders become filled with an illicit passion for their beliefs when anyone proposes to rob them of their companionship.

The Mahatma is no exception. The Mahatma appears not to believe in thinking. He prefers to follow the saints. Like a conservative with his reverence for consecrated notions, he is afraid that if he once starts thinking, many ideals and institutions to which he clings will be doomed. One must sympathize with him. For every act of independent thinking puts some portion of an apparently stable world in peril.

But it is equally true that dependence on saints cannot lead us to know the truth. The saints are after all only human beings, and as Lord Balfour said, 'The human mind is no more a truth-finding apparatus than the snout of a pig.'[119] In so far as he does think, to me he really appears to be prostituting his intelligence to find reasons for supporting this archaic social structure of the Hindus. He is the most influential apologist of it and therefore the worst enemy of the Hindus.

Unlike the Mahatma, there are Hindu leaders who are not content merely to believe and follow. They dare to think, and act in accordance with the result of their thinking. But unfortunately they are either a dishonest lot, or an indifferent lot when it comes to the question of giving right guidance to the mass of the people. Almost every Brahmin has transgressed the rule of caste. The number of Brahmins who sell shoes is far greater than those who practise priesthood. Not only have the Brahmins given up their ancestral calling of priesthood for trading, but they have entered trades which are prohibited to them by the shastras. Yet how many Brahmins who break caste every day will preach against caste and against the shastras?

---

[119]Lord (Arthur James) Balfour was a British conservative politician who served as Prime Minister between 1902 and 1905 and as Foreign Secretary between 1916 and 1919. It is not clear where Lord Balfour spoke these words, but there are other citations of this from the same period, each slightly differing in detail. *The World Review* (1936, 67) cites Balfour thus: 'Lord Balfour has wisely said that "The human brain is as much an organ for seeking food as the pig's snout." After all, the human brain is only an enlarged piece of the spinal column, whose first function is to sense danger and preserve life.'

For one honest Brahmin preaching against caste and shastras because his practical instinct and moral conscience cannot support a conviction in them, there are hundreds who break caste and trample upon the shastras every day, but who are the most fanatic upholders of the theory of caste and the sanctity of the shastras. Why this duplicity? Because they feel that if the masses are emancipated from the yoke of caste, they would be a menace to the power and prestige of the Brahmins as a class. The dishonesty of this intellectual class, who would deny the masses the fruits of their thinking, is a most disgraceful phenomenon.

The Hindus, in the words of Matthew Arnold, are 'wandering between two worlds, one dead, the other powerless to be born.'[120] What are they to do? The Mahatma to whom they appeal for guidance does not believe in thinking, and can therefore give no guidance which can be said to stand the test of experience. The intellectual classes to whom the masses look for guidance are either too dishonest or too indifferent to educate them in the right direction. We are indeed witnesses to a great tragedy. In the face of this tragedy all one can do is to lament and say—such are thy leaders, O Hindus!

◆

---

[120]These lines are from the poem 'Stanzas from the Grande Chartreuse' by Matthew Arnold (1822–88), English poet and literary critic, reflecting the inner conflict of the Victorian era between scientific progress on the one hand, and religion, identity and values on the other. Ambedkar cites Arnold in 'castes in India' (1916) as well, written during his years at Columbia University. It is possible that Ambedkar often turned to Arnold thanks to his mentor Dewey, who was fond of quoting him. According to S. Morris Eames (1969, xxxvii), Dewey's essay 'Poetry and Philosophy' (1890) begins with a long epigraph from Arnold. Eames says: 'Dewey is appreciative of many of the insights of Matthew Arnold, and in later years he turns again and again to ideas he attributed to this poet and critic. Arnold once wrote that 'poetry is a criticism of life', and while Dewey thinks that poetry is more than this, he was influenced by Arnold's view in transferring it into philosophy, for he later writes that philosophy 'is inherently criticism', and in his own method makes philosophy 'a criticism of criticisms'.' This idea is also echoed by the Italian political thinker Antonio Gramsci (1891–1937), a contemporary of Ambedkar: 'The crisis consists precisely in the fact that the old is dying and the new cannot be born; in this interregnum a great variety of morbid symptoms appear' (1971, 276).

What is Gandhism? What does it stand for? What are its teachings about economic problems? What are its teachings about social problems? At the outset, it is necessary to state that some Gandhists have conjured up a conception of Gandhism which is purely imaginary. According to this conception, Gandhism means return to the village and making the village self-sufficient. It makes Gandhism a mere matter of regionalism. Gandhism, I am sure, is neither so simple nor so innocent as regionalism is. Gandhism has a much bigger content than regionalism. Regionalism is a small insignificant part of it. It has a social philosophy and it has an economic philosophy. To omit to take into account the economic and social philosophy of Gandhism is to present deliberately a false picture of Gandhism. The first and foremost requisite is to present a true picture of Gandhism.

To start with Mr Gandhi's teachings on social problem. Mr Gandhi's views on the caste system—which constitutes the main social problem in India—were fully elaborated by him in 1921–22 in a Gujarathi Journal called *Navajivan*. The article[121] is written in Gujarathi. I give below an English translation of his views as near as possible in his own words. Says Mr Gandhi:

'1. I believe that if Hindu Society has been able to stand, it is because it is founded on the caste system.

2. The seeds of Swaraj are to be found in the caste system. Different castes are like different sections of military division. Each division is working for the good of the whole.

3. A community which can create the caste system must be said to possess unique power of organization.

4. caste has a ready made means for spreading primary education. Every caste can take the responsibility for the education of the children of the caste. Caste has a political basis. It can work as an electorate for a representative body. Caste can perform judicial functions by electing persons to act as judges to decide disputes among members of the same caste. With castes it is easy to raise a defence force by requiring each caste to raise a brigade.

---

[121]It is reprinted in Vol. II of the series called Gandhi Sikshan as No. 18.

5. I believe that inter-dining or inter-marriage are not necessary for promoting national unity. That dining together creates friendship is contrary to experience. If this was true, there would have been no war in Europe... Taking food is as dirty an act as answering the call of nature. The only difference is that after answering the call of nature we get peace while after eating food we get discomfort. Just as we perform the act of answering the call of nature in seclusion, so also the act of taking food must also be done in seclusion.

6. In India, children of brothers do not inter-marry. Do they cease to love because they do not inter-marry? Among the Vaishnavas, many women are so orthodox that they will not eat with the members of the family nor will they drink water from a common water pot. Have they no love? The caste system cannot be said to be bad because it does not allow inter-dining or inter-marriage between different castes.

7. caste is another name for control. Caste puts a limit on enjoyment. Caste does not allow a person to transgress caste limits in pursuit of his enjoyment. That is the meaning of such caste restrictions as inter-dining and inter-marriage.

8. To destroy caste system and adopt Western European social system means that Hindus must give up the principle of hereditary occupation which is the soul of the caste system. Hereditary principle is an eternal principle. To change it is to create disorder. I have no use for a Brahmin if I cannot call him a Brahmin for my life. It will be a chaos if every day a Brahmin is to be changed into a Shudra and a Shudra is to be changed into a Brahmin.

9. The caste system is a natural order of society. In India, it has been given a religious coating. Other countries not having understood the utility of the caste system, it existed only in a loose condition and consequently those countries have not derived from caste system the same degree of advantage which India has derived.

These being my views, I am opposed to all those who are out to destroy the caste system.'

In 1922, Mr Gandhi was a defender of the caste system. Pursuing the inquiry, one comes across a somewhat critical view of the caste system by Mr Gandhi in the year 1925. This is what Mr Gandhi said on 3rd February 1925:

> 'I gave support to caste because it stands for restraint. But, at present, caste does not mean restraint, it means limitations. Restraint is glorious and helps to achieve freedom. But limitation is like chain. It binds. There is nothing commendable in castes as they exist today. They are contrary to the tenets of the shastras. The number of castes is infinite and there is a bar against inter-marriage. This is not condition of elevation. It is a state of fall.'

In reply to the question: What is the way out? Mr Gandhi said:

> 'The best remedy is that small castes should fuse themselves into one big caste. There should be four such big castes so that we may reproduce the old system of four varnas.'

In short, in 1925, Mr Gandhi became an upholder of the varna system.

The old varna system prevalent in ancient India had society divided into four orders: (1)Brahmins, whose occupation was learning; (2)Kshatriyas, whose occupation was warfare; (3)Vaishyas, whose occupation was trade, and (4)Shudras, whose occupation was service of the other classes. Is Mr Gandhi's varna system the same as this old varna system of the orthodox Hindus? Mr Gandhi explained his varna system in the following terms:[122]

> '1. I believe that the divisions into varna is based on birth.
>
> 2. There is nothing in the varna system which stands in the way of the Shudra acquiring learning or studying military art of offence or defence. Contra it is open to a Kshatriya to serve. The varna system is no bar to him. What the varna system enjoins is that a Shudra will not make learning a way of earning a living. Nor will a Kshatriya adopt service as a way of earning a living. (Similarly a Brahmin may learn the art of war or trade. But he must not make them a way of earning his living. Contra a Vaishya may acquire learning or may

[122]The extracts are taken from an article by Mr Gandhi on the subject and is reproduced in the *Varna Vyavastha*—a book which contains Mr Gandhi's writings in original Gujarathi.

cultivate the art of war. But he must not make them a way of earning his living.)

3. The varna system is connected with the way of earning a living. There is no harm if a person belonging to one varna acquires the knowledge or science and art specialised in by persons belonging to other varnas. But as far as the way of earning his living is concerned, he must follow the occupation of the varna to which he belongs, which means he must follow the hereditary profession of his forefathers.

4. The object of the varna system is to prevent competition and class struggle and class war. I believe in the varna system because it fixes the duties and occupations of persons.

5. Varna means the determination of a man's occupation before he is born.

6. In the varna system, no man has any liberty to choose his occupation. His occupation is determined for him by heredity.'

Turning to the field of economic life, Mr Gandhi stands for two ideals: One of these is the opposition to machinery. As early as 1921, Mr Gandhi gave vent to his dislike for machinery. Writing in the *Young India* of 19 January 1921, Mr Gandhi said:

'Do I want to put back the hand of the clock of progress? Do I want to replace the mills by hand-spinning and hand-weaving? Do I want to replace the railway by the country-cart? Do I want to destroy machinery altogether? These questions have been asked by some journalists and public men. My answer is: I would not weep over the disappearance of machinery or consider it a calamity.'

His opposition to machinery is well-evidenced by his idolization of charkha (the spinning wheel) and by insistence upon hand-spinning and hand-weaving. This opposition to machinery and his love for charklia is riot a matter of accident. It is a matter of philosophy. This philosophy Mr Gandhi took special occasion to propound in his presidential address at the Kathiawad Political Conference held on 8 January 1925. This is what Mr Gandhi said:

'Nations are tired of the worship of lifeless machines multiplied ad infinitum. We are destroying the matchless living machines viz., our own bodies by leaving them to rust and trying to substitute lifeless machinery for them. It is a law of God that the body must be fully worked and utilized. We dare not ignore it. The spinning wheel is the auspicious symbol of Sharir Yajna—body labour. He who eats his food without offering this sacrifice steals it. By giving up this sacrifice we, became traitors to the country, and banged the door in the face of the Goddess of Fortune.'

Anyone who has read Mr Gandhi's booklet on Hind Swaraj (Indian Home Rule) will know that Mr Gandhi is against modern civilization. The book was first published in 1908. But, there has been no change in his ideology. Writing in 1921, Mr Gandhi said:[123]

'The booklet is a severe condemnation of "modern civilization." It was written in 1908. My conviction is deeper today than ever. I feel that, | if India would discard "Modern civilization, She can only gain by doing so."'

In Mr Gandhi's view:[124] 'Western civilization is the creation of satan.'

The second ideal of Mr Gandhi is the elimination of class-war and even class struggle in the relationship between employers and employees and between landlords and tenants. Mr Gandhi's views on the relationship between employers and employees were set forth by him in an article on the subject which appeared in the *Navajivan* of the 8 June 1921 from which the following is an extract:

'Two paths are open before India, either to introduce the Western principle of "Might is right" or to uphold the Eastern principle that truth alone conquers, that truth knows no mishap, that the strong and the weak have alike a right to secure justice. The choice is to begin with the labouring class. Should the labourers obtain an increment in their wages by violence? Even if that be possible, they cannot resort to anything like violence, howsoever legitimate may be their claims. To use violence for securing rights may seem an easy path, but it proves to be

---

[123] *Young India*, 26 January 1921.
[124] *Dharma Manthan*, p 65.

thorny in the long run. Those who live by sword die also by sword. The swimmer often dies by drowning. Look at Europe. No one seems to be happy there, for, not one is contented. The labourer does not trust the capitalist and the capitalist has no faith in the labourer. Both have a sort of vigour and strength but even the bulls have it. They fight to the very bitter end. All motion is not progress. We have got no reason to believe that the people of Europe are progressing. Their possession of wealth does not argue the possession of any moral or spiritual qualities.

'What shall we do then? The labourers in Bombay made a fine stand. I was not in a position to know all the facts. But, this much I could see that they could fight in a better way. The mill-owner may be wholly in the wrong. In the struggle between capital and labour, it may be generally said that more often than not the capitalists are in the wrong box. But, when labour comes fully to realize its strength, I know it can become more tyrannical than capital. The millowners will have to work on the terms dictated by labour, if the latter could command intelligence of the former. It is clear, however, that labour will never attain to that intelligence. If it does, labour will cease to be labour and become itself the master. The capitalists do not fight on the strength of money alone. They do possess intelligence and tact.

'The question before us is this: When the labourers, remaining what they are, develop a certain consciousness, what should be their course? It would be suicidal if the labourers rely upon their numbers or brute-force, i.e., violence. By so doing, they will do harm to industries in the country. If, on the other hand, they take their stand on pure justice and suffer in their person to secure it, not only will they always succeed but they will reform their masters, develop industries and both master and men will be as members of one and the same family.'

Referring to the same theme on another occasion, Mr Gandhi said:[125]

'Nor was it otherwise before. Indian history is not one of strained relations between capital and labour.'

Particularly noteworthy are the views of Mr Gandhi on strike as a weapon in the hand of the workers to improve their economic

---

[125] *Young India*, 23 February 1922.

condition. Mr Gandhi says:

'Speaking, therefore, as one having handled large successful strikes, I repeat the following maxims, already stated in these pages, for the guidance of all strike leaders:

(1) There should be no strike without a real grievance.
(2) There should be no strike if the persons concerned are not able to support themselves out of their own savings or by engaging in some temporary occupation, such as carding, spinning and weaving. Strikers should never depend upon public subscriptions or other charity.
(3) Strikers must fix an unalterable minimum demand, and declare it before embarking upon their strike.

'A strike may fail in spite of a just grievance and the ability of strikers to hold out indefinitely, if there are workers to replace them. A wise man, therefore, will not strike for increase of wages or other comforts if he feels that he can be easily replaced. But, a philanthropic or patriotic man will strike in spite of supply being greater than the demand when he feels for and wishes to associate himself with his neighbour's distress. Needless to say, there is no room in a civil strike of the nature described by me for violence in the shape of intimidation, incendiarism or otherwise. Judged by the tests suggested by me, it is clear that friends of the strikers could never have advised them to apply for or receive Congress or any other public funds for their support. The value of the strikers' sympathy was diminished to the extent that they received or accepted financial aid. The merit of a sympathetic strike lies in the inconvenience and the loss suffered by the sympathizers.'

Mr Gandhi's view on the relationship between landlords and tenants were expounded by him in the *Young India* of 18 May 1921 in the form of instructions[126] to the tenants of UP, who had risen against their landlords. Mr Gandhi said:

'Whilst the UP Government is crossing the bounds of propriety, and intimidating people, there is little doubt that the Kisans too are not

---

[126] *Young India*, 11 August 1921.

making wise use of their newly found power. In several Zamindaries, they are said to have overstepped the mark, taken the law into their own hands, and to have become impatient of anybody who would not do as they wish. They are abusing social boycott and are turning it into an instrument of violence. They are reported to have stopped the supply of water, barber and other paid services to their Zamindars in some instances and even suspended payment of the rent due to them. The Kisan movement has received an impetus from non-cooperation but it is anterior to and independent of it. Whilst we will not hesitate to advise the Kisans, when the moment comes, to suspend payment of taxes to Government, it is not contemplated that at any stage of non-cooperation we would seek to deprive the Zamindars of their rent. The Kisan movement must be confined to the improvement of status of the Kisans and the betterment of the relations between the Zamindars and them. The Kisans must be advised scrupulously to abide by the terms of their agreement with the Zamindars, whether such is written or inferred from custom. Where a custom or even a written contract is bad, they may not try to uproot it by violence or without previous reference to the Zamindars. In every case, there should be a friendly discussion with the Zamindars and an attempt made to arrive at a settlement.'

Mr Gandhi does not wish to hurt the propertied class. He is even opposed to a campaign against them. He has no passion for economic equality. Referring to the propertied class, Mr Gandhi said quite recently that he does not wish to destroy the hen that lays the golden egg. His solution for the economic conflict between the owners and workers, between the rich and the poor, between landlords and tenants, and between the employers and the employees is very simple.

The owners need not deprive themselves of their property. All that they need do is to declare themselves Trustees for the poor. Of course the Trust is to be a voluntary one carrying only a spiritual obligation.

◆

Is there anything new in the Gandhian analysis of economic ills? Are the economics of Gandhism sound? What hope does Gandhism hold out to the common man, to the down and out? Does it promise him a better life, a life of joy, and culture, a life of freedom, not merely freedom from want but freedom to rise, to grow to the full stature which his capacities can reach?

There is nothing new in the Gandhian analysis of economic ills in so far as it attributes them to machinery and the civilization that is built upon it. The arguments that machinery and modern civilization help to concentrate management and control into relatively few hands, and with the aid of banking and credit facilitate the transfer into still fewer hands of all materials and factories and mills in which millions are bled white in order to support huge industries thousands of miles away from their cottages, or that machinery and modern civilization cause deaths, maimings and cripplings far in excess of the corresponding injuries by war, and are responsible for disease and physical deterioration caused directly and indirectly by the development of large cities with their smoke, dirt, noise, foul air, lack of sunshine and outdoor life, slums, prostitution and unnatural living which they bring about, are all old and worn out arguments. There is nothing new in them. Gandhism is merely repeating the views of Rousseau, Ruskin, Tolstoy and their school.

The ideas which go to make up Gandhism are just primitive. It is a return to nature, to animal life. The only merit is their simplicity. As there is always a large corps of simple people who are attracted by them, such simple ideas do not die, and there is always some simpleton to preach them. There is, however, no doubt that the practical instincts of men—which seldom go wrong—have found them unfruitful and which society in search of progress has thought it best to reject.

The economics of Gandhism are hopelessly fallacious. The fact that machinery and modern civilization have produced many evils may be admitted. But these evils are no argument against them. For, the evils are not due to machinery and modern civilization. They are due to wrong social organization which has made private property and pursuit of personal gain matters of absolute sanctity. If machinery and civilization have not benefited everybody, the remedy is not to condemn machinery and civilization, but to alter the organization of society so that the benefits will not be usurped by the few but will accrue to all.

In Gandhism, the common man has no hope. It treats man as an animal and no more. It is true that man shares the constitution and functions of animals, nutritive, reproductive, etc. But, these are not distinctively human functions. The distinctively human function is reason, the purpose of which is to enable man to observe, meditate, cogitate, study and discover the beauties of the universe and enrich his life and control the animal elements in his life. Man thus occupies the highest place in the scheme of animate existence. If this is true, what is the conclusion that follows? The conclusion that follows is that while the ultimate goal of a brute's life is reached once his physical appetites are satisfied, the ultimate goal of man's existence is not reached unless and until he has fully cultivated his mind. In short, what divides the brute from man is culture. Culture is not possible for the brute, but it is essential for man. That being so, the aim of human society must be to enable every person to lead a life of culture, which means the cultivation of the mind as distinguished from the satisfaction of mere physical wants. How can this happen?

Both for society and as well as for the individual, there is always a gulf between merely living and living worthily. In order that one may live worthily, one must first live. The time and energy spent upon mere life, upon gaining of subsistence, detracts from that available for activities of a distinctively human nature, and which go to make up a life of culture. How, then, can a life of culture be made possible? It is not possible unless there is sufficient leisure. For, it is only when there is leisure that a person is free to devote himself to a life of culture. The problem of all problems which human society has to face is how to provide leisure to every individual. What does leisure mean? Leisure means the lessening of the toil and effort necessary for satisfying the physical wants of life. How can leisure be made possible? Leisure is quite impossible unless some means are found whereby the toil required for producing goods necessary to satisfy human needs is lessened. What can lessen such toil? Only when machine takes the place of man. There is no other means of producing leisure. Machinery and modern civilization are thus indispensable for emancipating man from leading the life of a brute, and for providing him with leisure and making a life of culture possible. The man who condemns machinery and modern civilization simple does not understand their purpose and the ultimate aim which human society must strive to achieve.

Gandhism may be well-suited to a society which does not accept democracy as its ideal. A society which does not believe in democracy may be indifferent to machinery and the civilization based upon it. But, a democratic society cannot. The former may well content itself with life of leisure and culture for the few and a life of toil and drudgery for the many. But, a democratic society must assure a life of leisure and culture to each one of its citizens. If the above analysis is correct, then the slogan of a democratic society must be machinery, and more machinery, civilization and more civilization. Under Gandhism, the common man must keep on toiling ceaselessly for a pittance and remain a brute. In short, Gandhism, with its call of back to nature, means back to nakedness, back to squalor, back to poverty, and back to ignorance for the vast mass of the people.

The division of life into separate functions and of society into separate classes may not be altogether obliterated. Inspite of many social and economic changes, in spite of the abolition of legal serfdom, legal slavery, and the spread of the notion of democracy, with the extension of science, of general education through books, newspapers, travel and general intercourse in schools and factories, there remains, and perhaps will remain, enough cleavage in society into a learned and an ignorant class, a leisure and a labouring class.

But, Gandhism is not satisfied with only notional class distinctions. Gandhism insists upon class structure. It regards the class structure of society and also the income structure as sacrosanct with the consequent distinctions of rich and poor, high and low, owners and workers as permanent parts of social organization. From the point of view of social consequences, nothing can be more pernicious. Psychologically, class structure sets in motion influences which are harmful to both the classes. There is no common plane on which the privileged and the subject classes can meet. There is no endosmosis, no give and take of life's hopes and experiences. The social and moral evils of this separation to the subject class are, of course, real and obvious. It educates them into slaves and creates all the psychological complex which follows from a slave mentality. But, those affecting the privileged class, though less material arid less perceptible, are equally real. The isolation and exclusiveness following upon the class structure creates in the privileged classes the anti-social spirit of a gang. It feels it has interests of its own which it makes its prevailing purpose to protect against everybody even against the interests of the State. It makes their culture sterile, their art showy, their wealth luminous, and their manners fastidious. Practically speaking, in a class structure, there is, on the one hand, tyranny, vanity, pride, arrogance, greed, selfishness and, on the other, insecurity, poverty, degradation, loss of liberty, self-reliance, independence, dignity and self-respect. Democratic society cannot be indifferent to such consequences. But, Gandhism does not mind these consequences in the least. It is not enough to say that Gandhism is not satisfied with mere class distinctions. It is not enough to say that Gandhism believes in a class structure. Gandhism stands for more than that. A class structure which is a faded, jejune, effete thing, a mere sentimentality, a mere skeleton is not what Gandhism wants. It wants class structure to function as a living faith. In this, there is nothing to be surprised at. For, class structure in Gandhism is not a mere accident. It is its official doctrine.

The idea of trusteeship which Gandhism proposes as a panacea by which the moneyed classes will hold their properties in trust for the poor is the most ridiculous part of it. All that one can say about it is that if anybody else had propounded it, the author would have been laughed at as a silly fool who had not known the hard realities of life and was deceiving the servile classes by telling them that a little dose of moral rearmament to the propertied classes—those who by their insatiable cupidity and indomitable arrogance have made and will always make this world a vale of tears for the toiling millions—will recondition them to such an extent that they will be able to withstand the temptation to misuse the tremendous powers which the class structure gives them over servile classes.

The social ideal of Gandhism is either caste or varna. Though it may be difficult to say which, there can be no doubt that the social ideal of Gandhism is not democracy. For, whether one takes for comparison caste or varna, both are fundamentally opposed to democracy. It would have been some tiling if the defence of caste system which Gandhism offers was strong and honest. But, his defence of the caste system is the most insensible piece of rhetoric one can think of. Examine Mr Gandhi's arguments in support of caste and it will be found that everyone of them is specious if not puerile.

The first three arguments call for pity. That the Hindu society has been able to stand while others have died out or disappeared is hardly a matter for congratulation. If it has survived it is not because of caste but because the foreigner who conquered the Hindus did not find it necessary to kill them wholesale. There is no honour in mere survival. What matters is the plane of survival. One can survive by unconditional surrender. One can survive by beating a cowardly retreat, and one can survive by fighting. On what plane have the Hindus survived? If they can be said to have survived after fighting and beating their enemies, the virtue ascribed to the caste system by Mr Gandhi could be admitted. The history of the Hindus has been one of surrender—abject surrender. It is true others have surrendered to their invaders. But, in their case, surrender is followed by a revolt against the foreign ruler.

The Hindus have not only never withstood the onslaught of the foreign invader, they have never even shown the capacity to organize a rebellion to throw off the foreign yoke. On the other hand, the Hindus have tried to make slavery comfortable. On this, one may well argue the contrary, namely, that this helpless condition of the Hindus is due entirely to the caste system.

The argument in para 4 is plausible. But, it cannot be said that caste is the only machinery for discharging such functions as the spread of primary education or the judicial settlement of disputes. Caste is probably the worst instrument for the discharge of such functions. It can be easily influenced and easily corrupted. Such functions have been discharged in other countries much better than they have been in India although they have had no caste system. As to using the caste as basis for raising military units, the idea is simply fantastic. Under the occupational theory underlying the caste system, this is unthinkable. Mr Gandhi knows that not a single caste in his own province of Gujarat has ever raised a military unit. It did not do it in the present World War. But it did not do so even in the last

World War, when Mr Gandhi toured through Gujarat as a recruiting agent of British Imperialism. In fact, under the caste system, a general mobilization of the people for defence is impossible since mobilization requires a general liquidation of the occupational theory underlying the caste system.

The arguments contained in paras 5 and 6 are as stupid as they are revolting. The argument in para 5 is hardly a good argument. It is quite true the family is an ideal unit in which every member is charged with love and affection for another member although there is no inter-marriage among members of a family. It may even be conceded that in a Vaishnava family, members of the family do not inter-dine and yet they are full of love and affection for one another. What does all this prove?

It does not prove that inter-dining and inter-marrying are not necessary for establishing fraternity. What it proves is that where there are other means of maintaining fraternity—such as consciousness of family tie—inter-dining and inter-marriage are not necessary. But, it cannot be denied that where—as in the caste system—no binding force exists, inter-marriage and inter-dining are absolutely essential. There is no analogy between family and caste, inter-caste dinner and inter-caste marriage are necessary because there are no other means of binding the different castes together while in the case of a family there exists other forces to bind them together. Those who have insisted upon the ban against inter-dining and inter-marriage have treated it as a question of relative values. They have never elevated it to the level of a question of absolute value. Mr Gandhi is the first one to do it. Inter-dining is bad and—even if it was capable of producing good—it should not be resorted to, and why? Because eating is a filthy act, as filthy as answering the call of nature! The caste system has been defended by others. But, this is the first time I have seen such an extraordinary, if not a shocking, argument used to support it. Even the orthodox may say, 'Save us from Mr Gandhi.' It shows what a deep-dyed Hindu Mr Gandhi is. He has outdone the most orthodox of orthodox Hindus. It is not enough to say that it is an argument of a cave man. It is really an argument of a mad man.

The argument in favour of the caste system outlined in para 7 is not worth much in terms of building up moral strength. The caste system, no doubt, prohibits a man from satisfying his lust for a woman who is not of his caste. The caste system, no doubt, prohibits a man from satisfying his craving for food cooked in the house of a man who is not of his caste. If morality consists of observing restraints without regard to the sense or sensibility of restraints, then the caste system may be admitted to be a moral system. But, Mr Gandhi does not see that these easy restraints are more than balanced by vast liberties permitted by Hinduism. For, Hinduism places no restraint upon a man marrying hundred women and keeping hundred prostitutes within the ambit of his caste. Nor does it stop him from indulging in his appetite with his castemen to any degree.

The argument in para 8 begs the whole question. The hereditary system may be good or may not be good. It may be agreeable to some. It may be disagreeable to others. Why elevate it into an official doctrine? Why make it compulsory? In Europe, it is not an official doctrine and it is not compulsory. It is left to the choice of an individual, most of whom do follow the profession of their ancestors, and some don't. Who can say that compulsory system has worked better than the voluntary system? If a comparison of the economic condition of the people in India and the people of Europe is any guide, there would be very few rationally-minded people who would be found to support the caste system on this ground. As to the difficulty in changing nomenclature to keep pace with frequent changes in occupation, it is only artificial, it arises out of the supposed necessity of having labels for designating persons following a particular profession. The class labels are quite unnecessary and could well be abolished altogether without causing difficulty. Besides, what happens today in India? Men's callings and their class labels are not in accord. A Brahmin sells shoes. Nobody is disturbed because he is not called a Chamar. A Chamar becomes an officer of the State. Nobody is disturbed because he is not called a Brahmin. The whole argument is based on a misunderstanding. What matters to society is not the label by which the individual's class is known, but the service he offers.

The last argument set out in para 9 is one of the most astounding arguments I have heard in favour of the caste system. It is historically false. No one who knows anything about the Manusmritii can say that the caste system is a natural system. What does Manusmritii show? It shows that the caste system is a legal system maintained at the point of a bayonet. If it has survived, it is due to (1)prevention of the masses from the possession of arms; (2)denying to the masses the right to education; and (3)depriving the masses of the right to property. The caste system, far from natural, is really an imposition by the ruling classes upon the servile classes.

That Mr Gandhi changed over from the caste system to the varna system does not make the slightest difference to the charge that Gandhism is opposed to democracy. In the first place, the idea of varna is the parent of the idea of caste. If the idea of caste is a pernicious idea, it is entirely because of the viciousness of the idea of varna. Both are evil ideas, and it matters very little whether one believes in varna or in caste. The idea of varna was most mercilessly attacked by the Buddhists who did not believe in it. Orthodox or the Sanatan Vedic Hindus had no rational defence to offer. All that they could say was that it was founded on the authority of the Vedas and that as the Vedas were infallible so was the varna system. This argument was not enough to save the varna system against the rationalism of the Buddhists. If the idea of the varna survived, it was because of the Bhagvat Gita, which gave a philosophical foundation to the varna system by arguing that the varna was based on the innate qualities of man. The Bhagvat Gita made use of the Sankhya philosophy to bolster and buttress the varna idea which would have otherwise petered away by making sense of a thing that is absolute nonsense. The Bhagvat Gita had done enough mischief by giving a fresh lease of life to the varna system by basing it upon a new and plausible foundation, namely, that of innate qualities.

The varna system of the Bhagvat Gita has at least two merits. It does not say that it is based on birth. Indeed, it makes a special point that each man's varna is fixed according to his innate qualities. It does not say that the occupation of the son shall be that of the father. It says that the profession of a person shall be according to his innate qualities, the profession of the father according to the father's innate quality, and that of the son according to the son's innate qualities. But

Mr Gandhi has given a new interpretation of the varna system. He has changed it out of recognition. Under the old orthodox interpretation, caste connoted hereditary occupation, but varna did not. Mr Gandhi, by his own whim, has given a new connotation to the varna. With Mr Gandhi, varna is determined by birth and the profession of a varna is determined by the principle of heredity so that varna is merely another name for caste. That Mr Gandhi changed from caste to varna does not indicate the growth of any new revolutionary ideology. The genius of Mr Gandhi is elvish, always and throughout. He has all the precocity of an elf with no little of its outward guise. Like an elf, he can never grow up and grow out of the caste ideology.

Mr Gandhi sometimes speaks on social and economic subjects as though he was a blushing red. Those who will study Gandhism will not be deceived by the occasional aberrations of Mr Gandhi in favour of democracy and against capitalism. For, Gandhism is in no sense a revolutionary creed. It is conservatism in excelsis. So far as India is concerned, it is a reactionary creed blazoning on its banner the call of Return to Antiquity. Gandhism aims at the resuscitation and reanimation of India's dread, dying past.

Gandhism is a paradox. It stands for freedom from foreign domination, which means the destruction of the existing political structure of the country. At the same time, it seeks to maintain intact a social structure which permits the domination of one class by another on a hereditary basis, which means a perpetual domination of one class by another. What is the explanation of this paradox? Is it a part of a strategy by Mr Gandhi to win the whole-hearted support of the Hindus, orthodox and unorthodox, to the campaign of Swaraj? If it is the latter, can Gandhism be regarded as honest and sincere? Be that as it may, there are two features of Gandhism which are revealing but to which unfortunately no attention has so far been paid. Whether they will make Gandhism more acceptable than Marxism is another matter. But, as they do help to distinguish Gandhism from Marxism, it may be well to refer to them.

The first special feature of Gandhism is that its philosophy helps those who have to keep what they have, and to prevent those who have not from getting what they have a right to get. No one who examines the Gandhian attitude to strikes, the Gandhian reverence for caste, and the Gandhian doctrine of trusteeship by the rich for the benefit of the poor can deny that this is upshot of Gandhism. Whether this is the calculated result of a deliberate design or whether it is a matter of accident may be open to argument. But, the fact remains that Gandhism is the philosophy of the well-to-do and the leisure class.

The second special feature of Gandhism is to delude people into accepting their misfortunes by presenting them as best of good fortunes. One or two illustrations will suffice to bring out the truth of this statement.

The Hindu sacred law penalized the Shudras (Hindus of the fourth class) from acquiring wealth. It is a law of enforced poverty unknown in any other part of the world. What does Gandhism do? It does not lift the ban. It blesses the Shudra for his moral courage to give up property! It is well-worth quoting Mr Gandhi's own words. Here they are:[127]

> 'The Shudra who only serves (the higher caste) as a matter of religious duty, and who will never own any property, who indeed has not even the ambition to own anything, is deserving of thousand obeisance. The very Gods will shower down flowers on him.'

Another illustration in support is the attitude of Gandhism towards the [human] scavenger. The sacred law of the Hindus lays down that a scavenger's progeny shall live by scavenging. Under Hinduism, scavenging was not a matter of choice, it was a matter of force.[128] What does Gandhism do? It seeks to perpetuate this system by praising scavenging as the noblest service to society! Let me quote Mr Gandhi. As a President of a Conference of the Untouchables, Mr Gandhi said:[129]

> 'I do not want to attain Moksha. I do not want to be reborn. But, if I have to be reborn, I should be born an Untouchable, so that I may share their sorrows, sufferings and the affronts levelled at them, in order that I may endeavour to free myself and them from that miserable condition.

---

[127]Quoted from *Varna Vyavastha*, p 51.
[128]Ibid.
[129]*Young India*, 27 April 1921.

I, therefore, prayed that if I should be born again, I should do so not as a Brahmin, Kshatriya, Vaishya, or Shudra, but as an Atishudra.

'I love scavenging. In my Ashram, an eighteen years old Brahmin lad is doing the scavenger's work in order to teach the Ashram scavenger cleanliness. The lad is no reformer. He was born and bred in orthodoxy. But, he felt that his accomplishments were incomplete until he had become also a perfect sweeper, and that, if he wanted the Ashram sweeper to do his work well, he must do it himself and set an example. 'You should realize that you are cleaning Hindu Society.'

Can there be a worse example of false propaganda than this attempt of Gandhism to perpetuate evils which have been deliberately imposed by one class over another? If Gandhism preached the rule of poverty for all and not merely for the Shudra, the worst that could be said about it is that it is a mistaken idea. But, why preach it as good for one class only? Why appeal to the worst of human failings, namely, pride and vanity, in order to make him voluntarily accept what on a rational basis he would resent as a cruel discrimination against him? What is the use of telling the scavenger that even a Brahmin is prepared to do scavenging, when it is clear that according to Hindu Shastras and Hindu notions even if a Brahmin did scavenging he would never be subject to the disabilities of one who is a born scavenger? For, in India, a man is not a scavenger because of his work. He is a scavenger because of his birth irrespective of the question whether he does scavenging or not. If Gandhism preached that scavenging is a noble profession with the object of inducing those who refuse to engage in it, one could understand it. But, why appeal to the scavenger's pride and vanity in order to induce him and him only to keep on to scavenging by telling him that scavenging is a noble profession and that he need not be ashamed of it? To preach that poverty is good for the Shudra and for none else, to preach that scavenging is good for the Untouchables and for none else, and to make them accept these onerous impositions as voluntary purposes of life, by appeal to their failings, is an outrage and a cruel joke on the helpless classes which none but Mr Gandhi can perpetuate with equanimity and impunity.

In this connection, one is reminded of the words of Voltaire who in repudiation of an 'ism' very much like Gandhism said: 'Oh! mockery to say to people that the suffering of some brings joy to others and works good to the whole! What solace is it to a dying man to know that from his decaying body a thousand worms will come into life?'

Criticism apart, this is the technique of Gandhism to make wrongs done appear to the very victim as though they were his privileges. If there is an 'ism' which has made full use of religion as an opium to lull the people into false beliefs and false security, it is Gandhism. Following Shakespeare, one can well say: Plausibility! Ingenuity! Thy name is Gandhism.

Such is Gandhism. Having known what is Gandhism, the answer to the question, 'Should Gandhism become the law of the land what would be the lot of the Untouchables under it,' cannot require much scratching of the brain. How would it compare with the lot of the lowest Hindu? Enough has been said to show what would be his lot should the Gandhian social order come into being. In so far as the lowest Hindu and the Untouchable belong to the same disinherited class, the Untouchable's lot cannot be better. If anything, it might easily be worse. Because in India even the lowest man among the Caste Hindus—why even the aboriginal and hill tribe man—though educationally and economically not very much above the Untouchables, is still superior to the Untouchables. It is not he who regards himself as superior to the Untouchables. The Hindu society accepts his claim to superiority over the Untouchables. The Untouchable will, therefore, continue to suffer the worst fate as he does now, namely, in prosperity he will be the last to be employed and in depression the first to be fired.

What does Gandhism do to relieve the Untouchables from this fate? Gandhism professes to abolish Untouchability. That is hailed as the greatest virtue of Gandhism. But, what does this virtue amount to in actual life? To assess the value of this anti-Untouchability which is regarded as a very big element in Gandhism, it is necessary to understand fully the scope of Mr Gandhi's programme for the removal of Untouchability. Does it mean anything more than that the Hindus will not mind touching the Untouchables? Does it mean the removal of the ban on the right of the Untouchables to education? It would be better to take the two questions separately.

To start with the first question, Mr Gandhi does not say that a Hindu should not take a bath after touching the Untouchables. If Mr Gandhi does not object to it as a purification of pollution, then it is difficult to see how Untouchability can be said to vanish by touching the Untouchables. Untouchability centres round the idea of pollution by contact and purification by bath to remove the pollution. Does it mean social assimilation with the Hindus? Mr Gandhi has most categorically stated that removal of Untouchability does not mean inter-dining or inter-marriage between the Hindus and the Untouchables. Mr Gandhi's anti-Untouchability means that the Untouchables will be classed as Shudras instead of being classed as Ati-Shudras.[130] There is nothing more in it. Mr Gandhi has not considered the question whether the old Shudras will accept the new Shudras into their fold. If they don't, then the removal of Untouchability is a senseless proposition for it will still keep the Untouchables as a separate social category. Mr Gandhi probably knows that the abolition of Untouchability will not bring about the assimilation of the Untouchables by the Shudras. That seems to be the reason why Mr Gandhi himself has given a new and a different name to the Untouchables. The new name registers by anticipation what is likely to be the fact. By calling the Untouchables Harijans, Mr Gandhi has killed two birds with one stone. He has shown that assimilation of the Untouchables by the Shudras is not possible. He has also by his new name counteracted assimilation and made it impossible.

Regarding the second question, it is true that Gandhism is prepared to remove the old ban placed by the Hindu Shastras on the right of the Untouchables to education and permit them to acquire knowledge and learning. Under Gandhism, the Untouchables may study law, they may study medicine, they may study engineering or anything else they may fancy. So far so good. But, will the Untouchables be free to make use of their knowledge and learning? Will they have the right to choose their profession? Can they adopt the career of lawyer, doctor or engineer? To these questions, the answer which Gandhism gives is an emphatic 'No'. The Untouchables must follow their hereditary

---

[130] *Young India*, 5 February 1925.

professions. That those occupations are unclean is no answer. That before the occupation became hereditary it was the result of force and not volition does not matter. The argument of Gandhism is that what is once settled is settled for ever even if it was wrongly settled. Under Gandhism, the Untouchables are to be eternal scavengers. There is no doubt that the Untouchables would much prefer the orthodox system of Untouchability. A compulsory state of ignorance imposed upon the Untouchables by the Hindu Shastras made scavenging bearable. But, Gandhism, which compels an educated Untouchable to do scavenging, is nothing short of cruelty. The grace in Gandhism is a curse in its worst form. The virtue of the anti-Untouchability plank in Gandhism is quite illusory. There is no substance in it.

What else is there in Gandhism which the Untouchables can accept as opening a way for their ultimate salvation? Barring this illusory campaign against Untouchability, Gandhism is simply another form of Sanatanism, which is the ancient name for militant orthodox Hinduism. What is there in Gandhism which is not to be found in orthodox Hinduism? There is caste in Hinduism, there is caste in Gandhism. Hinduism believes in the law of hereditary profession, so does Gandhism. Hinduism enjoins cow-worship. So does Gandhism. Hinduism upholds the law of karma, predestination of man's condition in this world, so does Gandhism. Hinduism accepts the authority of the Shastras. So does Gandhism. Hinduism believes in avatar or incarnations of God. So does Gandhism. Hinduism believes in idols, so does Gandhism.[131] All that Gandhism has done is to find a philosophic justification for Hinduism and its dogmas. Hinduism is bald in the sense that it is just a set of rules which bear on their face the appearance of a crude and cruel system. Gandhism supplies the philosophy which smoothens its surface and gives it the appearance of decency and respectability and so alters it and embellishes it as to make it even attractive. What philosophy does Gandhism propound to cover the nudity of Hinduism? This philosophy can be put in a nutshell. It is a philosophy which says that 'All that is in Hinduism

---

[131]Mr Gandhi's articles of faith have been outlined by him in *Young India* of 6 October 1921.

is well, all that is in Hinduism is necessary for public good.' Those who are familiar with Voltaire's Candide will recognize that it is the philosophy of Master Pangloss and recall the mockery Voltaire made of it. The Hindus are, of course, pleased with it. No doubt, it suits them and accords with their interest. Prof. Radhakrishnan—whether out of genuine feeling or out of sycophancy we need not stop to inquire—has gone to the length of describing Mr Gandhi as 'God on earth'. What do the Untouchables understand this to mean? To them, it means that: This God by name Gandhi came to console an afflicted race. He saw India and changed it not saying all is well and will be, if the Hindus will only fulfil the law of caste. He told the afflicted race, 'I have come to fulfil the law of caste.' Not a little, not a jot shall I allow to abate from it.

What hope can Gandhism offer to the Untouchables? To the Untouchables, Hinduism is a veritable chamber of horrors. The sanctity and infallibility of the Vedas, Smritis and Shastras, the iron law of caste, the heartless law of karma and the senseless law of status by birth are to the Untouchables veritable instruments of torture which Hinduism has forged against the Untouchables. These very instruments, which have mutilated, blasted and blighted the life of the Untouchables, are to be found intact and untarnished in the bosom of Gandhism. How can the Untouchables say that Gandhism is a heaven and not a chamber of horrors as Hinduism has been? The only reaction, and a very natural reaction, of the Untouchables would be to run away from Gandhism.

Gandhists may say that what I have stated applies to the old type of Gandhism. There is a new Gandhism, Gandhism without caste. This has reference to the recent statement[132] of Mr Gandhi that caste is an anachronism. Reformers were naturally gladdened by this declaration of Mr Gandhi. And, who would not be glad to see that a man like Mr Gandhi having such terrible influence over the Hindus, after having played the most mischievous part of a social reactionary, after having stood out as the protagonist of the caste system, after having beguiled and befooled the unthinking Hindus with arguments which made no

---

[132] *The Hindustan Times*, 15 April 1945.

distinction between what is fair and foul, should have come out with this recantation? But, is this really a matter for jubilation? Does it change the nature of Gandhism? Does it make Gandhism a new and a better 'ism'[133] than it was before? Those who are carried away by this recantation of Mr Gandhi, forget two things. In the first place, all that Mr Gandhi has said is that caste is an anachronism. He does not say it is an evil. He does not say it is anathema. Mr Gandhi may be taken to be not in favour of caste. But, Mr Gandhi does not say that he is against the varna system. And what is Mr Gandhi's varna system? It is simply a new name for the caste system and retains all the worst features of the caste system.

The declaration of Mr Gandhi cannot be taken to mean any fundamental change in Gandhism. It cannot make Gandhism acceptable to the Untouchables. The Untouchables will still have ground to say: 'Good God! Is this man, Gandhi, our Saviour?'

I appreciate greatly the honour done me by the Mahatma in taking notice in his Harijan of the speech on caste which I had prepared for the Jat-Pat-Todak Mandal. From a perusal of his review of my speech, it is clear that the Mahatma completely dissents from the views I have expressed on the subject of caste. I am not in the habit of entering into controversy with my opponents unless there are special reasons which compel me to act otherwise. Had my opponent been some mean and obscure person, I would not have pursued him. But my opponent being the Mahatma himself, I feel I must attempt to meet the case to the contrary which he has sought to put forth.

While I appreciate the honour he has done me, I must confess to a sense of surprise on finding that of all people the Mahatma should accuse me of a desire to seek publicity, as he seems to do when he suggests that in publishing the undelivered speech my object was to see that I was not 'forgotten.' Whatever the Mahatma may choose to say, my object in publishing the speech was to provoke the Hindus to think, and to take stock of their position. I have never hankered for publicity, and if I may say so, I have more of it than I wish or need. But supposing it was out of the motive of gaining publicity that

---

[133]Ibid.

I printed the speech, who could cast a stone at me? Surely not those who, like the Mahatma, live in glass houses.

Motive apart, what has the Mahatma to say on the question raised by me in the speech? First of all, anyone who reads my speech will realize that the Mahatma has entirely missed the issues raised by me, and that the issues he has raised are not the issues that arise out of what he is pleased to call my indictment of the Hindus. The principal points which I have tried to make out in my speech may be catalogued as follows:

1. That caste has ruined the Hindus;
2. That the reorganization of the Hindu Society on the basis of Chaturvarnya is impossible because the Varnavyavastha is like a leaky pot or like a man running at the nose. It is incapable of sustaining itself by its own virtue, and has an inherent tendency to degenerate into a caste system unless there is a legal sanction behind it which can be enforced against everyone transgressing his varna;
3. That the reorganization of the Hindu society on the basis of Chaturvarnya would be harmful, because the effect of the Varnavyavastha would be to degrade the masses by denying them opportunity to acquire knowledge, and to emasculate them by denying them the right to be armed;
4. That the Hindu society must be reorganized on a religious basis which would recognize the principles of Liberty, Equality and Fraternity;
5. That in order to achieve this object the sense of religious sanctity behind caste and varna must be destroyed;
6. That the sanctity of caste and varna can be destroyed only by discarding the divine authority of the Shastras.

It will be noticed that the questions raised by the Mahatma are absolutely beside the point, and show that the main argument of the speech was lost upon him.

Let me examine the substance of the points made by the Mahatma. The first point made by the Mahatma is that the texts cited by me are not authentic. I confess I am no authority on this matter. But I should like to state that the texts cited by me are all taken from the writings of the late Mr Tilak, who was a recognized authority on the Sanskrit language and on the Hindu Shastras. His second point is that these Shastras should be interpreted not by the learned but by the saints; and that as the saints have understood them, the Shastras do not support caste and Untouchability.

As regards the first point, what I would like to ask the Mahatma is, what does it avail to anyone if the texts are interpolations, and if they have been differently interpreted by the saints? The masses do not make any distinction between texts which are genuine and texts which are interpolations. The masses do not know what the texts are. They are too illiterate to know the contents of the Shastras. They have believed what they have been told, and what they have been told is that the Shastras do enjoin as a religious duty the observance of caste and Untouchability.

With regard to the saints, one must admit that howsoever different and elevating their teachings may have been as compared to those of the merely learned, they have been lamentably ineffective. They have been ineffective for two reasons. Firstly, none of the saints ever attacked the caste system. On the contrary—they were staunch believers in the system of castes. Most of them lived and died as members of the castes to which they respectively belonged. So passionately attached was Jnyandeo to his status as a Brahmin that when the Brahmins of Paithan would not admit him to their fold, he moved heaven and earth to get his status as a Brahmin recognized by the Brahmin fraternity.

And even the saint Eknath, who now figures in the film 'Dharmatma' as a hero for having shown the courage to touch the Untouchables and dine with them, did so not because he was opposed to caste and Untouchability, but because he felt that the pollution caused thereby could be washed away by a bath in the sacred waters of the river Ganges [भंलनचा निढाल ज्यासी। गंगास्नानि घूद्रष्ठव त्यासी।। एकनायो प्राणदण्ड, ब 28, औ. 191]. The saints have never, according to my study, carried on a campaign against caste and Untouchability. They were not concerned with the struggle between men. They were concerned with the relation between man and God. They did not preach that all men were equal. They preached that all men were equal in the eyes of God—a very different and a very innocuous proposition, which nobody can find difficult to preach or dangerous to believe in.

The second reason why the teachings of the saints proved ineffective was because the masses have been taught that a saint might break caste, but the common man must not. A saint therefore never became an example to follow. He always remained a pious man to be honoured. That the masses have remained staunch believers in caste and Untouchability shows that the pious lives and noble sermons of the saints have had no effect on their life and conduct, as against the teachings of the Shastras. Thus it can be a matter of no consolation that there were saints, or that there is a Mahatma who understands the Shastras differently from the learned few or ignorant many.

That the masses hold a different view of the Shastras is a fact which should and must be reckoned with. How that is to be dealt with, except by denouncing the authority of the Shastras which continue to govern their conduct, is a question which the Mahatma has not considered. But whatever the plan the Mahatma puts forth as an effective means to free the masses from the teachings of the Shastras, he must accept that the pious life led by one good Samaritan may be very elevating to himself, but in India, with the attitude the common man has to saints and to Mahatmas—to honour but not to follow—one cannot make much out of it.

The third point made by the Mahatma is that a religion professed by Chaitanya, Jnyandeo, Tukaram, Tiruvalluvar, Ramkrishna Paramahansa, etc., cannot be devoid of merit as is made out by me, and that a religion has to be judged not by its worst specimens but by the best it might have produced. I agree with every word of this statement. But I do not quite understand what the Mahatma wishes to prove thereby. That religion should be judged not by its worst specimens but by its best is true enough, but does it dispose of the matter? I say it does not.

The question still remains, why the worst number so many and the best so few. To my mind there are two conceivable answers to this question: (1) That the worst by reason of some original perversity of theirs are morally uneducable, and are therefore incapable of making the remotest approach to the religious ideal. Or: (2) That the religious ideal is a wholly wrong ideal which has given a wrong moral twist to the lives of the many, and that the best have become best in spite of the wrong ideal—in fact, by giving to the wrong twist a turn in the right direction.

Of these two explanations I am not prepared to accept the first, and I am sure that even the Mahatma will not insist upon the contrary. To my mind the second is the only logical and reasonable explanation, unless the Mahatma has a third alternative to explain why the worst are so many and the best so few. If the second is the only explanation, then obviously the argument of the Mahatma that a religion should be judged by its best followers carries us nowhere—except to pity the lot of the many who have gone wrong because they have been made to worship wrong ideals.

The argument of the Mahatma that Hinduism would be tolerable if only many were to follow the example of the saints is fallacious for another reason. (In this connection, see the illuminating article on 'Morality and the Social Structure' by Mr H.N. Brailsford in the Aryan Path for April, 1936.) By citing the names of such illustrious persons as Chaitanya, etc,. what the Mahatma seems to me to suggest in its broadest and simplest form is that Hindu society can be made tolerable and even happy without any fundamental change in its structure, if all the high-caste Hindus can be persuaded to follow a high standard of morality in their dealings with the low-caste Hindus. I am totally opposed to this kind of ideology.

I can respect those of the Caste Hindus who try to realize a high social ideal in their life. Without such men, India would be an uglier and a less happy place to live in than it is. But nonetheless, anyone who relies on an attempt to turn the members of the Caste Hindus into better men by improving their personal character is, in myjudgement, wasting his energy and hugging an illusion. Can personal character make the maker of armaments a good man, i.e., a man who will sell shells that will not burst and gas that will not poison? If it cannot, how can you accept personal character [as sufficient] to make a man loaded with the consciousness of caste a good man, i.e., a man who would treat his fellow-men as his friends and equals? To be true to himself, he must deal with his fellow-man either as a superior or inferior, according as the case may be; at any rate, differently from his own caste-fellows. He can never be expected to deal with his fellow-men as his kinsmen and equals.

As a matter of fact, a Hindu does treat all those who are not of his caste as though they were aliens, who could be discriminated against with impunity, and against whom any fraud or trick may be practised without shame. *This is to say that there can be a better or a worse Hindu. But a good Hindu there cannot be.* This is so not because there is anything wrong with his personal character. In fact what is wrong is the entire basis of his relationship to his fellows. The best of men cannot be moral if the basis of relationship between them and their fellows is fundamentally a wrong relationship. To a slave, his master may be better or worse. But there cannot be a good master. A good man cannot be a master, and a master cannot be a good man.

The same applies to the relationship between high-caste and low-caste. To a low-caste man, a high-caste man can be better or worse as compared to other high-caste men. A high-caste man cannot be a good man, insofar as he must have a low-caste man to distinguish him as a high-caste man. It cannot be good to a low-caste man to be conscious that there is a high-caste man above him. I have argued in my speech that a society based on varna or caste is a society which is based on a wrong relationship. I had hoped that the Mahatma would attempt to demolish my argument. But instead of doing that, he has merely reiterated his belief in Chaturvarnya without disclosing the ground on which it is based.

Does the Mahatma practise what he preaches? One does not like to make personal reference in an argument which is general in its application. But when one preaches a doctrine and holds it as a dogma, there is a curiosity to know how far he practises what he preaches. It may be that his failure to practise is due to the ideal being too high to be attainable; it may be that his failure to practise is due to the innate hypocrisy of the man. In any case he exposes his conduct to examination, and I must not be blamed if I ask, how far has the Mahatma attempted to realize his ideal in his own case?

The Mahatma is a Bania by birth. His ancestors had abandoned trading in favour of ministership, which is a calling of the Brahmins.

In his own life, before he became a Mahatma, when the occasion came for him to choose his career he preferred law to [a merchant's] scales. On abandoning law, he became half-saint and half-politician. He has never touched trading, which is his ancestral calling.

His youngest son—I take one who is a faithful follower of his father—was born a Vaishya, has married a Brahmin's daughter, and has chosen to serve a newspaper magnate. The Mahatma is not known to have condemned him for not following his ancestral calling. It may be wrong and uncharitable to judge an ideal by its worst specimens. But surely the Mahatma as a specimen has no better, and if he even fails to realize the ideal then the ideal must be an impossible ideal, quite opposed to the practical instincts of man.

Students of Carlyle know that he often spoke on a subject before he thought about it. I wonder whether such has not been the case with the Mahatma, in regard to the subject matter of caste. Otherwise, certain questions which occur to me would not have escaped him. When can a calling be deemed to have become an ancestral calling, so as to make it binding on a man? Must a man follow his ancestral calling even if it does not suit his capacities, even when it has ceased to be profitable? Must a man live by his ancestral calling even if he finds it to be immoral? If everyone must pursue his ancestral calling, then it must follow that a man must continue to be a pimp because his grandfather was a pimp, and a woman must continue to be a prostitute because her grandmother was a prostitute. Is the Mahatma prepared to accept the logical conclusion of his doctrine? To me his ideal of following one's ancestral calling is not only an impossible and impractical ideal, but it is also morally an indefensible ideal.

Chapter 10

THE ANNIHILATION OF CASTE

Friends,

I am really sorry for the members of the Jat-Pat-Todak Mandal who have so very kindly invited me to preside over this Conference. I am sure they will be asked many questions for having selected me as the President. The Mandal will be asked to explain as to why it has imported a man from Bombay to preside over a function which is held in Lahore. I believe the Mandal could easily have found someone better qualified than myself to preside on the occasion. I have criticized the Hindus. I have questioned the authority of the Mahatma whom they revere. They hate me. To them I am a snake in their garden. The Mandal will no doubt be asked by the politically-minded Hindus to explain why it has called me to fill this place of honour. It is an act of great daring. I shall not be surprised if some political Hindus regard it as an insult. This selection of me certainly cannot please the ordinary religious-minded Hindus.

The Mandal may be asked to explain why it has disobeyed the Shastric injunction in selecting the President. According to the Shastras, the Brahmin is appointed to be the Guru for the three varnas,[134] is a direction of the Shastras. The Mandal therefore knows from whom a Hindu should take his lessons and from whom he should not. The Shastras do not permit a Hindu to accept anyone as his Guru merely

---

[134]'Varnanam Brahmano Guru.' This is Manusmriti 10.3. Bibek Debroy's translation: 'Among varnas, the Brahman is the teacher/preceptor.' There is no standardized text of the Manusmriti; in some versions, the text mentions prabhu (lord) instead of guru (teacher). George Buhler renders the entire couplet at 10.3 as follows: 'On account of his pre-eminence, on account of the superiority of his origin, on account of his observance of (particular) restrictive rules, and on account of his particular sanctification the Brahmana is the lord of (all) castes (varna)' (1886/2004, 276). Chapter 10 of the Manusmriti discusses varnas and their duties at length and lists out dos and don'ts.

because he is well-versed. This is made very clear by Ramdas,[135] a Brahmin saint from Maharashtra, who is alleged to have inspired Shivaji to establish a Hindu Raj. In his Dasbodh, a socio-politico-religious treatise in Marathi verse, Ramdas asks, addressing the Hindus, can we accept an Antyaja[136] to be our Guru because he is a Pandit (i.e. learned)? He gives an answer in the negative.

---

[135]Ramdas (1608–81) was a seventeenth-century coeval of the Maratha king Shivaji (1627/30–80), and is said to have been his Brahmin guru. Bhakti poet Tukaram, Shudra by birth and trader by profession, was also his contemporary. Bhakti is devotional love for a personal god experienced without the mediation of the priest or ritual. The progenitors of the Bhakti movement, the Alvars (sixth to ninth centuries) and Nayanmars (twelfth century) of the Tamil country, were fiercely monotheistic in their expression of love for Vishnu and Siva or their forms, and this happened at the expense and persecution of Jains and Buddhists (see: Monius 2011). What was crucial, however, was that anyone from any strata of society—men and women—could aspire to reach god. The twelfth-century Basava-led Veerashaiva movement in the Kannada-speaking South, that launched the literary vachana tradition, reoudiated the caste system and the primacy of the Brahmin. Between the fourteenth and eighteenth centuries, sometimes fusing with elements of Islam and Sufism, the Bhakti movement manifested itself variously in the western, northern and eastern parts of the subcontinent through the work of sants, or teachers, who were largely from working-caste backgrounds but also included Brahmins (like Dnyaneshwar in western India or Chaitanya in Bengal) who embraced Bhakti's egalitarian credo. According to the scholar Veena Naregal (2001, 12), Ramdas's 'religious and political pragmatism were quite at variance with the inspiration of the Bhakti poets'. Dasbodh, composed of 70,000 ovis over twenty sections, offers an interpretation of vedantic philosophy. Ramdas talked of the need for the return of Brahmin supremacy and viewed the crisis in Maratha society as a breakdown in the social order due to 'Muslim oppression', Hindu conversions to Islam, and the usurpation of Brahmin spiritual leadership by the non-Brahmin Varkari saints and gurus (Ranade, 1983). Ramdas today is a hero for Hindu nationalists, especially the Chitpavan Brahmins of Maharashtra. See also Note 32 on the Varkari tradition. Also see Gail Omvedt's account (1976) of the differences between Mahanubhav Bhakti and Ramdas's version of it, which she argues blunted the radical potential of Mahanubhav.

[136]Antyaja: last-born; a term used for those outside the pale of the fourfold varna system which comprises Brahmin (priests), Kshatriya (warriors), Vaishya (merchants and farmers) and Shudra (menials). Of these, the first three groups are considered dwija, twice-born. The Shudra are the servile class meant to serve the top three varnas. The antyaja are outside the pale—Untouchables meant to live outside the village.

What replies to give to these questions is a matter which I must leave to the Mandal. The Mandal knows best the reasons which led it to travel to Bombay to select a president, to fix upon a man so repugnant to the Hindus, and to descend so low in the scale as to select an Antyaja—an untouchable—to address an audience of the Savarnas.[137] As for myself, you will allow me to say that I have accepted the invitation much against my will, and also against the will of many of my fellow Untouchables. I know that the Hindus are sick of me. I know that I am not a persona grata [someone welcome] with them. Knowing all this, I have deliberately kept myself away from them. I have no desire to inflict myself upon them. I have been giving expression to my views from my own platform. This has already caused a great deal of heart-burning[138] and irritation.

I have no desire to ascend the platform of the Hindus, to do within their sight what I have been doing within their hearing. If I am here it is because of your choice and not because of my wish. Yours is a cause of social reform. That cause has always made an appeal to me, and it is because of this that I felt I ought not to refuse an opportunity of helping the cause—especially when you think that I can help it. Whether what I am going to say today will help you in any way to solve the problem you are grappling with, is for you to judge. All I hope to do is to place before you my views on the problem.

The path of social reform, like the path to heaven (at any rate, in India), is strewn with many difficulties. Social reform in India has few friends and many critics. The critics fall into two distinct classes. One class consists of political reformers, and the other of the socialists.

It was at one time recognized that without social efficiency,[139] no

---

[137]Savarna: those with varna, a Caste Hindu; a term used for those within the fourfold varna system. A Shudra is also a savarna; the opposite of savarna is avarna, the Untouchable.

[138]'Heart-burning' in AoC 1936 and subsequent editions.

[139]Ambedkar is borrowing this term from John Dewey (1859–1952), the prominent American pragmatist philosopher, radical democrat and educational theorist who taught Ambedkar at Columbia University and influenced him deeply. Dewey, author of about forty books, helped create some of the most prominent political and educational organizations of his time: the American Civil Liberties Union,

permanent progress in the other fields of activity was possible; that owing to mischief wrought by evil customs, Hindu Society was not in a state of efficiency; and that ceaseless efforts must be made to eradicate these evils. It was due to the recognition of this fact that the birth of the National Congress was accompanied by the foundation of the Social Conference.[140] While the Congress was concerned with defining the weak points in the political organization of the country, the Social Conference was engaged in removing the weak points in the social organization of the Hindu Society. For some time the Congress and the Conference worked as two wings of one common activity, and they held their annual sessions in the same pandal.

But soon the two wings developed into two parties, a 'political reform party' and a 'social reform party', between whom there raged a fierce controversy. The 'political reform party' supported the National Congress, and the 'social reform party' supported the Social Conference. The two bodies thus became two hostile camps. The point at issue was

---

the National Association for the Advancement of Colored People (NAACP), the League for Industrial Democracy, the New York Teachers Union, the American Association of University Professors, and the New School for Social Research. 'Social efficiency' was a term that began its career in 1884 when it was introduced by British sociologist Benjamin Kidd (known for his work Social Evolution, 1884) who used it in a social Darwinist sense, but Dewey and others sought to rescue the term from a narrow, utilitarian approach and imbue it with humanitarian value. In the field of education, the term acquired currency in the 1920s. Arun P. Mukherjee (2009), who offers a fine analysis of Ambedkar's refashioning of Deweyan thought into a tool for his own investigations of Indian society, argues that for Dewey and Ambedkar social efficiency lies in the individual being able to choose and develop his/her competencies to the fullest and thus mindfully contribute to the functioning of society. For a system that predetermines a person's occupation on the basis of caste or class affiliations cannot but result in inefficiency. The term has its origins in early-twentieth-century attempts at reorganizing society, politics and the economy for 'efficiency' based on 'scientific principles'. For more on this, see Knoll (2009) and Holt (1994).

[140]The (Indian National) Social Conference was founded by Mahadev Govind Ranade (1842–1901) in 1887, two years after the founding of the Indian National Congress. It was meant to serve as the social arm of the Congress, and it focused mainly on women's uplift. Conservative leaders like B.G. Tilak were staunchly opposed to even the mild reforms suggested by votaries of the Social Conference.

whether social reform should precede political reform. For a decade the forces were evenly balanced, and the battle was fought without victory to either side.

It was, however, evident that the fortunes of the Social Conference were ebbing fast. The gentlemen who presided over the sessions of the Social Conference lamented that the majority of the educated Hindus were for political advancement and indifferent to social reform; and that while the number of those who attended the Congress was very large, and the number who did not attend but who sympathized with it was even larger, the number of those who attended the Social Conference was very much smaller.

This indifference, this thinning of its ranks, was soon followed by active hostility from the politicians. Under the leadership of the late Mr Tilak,[141] the courtesy with which the Congress allowed the Social Conference the use of its pandal was withdrawn, and the spirit of enmity went to such a pitch that when the Social Conference desired to erect its own pandal, a threat to burn the pandal was held out by its opponents.[142] Thus in the course of time the party in favour of political reform won, and the Social Conference vanished and was forgotten.

---

[141]Bal Gangadhar 'Lokmanya' Tilak (1865–1920) was a Chitpavan Brahmin and a social conservative who sought to imbue Congress nationalism with a distinct right-wing hue. He published two newspapers, the Marathi-language/Cesar/and Mahratta in English. Jaffrelot (2005, 44) calls him 'the Congress leader from Poona who tended not to put in practice the social reforms he articulated' (emphasis added). Tilak saw even the education of women and non-Brahmins as 'a loss of nationality' and consistently opposed the establishment of girls' schools at a time when his coeval Jotiba Phule launched a full-scale attack on Brahminism, educated his wife Savitri, and established a school for girls which also admitted Untouchable children. See Rao (n.d.). For an account of the Phule-led non-Brahmin movement, see O'Hanjon (2002).

[142]For a chronicle of the tussles between the Social Conference and conservative forces within the Congress, see John R. McLane (1988, 47–61). McLane writes: 'In Maharashtra, Tilak demonstrated the potent political appeal of Hindu symbolism with the Ganapati and Shivaji festivals. In 1895, when the Congress met in Poona, the rowdyism of Tilak's anti-reformer allies forced the Social Conference to abandon the use of the Congress enclosure for its meeting' (55).

The speech delivered by Mr W.C. Bonnerji[143] in 1892 at Allahabad, as President of the eighth session of the Congress, sounds like a funeral oration on the death of the Social Conference, and is so typical of the Congress attitude that I venture to quote from it the following extract. Mr Bonnerji said:

'I for one have no patience with those who say we shall not be fit for political reform until we reform our social system. I fail to see any connection between the two... Are we not fit (for political reform) because our widows remain unmarried and our girls are given in marriage earlier than in other countries? because our wives and daughters do not drive about with us visiting our friends? because we do not send our daughters to Oxford and Cambridge?' (Cheers [from the audience])

I have stated the case for political reform as put by Mr Bonnerji. There were many who were happy that the victory went to the Congress. But those who believe in the importance of social reform may ask, is an argument such as that of Mr Bonnerji final? Does it prove that the victory went to those who were in the right? Does it prove conclusively that social reform has no bearing on political reform? It will help us to understand the matter if I state the other side of the case. I will draw upon the treatment of the Untouchables for my facts.

Under the rule of the Peshwas in the Maratha country,[144] the

---

[143]Womesh Chunder Bonnerjee was amongst the founders of the Indian National Congress and became its first president. As a lawyer, he divided his life between England and Calcutta, and on retirement settled in Croydon, England. See the account of his daughter Janaki Agnes Penelope Majumdar (2003). While studying in England, in 1865, Bonnerjee wrote in a letter to his uncle: 'I have discarded all ideas of caste, I have come to hate all the demoralising practices of our countrymen and I write this letter an entirely altered man' (Kumar 1989, 48). Since he had 'lost caste' by crossing the seas, Bonnerjee was regarded an outcaste by his family. He set up a separate household refusing to undergo penance, and renounced Hindu customs. He brought his wife out of purdah, made her eat beef and wear English clothes, and sent his children to England for education (Majumdar 2003).

[144]The Peshwas were initially ministers under Shivaji who founded the Maratha empire in seventeenth-century western India. After the death of Shivaji in 1680, the Peshwas, who were Chitpavan Brahmins, turned into a military-bureaucratic

untouchable was not allowed to use the public streets if a Hindu was coming along, lest he should pollute the Hindu by his shadow. The untouchable was required to have a black thread either on his wrist or around his neck, as a sign or a mark to prevent the Hindus from getting themselves polluted by his touch by mistake. In Poona, the capital of the Peshwa, the untouchable was required to carry, strung from his waist, a broom to sweep away from behind himself the dust he trod on, lest a Hindu walking on the same dust should be polluted. In Poona, the untouchable was required to carry an earthen pot hung around his neck wherever he went—for holding his spit, lest his spit falling on the earth should pollute a Hindu who might unknowingly happen to tread on it.

Let me take more recent facts. The tyranny practised by the Hindus upon the Balais, an untouchable community in Central India, will serve my purpose. You will find a report of this in the *Times of India* of 4 January 1928. The correspondent of the *Times of India* reported that high-caste Hindus—viz., Kalotas, Rajputs and Brahmins, including the Patels and Patwaris of the villages of Kanaria, Bicholi-Hafsi, Bicholi-Mardana, and about fifteen other villages in the Indore district (of the Indore State)—informed the Balais of their respective villages that if they wished to live among them, they must conform to the following rules:

1. Balais must not wear gold-lace-bordered pugrees.
2. They must not wear dhotis with coloured or fancy borders.
3. They must convey intimation [information] of the death of any Hindu to relatives of the deceased—no matter how far away these relatives may be living.

elite, and, in one of those rare instances, both ritual and secular power were vested with Brahmins. The reign of the Peshwas witnessed what feminist scholar Uma Chakravarti (1995, 3–21) terms 'the consolidation of Brahmanya-raj'. In 1818, the 30,000-strong army of the last Peshwa, Bajirao II (1795–1818), was defeated by the 500-member regiment of Untouchable Mahar soldiers led by Capt F.F. Staunton. This is known as the Battle of Koregaon, along the river Bhima, northwest of Poona. For an account of the rise of the Brahmins in western India, see Eaton (2005).

4. In all Hindu marriages, Balais must play music before the processions and during the marriage.
5. Balai women must not wear gold or silver ornaments; they must not wear fancy gowns or jackets.
6. Balai women must attend all cases of confinement [childbirth] of Hindu women.[145]
7. Balais must render services without demanding remuneration, and must accept whatever a Hindu is pleased to give.
8. If the Balais do not agree to abide by these terms, they must clear out of the villages.

The Balais refused to comply; and the Hindu element proceeded against them. Balais were not allowed to get water from the village wells; they were not allowed to let go their cattle to graze. Balais were prohibited from passing through land owned by a Hindu, so that if the field of a Balai was surrounded by fields owned by Hindus, the Balai could have no access to his own field. The Hindus also let their cattle graze down the fields of Balais. The Balais submitted petitions to the Darbar[146] [Court of Indore] against these persecutions; but as they could get no timely relief, and the oppression continued, hundreds of Balais with their wives and children were obliged to abandon their homes—in which their ancestors had lived for generations—and to migrate to adjoining States: that is, to villages in Dhar, Dewas, Bagli, Bhopal, Gwalior and other States. What happened to them in their new homes may for the present be left out of our consideration.

The incident at Kavitha[147] in Gujarat happened only last year.

---

[145]In large parts of India, Dalit women act as dais (midwives) and are expected to help with childbirth in privileged-caste households.

[146]Ambedkar is referring here to the court of Indore. This can be inferred from a citation of the same *Times of India* article in the posthumously published *Untouchables or the Children of India's Ghetto* (BAWS 5, 48–9).

[147]Following a Bombay government ruling, in August 1935, that Untouchable students should be admitted to schools, the Untouchables of Kavitha village enrolled four children in the local school. This invoked both physical assaults and social boycott, and the Untouchables turned to the Harijan Sevak Sangh, an organisation founded by M.K. Gandhi, for help. Gandhi and 'Sardar' Vallabhbhai Patel opposed the Untouchables' efforts at taking recourse to law, and forced

The Hindus of Kavitha ordered the Untouchables not to insist upon sending their children to the common village school maintained by Government. What sufferings the Untouchables of Kavitha had to undergo, for daring to exercise a civic right against the wishes of the Hindus, is too well-known to need detailed description. Another instance occurred in the village of Zanu, in the Ahmedabad district of Gujarat. In November 1935 some untouchable women of well-to-do families started fetching water in metal pots. The Hindus looked upon the use of metal pots by Untouchables as an affront to their dignity, and assaulted the untouchable women for their impudence.

A most recent event is reported from the village of Chakwara in Jaipur State. It seems from the reports that have appeared in the newspapers that an untouchable of Chakwara who had returned from a pilgrimage had arranged to give a dinner to his fellow Untouchables of the village, as an act of religious piety. The host desired to treat the guests to a sumptuous meal, and the items served included ghee (butter) also. But while the assembly of Untouchables was engaged in partaking of the food, the Hindus in their hundreds, armed with lathis, rushed to the scene, despoiled the food, and belaboured the Untouchables—who left the food they had been served with and ran[148] away for their lives. And why was this murderous assault committed

---

them to withdraw their complaint. Ambedkar, while recounting this incident, does not mince words (BAWS 5, 43): 'With all the knowledge of tyranny and oppression practised by the caste Hindus of Kavitha against the Untouchables all that Mr Gandhi felt like doing was to advise the Untouchables to leave the village. He did not even suggest that the miscreants should be hauled up before a court of law. His henchman, Mr Vallabhbhai Patel, played a part which was still more strange. He had gone to Kavitha to persuade the caste Hindus not to molest the Untouchables. But they did not even give him a hearing. Yet this very man was opposed to the Untouchables hauling them up in a court of law and getting them punished. The Untouchables filed the complaint notwithstanding his opposition. But he ultimately forced them to withdraw the complaint on the caste Hindus making some kind of a show of an understanding not to molest, an undertaking, which the Untouchables can never enforce. The result was that the Untouchables suffered and their tyrants escaped with the aid of Mr Gandhi's friend, Mr Vallabhbhai Patel.'

[148]'Ran away' in AoC 1936 and subsequent editions.

on defenceless Untouchables? The reason given is that the untouchable host was impudent enough to serve ghee, and his untouchable guests were foolish enough to taste it. Ghee is undoubtedly a luxury for the rich. But no one would think that consumption of ghee was a mark of high social status. The Hindus of Chakwara thought otherwise, and in righteous indignation avenged themselves for the wrong done to them by the Untouchables, who insulted them by treating ghee as an item of their food—which they ought to have known could not be theirs, consistently with the dignity of the Hindus. This means that an untouchable must not use ghee, even if he can afford to buy it, since it is an act of arrogance towards the Hindus. This happened on or about the 1st of April 1936![149]

Having stated the facts, let me now state the case for social reform. In doing this, I will follow Mr Bonnerji as nearly as I can, and ask the political-minded Hindus, 'Are you fit for political power even though you do not allow a large class of your own countrymen like the Untouchables to use public schools? Are you fit for political power even though class of your own countrymen like the Untouchables to use public schools? Are you fit for political power even though you do not allow them the use of public wells? Are you fit for political power even though you do not allow them the use of public streets? Are you fit for political power even though you do not allow them to wear what apparel or ornaments they like? Are you fit for political power even though you do not allow them to eat any food they like?' I can ask a string of such questions. But these will suffice.

I wonder what would have been the reply of Mr Bonnerji. I am sure no sensible man will have the courage to give an affirmative answer. Every Congressman who repeats the dogma of Mill[150] that

---

[149]The state of affairs in Chakwara has far from improved. Dalits in this village, denied access to the local pond, have been waging a struggle since 1980. In 2001, two Dalits were fined Rs 50,000 by the Jat- and Brahmin-dominated village panchayat for using water from the Chakwara pond (Usmani, 2008).

[150]John Stuart Mill (1806–73) in the last chapter of Considerations on Representative Government (1861/2004) poses a critique of the colonial administration of the British empire. However, Mill's criticism has to be seen in the context of his advocating 'representative government' for the Americas and Australia for they

one country is not fit to rule another country, must admit that one class is not fit to rule another class. How is it then that the 'social reform party' lost the battle? To understand this correctly it is necessary to take note of the kind of social reform which the reformers were agitating for. In this connection it is necessary to make a distinction between social reform in the sense of the reform of the Hindu family, and social reform in the sense of the reorganization and reconstruction of the Hindu Society. The former has a relation to widow remarriage, child marriage, etc., while the latter relates to the abolition of the caste system.

The Social Conference was a body which mainly concerned itself with the reform of the high-caste[151] Hindu family. It consisted mostly of enlightened high-caste Hindus who did not feel the necessity for agitating for the abolition of caste, or had not the courage to agitate for it. They felt quite naturally a greater urge to remove such evils as enforced widowhood, child marriages, etc.—evils which prevailed among them and which were personally felt by them. They did not stand up for the reform of the Hindu Society. The battle that was fought centered round the question of the reform of the family. It did not relate to social reform in the sense of the break-up of the caste system. It [the break-up of the caste system] was never put in issue by the reformers. That is the reason why the Social Reform Party lost.

I am aware that this argument cannot alter the fact that political reform did in fact gain precedence over social reform. But the argument has this much value (if not more): it explains why social reformers

---

are 'composed of people of similar civilisation to the ruling country', and 'whose population', he says, 'is in a sufficiently advanced state', compared to which 'others, like India, are still at a great distance from that state'. Here, Mill argues, the coloniser must rule to introduce a higher form of civilisation. Ambedkar is alluding here to his contemporaries' reverence for a complex figure who on the one hand championed the cause of individual freedom and liberty, and on the other, defended British imperialism by justifying the right of 'civilised' nations to rule over 'barbarians'. In his essay, 'A Few Words on Non-Intervention' (1859/1984), Mill outlines the circumstances under which states should be allowed to intervene in the sovereign affairs of another country.

[151]Term added in 1937.

lost the battle. It also helps us to understand how limited was the victory which the 'political reform party' obtained over the 'social reform party', and to understand that the view that social reform need not precede political reform is a view which may stand only when by social reform is meant the reform of the family. That political reform cannot with impunity take precedence over social reform in the sense of the reconstruction of society, is a thesis which I am sure cannot be controverted.

That the makers of political constitutions must take account of social forces is a fact which is recognized by no less a person than Ferdinand Lassalle,[152] the friend and co-worker of Karl Marx. In addressing a Prussian audience in 1862, Lassalle said:

> 'The constitutional questions are in the first instance not questions of right but questions of might. The actual constitution of a country has its existence only in the actual condition of force which exists in the country: hence political constitutions have value and permanence only when they accurately express those conditions of forces which exist in practice within a society.'[153]

But it is not necessary to go to Prussia.[154] There is evidence at home. What is the significance of the Communal Award,[155] with its

---

[152]Ferdinand Lassalle (1825–64) was a philologist, legal expert and social agitator, the first to organise a socialist party in Germany and rally the workers to assert their rights. He came to prominence as an interpreter of Marxism for the workers. However, from a letter written by Marx to Ludwig Kugelmann on 23 February 1865 it is clear that Marx considered Lassalle's interpretation plagiarism. In the same letter he also expresses his condemnation of Lassalle's attempt at striking a deal with Bismarck urging him to introduce universal adult suffrage in exchange of working-class support for the government.

[153]Ambedkar is quoting from 'On the Essence of Constitutions', the famous speech Lassalle delivered on 16 April 1862 in Berlin.

[154]Rendered as 'Lasalle' in AoC 1936.

[155]The Communal Award, also known as the Ramsay Macdonald Award after the British Prime Minister, issued on 16 August 1932, was the result of the Second Round Table Conference (September–December 1931) that granted separate electorates to minorities in the dominion of India. Besides Muslims and Sikhs, the Depressed Classes were also granted a separate electorate for twenty years. The

allocation of political power in defined proportions to diverse classes and communities? In my view, its significance lies in this: that political constitution must take note of social organization. It shows that the politicians who denied that the social problem in India had any bearing on the political problem were forced to reckon with the social problem in devising the Constitution. The Communal Award is, so to say, the nemesis following upon the indifference to and neglect of social reform. It is a victory for the Social Reform Party which shows that, though defeated, they were in the right in insisting upon the importance of social reform. Many, I know, will not accept this finding. The view is current—and it is pleasant to believe in it—that the Communal Award is unnatural and that it is the result of an unholy alliance between the minorities and the bureaucracy.[156] I do not wish to rely on the Communal Award as a piece of evidence to support my contention, if it is said that it is not good evidence.

Let us turn to Ireland. What does the history of Irish Home Rule show? It is well-known that in the course of the negotiations between the representatives of Ulster and Southern Ireland, Mr Redmond, the representative of Southern Ireland, in order to bring Ulster into a Home Rule Constitution common to the whole of Ireland, said to the Ireland, in order to bring Ulster into a Home Rule Constitution common to the whole of Ireland, said to the representatives of Ulster: 'Ask any political safeguards you like and you shall have them.' What was the reply that Ulstermen gave? Their reply was, 'Damn your safeguards, we

---

award granted a double vote to Untouchables that allowed them to choose their own representatives from special constituencies, as well as to cast their vote in general constituencies. The Congress and Gandhi opposed this, and Gandhi went on indefinite hunger strike in Poona jail. A compromise was reached with the signing of the Poona Pact on 24 September 1932, under which the Untouchables were allotted reserved constituencies but not separate electorates. See the text of the Communal Award in B.R. Ambedkar (BAWS 9, 81). For a further delineation of the Communal Award and the Poona Pact and their implications, see 'A Note on the Poona Pact' in this book (357–76).

[156]For an analysis and discussion of the Communal Award and the Poona Pact, see Zelliot (2013, 128–42); Jaffrelot (2005, 52–73); Kumar (1985).

don't want to be ruled by you on any terms.'[157] People who blame the minorities in India ought to consider what would have happened to the political aspirations of the majority, if the minorities had taken the attitude which Ulster took. Judged by the attitude of Ulster to Irish Home Rule, is it nothing that the minorities agreed to be ruled by the majority (which has not shown much sense of statesmanship), provided some safeguards were devised for them? But this is only incidental. The main question is, why did Ulster take this attitude? The only answer I can give is that there was a social problem between Ulster and Southern Ireland: the problem between Catholics and Protestants, which is essentially a problem of caste. That Home Rule in Ireland would be Rome Rule was the way in which the Ulstermen had framed their answer. But that is only another way of stating that it was the social problem of caste between the Catholics and Protestants which prevented the solution of the political problem. This evidence again is sure to be challenged. It will be urged that here too the hand of the Imperialist was at work.

But my resources are not exhausted. I will give evidence from the History of Rome. Here no one can say that any evil genius was at work. Anyone who has studied the History of Rome will know that the Republican Constitution of Rome bore marks having strong resemblance to the Communal Award. When the kingship in Rome was abolished, the kingly power (or the Imperium) was divided between the Consuls and the Pontifex Maximus.[158] In the Consuls was vested the

---

[157]The Irish Home Rule movement was launched in the second half of the nineteenth century to recover legislative independence from the British after Ireland had become part of the Union. See more in Alan O'Day (1998) and Alvin Jackson (2003). Howard Brasted (1980) argues that the precedent of the Irish Home Rule movement awoke the nationalist spirit amongst the educated Indian elite and provided a model for the Congress. Home Rule could never be implemented in Ireland due to the strong opposition by the Protestant Unionists of Northern Ireland (Ulstermen). Here, it is not clear if Ambedkar is referring to John Edward Redmond (1856–1918), Member of Parliament and leader of the Irish Parliamentary Party and the National League, or his brother, William (Willie) Redmond (1861–1917), also an MP and nationalist politician.
[158]Pontifex Maximus was the highest priest of the college of pontiffs in ancient Rome.

secular authority of the king, while the latter took over the religious authority of the king. This Republican Constitution had provided that of the two Consuls, one was to be Patrician and the other Plebian.[159] The same Constitution had also provided that of the Priests under the Pontifex Maximus, half were to be Plebians and the other half Patricians. Why is it that the Republican Constitution of Rome had these provisions—which, as I said, resemble so strongly the provisions of the Communal Award? The only answer one can get is that the Constitution of Republican Rome had to take account of the social division between the Patricians and the Plebians, who formed two distinct castes.[160] To sum up, let political reformers turn in any direction they like: they will find that in the making of a constitution, they cannot ignore the problem arising out of the prevailing social order.

The illustrations which I have taken in support of the proposition that social and religious problems have a bearing on political constitutions seem to be too particular. Perhaps they are. But it should not be supposed that the bearing of the one on the other is limited. On the other hand, one can say that generally speaking, History bears

---

[159]Patricians (derived from the root patre, meaning 'father') were the upper class in ancient Rome. Their ancestry was traced back by Roman historians such as Livy to the legend of Romulus, the mythical founder of Rome, who is said to have appointed one hundred men as senators. Patricians claimed to be descendants of these first senators and the Sabine women kidnapped and raped for procreation. Plebeians were the general body of lower-class, free citizens. There were other lower classes like the peregrini and slaves. Most historians agree that the distinction between patricians, plebeians and other classes was based purely on birth. The most readily available tool to distinguish between the classes was gentes, family names. See Livy (2006).

[160]In his speech during the second leg of the Mahad Satyagraha on 25 December 1927, Ambedkar refers to the patrician-plebeian struggle, or 'the Conflict of the Orders' as it is more commonly known, in greater detail. The Conflict of the Orders, in which the plebeians sought political equality with the patricians, lasted between 494 and 2–87 BCE. In this protracted conflict, the patricians were occasionally forced to give some concession to the plebeians, but always sought to retain the final authority. Thus the provisions for economic reform in laws like Lex Licinia Sextia (367 BCE) and Leges. Genuciae (342 BCE)—ceiling on the ownership of land by a single person, ban on lending that carried interest, etc.—were largely ignored by the patricians. In his Mahad speech, Ambedkar gives a very interesting

out the proposition that political revolutions have always been preceded by social and religious revolutions. The religious Reformation started by Luther[161] was the precursor of the political emancipation of the European people. In England, Puritanism led to the establishment of political liberty. Puritanism founded the new world. It was Puritanism that won the war of American Independence, and Puritanism was a religious movement.[162]

The same is true of the Muslim Empire. Before the Arabs became a political power, they had undergone a thorough religious revolution started by the Prophet Mohammad.[163] Even Indian History supports

---

[161]Martin Luther (1483–1546), German monk who held the chair of Theology at the University of Wittenberg, was a key figure (along with John Calvin, John Wycliffe and Jan Hus) in the sixteenth-century Reformation movement. He sought to shift the religious leadership's focus away from fees and payments as part of a renewal of the medieval Church. The reformers hoped to restore and clarify the core tenets of the faith, which they would then make accessible to all Christians. For a history of European Reformation, see Peter G. Wallace (2004).

[162]The English Civil War (1642–51), which questioned the prerogative of the king and challenged the theory of divine right, owed much to the spirit of European Reformation. The Puritans—who espoused a militant, biblically based Calvinistic Protestantism—sought to 'purify' the Church of England of remnants of the Catholic popery, and argued that the Anglican Church established by Queen Elizabeth was far too close to Roman Catholicism. ('Puritan' means that the followers had a pure soul and lived a good life.) Alexis de Tocqueville (1805–59), the French political thinker best known for his two-volume Democracy in America (1835, 1840), argued that the tradition of political liberty in the United States of America began with the settling of New England by the Puritans from England. For an in-depth study of debates around puritanism and liberty in England, see Puritanism and Liberty, being the Army Debates (1647–9) from the Clarke Manuscripts with Supplementary Documents in A.S.P. Woodhouse (1951). This contains the Putney Debates, the Whitehall Debates, and numerous other documents about Puritan religious and political views during the English Revolution.

[163]Prophet Muhammad (570–632 CE) unified scores of warring Arab tribes into a single religious polity (ummah, community) under Islam (which means to submit, surrender). For a concise history of Islam, see Karen Armstrong (2000), who writes: "Muhammad had become the head of a collection of tribal groups that were not bound together by blood but by a shared ideology, an astonishing innovation in Arabian society' (14). Nobody was forced to convert, but all Muslims belonged

the same conclusion. The political revolution led by Chandragupta was preceded by the religious and social revolution of Buddha.[164] The political revolution led by Shivaji was preceded by the religious and social reform brought about by the saints of Maharashtra.[165] The political revolution of the Sikhs was preceded by the religious and social revolution led by Guru Nanak.[166] It is unnecessary to add more

---

to one ummah, they could not attack one another, and they vowed to give one another protection.

[164]Chandragupta Maurya (340–298 BCE), founder of the Mauryan dynasty, is credited with being the first emperor to rule large parts of the Indian subcontinent as one state. Gautama Buddha (c. 563–483 BCE), on whose teachings Buddhism was founded, preceded him. Chandragupta's grandson was the emperor Ashoka (304–232 BCE), who turned from a warmonger to an advocate of Buddhism and pacifism (though he continued to give the death penalty till the end of his reign).

[165]The allusion here is to the Varkari tradition that was established in western India with the Brahmin Dnyandev or Dnyaneswar, and the Untouchable Cokhamela in the fourteenth century, and was followed by saint-poets from the subaltern castes like Namdeo, Bahinabai and Tukaram into the seventeenth century. While Ambedkar disregarded the piety of Cokhamela, he quite often quoted the radical Tukaram who was Shivaji's contemporary. For a discussion of the political aspects of Tukaram, who was of the Kunabi peasant caste, and his influence on Shivaji, see Gail Omvedt (2008, 109–32). A varkar is a pilgrim, and the Varkari tradition revolves around the god Vithoba or Vitthala in Pandharpur (in Maharashtra's Solapur district). In popular lore Vitthala has come to be regarded as a form of Krishna and this tradition is seen as Vaishnavite. The Varkari cult is seven hundred years old, and with it begins the Marathi literary tradition, according to Omvedt (85). She discusses how scholars believe Vitthala could have had origins in Saivism, Buddhism or even among pastoral nomadic tribes. Omvedt discusses the Sanskritisation and Vishnu-isation of Vitthala and believes the god could have been originally female ('wide hips, narrow waist, busty, long hair, straight though harsh face') and that contemporary Dalit Buddhists point to 'the god's blackness as evidence of indigenous origins' based on iconography (see 85–90). For an overview of the Bhakti tradition and sants in Maharashtra, see Zelliot and Berntsen (1998). Also see the volume edited by Lele (1981).

[166]Guru Nanak (1469–1539) was the first of the ten gurus and founder of the Sikh religion. He started a strand of nirguni (without attributes) Bhakti tradition that advocated spending one's life immersed in nam simran (remembrance of the divine name). Guru Nanak and the gurus that followed him preached spiritual equality against varnashrama dharma and imparted their teaching to devotees from

illustrations. These will suffice to show that the emancipation of the mind and the soul is a necessary preliminary for the political expansion of the people.

Let me now turn to the socialists. Can the socialists ignore the problem arising out of the social order? The socialists of India, following their fellows in Europe, are seeking to apply the economic interpretation of history to the facts of India.[167] They propound that man is an economic creature, that his activities and aspirations are bound by economic facts, that property is the only source of power. They therefore preach that political and social reforms are but gigantic illusions, and that economic reform by equalization of property must have precedence over every other kind of reform. One may take issue with every one of these premises—on which rests the socialists' case for economic reform as having priority over issue with every one of these premises—on which rests the socialists' case for economic reform as having priority over every other kind of reform. One may contend that the economic motive is not the only motive by which man is actuated [motivated]. That economic power is the only kind of power, no student of human society can accept.

That the social status of an individual by itself often becomes a source of power and authority, is made clear by the sway which the Mahatmas have held over the common man. Why do millionaires in India obey penniless Sadhus and Fakirs? Why do millions of paupers in India sell their trifling trinkets which constitute their only wealth, and go to Benares and Mecca? That religion is the source of power is illustrated by the history of India, where the priest holds a sway over

---

all castes. Puri (2003, 2694) writes that while the Sikh holy book, Guru Granth Sahib, includes compositions by Kabir, a weaver, and Ravidas, a tanner (Chamar), the ten gurus of Sikhism came from Khatri families—the highest caste among Sikhs—and married their children within their caste. Despite the preaching of spiritual equality in the eyes of god, there was no expectation on the part of the gurus or their devotees to give up caste identity and thus the doctrine was not translated into social equality.

[167]Ambedkar is referring here to the socialists within the Congress who in 1934 formed a faction called the Congress Socialist Party (CSP). Jawaharlal Nehru, at this juncture, was also actively advocating socialist ideas but did join the CSP.

the common man often greater than that of the magistrate, and where everything, even such things as strikes and elections, so easily takes a religious turn and can so easily be given a religious twist.

Take the case of the Plebians of Rome, as a further illustration of the power of religion over man. It throws great light on this point. The Plebians had fought for a share in the supreme executive under the Roman Republic, and had secured the appointment of a Plebian Consul elected by a separate electorate constituted by the Commitia Centuriata,[168] which was an assembly of Plebians. They wanted a Consul of their own because they felt that the Patrician Consuls used to discriminate against the Plebians in carrying on the administration. They had apparently obtained a great gain, because under the Republican Constitution of Rome one Consul had the power of vetoing an act of the other Consul.

But did they in fact gain anything? The answer to this question must be in the negative. The Plebians never could get a Plebian Consul who could be said to be a strong man, and who could act independently of the Patrician Consul. In the ordinary course of things the Plebians should have got a strong Plebian Consul, in view of the fact that his election was to be by a separate electorate of Plebians. The question is, why did they fail in getting a strong Plebian to officiate as their Consul?

The answer to this question reveals the dominion which religion exercises over the minds of men. It was an accepted creed of the

---

[168]Comitia Centuriata, or the Century Assembly, was originally an assembly of the Roman military, but soon turned into a political assembly, and became one of the three public assemblies of the Republic of Rome where citizens, grouped into 'centuries', voted on legislative, electoral and judicial matters. In the early days, entry to the Senate was only by birth and rank—so the patricians called the shots. Even in the Comitia Centuriata, instituted in about 450 BCE, entry was restricted initially to the patricians and the plebeians were kept at bay. Even after the Comitia Centuriata came to include plebeians, its organization and voting system nevertheless gave greater influence to the rich than to the poor, which as Ambedkar points out, resembled the Communal Award. Ambedkar understands, in the caste context, the plight of plebeians with voting rights as being similar to that of Untouchables who were denied a separate electorate—the mere right to vote does not necessarily empower them. For more on the evolution of the Roman republic, see Olga Tellegen-Couperus (1993).

whole Roman populus [people] that no official could enter upon the duties of his office unless the Oracle of Delphi[169] declared that he was acceptable to the Goddess. The priests who were in charge of the temple of the Goddess of Delphi were all Patricians. Whenever therefore the Plebians elected a Consul who was known to be a strong party man and opposed to the Patricians—or 'communal,' to use the term that is current in India—the Oracle invariably declared that he was not acceptable to the Goddess. This is how the Plebians were cheated out of their rights.

But what is worthy of note is that the Plebians permitted themselves to be thus cheated because they too, like the Patricians, held firmly the belief that the approval of the Goddess was a condition precedent to the taking charge by an official of his duties, and that election by the people was not enough. If the Plebians had contended that election was enough and that the approval by the Goddess was not necessary, they would have derived the fullest benefit from the political right which they had obtained. But they did not. They agreed to elect another, less suitable to themselves but more suitable to the Goddess—which in fact meant more amenable to the Patricians. Rather than give up religion, the Plebians give up the material gain for which they had fought so hard. Does this not show that religion can be a source of power as great as money, if not greater?

The fallacy of the socialists[170] lies in supposing that because in

---

[169]While Delphi, associated with the Greek god Apollo, was an important site in Hellenic political life, the Romans did not seem to consult the Oracle regularly owing to its considerable distance from Rome. They, however, tended to refer to the Sibylline Books, kept at the Capitolium. See: Fontenrose (1978). For an account of the hold of religion on the Romans, see: Rupke (2007).

[170]Ambedkar's ire here is likely directed at the socialist turn within the Congress. Following the 1936 Congress session in Lucknow, where Nehru took over as party president at Gandhi's behest, the Agrarian Resolution declared that "the most important and urgent problem of the country is the appalling poverty, unemployment and indebtedness of the peasantry, fundamentally due to the antiquated and repressive land revenue system'. Nehru and the few socialists he managed to sneak into the thirteen-member Congress Working Committee (CWC)—Acharya Narayan Dev, Jayaprakash Narayan and Achyut Patwardhan—sought to end the 'middle-class domination' of the Congress and sought direct

the present stage of European Society property as a source of power is predominant, that the same is true of India, or that the same was true of Europe in the past. Religion, social status, and property are all sources of power and authority, which one man has, to control the liberty of another. One is predominant at one stage; the other is predominant at another stage. That is the only difference. If liberty is the ideal, if liberty means the destruction of the dominion which one man holds over another, then obviously it cannot be insisted upon that economic reform must be the one kind of reform worthy of pursuit. If the source of power and dominion is, at any given time or in any given society, social and religious, then social reform and religious reform must be accepted as the necessary sort of reform.

One can thus attack the doctrine of the Economic Interpretation of History adopted by the socialists of India. But I recognize that the economic interpretation of history is not necessary for the validity of the Socialist contention that equalization of property is the only real reform and that it must precede everything else. However, what I would like to ask the socialists is this: Can you have economic reform without first bringing about a reform of the social order? The socialists of India do not seem to have considered this question. I do not wish to do them an injustice. I give below a socialists of India do not seem to have considered this question.[171] I do not wish to

---

representation for peasants and workers in the party. But tacitly backed by Gandhi, the right wing within the Congress opposed Nehru's socialist tendencies. On 29 June 1936, CWC members Babu Rajendra Prasad, Jairamdas Daulatram, Jamnalal Bajaj, Acharya Kripalani and S.D. Dev submitted their resignations from the CWC in a joint letter, contending that Nehru's preaching of socialism in his election speeches was 'prejudicial to the interests of the country and to the success of the national struggle for freedom'. Gandhi backed the conservatives, as did the business classes. Subsequently Nehru recanted. For a detailed account of Nehru and socialism, see R.C. Dutt (1980, 30–90).

[171]Ambedkar (in Das, 2010b, 49–68) mounts a more direct attack on the socialists in the presidential address delivered on 12 and 13 February 1938 to the GIP (Great Indian Peninsular) Railway Depressed Classes Workmen's Conference held in Nashik, Manmad district. In this speech he offers a trenchant critique of capitalism and Brahminism, and examines the problems with Indian socialists at greater length. Ambedkar was addressing the GIP conference in his capacity as

do them an injustice. I give below a quotation from a letter which a prominent Socialist wrote a few days ago to a friend of mine, in which he said, 'I do not believe that we can build up a free society in India so long as there is a trace of this ill-treatment and suppression of one class by another. Believing as I do in a socialist ideal, inevitably I believe in perfect equality in the treatment of various classes and groups. I think that Socialism offers the only true remedy for this as well as other problems.'

Now the question that I would like to ask is: Is it enough for a Socialist to say, 'I believe in perfect equality in the treatment of the various classes?' To say that such a belief is enough is to disclose a complete lack of understanding of what is involved in Socialism. If Socialism is a practical programme and is not merely an ideal, distant and far off, the question for a Socialist is not whether he believes in equality. The question for him is whether he minds one class illtreating and suppressing another class as a matter of system, as a matter of principle—and thus allowing tyranny and oppression to continue to divide one class from another.

Let me analyse the factors that are involved in the realization of Socialism, in order to explain fully my point. Now it is obvious that the economic reform contemplated by the socialists cannot come about unless there is a revolution resulting in the seizure of power. That seizure of power must be by a proletariat. The first question I ask is: Will the proletariat of India combine to bring about this revolution? What will move men to such an action? It seems to me that, other things being equal, the only thing that will move one man to take such an action is the feeling that other men with whom he is acting are actuated by a feeling of equality and fraternity and—above all—of justice. Men will not join in a revolution for the equalization of property unless they know that after the revolution is achieved they will be treated equally, and that there will be no discrimination of caste and creed.

The assurance of a Socialist leading the revolution that he does not believe in caste, I am sure will not suffice. The assurance must be the

president of the Independent Labour Party, the first political party founded by him in August 1936, a few months after the publication of *Annihilation of Caste*.

assurance proceeding from a much deeper foundation—namely, the mental attitude of the compatriots towards one another in their spirit of personal equality and fraternity. Can it be said that the proletariat of India, poor as it is, recognizes no distinctions except that of the rich and the poor? Can it be said that the poor in India recognize no such distinctions of caste or creed, high or low? If the fact is that they do, what unity of front can be expected from such a proletariat in its action against the rich? How can there be a revolution if the proletariat cannot present a united front?

Suppose for the sake of argument that by some freak of fortune a revolution does take place and the socialists come into power; will they not have to deal with the problems created by the particular social order prevalent in India? I can't see how a Socialist State in India can function for a second without having to grapple with the problems created by the prejudices which make Indian people observe the distinctions of high and low, clean and unclean. If socialists are not to be content with the mouthing of fine phrases, if the socialists wish to make Socialism a definite reality, then they must recognize that the problem of social reform is fundamental, and that for them there is no escape from it.

That the social order prevalent in India is a matter which a Socialist must deal with; that unless he does so he cannot achieve his revolution; and that if he does achieve it as a result of good fortune, he will have to grapple with the social order if he wishes to realize his ideal—is a proposition which in my opinion is incontrovertible. He will be compelled to take account of caste after the revolution, if he does not take account of it before the revolution. This is only another way of saying that, turn in any direction you like, caste is the monster that crosses your path. You cannot have political reform, you cannot have economic reform, unless you kill this monster.

It is a pity that caste even today has its defenders. The defences are many. It is defended on the ground that the caste system is but another name for division of labour; and if division of labour is a necessary feature of every civilized society, then it is argued that there is nothing wrong in the caste system. Now the first thing that is to be urged against this view is that the caste system is not merely a division of labour. *It is also a division of labourers.*[172] Civilized society undoubtedly needs division of labour. But in no civilized society is division of labour accompanied by this unnatural undoubtedly needs division of labour. But in no civilized society is division of labour accompanied by this unnatural division of labourers into watertight compartments. The caste system is not merely a division of labourers which is quite different from division of labour—it is a hierarchy in which the divisions of labourers are graded one above the other. In no other country is the division of labour accompanied by this gradation of labourers.

There is also a third point of criticism against this view of the caste system. This division of labour is not spontaneous, it is not based on natural aptitudes. Social and individual efficiency requires us to develop the capacity of an individual to the point of competency to choose and to make his own career. This principle is violated in the caste system, in so far as it involves an attempt to appoint tasks to individuals in advance—selected not on the basis of trained original capacities, but on that of the social status of the parents.[173]

Looked at from another point of view, this stratification of occupations which is the result of the caste system is positively pernicious. Industry is never static.[174] It undergoes rapid and abrupt

---

[172]Emphasis in original.

[173]Ambedkar is echoing the words of Dewey. According to Mukherjee (2009, 347): 'So deeply embedded is Dewey's thought in Ambedkar's consciousness that quite often his words flow through Ambedkar's discourse without quotation marks.' She also notes 'how Ambedkar culled sentences from Democracy and Education to describe his version of the ideal society' (351). Ambedkar expresses his debt to Dewey in section 25.4 of AoC The relevant paragraph from Dewey's Democracy and Education, quoted by Mukherjee, reads: 'A democratic criterion requires us to develop capacity to the point of competency to choose and make its own career. This principle is violated when the attempt is made to fit individuals in advance for definite industrial callings, selected not on the basis of trained original capacities, but on that of the wealth or social status of parents' (364). See Dewey (1916). All further citations from Democracy and Education are from the online edition.

[174]John Dewey was an advocate of industrial democracy, which, in Noam Chomsky's (2003) words 'means democratising production, commerce, and so on, which means eliminating the whole structure of capitalist hierarchy'. Chomsky terms Dewey a

changes. With such changes, an individual must be free to change his occupation. Without such freedom to adjust himself to changing circumstances, it would be impossible for him to gain his livelihood. Now the caste system will not allow Hindus to take to occupations where they are wanted, if they do not belong to them by heredity. If a Hindu is seen to starve rather than take to new occupations not assigned to his caste, the reason is to be found in the caste system. By not permitting readjustment of occupations, caste becomes a direct cause of much of the unemployment we see in the country.

As a form of division of labour, the caste system suffers from another serious defect. The division of labour brought about by the caste system is not a division based on choice. Individual sentiment, individual preference, has no place in it. It is based on the dogma of predestination. Considerations of social efficiency would compel us to recognize that the greatest evil in the industrial system is not so much poverty and the suffering that it involves, as the fact that so many persons have callings [occupations]which make no appeal to those who are engaged in them. Such callings constantly provoke one to aversion, ill will, and the desire to evade.[175]

There are many occupations in India which, on account of the fact that they are regarded as degraded by the Hindus, provoke those who are engaged in them to aversion. There is a constant desire to evade and escape from such occupations, which arises solely because of the blighting effect which they produce upon those who follow them, owing to the slight and stigma cast upon them by the Hindu religion.

'radical' in this interview. In another essay, Chomsky (2013) says: 'Dewey called for workers to be 'masters of their own industrial fate' and for all institutions to be brought under public control, including the means of production, exchange, publicity, transportation and communication. Short of this, Dewey argued, politics will remain "the shadow cast on society by big business."'

[175]This latter sentence also echoes Dewey (1916): 'Sentimentally, it may seem harsh to say that the greatest evil of the present regime is not found in poverty and in the suffering which it entails, but in the fact that so many persons have callings which make no appeal to them, which are pursued simply for the money reward that accrues. For such callings constantly provoke one to aversion, ill will, and a desire to slight and evade' (cited in Mukherjee 2009, 364).

What efficiency can there be in a system under which neither men's hearts nor their minds are in their work? As an economic organization caste is therefore a harmful institution, inasmuch as it involves the subordination of man's natural powers and inclinations to the exigencies of social rules.

Some have dug a biological trench in defence of the caste system. It is said that the object of caste was to preserve purity of race and purity of blood. Now ethnologists[176] are of the opinion that men of pure race exist nowhere and that there has been a mixture of all races in all parts of the world. Especially is this the case with the people of India. Mr D.R. Bhandarkar in his paper on 'Foreign Elements in the Hindu Population' has stated that 'There is hardly a class or caste in India which has not a foreign strain in it. There is an admixture of alien blood not only among the warrior classes—the Rajputs and the Marathas—but also among the Brahmins who are under the happy delusion that they are free from all foreign elements.'[177] The caste system cannot be said to have grown as a means of preventing the admixture of races, or as a means of maintaining purity of blood.

---

[176]Ethnology draws upon ethnographic material to compare and contrast different cultures. Ethnography is the study of single groups through direct contact with their cultures. In the nineteenth century, ethnologists and ethnographers studied caste mainly as a subsidiary exercise in the supposedly higher and grander task of uncovering the evolutionary heritage of all humanity. In doing so they contributed to the 'Orientalist' exercise of the census and gazetteers and to the racial understanding of caste. Caste was thus subsumed into theories of biologically determined race essences. Ambedkar, in fact, begins his 1916 essay, 'Castes in India', with a reference to ethnology. Further, on caste and ethnology, see Bayly (1999, 11–19); and Dirks (2001, 126–38). See also Ketkar (1909/1998, 165–70).
[177]Devadatta Ramakrishna Bhandarkar (1875–1950) was an epigraphist and archaeologist who worked for the Archaeological Survey of India. Ambedkar is citing from p.37 of this 1911 essay. Based on epigraphic research, Bhandarkar uses evidence from the Vedas and the epics of the Hindu tradition, such as the Rig Veda and the Mahabharata, to disprove the 'purity of blood' myth attributed to Brahmins. 'It may be said that after all the Mahabharata…is a conglomeration of legends, which are not of much historical importance, though they cannot be objected to by an orthodox Brahmana and consequently may be adduced to silence his pretensions to purity of origin and the consequent highest place in Hindu society' (1911, 10).

As a matter of fact [the] caste system came into being long after the different races of India had commingled in blood and culture.[178] To hold that distinctions of castes are really distinctions of race, and to treat different castes as though they were so many different races, is a gross perversion of facts. What racial affinity is there between the Brahmin of the Punjab and the Brahmin of Madras? What racial affinity is there between the untouchable of Bengal and the untouchable of Madras? What racial difference is there between the Brahmin of the Punjab and the Chamar of the Punjab? What racial difference is there between the Brahmin of Madras and the Pariah of Madras? The Brahmin of the Punjab is racially of the same stock as the Chamar of the Punjab, and the Brahmin of Madras is of the same race as the Punjab is racially of the same stock as the Chamar of the Punjab, and the Brahmin of Madras is of the same race as the Pariah of Madras.

[The] caste system does not demarcate racial division. [The] caste system is a social division of people of the same race. Assuming it,

---

[178]In his understanding of the caste system and its evolution, Ambedkar here differs strongly from Brahminic appropriations (such as by B.G. Tilak who authored *The Arctic Home in the Vedas*, 1903) of the racial theory of Aryans and Dravidians propounded by European Indologists. In fact, as seen in Roy's introduction to this edition, even Gandhi, in his South Africa years, strongly believed in the British and India's ruling classes both being 'Aryan'. Ambedkar, however, also differs on this front from his predecessor and radical thinker Jotiba Phule and his contemporary fellow-traveller 'Periyar' E.V. Ramasamy Naicker (1879–1973) who turned the racial theory inside out, postulated a pre-Aryan golden age, and regarded the Brahmins as Aryans, and hence foreigners, who imposed the caste system upon the non-Brahmins who were seen as an indigenous race. For Phule's writings, especially Gulamgiri (Slavery, 1873), see G.P. Deshpande (2002, 23–101). Periyar, on the eve of independence, quite radically called upon the Dravidian people of South India to 'guard against the transfer of power from the British to the Aryans' (*The Hindu*, 11 February 1946). As sociologist T.K. Oommen (2005, 99) argues, 'According to Periyar, Brahmins had tried to foist their language and social system on Dravidians to erase their race consciousness and, therefore, he constantly reminded the Dravidians to uphold their "race consciousness". However, Periyar did not advocate the superiority of one race over the other but insisted on [the] equality of all races. Thus the fundamental difference between Aryan Hinduism and Dravidian Hinduism is crucial: the former [is] hegemonic, but the latter is emancipatory.'

however, to be a case of racial divisions, one may ask: What harm could there be if a mixture of races and of blood was permitted to take place in India by inter-marriages between different castes? Men are no doubt divided from animals by so deep a distinction that science recognizes men and animals as two distinct species. But even scientists who believe in purity of races do not assert that the different races constitute different species of men. They are only varieties of one and the same species. As such they can inter-breed and produce an offspring which is capable of breeding and which is not sterile.

An immense lot of nonsense is talked about heredity and eugenics[179] in defence of the caste system. Few would object to the caste system if it was in accord with the basic principle of eugenics, because few can object to the improvement of the race by judicious mating. But one fails to understand how the caste system secures judicious mating. [The] caste system is a negative thing. It merely prohibits persons belonging to different castes from inter-marrying. It is not a positive method of selecting which two among a given caste should marry.

If caste is eugenic in origin, then the origin of sub-castes must also be eugenic. But can anyone seriously maintain that the origin of sub-castes is eugenic? I think it would be absurd to contend for such a proposition, and for a very obvious reason. If caste means race, then differences of sub-castes cannot mean differences of race, because sub-castes become ex hypothesia [by hypothesis] sub-divisions of one and the same race. Consequently the bar against intermarrying and inter-dining between sub-castes cannot be for the purpose of maintaining

---

[179]Eugenics is the 'science' of predicting and controlling heredity that was popular at the turn of the twentieth century, in that it was perceived to be an effort at the 'improvement' of the human species. The term was coined by Francis Galton inspired by Darwin's theory of natural selection as well as the rediscovery of Mendel's work on heredity (see also Note 47). Galton advocated that only the best and most meritorious should be encouraged to breed; a more disastrous strand of his theory led to Hitler's 'final solution'. According to Mark Singleton (2007, 125–46), the popularity of eugenics in India can be understood by the place it occupied as a 'scientific explanation' for the 'degeneration' of Hindu society and colonial subjugation by the British. Another reason for the popularity of eugenics was its valorisation of the endogamy of the caste system as a mechanism of racial purity.

purity of race or of blood. If sub-castes cannot be eugenic in origin, there cannot be any substance in the contention that caste is eugenic in origin.

Again, if caste is eugenic in origin[180] one can understand the bar against inter-marriage. But what is the purpose of the interdict placed on inter-dining between castes and sub-castes alike? Interdining cannot infect blood, and therefore cannot be the cause either of the improvement or of [the] deterioration of the race.

This shows that caste has no scientific origin, and that those who are attempting to give it an eugenic basis are trying to support by science what is grossly unscientific. Even today, eugenics cannot become a practical possibility unless we have definite knowledge regarding the laws of heredity. Prof. Bateson in his Mendel's Principles of Heredity says, 'There is nothing in the descent of the higher mental qualities to suggest that they follow any single system of transmission. It is likely that both they and the more marked developments of physical powers result rather from the coincidence of numerous factors than from the possession of any one genetic element.'[181] To argue that the caste system was eugenic in its conception is to attribute to the forefathers of present-day Hindus a knowledge of heredity which even

---

[180]For a good example of the use of eugenics to defend caste, see T.N. Roy (1927, 67–72), who begins with this assertion: 'The greatest eugenic movement that the world has as yet witnessed originated in India. It was the institution of the caste system.' Arguing that 'the earliest eugenic movement began with the institution of what is known as Gotra', Roy blames the 'downfall of Hinduism' on not observing caste distinctions well enough. 'The Brahmin was originally created by eugenic selection,' he argues, and gives the finest examples of intellect in Bengal as being all Brahmin men—Raja Ram Mohan Roy, Ishwar Chandra Vidyasagar and Bankim Chandra Chatterjee.

[181]William Bateson (1861–1926) was a British scientist and is considered the founder of genetics. He wrote Mendel's Principles of Heredity (1909) after the discovery of Gregor Mendel's article written in 1866. Ambedkar is citing from p.205 of Bateson's book. Bateson elaborated his own research findings following the investigation of Mendel's theories. This discovery laid down the basis for not only genetics but also eugenics. However, early into his research Bateson had recognised the dangers of the application of genetics to social engineering and warned against the uniformizing tendencies of eugenic thinking. See: Harvey (1995).

the modern scientists do not possess.

A tree should be judged by the fruits it yields. If caste is eugenic, what sort of a race of men should it have produced? Physically speaking the Hindus are a C3 people.[182] They are a race of Pygmies and dwarfs, stunted in stature and wanting in stamina. It is a nation 9/10ths of which is declared to be unfit for military service. This shows that the caste system does not embody the eugenics of modern scientists. It is a social system which embodies the arrogance and selfishness of a perverse section of the Hindus who were superior enough in social status to set it in fashion, and who had the authority to force it on their inferiors.

Caste does not result in economic efficiency. Caste cannot improve, and has not improved, the race.[183] Caste has however done one thing. It has completely disorganized and demoralized the Hindus.

The first and foremost thing that must be recognized is that Hindu Society is a myth. The name Hindu is itself a foreign name. [184]It

---

[182]Ambedkar here slips into an essentialist understanding of caste, race and morphology. He is drawing upon a British military categorization of working class soldiers during the First World War. Then British Prime Minister David Lloyd George lamented: 'How can Britain run an A1 empire with a C3 population?' Ina Zweiniger-Bargielowska (2006) argues that though the obsession with a deteriorating national health and physical fitness echoed fascist narratives, these eugenic categories were used as metaphors across the political spectrum in Britain. Ambedkar is using this premise to dismiss the 'biological' defence of the caste system. See also the work of Heather Streets (2004), who discusses how the British, from 1857 to 1914, identified and taxonomized 'martial races' that are believed to possess a biological or cultural disposition to the racial and masculine qualities necessary for the arts of war.

[183]In AoC 1936 and subsequent editions, this reads as: 'Caste cannot and has not improved race.'

[184]Derived from Sindhu, the native name for the Indus river, the term Hind was first used in Persian and came to be established after the eleventh-century polymath Al-Biruni (973–1048), commissioned by the King Mahmud of Ghazni (in present-day Afghanistan), travelled to the Indian subcontinent in 1017 and wrote the famous encyclopedic account of India called *Tarikh al-Hind*. The word 'Hindu', derived thus, did not indicate a religious group but was used as a geographical demarcator for the inhabitants of the land near and east of the Indus. Later, the word may have been adopted by those inhabitants to distinguish themselves from the Muslims who came to initially rule the northern parts of India. The ancient

was given by the Mohammedans to the natives for the purpose of distinguishing themselves from foreign name. It was given by the Mohammedans to the natives for the purpose of distinguishing themselves [from them]. It does not occur in any Sanskrit work prior to the Mohammedan invasion. They did not feel the necessity of a common name, because they had no conception of their having constituted a community. Hindu Society as such does not exist. It is only a collection of castes. Each caste is conscious of its existence. Its survival is the be-all and end-all of its existence. Castes do not even form a federation. A caste has no feeling that it is affiliated to other castes, except when there is a Hindu–Muslim riot. On all other occasions each caste endeavours to segregate itself and to distinguish itself from other castes.

Each caste not only dines among itself and marries among itself, but each caste prescribes its own distinctive dress. What other explanation can there be of the innumerable styles of dress worn by the men and women of India, which so amuse the tourists? Indeed the ideal Hindu must be like a rat living in his own hole, refusing to have any contact with others. There is an utter lack among the Hindus of what the sociologists call 'consciousness of kind'.[185] There is no Hindu consciousness of kind. In every Hindu the consciousness that exists is the consciousness of his caste. That is the reason why the Hindus

---

texts that so-called Hindus today claim their roots from—the Vedas, Ramayana, Mahabharata, Bhagvad Gita, Upanishads—do not ever use the terms Hindu or Hindusim. Recent research argues that the terms came into vogue with Orientalist and colonial scholarship. For an overview of the debates around 'Hindu' and 'Hinduism' and a nuanced counter-argument see D.N. Lorenzen (2006, 7–10). See also Romila Thapar's essay, 'Syndicated Hinduism' (1989/2001, 54) where she says, 'The term Hinduism as we understand it today to describe a particular religion is modern.' Ambedkar, for his times, was far-sighted in jettisoning a term around which Indian nationalism and anti-colonialism came to be constructed.

[185]The phrase 'consciousness of kind' was coined by the American sociologist Franklin Henry Giddings (1855–1931), and was first elaborated in *The Principles of Sociology* (1896). Giddings sought to define the fundamental underlying law that defined human society. He defined 'consciousness of kind' as 'a state of consciousness in which any being, whether low or high in the scale of life, recognizes another conscious being as of like kind with itself.' See Giddings (1896/2004, 17).

cannot be said to form a society or a nation.

There are, however, many Indians whose patriotism does not permit them to admit that Indians are not a nation, that they are only an amorphous mass of people. They have insisted that underlying the apparent diversity there is a fundamental unity which marks the life of the Hindus, inasmuch as there is a similarity of those habits and customs, beliefs and thoughts, which obtain all over the continent of India. Similarity in habits and customs, beliefs and thoughts, there is. But one cannot accept the conclusion that therefore, the Hindus constitute a society. To do so is to misunderstand the essentials which go to make up a society. Men do not become a society by living in physical proximity, any more than a man ceases to be a member of his society by living so many miles away from other men.

Secondly, similarity in habits and customs, beliefs and thoughts, is not enough to constitute men into society. Things may be passed physically from one to another like bricks. In the same way habits and customs, beliefs and thoughts of one group may be taken over by another group, and there may thus appear a similarity between the two. Culture spreads by diffusion, and that is why one finds similarity between various primitive tribes in the matter of their habits and customs, beliefs and thoughts, although they do not live in proximity. But no one could say that because there was this similarity, the primitive tribes constituted one society. This is because similarity in certain things is not enough to constitute a society.

Men constitute a society because they have things which they possess in common. To have similar things is totally different from possessing things in common. And the only way by which men can come to possess things in common with one another is by being in communication[186] with one another. This is merely another way of saying that society continues to exist by communication—indeed, in communication.[187] To make it concrete, it is not enough if men act

---

[186]Rendered as 'communion' in AoC 1936 and subsequent editions.

[187]This echoes Dewey's words in *Democracy and Education* (1916): 'Society exists not only by transmission, by communication, but it may fairly be said to exist in transmission, in communication.'

in a way which agrees with the acts of others. Parallel activity, even if similar, is not sufficient to bind men into a society.

This is proved by the fact that the festivals observed by the different castes amongst the Hindus are the same. Yet these parallel performances of similar festivals by the different castes have not bound them into one integral whole. For that purpose what is necessary is for a man to share and participate in a common activity, so that the same emotions are aroused in him that animate the others. Making the individual a sharer or partner in the associated activity, so that he feels its success as his success, its failure as his failure, is the real thing that binds men and makes a society of them. The caste system prevents common activity; and by preventing common activity, it has prevented the Hindus from becoming a society with a unified life and a consciousness of its own being.

The Hindus often complain of the isolation and exclusiveness of a gang or a clique and blame them for anti-social spirit. But they conveniently forget that this anti-social spirit is the worst feature of their own caste system. One caste enjoys singing a hymn of hate against another caste as much as the Germans enjoyed singing their hymn of hate against the English during the last war [World War I]. The literature of the Hindus is full of caste genealogies in which an attempt is made to give a noble origin to one caste and an ignoble origin to other castes. The Sahyadrikhand is a attempt is made to give a noble origin to one caste and an ignoble origin to other castes. The Sahyadrikhand is a notorious instance of this class of literature.[188]

---

[188]The Sahyadrikhand is a latter-day addition to the Skanda Purana, the most volatile of Sanskrit texts, continuously expanding and incorporating new traditions. Wendy Doniger (1993, 60) terms it 'surely the shiftiest, or sandiest, of all', puranas (collections of stories revolving around divinities and myths that allude to history though they cannot be accused of historicity). The Sahyadrikhand recounts the genealogy of several Maharashtrian Brahmin sub-castes to incorporate them into caste hierarchy. See also Rao (2009, 55). Ambedkar (BAWS 3, 48) elsewhere writes of the Sahyadrikhand: 'It assigns noble origin to other castes while it assigns to the Brahmin caste the filthiest origin. It was a revenge on Manu. It was the worst lampoon on the Brahmins as a caste. The Peshwas very naturally ordered its destruction. Some survived the general destruction.'

This anti-social spirit is not confined to caste alone. It has gone deeper and has poisoned the mutual relations of the sub-castes as well. In my province the Golak Brahmins, Deorukha Brahmins, Karada Brahmins, Palshe Brahmins,[189] and Chitpavan Brahmins[190] all claim to be sub-divisions of the Brahmin caste. But the anti-social spirit that prevails between them is quite as marked and quite as virulent as the anti-social spirit that prevails between them and other non-Brahmin castes. There is nothing strange in this. An anti-social spirit is found wherever one group has 'interests of its own' which shut it out from full interaction with other groups, so that its prevailing purpose is protection of what it has got.

---

[189]Golak or Govardhan Brahmins are a sub-caste in western India (largely Maharashtra) considered of inferior birth by other Brahmin communities of the region. See: Hassan (1920). Deorukha (Devrukhe) Brahmins and Karada (Karhade) are sub-castes of the Panchadravid (living south of the Vindhya mountains) Maharashtrian Brahmins. Palshe is another Maharashtrian Brahmin sub-caste considered inferior by Chitpavan Brahmins. In Anandrav Bhikaji Phadke versus Shankar Daji Charye (1883 ILR 7 Bom 323) the Bombay Court upheld the right of Chitpavan Brahmins to exclude Palshe Brahmins from worshipping at a temple, on the ground that such an exclusive right is one which the courts must guard, as otherwise all 'high-caste Hindus' would hold their sanctuaries and perform their worship only so far as those of the lower castes' chose to allow them (Naval 2004, 14).

[190]The origin of the Chitpavan Brahmins is traced to the myth of Parashurama, believed to be an 'immortal' Brahmin incarnation of Vishnu. Parashurama is said to have burned the bodies of fourteen people who were washed ashore on a funeral pyre, purifying them, and then restored them to life—thus the name chita (pyre) pavan (purified). These fourteen people are said to be of Jewish, Persian or, in some versions, Berber descent. Another version gives the etymology of their name as 'pure of the mind' (Figueira 2002, 121–33). Their recorded history, however, begins in the eighteenth century, when Chattrapati Shahu, grandson of Shivaji, appointed Balaji Vishwanath Bhat, a Chitpavan Brahmin, as Peshwa (Johnson 2005, 58). M.G. Ranade, founder-member of the Indian National Congress; G.K. Gokhale, 'moderate' Congress leader and mentor to M.K. Gandhi; Pandita Ramabai, a pioneer of education and women's rights; B.G. Tilak, Hindu nationalist leader; Vinoba Bhave, 'spiritual successor' to Gandhi; V.D. Savarkar, who coined the term Hindutva, and who was one of the co-accused in Gandhi's assassination; and Nathuram Godse, who assassinated Gandhi, were all Chitpavan Brahmins.

This anti-social spirit, this spirit of protecting its own interests, is as much a marked feature of the different castes in their isolation from one another as it is of nations in their isolation. The Brahmin's primary concern is to protect 'his interest' against those of the non-Brahmins; and the non-Brahmin's primary concern is to protect their interests against those of the Brahmins. The Hindus, therefore, are not merely an assortment of castes, but are so many warring groups, each living for itself and for its selfish ideal.

There is another feature of caste which is deplorable. The ancestors of the present-day English fought on one side or the other in the Wars of the Roses and the Cromwellian War.[191] But the descendants of those who fought on the one side do not bear any animosity—any grudge—against the descendents of those who fought on the other side. The feud is forgotten. But the present-day non-Brahmins cannot forgive the present-day Brahmins for the insult their ancestors gave to Shivaji.[192] The present-day Kayasthas will not forgive the present-day Brahmins for the infamy cast upon their forefathers by the forefathers of the latter.[193] To what is this difference due? Obviously to the caste

---

[191]The Wars of the Roses were fought between 1455 and 1485 between Lancaster and York, two houses of the royal line Plantagenet. Ambedkar most probably is referring to the Second English Civil War as the Cromwellian war which was fought between the parliamentarians and the royalists in 1648–59, in which Cromwell and his parliamentarian forces defeated the royalists and established the precedent that the king can only rule with the Parliament's consent.

[192]In 1674, the Deccan Brahmins refused to allow the coronation of Shivaji, the Maratha king (1627/30–80), according to Vedic rites. They doubted his Kshatriya origins and saw him as a Shudra claimant. As Rao (2009, 42) says: 'A Brahmin from Benares, Gaga Bhatta, supported Shivaji's claim to Kshatriya status after much persuasion and traced the Bhosle lineage to the Sisodia Rajputs of Udaipur.' Gaga Bhatta is also said to have charged a hefty fee for legitimizing Shivaji's claim. On Shivaji's coronation story, see V.S. Bendrey (1960); see also Laine (2003), a book that was banned in Maharashtra in 2004. (The ban was lifted in 2007 by the Bombay High Court and this was upheld by the Supreme Court of India in 2010.) A recent paper by Rosalind O'Hanlon (2010a) throws light on the migration of several Maratha Brahmins to Benares in the sixteenth century and the story behind Gaga Bhatta's return to the Konkan region in the mid-seventeenth century.

[193]Kayasthas are a caste of scribes whose varna status has been the subject of a

system. The existence of caste and caste-consciousness has served to keep the memory of past feuds between castes green, and has prevented solidarity.

The recent [constitutional] discussion about the excluded[194] and partially included areas has served to draw attention to the position of what are called the aboriginal tribes in India.[195] They number about 13 million, if not more. Apart from the question of whether their exclusion from the new Constitution[196] is proper or improper, the fact

---

raging debate. While they trace their origin to Chitragupta, the scribe of god Yama, and claim a status equal to Brahmins, or to Kshatriyas, many Brahmin texts position them as Shudras. The poet (and Kayastha) Harivansh Rai Bachchan (1998, 7) writes that Brahmins 'have sought to degrade the Kayasthas in many a Sanskrit verse such as the following: That the foetal Kayastha eats not his mother's flesh/speaks not of tenderness, but of toothlessness.' The Peshwa Brahmins of the Deccan had resented the Kayasthas' right to learning and becoming scribes and record-keepers in the seventeenth century. 'The head of the state, though a Brahman, was despised by his other Brahman servants, because the first Peshwa's great-grandfather's great-grandfather had once been lower in society than the Desh Brahmans' great-grandfathers' great-grandfathers. While the Chitpavan Brahmans were waging social war with the Deshastha Brahmans, a bitter jealousy raged between the Brahman ministers and governors and the Kayastha secretaries' (Sarkar 1948, 357). See also Sections 9.1–3 of AoC Further, see O'Hanlon (2010b) who says from the mid-fifteenth century, periodic but intense disputes developed over Kayastha entitlement to the rituals of the twice-born. 'Often migrants who had come into the Maratha regions as servants of the Bahmani kings and to Deccan Sultanate states, Kayasthas were intruders into local societies whose Brahmin communities had hitherto commanded more exclusive possession of scribal skills' (566). See also Note 108 at 18.1.

[194]In AoC 1936 and 1937, Ambedkar uses 'excluded and partially excluded areas'; whereas the 1944 edition uses 'excluded and partially included areas'. Since the latter is incorrect, the former has been retained.

[195]Ambedkar is referring to the constitutional discussions culminating in the Government of India Act of 1935 in which areas inhabited by tribals were classified as 'excluded' and 'partially excluded areas' for the purpose of administration. Laws were only applicable in these areas when the governor approved it, purportedly not to harm these "backward' societies with the implementation of laws instituted for the more 'developed' parts of India. See also Chandra (2013).

[196]Ambedkar is referring to the Government of India Act of 1935 as the new Constitution.

still remains that these aborigines have remained in their primitive uncivilized state[197] in a land which boasts of a civilization thousands

---

[197]Ambedkar's views on Adivasis—officially classified as Scheduled Tribes—are problematic. Even as he appears well intentioned and protectionist, he argues for 'civilising the savages' and looks at them as leading the life of 'hereditary animals', and even warns 'the Hindus' that the 'aborigines are a source of potential danger'. Later, in his address to the All India Scheduled Castes Federation held in Bombay on 6 May 1945, ('The Communal Deadlock and a Way to Solve It'), while discussing the issue of proportionate representation, he says: 'My proposals do not cover the Aboriginal Tribes although they are larger in number than the Sikhs, Anglo-Indians, Indian Christians and Parsees... [T]he Aboriginal Tribes have not as yet developed any political sense to make the best use of their political opportunities and they may easily become mere instruments in the hands either of a majority or a minority and thereby disturb the balance without doing any good to themselves...the proper thing to do for these backward communities is to establish a Statutory Commission to administer what are now called the 'excluded areas' on the same basis as was done in the case of the South African Constitution. Every Province in which these excluded areas are situated should be compelled to make an annual contribution of a prescribed amount for the administration of these areas' (BAWS 1, 375, emphasis added). Ironically, Gandhi used a similar logic to argue that the Untouchables had not yet developed the political sense to use the vote, let alone make use of separate electorates that Ambedkar had championed and won for the Untouchables in the 1931 Round Table Conferences. Shashank Kela (2012, 297–8) says, 'Racism and prejudice marked the Constituent Assembly's 'adivasi' debates. Members referred to their subhuman existence, primitiveness and propensity for summary justice; invoked the threat of separatism; and adduced arguments of the greatest good of the greatest numbers.' Uday Chandra (2013) has argued how both Ambedkar and Jawaharlal Nehru partook of a liberalist-colonial understanding, and fear, of the 'primitive' during the making of the Constitution of Independent India, almost retaining the colonialist approach to so-called tribals. In contrast, the Adivasi leader from Jharkhand and member of the Constituent Assembly (CA), Jaipal Singh, had argued on 19 December 1946: 'What my people require, Sir, is not adequate safeguards... We do not ask for any special protection. We want to be treated like every other Indian.' As Chandra points out, this was a perception shared by Vallabhbhai Patel, Chairman of the Tribal and Excluded Areas Committee and future Home Minister. However, later, during the CA debates on the Sixth Schedule, the Ambedkar-led proposal to allow Scheduled Tribes to function from excluded areas found favour with Adivasi spokespersons such as Rev. J.J.M. Nichols-Roy, who said on 19 November 1949: 'The Sixth Schedule concerns the hill-districts of

of years old. Not only are they not civilized, but some of them follow pursuits which have led to their being classified as criminals.[198]

Thirteen million people living in the midst of civilization are still in a savage state, and are leading the life of hereditary criminals! But the Hindus have never felt ashamed of it. This is a phenomenon which in my view is quite unparalleled. What is the cause of this shameful state of affairs? Why has no attempt been made to civilize these aborigines and to lead them to take to a more honourable way of making a living?

The Hindus will probably seek to account for this savage state of the aborigines by attributing to them congenital stupidity. They will probably not admit that the aborigines have remained savages because they had made no effort to civilize them, to give them medical aid, to reform them, to make them good citizens. But supposing a Hindu wished to do what the Christian missionary is doing for these aborigines, could he have done it? I submit not. Civilizing the aborigines means adopting them as your own, living in their midst, and cultivating fellow-feeling—in short, loving them. How is it possible for a Hindu to do this? His whole life is one anxious effort to preserve his caste. Caste is his precious possession which he must save at any cost. He cannot consent to lose it by establishing contact with the aborigines, the remnants of the hateful Anaryas[199] of the Vedic days.

Assam in which the hill men in Assam live by themselves in their own territories, who have their own language and their culture and the Constituent Assembly has rightly agreed…that there should be councils for these different districts in order to enable the people who live in those areas to develop themselves according to their genius and culture.' For the workings of autonomous district councils established under the Sixth Schedule in the Northeastern states, see Bengt G. Karlsson (2011) and Sanjib Baruah (2007).

[198]By the beginning of the twentieth century, huge sections of the population, mostly itinerant, were labelled criminal under the Criminal Tribes Acts of 1871 and 1911. Seeing criminality as hereditary was a logical outcome of the caste system. If people could be born scholars, weavers and cobblers they could also be born thieves and thugs. See: D'Souza (2001) and Radhakrishna (2001).

[199]Anaryas: Sanskrit for non-Aryans. Anasa (literally those without a nose, figuratively those without an aquiline nose) is another term frequently used in the Vedas to refer to the local, indigenous populations, whom the Aryas regarded

Not that a Hindu could not be taught the sense of duty to fallen humanity, but the trouble is that no amount of sense of duty can enable him to overcome his duty to preserve his caste. Caste is, therefore, the real explanation as to why the Hindu has let the savage remain a savage in the midst of his civilization without blushing, or without feeling any sense of remorse or repentance. The Hindu has not realized that these aborigines are a source of potential danger. If these savages remorse or repentance. The Hindu has not realized that these aborigines are a source of potential danger. If these savages remain savages, they may not do any harm to the Hindus. But if they are reclaimed by non-Hindus and converted to their faiths, they will swell the ranks of the enemies of the Hindus. If this happens, the Hindu will have to thank himself and his caste system.

Not only has the Hindu made no effort for the humanitarian cause of civilizing the savages, but the higher-caste Hindus have deliberately prevented the lower castes who are within the pale of Hinduism from rising to the cultural level of the higher castes. I will give two instances, one of the Sonars and the other of the Pathare Prabhus.[200] Both are communities quite well-known in Maharashtra. Like the rest of the

---

as different from them and therefore to be stigmatized.

[200]Pathare means stone and prabhu means lord. This caste claims to have descended from the Kshatriyas. The mythological claim around origins goes thus: 'The first of them was Ashvapati (700 BCE), a lineal descendant of Rama and Prithu, who, as is stated in the local chronology, governed India in the Dvapara and Treta Yugas, which is a good while ago! The Patarah Prabhus are the only caste within which Brahmans have to perform certain purely Vedic rites known under the name of the "Kshatriya rites"' (Blavatsky, 1892/2010, 145–6). Veena Naregal (2001, 168–9) says: 'In western India it was mainly brahmins and some sub-brahmin groups like the prabhus and shenvis who were among the first to perceive the benefits of the new literate order and respond to the opportunities it created. The prabhus and the shenvis were traditionally trained scribes who had a long and successful history of employment as karkuns in different parts of the Peshwa kingdom and in the offices of the colonial trading houses of Bombay. The possession of uncommon literate skills had also allowed the prabhus to be closely associated with pre-modern book production.' See also Uma Chakravarti (2000) for a discussion of the Peshwa intervention on norms for widows and enforced widowhood claims of upwardly mobile middle caste groups.

communities desiring to raise their status, these two communities were at one time endeavouring to adopt some of the ways and habits of the Brahmins.

The Sonars were styling themselves Daivadnya Brahmins[201] and were wearing their 'dhotis' with folds in them, and using the word 'namaskar' for salutation. Both the folded way of wearing the dhoti and the namaskar were special to the Brahmins. The Brahmins did not like this imitation and this attempt by Sonars to pass off as Brahmins. Under the authority of the Peshwas, the Brahmins successfully put down this attempt on the part of the Sonars to adopt the ways of the Brahmins. They even got the President of the Councils of the East India Company's settlement in Bombay to issue a prohibitory order against the Sonars residing in Bombay.

At one time the Pathare Prabhus had widow-remarriage as a custom of their caste. This custom of widow-remarriage was later on looked upon as a mark of social inferiority by some members of the caste, especially because it was contrary to the custom prevalent among the Brahmins. With the object of raising the status of their community, some Pathare Prabhus sought to stop this practice of widow-remarriage that was prevalent in their caste. The community was divided into two camps, one for and the other against the innovation. The Peshwas took the side of those in favour of widow-remarriage, and thus virtually prohibited the Pathare Prabhus from following the ways of the Brahmins.

The Hindus criticize the Mohammedans for having spread their religion by the use of the sword. They also ridicule Christianity on the score of the Inquisition.[202] But really speaking, who is better and

---

[201]On Daivadnya (also Daivajna) Brahmins, the Census of India (1961, 14) says: 'They are locally known as "Sonars" and "Sonagars" and are the traditional goldsmiths. They are found in almost all the towns and big villages of North Kanara District. They are said to have migrated from Goa.'

[202]Here Ambedkar is referring to the polemics used by the Vedic missionaries of the Arya Samaj to counter the influence of Muslim and Christian preachers and missionaries—adopting their established practices of preaching at religious fairs, challenging missionaries in pamphlets and on the streets. The rise of the Arya Samaj owed much to the demographic shifts that characterized the history of the

more worthy of our respect—the Mohammedans and Christians who attempted to thrust down the throats of unwilling persons what they regarded as necessary for their salvation, or the Hindu who would not spread the light, who would endeavour to keep others in darkness, who would not consent to share his intellectual and social inheritance with those who are ready and willing to make it a part of their own make-up? I have no hesitation in saying that if the Mohammedan has been cruel, the Hindu has been mean; and meanness is worse than cruelty.

Whether the Hindu religion was or was not a missionary religion has been a controversial issue.[203] Some hold the view that it was never a missionary religion. Others hold that it was. That the Hindu religion was once a missionary religion must be admitted. It could not have spread over the face of India, if it was not a missionary religion. That today it is not a missionary religion is also a fact which must be accepted. The question therefore is not whether or not the Hindu religion was a missionary religion. The real question is, why did the Hindu religion cease to be a missionary religion?[204]

My answer is this: the Hindu religion ceased to be a missionary

---

Punjab due to its proximity to Central Asia and the predominance of Sikh and Muslim rulers. In the nineteenth century, British rule added to this list, and the conversions of the oppressed castes in large numbers to Islam and Christianity exacerbated the situation. See: Jones (2006, 139–45). According to Gopal Krishan (2004, 77–89), in 1881, the Hindus constituted 43.8 per cent of the population, the Sikhs 8.2 per cent and Christians 0.1 per cent. The Muslims, at 47.6 per cent, were well short of an absolute majority. But by 1941, the Muslims were in absolute majority in the Punjab accounting for 53.2 per cent of the total population. The Hindus made 29.1 per cent of the total, the Sikhs 14.9 per cent, Christians 1.9 per cent and others 1.3 per cent. The erosion in the percentage share of the Hindus was caused by the conversion of many Hindus—especially the lower castes', such as Chuhras, Chamars, Jhiwars and Malis—to Islam, Sikhism and Christianity.
[203]Reads in AoC 1936 as: 'Whether the Hindu religion is a missionary religion is a question which was once a subject of controversy.' Amended in 1937.
[204]For a discussion of conversion during the colonial period, see Gauri Viswanathan (1998), especially the chapter 'Conversion to Equality' (211–40) that discusses Ambedkar's quest for equality through conversion. Also see Chakravarti (2000), where she alludes to the problems of the convert, Pandita Ramabai, in terms of cultural and 'nationalist' positions vis-a-vis the colonial structure which bear out Ambedkar's point.

religion when the caste system grew up among the Hindus. Caste is inconsistent with conversion. Inculcation of beliefs and dogmas is not the only problem that is involved in conversion. To find a place for the convert in the social life of the community is another, and a much more important, problem that arises in connection with conversion. That problem is where to place the convert, in what caste? It is a problem that arises in connection with conversion. That problem is where to place the convert, in what caste? It is a problem which must baffle every Hindu wishing to make aliens converts to his religion.

Unlike a club, the membership of a caste is not open to all and sundry.[205] The law of caste confines its membership to persons born in the caste. Castes are autonomous, and there is no authority anywhere to compel a caste to admit a newcomer to its social life. Hindu Society being a collection of castes, and each caste being a closed corporation, there is no place for a convert. Thus it is the caste which has prevented the Hindus from expanding and from absorbing other religious communities. So long as caste remains, Hindu religion cannot be made a missionary religion, and Shudhi[206] will be both a folly and a futility.

The reasons which have made Shudhi impossible for Hindus are also responsible for making Sanghatan[207] impossible. The idea underlying

---

[205]Phrase added in AoC 1937.

[206]Shuddhi or shuddhikaran—a movement for 'reconversion' to Hinduism—was initiated by Dayananda Saraswati, founder of the Arya Samaj. In 1877, two years after founding the Arya Samaj, Dayananda is said to have performed the first-ever shuddhi of a Muslim man (Parel 2000, 122). Swami Shraddhananda (1856–1926) carried on this legacy more militantly in the early twentieth century in the Punjab and the United Provinces. For an account, see Jaffrelot (1995). However, as Ambedkar points out, shuddhi created many problems since the privileged castes were not willing to mingle with newly 'purified' lower caste members. See also Jones (2006, 129–35, 202–14).

[207]The Hindu Mahasabha launched the sangathan movement in the early 1920s in response to the Khilafat Movement (1918–24), which had Gandhi's support, aimed at a pan-Islamic mobilization to save the Ottoman Empire from dismemberment and to secure political reforms for India. The underlying logic of sangathan was to defend the Hindu community from so-called foreign forces through organization and unification. It aimed to integrate the different sections

Sanghatan is to remove from the mind of the Hindu that timidity and cowardice which so painfully mark him off from the Mohammedan and the Sikh, and which have led him to adopt the low ways of treachery and cunning for protecting himself. The question naturally arises: From where does the Sikh or the Mohammedan derive his strength, which makes him brave and fearless? I am sure it is not due to relative superiority of physical strength, diet, or drill. It is due to the strength arising out of the feeling that all Sikhs will come to the rescue of a Sikh when he is in danger, and that all Mohammedans will rush to save a Muslim if he is attacked.

The Hindu can derive no such strength. He cannot feel assured that his fellows will come to his help. Being one and fated to be alone, he remains powerless, develops timidity and cowardice, and in a fight surrenders or runs away. The Sikh as well as the Muslim stands fearless and gives battle, because he knows that though one he will not be alone. The presence of this belief in the one helps him to hold out, and the absence of it in the other makes him to give way.

If you pursue this matter further and ask what is it that enables the Sikh and the Mohammedan to feel so assured, and why is the Hindu filled with such despair in the matter of help and assistance, you will find that the reasons for this difference lie in the difference in their associated mode of living.[208] The associated mode of life practised by the Sikhs and the Mohammedans produces fellow-feeling. The associated mode of life of the Hindus does not. Among Sikhs and Muslims there is a social cement which makes them 'Bhais'.[209] Among Hindus

---

of the Hindu community, including the Untouchables. The main proponents of sangathan were Bhai Parmanand (see Note 11 in Prologue) and V.D. Savarkar. See Jaffrelot (1999a, 19–24) and also Bapu (2013, 47–60).

[208]Ambedkar is invoking the Deweyan concept of 'associated life', which he picks up and develops further into a political tool. Both Dewey and Ambedkar believed that democracy should not be restricted to the political realm, but should also manifest itself in other areas, such as education, industry and the public sphere. See Mukherjee (2009, 356).

[209]A feeling of brotherhood (ikhwaan) among Muslims across the world (ummat) is an important conceptual category in Islam. Sikhs are also enjoined by their religion to practise universal brotherhood and often address each other as bhai (brother).

there is no such cement, and one Hindu does not regard another Hindu as his Bhai. This explains why a Sikh says and feels that one Sikh, or one Khalsa, is equal to 'sava lakh' men.[210] This explains why one Mohammedan is equal to a crowd of Hindus. This difference is undoubtedly a difference due to caste. So long as caste remains, there will be no Sanghatan; and so long as there is no Sanghatan the Hindu will remain weak and meek.

The Hindus claim to be a very tolerant people. In my opinion this is a mistake. On many occasions they can be intolerant, and if on some occasions they are tolerant, that is because they are too weak to oppose or too indifferent to oppose. This indifference of the Hindus has become so much a part of their nature that a Hindu will quite meekly tolerate an insult as well as a wrong. You see amongst them, to use the words of Morris, 'The great treading down the little, the strong beating down the weak, cruel men fearing not, kind men daring not and wise men caring not.'[211] With the Hindu Gods all-forbearing, it is not difficult to imagine the pitiable condition of the wronged and the oppressed among the Hindus. Indifferentism is the worst kind of disease that can infect a people. Why is the Hindu so indifferent? In my opinion this indifferentism is the result of the caste system, which has made Sanghatan and cooperation even for a good cause impossible.

The assertion by the individual of his own opinions and beliefs, his own independence and interest—as over against group standards, group authority, and group interests—is the beginning of all reform. But whether the reform will continue depends upon what scope the group affords for such individual assertion. If the group is tolerant and fair-minded in dealing with such individuals, they will continue

---

[210]Sava lakh: 125,000. The complete phrase, 'Sava lakh se ek laraun' (My one follower will take on 125,000), is attributed to Govind Singh, the tenth Sikh Guru, who is said to have given this battle cry at Chamkaur in 1704.

[211]William Morris (1834–96) was a poet, author, leader of the early British socialist movement, and the founder of the Arts and Crafts Movement in Britain. The quote is from A Dream of John Ball (1888), a dream travel in time to the Peasants' Revolt of 1381 (also known as Wat Tyler's Rebellion or the Great Rising). Ambedkar here is quoting from the speech given by the character of John Ball, a radical travelling priest excommunicated for his preaching of equality to the Kentish rebels.

to assert [their beliefs], and in the end will succeed in converting their fellows. On the other hand if the group is intolerant, and does not bother about the means it adopts to stifle such individuals, they will perish and the reform will die out.

Now a caste has an unquestioned right to excommunicate any man who is guilty of breaking the rules of the caste; and when it is realized that excommunication involves a complete cesser [cessation] of social intercourse, it will be agreed that as a form of punishment there is really little to choose between excommunication and death. No wonder individual Hindus have not had the courage to assert their independence by breaking the barriers of caste.

It is true that man cannot get on with his fellows. But it is also true that he cannot do without them. He would like to have the society of his fellows on his terms. If he cannot get it on his terms, then he will be ready to have it on any terms, even amounting to complete surrender. This is because he cannot do without society. A caste is ever ready to take advantage of the helplessness of a man, and to insist upon complete conformity to its code in letter and in spirit.

A caste can easily organize itself into a conspiracy to make the life of a reformer a hell; and if a conspiracy is a crime, I do not understand why such a nefarious act as an attempt to excommunicate a person for daring to act contrary to the rules of caste should not be made an offence punishable in law. But as it is, even law gives each caste an autonomy to regulate its membership and punish dissenters with excommunication. Caste in the hands of the orthodox has been a powerful weapon for persecuting the reformers and for killing all reform.

The effect of caste on the ethics of the Hindus is simply deplorable. Caste has killed public spirit. Caste has destroyed the sense of public charity. Caste has made public opinion impossible. A Hindu's public is his caste. His responsibility is only to his caste. His loyalty is restricted only to his caste. Virtue has become caste-ridden, and morality has become castebound. There is no sympathy for the deserving. There is no appreciation of the meritorious. There is no charity to the needy. Suffering as such calls for no response. There is charity, but it begins with the caste and ends with the caste. There is sympathy, but not for men of other castes.

Would a Hindu acknowledge and follow the leadership of a great and good man? The case of a Mahatma apart, the answer must be that he will follow a leader if he is a man of his caste. A Brahmin will follow a leader only if he is a Brahmin, a Kayastha if he is a Kayastha, and so on. The capacity to appreciate merits in a man, apart from his caste, does not exist in a Hindu. There is appreciation of virtue, but only when the man is a fellow caste-man. The whole morality is as bad as tribal morality. My caste-man, right or wrong; my caste-man, good or bad. It is not a case of standing by virtue or not standing by vice. It is a case of standing by, or not standing by, the caste. Have not Hindus committed treason against their country in the interests of their caste?

I would not be surprised if some of you have grown weary listening to this tiresome tale of the sad effects which caste has produced. There is nothing new in it. I will therefore turn to the constructive side of the problem. What is your ideal society if you do not want caste, is a question that is bound to be asked of you. If you ask me, my ideal would be a society based on *Liberty, Equality, and Fraternity.* And why not?

What objection can there be to fraternity? I cannot imagine any. An ideal society should be mobile, should be full of channels for conveying a change taking place in one part to other parts. In an ideal society there should be many interests channels for conveying a change taking place in one part to other parts. In an ideal society there should be many interests consciously communicated and shared. There should be varied and free points of contact with other modes of association. In other words there must be social endosmosis.[212] This is fraternity,

---

[212]Endosmosis was another Deweyan term that Ambedkar deployed and developed. It is derived from a biological term which means the passage of a fluid through a permeable membrane from a region of lower to a region of higher concentration. Mukherjee points out that the term was used originally by the French philosopher Henri Louis Bergson (1859–1941) and, after him, by American philosopher and psychologist William James (1842–1910), who was, like Dewey, a leading exponent of pragmatism, 'to describe the interaction of the mind with nature'. Dewey appropriated it as a descriptor for interaction between social groups. In Ambedkar and Dewey's work the term came to be a metaphor of the fluidity of

which is only another name for democracy. Democracy is not merely a form of government. It is primarily a mode of associated living, of conjoint communicated experience.[213] It is essentially an attitude of respect and reverence towards one's fellow men.

Any objection to liberty? Few object to liberty in the sense of a right to free movement, in the sense of a right to life and limb. There is no objection to liberty in the sense of a right to property, tools, and materials, as being necessary for earning a living, to keep the body in a due state of health. Why not allow a person the liberty to benefit from an effective and competent use of a person's powers? The supporters of caste who would allow liberty in the sense of a right to life, limb, and property, would not readily consent to liberty in this sense, inasmuch as it involves liberty to choose one's profession.

But to object to this kind of liberty is to perpetuate slavery. For slavery does not merely mean a legalized form of subjection. It means a state of society in which some men are forced to accept from others the purposes which control their conduct. This condition obtains even where there is no slavery in the legal sense. It is found where, as in the caste system, some persons are compelled to carry on certain prescribed callings which are not of their choice.

Any objection to equality? This has obviously been the most contentious part of the slogan of the French Revolution. The objections to equality may be sound, and one may have to admit that all men are not equal. But what of that? Equality may be a fiction, but nonetheless one must accept it as the governing principle. A man's power is dependent upon (1) physical heredity; (2) social inheritance or endowment in the form of parental care, education, accumulation of scientific knowledge, everything which enables him to be more efficient than the savage; and finally, (3) on his own efforts. In all these three respects men are undoubtedly unequal. But the question is, shall we

---

communications between social groups, in which, according to Mukherjee (2009, 352), they managed to reconcile the two extremes and give a sense of being both separate and connected.

[213] These lines appear almost exactly in Dewey's *Democracy and Education*, chapter 7: 'A democracy is more than a form of government; it is primarily a mode of associated living, of conjoint communicated experience.'

treat them as unequal because they are unequal? This is a question which the opponents of equality must answer.

From the standpoint of the individualist, it may be just to treat men unequally so far as their efforts are unequal. It may be desirable to give as much incentive as possible to the full development of everyone's powers. But what would happen if men were treated as unequally as they are unequal in the first two respects?[214] It is obvious that those individuals also in whose favour there is birth, education, family name, business connections, and inherited wealth, would be selected in the race. But selection under such circumstances would not be a selection of the able. It would be the selection of the privileged. The reason, therefore, which requires that in the third respect [of those described in the paragraph above] we should treat men unequally, demands that in the first two respects we should treat men as equally as possible.

On the other hand, it can be urged that if it is good for the social body to get the most out of its members, it can get the most out of them only by making them equal as far as possible at the very start of the race. That is one reason why we cannot escape equality. But there is another reason why we must accept equality. A statesman is concerned with vast numbers of people. He has neither the time nor the knowledge to draw fine distinctions and to treat each one equitably, i.e. according to need or according to capacity. However desirable or reasonable an equitable treatment of men may be, humanity is not capable of assortment and classification. The statesman, therefore, must follow some rough and ready rule, and that rough and ready rule is to treat all men alike, not because they are alike but because classification and assortment is impossible. The doctrine of equality is glaringly fallacious but, taking all in all, it is the only way a statesman can proceed in politics—which is a severely practical affair and which demands a severely practical test.

But there is a set of reformers who hold out a different ideal.

---

[214]In AoC 1936 this part reads as: 'men were treated unequally unequally as they are'; in 1937 as: 'men were treated unequally as they are'. The 1945 version is retained here.

They go by the name of the Arya Samajists,[215] and their ideal of social organization is what is called Chaturvarnya, or the division of society into four classes instead of the four thousand castes that we have in India. To make it more attractive and to disarm opposition, the protagonists of thousand castes that we have in India. To make it more attractive and to disarm opposition, the protagonists of Chaturvarnya take great care to point out that their Chaturvarnya is based not on birth but on guna (worth).[216] At the outset, I must confess that notwithstanding the worth-basis of this Chaturvarnya, it is an ideal to which I cannot reconcile myself.

In the first place, if under the Chaturvarnya of the Arya Samajists an individual is to take his place in the Hindu society according to his worth, I do not understand why the Arya Samajists insist upon labelling men as Brahmin, Kshatriya, Vaishya and Shudra. A learned man would be honoured without his being labelled a Brahmin. A soldier would be respected without his being designated a Kshatriya. If European society honours its soldiers and its servants[217] without giving them permanent labels, why should Hindu society find it difficult to do so, is a question which Arya Samajists have not cared to consider.

There is another objection to the continuance of these labels. All reform consists in a change in the notions, sentiments, and mental attitudes of the people towards men and things.[218] It is common

---

[215]It must be remembered that the Jat-Pat Todak Mandal, which invited Ambedkar for its annual conference, for which this address was prepared, was originally affiliated to the Arya Samaj and continued to have several important Arya Samaj leaders of the Punjab influencing it. Ambedkar chooses to take them on in this section of his speech, and this would likely have made them most uncomfortable, and caused them to withdraw their invitation to him. For a summary of the Arya Samaj's views on varnashrama (also known as chaturvarnya and varnavyavastha), based on Dayananda Saraswati's 'Vedic' approach, see Jones (2006).

[216]Refer to Note 161 at 24.3 on the guna-karma theory.

[217]'Savants' in 1936 and 1937; amended in 1944.

[218]Text in semi-bold in this paragraph does not appear in AoC 1936. In the first edition, the lines after the highlighted text appear thus: 'It is human experience that notions and sentiments associated with certain names become part of ourselves, stiffening into attitudes that which hold even trained minds in bondage. Intellectual servitude to old associations is very common and is more difficult to break than

experience that certain names become associated with certain notions and sentiments which determine a person's attitude towards men and things. The names Brahmin, Kshatriya, Vaishya and Shudra are names which are associated with a definite and fixed notion in the mind of every Hindu. That notion is that of a hierarchy based on birth.[219]

So long as these names continue, Hindus will continue to think of the Brahmin, Kshatriya, Vaishya, and Shudra as hierarchical divisions of high and low, based on birth, and to act accordingly. The Hindu must be made to unlearn all this. But how can this happen, if the old labels remain, and continue to recall to his mind old notions? If new notions are to be inculcated in the minds of people, it is necessary to give them new names. To continue the old names is to make the reform futile. To allow this Chaturvarnya based on worth to be designated by such stinking labels as Brahmin, Kshatriya, Vaishya and Shudra, indicative of social divisions based on birth, is a snare.

To me this Chaturvarnya with its old labels is utterly repellent, and my whole being rebels against it. But I do not wish to rest my objection to Chaturvarnya on mere grounds of sentiments. There are more solid grounds on which I rely for my opposition to it. A close examination of this ideal has convinced me that as a system of social organization, Chaturvarnya is impracticable, is harmful, and has turned out to be a miserable failure.[220] From a practical point of view, the system of Chaturvarnya raises several difficulties which its protagonists [advocates] do not seem to have taken into account. The principle underlying caste is fundamentally different from the principle

---

is generally thought. Facts may change, but if names remain the same, then the notions associated with those names linger not only in sentiments but also in practice. These labels have had all along in Indian history the de facto connotation of designating a hierarchy of castes based on birth. They were understood to be marks of superiority and inferiority.' These lines were amended in the 1937 edition used here.

[219]All of this paragraph, except its last sentence, does not appear in AoC 1936.
[220]The lines at the beginning of 16.1 till '...a miserable failure' figure under Section XV of AoC 1936. The lines that follow from here (beginning, 'From a practical...') till the first sentence of 16.3 (ending, '...chaturvarnya a success.') have been added in the 1937 edition.

underlying Chaturvarnya.[221] Not only are they fundamentally different, but they are also fundamentally opposed.

The former [Chaturvarnya] is based on worth. How are you going to compel people who have acquired a higher status based on birth, without reference to their worth, to vacate that status? How are you going to compel people to recognize the status due to a man, in accordance with his worth, who is occupying a lower status based on his birth? For this, you must first break up the caste system, in order to be able to establish the Chaturvarnya system. How are you going to reduce the four thousand castes, based on birth, to the four varnas, based on worth? This is the first difficulty which the protagonists of the Chaturvarnya must grapple with.

There is a second difficulty which the protagonists of Chaturvarnya must grapple with, if they wish to make the establishment of Chaturvarnya a success.[222] Chaturvarnya pre-supposes that you can classify people into four definite classes. Is this possible?[223] In this respect, the ideal of Chaturvarnya has, as you will see, a close affinity to the Platonic ideal. To Plato, men fell by nature into three classes. In some individuals, he believed,[224] mere appetites dominated. He assigned them to the labouring and trading classes. Others revealed to him that over and above appetites, they had a courageous disposition. He classed them as defenders in war and guardians of internal peace. Others showed a capacity to grasp the universal reason underlying things. He made them the law-givers of the people.

The criticism to which Plato's Republic is subject, is also the criticism which must apply to the system of Chaturvarnya, insofar as it proceeds upon the possibility of an accurate classification of men into four distinct classes.[225] The chief criticism against Plato is that his idea of

---

[221]This is given as 'varna' in AoC 1936 and 1937; Ambedkar changes it to 'chaturvarnya' in 1944.

[222]In AoC 1936, Section 16 begins here, with the sentence: 'The practicability of the chaturvarnya presupposes two things. It presupposes...'

[223]This question does not appear in AoC 1936.

[224]Phrase added in 1937.

[225]Plato's The Republic, addressing the question of justice, deduces that the human soul has three parts: the 'logical', thinking part; the 'spirited' part, by which we

lumping individuals into a few sharply-marked-off classes is a very superficial view of man and his powers. Plato had no perception of the uniqueness of every individual, of his incommensurability with others, of each individual as forming a class of his own. He had no recognition of the infinite diversity of active tendencies, and the combination of tendencies of which an individual is capable. To him, there were types of faculties or powers in the individual constitution.

All this is demonstrably wrong. Modem science has shown that the lumping together of individuals into a few sharply marked-off classes is a superficial view of man, not worthy of serious consideration. Consequently, the utilization of the qualities of individuals is incompatible with their stratification by classes, since the qualities of individuals are so variable. Chaturvarnya must fail for the very reason for which Plato's Republic must fail—namely, that it is not possible to pigeonhole men, according as they belong to one class[226] or the other.

---

develop anger and get into a temper; and the 'appetitive' part, by which we experience hunger, thirst, eroticism, love for moneymaking and other such desires. The book also categorizes men into three classes based on which part of their soul masks the others: the 'guardians' are persons in whom the logical part dominates, in the 'auxiliaries' spirit dominates, and the 'producers' are people who have let their appetite dominate. The guardians must rule, the auxiliaries must help in running the guardians' writ, and the producers must work. (See also Note 161 on the guna-karma theory.) Ambedkar disagrees with Plato on many levels. He is not convinced that there are only three qualities on the basis of which a soul can be divided. He believes that the multitude of human characteristics is so complex that it is impossible to identify and categorize them. He also points out that different characteristics become more or less important in the same person at different times. His criticism is also what was later popularized as the problem of the 'one-dimensional man' by Herbert Marcuse (1964/1991). From his experience of caste, Ambedkar's critique is that in such an arrangement where most of the power is vested with the guardians and the remaining with the auxiliaries (the 'twice-born' Brahmins, Kshatriyas and Vaishyas in the caste context), there is no mechanism to ensure that they will not oppress the producers (Shudras and Untouchables).

[226]In AoC 1936, this merely reads as 'not possible to pigeon men into holes'. In 1937, Ambedkar amends this to 'not possible to pigeon men into holes according as he belongs to one class or the other'. The subsequent lines, beginning 'That it is impossible...' till '... it was established?' in 16.6 are absent in AoC 1936.

That it is impossible to accurately classify people into four definite classes, is proved by the fact that the original four classes have now become four thousand castes.

There is a third difficulty in the way of the establishment of the system of Chaturvarnya. How are you going to maintain the system of Chaturvarnya, supposing it was established? One[227] important requirement for the successful working of Chaturvarnya is the maintenance[228] of the penal system which could maintain it by its sanction. The system of Chaturvarnya must perpetually face the problem of the transgressor. Unless there is a penalty attached to the act of transgression, men will not keep to their respective classes. The whole system will break down, being contrary to human nature. Chaturvarnya cannot subsist by its own inherent goodness. It must be enforced by law.

That without penal sanction the ideal of Chaturvarnya cannot be realized, is proved by the story in the Ramayana of Rama killing Shambuka.[229] Some people seem to blame Rama because he wantonly and without reason killed Shambuka. But to blame Rama for killing Shambuka is to misunderstand the whole situation. Ram Raj was a Raj based on Chaturvarnya. As a king, Rama was bound to maintain Chaturvarnya. It was his duty therefore to kill Shambuka, the Shudra who had transgressed his class and wanted to be a Brahmin. This is

---

[227]This sentence begins with 'Another' in AoC 1936; perhaps changed in the light of new sentences added in 1937.

[228]The word used is 'existence' in AoC 1936.

[229]The story of Shambuka is told in the seventh book, Uttarakanda, of the Valmiki Ramayana. Shambuka wants to achieve a higher status than the suras (devtas, gods) through meditation and austerities. On discovering that Shambuka, a Shudra, was indeed meditating, Rama promptly beheads him to restore varnasharma dharma. The story has been used by the Dravidian movement and in anti-caste literature to ridicule the idea of Rama as the embodiment of perfection. Kuvempu (Kuppalli Venkatappa Puttappa) (1904–94), a Jnanpith-winning Kannada author wrote *Sudra Tapasvi* (1944), a novel based on Shambuka's life. Sikhamani, a contemporary Telugu Dalit poet, writes: 'The sword that severed/ Shambuka's head could remain/ sharp and safe for centuries./ It has just changed hands/ and no longer recognises you./ No Manu to save you now!' See 'Steel Nibs are Sprouting...' in Satyanarayana and Tharu (2013, 554).

the reason why Rama killed Shambuka. But this also shows that penal sanction is necessary for the maintenance of Chaturvarnya. Not only penal sanction is necessary, but the penalty of death is necessary. That is why Rama did not inflict on Shambuka a lesser punishment. That is why the Manusmriti[230] prescribes such heavy sentences as cutting off the tongue, or pouring of molten lead in the ears, of the Shudra who recites or hears the Veda.[231] The supporters of Chaturvarnya must

---

[230]The Manusmriti represents itself as the dharma that Brahma declares to Manu, 'the first Man', and is passed on by him to Bhrigu, one of the ten 'great sages'. The text is believed to have attained its present form around the second century CE. Ambedkar writes in another, posthumously published work, *Revolution and Counter-Revolution in Ancient India* (BAWS 5, 273): 'Pushyamitra Sunga and his successors could not have tolerated these exaggerated claims of the Brahmins unless they themselves were Brahmins interested in the establishment of Brahmanism. Indeed it is quite possible that the Manusmriti was composed at the command of Pushyamitra Brahman king (185–149 BC) himself, and forms the book of the philosophy of Brahmanism.' In another work, *The Untouchables: Who Were They and Why They Became Untouchable*, Ambedkar (BAWS 9, 373) says: 'After taking all facts into consideration Prof Buhler has fixed a date which appears to strike the truth. According to Buhler, the Manusmriti, in the shape in which it exists now, came into existence in the Second Century AD.' A contemporary scholar, J.L. Brockington (1996, 92) arrives at a similar conclusion. Many editions of the Manusmriti have been published in Sanskrit since its first edition in 1813. The first translation was Institutes of Hindu law, or, The ordinances of Menu [sic], according to the gloss of Culluca: comprising the Indian system of duties, religious and civil: verbally translated from the original Sanscrit: with a preface, by Sir William Jones (1796). One of the best-known translations is George Buhler's Laws of Manu (1886/2004), which contains an exhaustive introduction and extracts from seven commentaries. In her modern translation, Wendy Doniger states that no work in the tradition of Western scholarship compares with the fame and sustained authority exercised across centuries by the Manusmriti. See Doniger and Smith (1991, xviii–xix). As C.J. Fuller (2003, 484) notes, British administrators depended on Dharmashastras such as the Manusmriti to develop a legal system for India, thus subjecting the Hindu population as a whole to a Brahminical legal code. For the most authoritative, exhaustively annotated edition (1,131 pages) of the Manusmriti, see Patrick Olivelle (2005).
[231]Such verses do not figure in the Manusmriti. Buhler's edition, which Ambedkar may have possibly accessed, offers two verses that come close to the import. 'A once-born man (a Shudra), who insults a twice-born man with gross invective,

give an assurance that they could successfully classify men, and that they could induce modern society in the twentieth century to re-forge the penal sanctions of the Manusmriti.

The protagonists of Chaturvarnya do not seem to have considered what is to happen to women in their system. Are they also to be divided into four classes, Brahmin, Kshatriya, Vaishya and Shudra? Or are they to be allowed to take the status of their husbands? If the status of the woman is to be the consequence of marriage, what becomes of the underlying principle of Chaturvarnya—namely, that the status of a person should be based upon the worth of that person? If they are to be classified according to their worth, is their classification to be nominal or real?

If it is to be nominal, then it is useless; and then the protagonists of Chaturvarnya must admit that their system does not apply to women. If it is real, are the protagonists of Chaturvarnya prepared to follow the logical consequences of applying it to women? They must be prepared to have women priests and women soldiers. Hindu society has grown accustomed to women teachers and women barristers. It may grow accustomed to women brewers and women butchers. But he would be a bold person who would say that it will allow women priests and women soldiers. But that will be the logical outcome of applying Chaturvarnya to women. Given these difficulties, I think no one except a congenital idiot could hope for and believe in a successful

shall have his tongue cut out; for he is of low origin' (8.270; 1886/2004, 211). And: 'If he arrogantly teaches Brahmins their duty, the king shall cause hot oil to be poured into his mouth and into his ears' (8.272; 2004, 211). For Ambedkar's extended discussion of the Manusmriti, see the annotated edition of 'Castes in India' in Rege (2013, 77–108). Ambedkar seems to be citing these punishments from chapter 12 of Gautama Dharma Sutra (600 BCE to 300 BCE, predating the Manusmriti) which he also cites in his posthumous work, Philosophy of Hinduism (BAWS 3). Buhler's translation (1898, 239) of Gautama Dharma Sutra talks of similar punishments for the Shudra: '4. Now if a Shudra listens intentionally to (a recitation of) the Veda, his ears shall be filled with (molten) tin or lac. 5. If he recites (Vedic texts), his tongue shall be cut out. 6. If he remembers them, his body shall be split in twain. 7. If he assumes a position equal (to that of twice-born men) in sitting, in lying down, in conversation or on the road, he shall undergo (corporal) punishment.'

regeneration of the Chaturvarnya.

Assuming that Chaturvarnya is practicable, I contend that it is the most vicious system. That the Brahmins should cultivate knowledge, that the Kshatriya should bear arms, that the Vaishya should trade, and that the Shudra should serve,[232] sounds as though it was a system of division of labour. Whether the theory was intended to state that the Shudra need not, or whether it was intended to lay down that he must not, is an interesting question. The defenders of Chaturvarnya give it the first meaning. They say, why need the Shudra trouble to acquire wealth, when the three [higher] varnas are there to support him? Why need the Shudra bother to take to education, when there is the Brahmin to whom he can go when the occasion for reading or writing arises? Why need the Shudra worry to arm himself, when there is the Kshatriya to protect him? The theory of Chaturvarnya, understood in this sense, may be said to look upon the Shudra as the ward and the three [higher] varnas as his guardians. Thus interpreted, it is a simple, elevating, and alluring theory.

Assuming this to be the correct view of the underlying conception of Chaturvarnya, it seems to me that the system is neither fool-proof nor knave-proof. What is to happen if the Brahmins, Vaishyas, and Kshatriyas fail to pursue knowledge, to engage in economic enterprise, and to be efficient soldiers, which are their respective functions? Contrarywise, suppose that they discharge their functions, but flout their duty to the Shudra or to one another; what is to happen to the

---

[232]In AoC 1936, after 'serve', it reads '—all this sounds very simple and appears to be perfect. But what does it all come to in practice? It means the pauperisation of the many for the sake of the few. It means the disarming of the many for the sake of the few. It means the deadening and darkening of the lives of the many in order that the few may have life and light. As has been observed, there is no country in the world which has suffered so much as a result of social evils of its own creation as India.' Ambedkar drops this passage in AoC 1937, and in its place offers an extended reflection—of 650 words—on the exploitative and illogical nature of the chaturvarnya system. This appears to be triggered by Gandhi's response to this speech-essay in *Harijan*, where he upholds the fourfold varnashrama dharma but denounces the proliferation of castes. In this edition, this new material appears from this point in 17.1 till the close of 17.4.

Shudra if the three classes refuse to support him on fair terms, or combine to keep him down? Who is to safeguard the interests of the Shudra—or for that matter, those of the Vaishya and Kshatriya—when the person who is trying to take advantage of his ignorance is the Brahmin? Who is to defend the liberty of the Shudra—and for that matter, of the Brahmin and the Vaishya—when the person who is robbing him of it is the Kshatriya?

Inter-dependence of one class on another class is inevitable. Even dependence of one class upon another may sometimes become allowable. But why make one person depend upon another in the matter of his vital needs? Education, everyone must have. Means of defence, everyone must have. These are the paramount requirements of every man for his self-preservation. How can the fact that his neighbour is educated and armed help a man who is uneducated and disarmed? The whole theory is absurd. These are the questions which the defenders of Chaturvarnya do not seem to be troubled about. But they are very pertinent questions. Assuming that in their conception of Chaturvarnya the relationship between the different classes is that of ward and guardian, and that this is the real conception underlying Chaturvarnya, it must be admitted that it makes no provision to safeguard the interests of the ward from the misdeeds of the guardian.

Whether or not the relationship of guardian and ward was the real underlying conception on which Chaturvarnya was based, there is no doubt that in practice the relation was that of master and servants. The three classes, Brahmins, Kshatriyas, and Vaishyas, although not very happy in their mutual relationship, managed to work by compromise. The Brahmin flattered the Kshatriya, and both let the Vaishya live in order to be able to live upon him. But the three agreed to beat down the Shudra. He was not allowed to acquire wealth, lest he should be independent of the three [higher] varnas. He was prohibited from acquiring knowledge, lest he should keep a steady vigil regarding his interests. He was prohibited from bearing arms, lest he should have the means to rebel against their authority. That this is how the Shudras were treated by the Tryavarnikas[233] is evidenced by the laws of Manu.

---

[233]Tryavarnikas: Sanskrit for 'three varnas'; refers to the dwija, 'twice-born', varnas.

There is no code of laws more infamous regarding social rights than the laws of Manu. Any instance from anywhere of social injustice must pale before it.

Why have the mass of people tolerated the social evils to which they have been subjected? There have been social revolutions in other countries of the world. Why have there not been social revolutions in India, is a question which has incessantly troubled me. There is only one answer which I can give, and it is that the lower classes of Hindus[234] have been completely disabled for direct action[235] on

---

[234]Highlighted words read in AoC 1936 as 'similar' (for social), 'occurred to' (troubled), 'have been able to' (can), and 'masses' (lower classes) respectively.

[235]'Direct action' is a method Ambedkar (BASWS 5, 375) advocated for the assertion of the civil rights of Untouchables. When Ambedkar was at Columbia University (1913–16), he was likely exposed to the views of American feminist anarchist Voltairine de Cleyre (1866–1912), whom the anarchist Emma Goldman called the 'most gifted and brilliant anarchist woman America ever produced'. In 1912, de Cleyre wrote a famous essay called 'Direct Action', which she defined as collective action against and mass resistance to state and capitalist oppression. 'Every person who ever had a plan to do anything, and went and did it, or who laid his plan before others, and won their cooperation to do it with him, without going to external authorities to please do the thing for them, was a direct actionist... Every person who ever in his life had a difference with anyone to settle, and went straight to the other persons involved to settle it, either by a peaceable plan or otherwise, was a direct actionist.' The term was also popularized by the Industrial Workers of the World founded in 1905 in Chicago; its mouthpiece was called Direct Action. On his part, Ambedkar called for 'open revolt in the form of direct action against the Hindu Established Order'. He lists the Chavadar Tank satyagraha in Mahad and the Kalaram temple satyagraha as instances of direct action which created a 'crisis' among Hindus. Ambedkar contrasts this method with that of Gandhi's Harijan Sevak Sangh that believed Caste Hindus must feel remorse and guilt (for practising untouchability) and thus voluntarily ask the Untouchables to participate in the general village life, that is, accessing waterbodies, roads or temples. Ambedkar here cites his letter to A.V. Thakkar, general secretary of the Harijan Sevak Sangh: 'The salvation of the Depressed Classes will come only when the Caste Hindu is made to think and is forced to feel that he must alter his ways. For that you must create a crisis by direct action against his customary code of conduct. The crisis will compel him to think and once he begins to think he will be more ready to change than he is otherwise likely to be. The great defect in the policy of least resistance and silent infiltration

account of this wretched caste system. They could not bear arms, and without arms they could not rebel. They were all ploughmen—or rather, condemned to be ploughmen—and they never were allowed to convert their ploughshares into swords. They had no bayonets, and therefore everyone who chose, could and did sit upon them. On account of the caste system,[236] they could receive no education. They could not think out or know the way to their salvation. They were condemned to be lowly; and not knowing the way of escape, and not having the means of escape, they became reconciled to eternal servitude,[237] which they accepted as their inescapable fate.[238]

It is true that even in Europe the strong has not shrunk from the exploitation—nay, the spoliation—of the weak. But in Europe, the strong have never contrived to make the weak helpless against exploitation so shamelessly as was the case in India among the Hindus. Social war has been raging between the strong and the weak far more violently in Europe than it has ever been in India. Yet the weak in Europe has had in his freedom of military service, his physical weapon; in suffering, his political weapon; and in education, his moral weapon. These three weapons for emancipation were never suffering, his political weapon; and in education, his moral weapon. These three weapons for emancipation were never withheld by the strong from the weak in Europe. All these weapons were, however, denied to the masses in

---

of rational ideas lies in that they do not "compel", for they do not produce a crisis. The direct action in respect of the Chavadar Tank in Mahad 1927, the Kalaram temple in Nasik 1930 and the Guruvayur temple in Malabar 1931–32 have done in a few days what million days of preaching by reformers would never have done.' In the 1920s, Ambedkar did invest a little faith in the Gandhian satyagraha method; as noted in Roy's introduction (p.107), Gandhi's portrait was displayed during the December leg of the Mahad satyagraha in 1927. Muhammad Ali Jinnah, founder of the All India Muslim League, also called for 'direct action' in 1946 if the Muslims were not granted Pakistan. For a discussion of Jinnah's lack of clarity on what he meant by direct action, see Ayesha Jalal (1985, 211–3).
[236]In AoC 1936, it is the 'wretched system of chaturvarnya'. Ambedkar in the next few passages of Section 17 consistently replaces references to chaturvarnya with 'caste system'—all these instances are highlighted with semibold text.
[237]In AoC 1936, this sentence ends with 'the fate of eternal servitude'.
[238] This paragraph does not appear in AoC 1936.

India by the caste system.

There cannot be a more degrading system of social organization than the caste system. It is the system which deadens, paralyses, and cripples the people, [keeping them] from helpful activity. This is no exaggeration. History bears ample evidence. There is only one period in Indian history which is a period of freedom, greatness and glory. That is the period of the Mourya Empire.[239] At all other times the country suffered from defeat and darkness. But the Mourya period was a period when the caste system was completely annihilated—when the Shudras, who constituted the mass of the people, came into their own and became the rulers of the country. The period of defeat and darkness is the period when the caste system flourished, to the damnation of the greater part of the people of the country.

Chaturvarnya is not new. It is as old as the Vedas. That is one of the reasons why we are asked by the Arya Samajists to consider its claims. Judging from the past, as a system of social organization it has been tried and it has failed. How many times have the Brahmins annihilated the seed of the Kshatriyas! How many times have the Kshatriyas annihilated the Brahmins! The Mahabharata and the Puranas are full of incidents of the strife between the Brahmins and the Kshatriyas. They even quarreled over such petty questions as to who should salute first, as to who should give way first, the Brahmins or the Kshatriyas, when

---

[239]The Mauryan empire lasted from 322 BCE to 185 BCE and reached its zenith under Ashoka, who, after securing the empire and extending its borders, embraced Buddhism and spread it through the territories under his control. He even sent ambassadors across Asia to spread the faith. Ambedkar (BAWS 3, 268) considered this Buddhist phase a 'revolution' in ancient India, and termed the re-emergence of Brahminism under the Brahmin King Pushyamitra Sunga (185–149 BCE) the 'counter-revolution': 'The Brahmins had not only lost state patronage but they lost their occupation which mainly consisted of performing sacrifices for a fee which oftentimes was very substantial and which constituted their chief source of living. The Brahmins therefore lived as the suppressed and Depressed Classes for nearly 140 years during which the Maurya Empire lasted. A rebellion against the Buddhist state was the only way of escape left to the suffering Brahmins and there is special reason why Pushyamitra should raise the banner of revolt against the rule of the Mauryas.'

the two met in the street.[240]

Not only was the Brahmin an eyesore to the Kshatriya and the Kshatriya an eyesore to the Brahmin, it seems that the Kshatriyas had become tyrannical, and the masses, disarmed as they were under the system of Chaturvarnya, were praying to Almighty God for relief from their tyranny. The Bhagwat[241] tells us very definitely that Krishna had taken avatar for one sacred purpose: and that was, to annihilate the Kshatriyas. With these instances of rivalry and enmity between the different varnas before us, I do not understand how anyone can hold out Chaturvarnya as an ideal to be aimed at,[242] or as a pattern on which the Hindu Society should be remodelled.

I have dealt with those, those who are outside your group [the Mandal] and whose hostility to your ideal [the destruction of caste] is quite open. There appear to be others who are neither without you nor with you. I was hesitating whether I should deal with their point of view. But on further consideration I have come to the conclusion that I must, and that for two reasons. Firstly, their attitude to the problem of caste is not merely an attitude of neutrality, but is an attitude of

---

[240]Ambedkar discusses the many conflicts between Brahmins and Kshatriyas at length elsewhere (BAWS 3, 392–415). Here, he is alluding to the mythical Brahmin warrior Parashurama's twenty-one wars of extermination against the Kshatriyas after Parashurama's father is killed by a Kshatriya and he sees his mother beating her chest twenty-one times. Mythical and legendary narratives asserting the authority of the Brahmins were in conflict with each other as Brahmin sub-castes tried to establish superiority over one another through competitive myth-making. See Figueira (2002). For a typical example of a legalistic inter-Brahmin conflict in modern India, see Notes 56–7 at 7.2. See Johnson (2005) for an account of how many of these factors played out in Bombay province in the formative years of Indian nationalism. The reference to 'who should salute first, as to who should give way first' pertains to the Brahmin-Kayastha conflict (see Note 60 to 7.4).

[241]The Bhagwat is the Bhagvad Gita. For a detailed discussion of the Bhagvad Gita by Ambedkar, see 'Krishna and His Gita' (BAWS 3). On how, for Ambedkar, the Bhagvad Gita is neither a book of religion nor a treatise on philosophy, see Pandit (1992). See also Kumar (2010) on 'Ambedkar's attempt to retrieve a counterhistory of Indian antiquity'.

[242]'To be copied' in AoC 1936.

armed neutrality.[243] Secondly, they probably represent a considerable body of people. Of these, there is one set which finds nothing peculiar nor odious in the caste system of the Hindus. Such Hindus cite the case of Muslims, Sikhs and Christians, and find comfort in the fact that they too have castes amongst them.

In considering this question, you must at the outset bear in mind that nowhere is human society one single whole. It is always plural. In the world of action, the individual is one limit and society the other. Between them lie all sorts of associative arrangements of lesser and larger scope—families, friendships, cooperative associations, business combines, political parties, bands of thieves and robbers. These small groups are usually firmly welded together, and are often as exclusive as castes. They have a narrow and intensive code, which is often anti-social. This is true of every society, in Europe as well as in Asia. The question to be asked in determining whether a given society is an ideal society is not whether there are groups in it, because groups exist in all societies.

The questions to be asked in determining what is an ideal society are: How numerous and varied are the interests which are consciously shared by the groups? How full and free is the interplay with other forms of associations? Are the forces that separate groups and classes more numerous than the forces that unite them? What social significance is attached to this group life? Is its exclusiveness a matter of custom and convenience, or is it a matter of religion? It is in the light of these questions that one must decide whether caste among non-Hindus is the same as caste among Hindus.[244]

---

[243]This is a war and diplomacy term. 'One speaks of an armed neutrality when a neutral State takes military measures for the purpose of defending its neutrality against possible or probable attempts of either belligerent [sic] to make use of the neutral territory' (Oppenheim 1905, 353).

[244]Ambedkar, once again, is drawing on his mentor John Dewey whom he mentions and acknowledges later in the essay. Discussing the 'need of a measure for the worth of any given mode of social life', Dewey writes (1916, ch. 7): 'How numerous and varied are the interests which are consciously shared? How full and free is the interplay with other forms of association? If we apply these considerations to, say, a criminal band, we find that the ties which consciously hold the members together

If we apply these considerations to castes among Mohammedans, Sikhs, and Christians on the one hand, and to castes among Hindus on the other, you will find that caste among non-Hindus is fundamentally different from caste among Hindus. First, the ties which consciously make the Hindus hold together are non-existent, while among non-Hindus there are many that hold them together. The strength of a society depends upon the presence of points of contact, possibilities of interaction, between different groups which exist in it. These are what Carlyle calls 'organic filaments'—i.e., the elastic threads which help to bring the disintegrating elements together and to reunite them.[245] There is no integrating force among the Hindus to counteract the disintegration caused by caste. While among the non-Hindus there are plenty of these organic filaments which bind them together.

Again it must be borne in mind that although there are castes among non-Hindus, as there are among Hindus, caste has not the same social significance for non-Hindus as it has for Hindus. Ask a Mohammedan or a Sikh who he is. He tells you that he is a Mohammedan or a Sikh, as the case may be. He does not tell you his caste, although he has one; and you are satisfied with his answer. When he tells you that he is a Muslim, you do not proceed to ask him whether he is a Shiya

---

are few in number, reducible almost to a common interest in plunder; and that they are of such a nature as to isolate the group from other groups with respect to give and take of the values of life.' See also Lenart Škof (2011) who maps the influence of Dewey's pragmatism on Ambedkar's political philosophy, tracks his debt to not just Dewey but also to British idealist and liberal T.H. Green (1836–82), and connects this to the work of contemporary Brazilian philosopher and social theorist Roberto Mangabeira Unger, who taught Barack Obama at Harvard.

[245]Thomas Carlyle (1795–1881) was a pre-eminent figure in Victorian letters. In History of the French Revolution (1837), he sympathized with the revolutionaries to an extent but despised anarchy, and appeared to fear the rule of the people. The concept of 'organic filaments' here is borrowed from Sartor Resartus (1833–4), a well-disguised autobiography and a critique of utilitarianism and British society, presenting fragments of Carlyle's philosophy in the form of a satire featuring a loose collection of papers written by a fictional German philosopher Diogenes Teufelsdrockh. In the seventh chapter of Book 3, Carlyle describes the world as a phoenix that begins to resurrect itself while dying. The 'organic filaments' are the processes of creation that hold together a world while it is destroying itself.

or a Suni; Sheikh or Saiyad; Khatik or Pinjari.[246] When he tells you he is a Sikh, you do not ask him whether he is Jat or Roda, Mazbi or Ramdasi.[247] But you are not satisfied, if a person tells you that he is a Hindu. You feel bound to inquire into his caste. Why? Because so essential is caste in the case of a Hindu, that without knowing it you do not feel sure what sort of a being he is.

That caste has not the same social significance among non-Hindus as it has among Hindus is clear, if you take into consideration the consequences which follow breach of caste. There may be castes among Sikhs and Mohammedans, but the Sikhs and the Mohammedans will not outcast a Sikh or a Mohammedan if he broke his caste. Indeed, the very idea of excommunication is foreign to the Sikhs and the Mohammedans. But with the Hindus the case is entirely different. A Hindu is sure to be outcasted if he broke caste. This shows the difference in the social significance of caste to Hindus and non-Hindus. This is the second point of difference.

But there is also a third and a more important one. Caste among the non-Hindus has no religious consecration; but among the Hindus most decidedly it has. Among the non-Hindus, caste is only a practice, not a sacred institution. They did not originate it. With them it is only a survival mechanism.[248] They do not regard caste as a religious dogma. Religion compels the Hindus to treat isolation and segregation of castes as a virtue. Religion does not compel the non-Hindus to take the same attitude towards caste. If Hindus wish to break caste,

---

[246]There has been a lot of recent research on caste among Muslims in India. Besides Imtiaz Ahmad (1978), see Ali Anwar's *Masawat ki Jung* [Battle for equality] (2005) and Masood Alam Falahi's *Hindustan Mein Zaat-Paat Aur Musalman* [Casteism in India and Muslims] (2007). For a quick overview, see Khalid Anis Ansari (2013) who chronicles the contemporary pasmanda movement: '"Pasmanda", a Persian term meaning "those who have fallen behind", refers to Muslims belonging to the Shudra (backward) and Ati-Shudra (Dalit) castes. It was adopted as an oppositional identity to that of the dominant ashraf Muslims (forward castes) in 1998 by the Pasmanda Muslim Mahaz, a group which mainly worked in Bihar. Since then, however, the pasmanda discourse has found resonance elsewhere too.'
[247]On the practice of caste in Sikhism, see Notes 33 and 168 at 2.22 and 26.3.
[248]This word does not figure in prior editions, and has been introduced for clarity.

their religion will come in their way. But it will not be so in the case of non-Hindus. It is, therefore, a dangerous delusion to take comfort in the mere existence of caste among non-Hindus, without caring to know what place caste occupies in their life and whether there are other 'organic filaments' which subordinate the feeling of caste to the feeling of community. The sooner the Hindus are cured of this delusion, the better.

The other set [of 'neutral' Hindus] denies that caste presents any problem at all for the Hindus to consider. Such Hindus seek comfort in the view that the Hindus have survived, and take this as a proof of their fitness to survive. This point of view is well expressed by Prof. S. Radhakrishnan in his *The Hindu View of Life*.[249] Referring to Hinduism he says,

> 'The civilization itself has not been a short-lived one. Its historic records date back for over four thousand years and even then it had reached a stage of civilization which has continued its unbroken, though at times slow and static, course until the present day. It has stood the stress and strain of more than four or five millenniums of spiritual thought and experience. Though peoples of different races and cultures have been pouring into India from the dawn of History, Hinduism has been able to maintain its supremacy and even the proselytizing creeds backed

---

[249]S. Radhakrishnan (1888–1975) was a prolific writer, an apologist of Hinduism, and the second president of Independent India. Ambedkar is citing from the book *The Hindu Way of Life* (1927, 12–13), a compilation of the lectures delivered at Oxford in 1926. Later in the work, Radhakrishnan says: 'In dealing with the problem of the conflict of the different racial groups, Hinduism adopted the only safe course of democracy, viz., that each racial group should be allowed to develop the best in it without impeding the progress of others. Every historical group is unique and specific and has an ultimate value, and the highest morality requires that we should respect its individuality. Caste, on its racial side, is the affirmation of the infinite diversity of human groups' (97). Furthermore, 'Caste was the answer of Hinduism to the forces pressing on it from outside. It was the instrument by which Hinduism civilised the different tribes it took in. Any group of people appearing exclusive in any sense is a caste. Whenever a group represents a type a caste arises' (104). Tellingly, his birth anniversary, 5 September, is celebrated as Teacher's Day in India.

by political power have not been able to coerce the large majority of Hindus to their views. The Hindu culture possesses some vitality which Hindus to their views. The Hindu culture possesses some vitality which seems to be denied to some other more forceful currents. It is no more necessary to dissect Hinduism than to open a tree to see whether the sap still runs.'

The name of Prof. Radhakrishnan is big enough to invest with profundity whatever he says, and impress the minds of his readers.[250] But I must not hesitate to speak out my mind. For I fear that his statement may become the basis of a vicious argument that the fact of survival is proof of fitness to survive.

It seems to me that the question is not whether a community lives or dies; the question is on what plane does it live. There are different modes of survival. But not all are equally honourable. For an individual as well as for a society, there is a gulf between merely living, and living worthily. To fight in a battle and to live in glory is one mode. To beat a retreat, to surrender, and to live the life of a captive is also a mode of survival. It is useless for a Hindu to take comfort in the fact that he and his people have survived. What he must consider is, what is the quality of their survival. If he does that, I am sure he will cease to take pride in the mere fact of survival. A Hindu's life has been a life of continuous defeat, and what appears to him to be life everlasting is not living everlastingly, but is really a life which is perishing everlastingly. It is a mode of survival of which every right-minded Hindu who is not afraid to own up to the truth will feel ashamed.

There is no doubt, in my opinion, that unless you change your social order you can achieve little by way of progress. You cannot mobilize the community either for defence or for offence. You cannot build anything on the foundations of caste. You cannot build up a nation, you cannot build up a morality. Anything that you will build on the foundations of caste will crack, and will never be a whole.

The only question that remains to be considered is—*How to bring*

---

[250]AoC 1936: 'impress the minds of many with the profundity of whatever he says.'

about the reform of the Hindu social order? How to abolish caste?[251] This is a question of supreme importance. There is a view that in the reform of caste, the first step to take is to abolish sub-castes. This view is based upon the supposition that there is a greater similarity in manners and status between sub-castes than there is between castes. I think this is an erroneous supposition. The Brahmins of Northern and Central India are socially of lower grade, as compared with the Brahmins of the Deccan and Southern India. The former are only cooks and water-carriers, while the latter occupy a high social position. On the other hand, in Northern India, the Vaishyas and Kayasthas are intellectually and socially on a par with the Brahmins of the Deccan and Southern India.

Again, in the matter of food there is no similarity between the Brahmins of the Deccan and Southern India, who are vegetarians, and the Brahmins of Kashmir and Bengal, who are non-vegetarians. On the other hand, the Brahmins of the Deccan and Southern India have more in common so far as food is concerned with such non-Brahmins as the Gujaratis, Marwaris, Banias, and Jains.

There is no doubt that from the standpoint of making the transition[252] from one caste to another easy, the fusion of the Kayasthas of Northern India and the other non-Brahmins of Southern India with the non-Brahmins of the Deccan and the Dravidian[253] country is more practicable than the fusion of the Brahmins of the South with the Brahmins of the North. But assuming that the fusion of sub-castes is possible, what guarantee is there that the abolition of subcastes will necessarily lead to the abolition of castes? On the contrary, it may happen that the process may stop with the abolition of sub-castes. In that case, the abolition of sub-castes will only help to strengthen the castes, and make them more powerful and therefore more mischievous. This remedy is therefore neither practicable nor effective, and may easily prove to be a wrong remedy.

Another plan of action for the abolition of caste is to begin with inter-caste dinners. This also, in my opinion, is an inadequate remedy.

---

[251]These questions are given in bold in AoC 1936.
[252]'Transit' in AoC 1936 and subsequent editions.
[253]'Dravid' in all previous editions.

There are many castes which allow inter-dining. But it is a common experience that inter-dining has not succeeded in killing the spirit of caste and the consciousness of caste. I am convinced that the real remedy is inter-marriage. Fusion of blood can alone create the feeling of being kith and kin, and unless this feeling of kinship, of being marriage. Fusion of blood can alone create the feeling of being kith and kin, and unless this feeling of kinship, of being kindred, becomes paramount, the separatist feeling—the feeling of being aliens—created by caste will not vanish. Among the Hindus, inter-marriage must necessarily be a factor of greater force in social life than it need be in the life of the non-Hindus. Where society is already well-knit by other ties, marriage is an ordinary incident of life. But where society is cut asunder, marriage as a binding force becomes a matter of urgent necessity. *The real remedy for breaking caste is inter-marriage. Nothing else will serve as the solvent of caste.*

Your Jat-Pat-Todak Mandal has adopted this line of attack. It is a direct and frontal attack, and I congratulate you upon a correct diagnosis, and more upon your having shown the courage to tell the Hindus what is really wrong with them. Political tyranny is nothing compared to social tyranny, and a reformer who defies society is a much more courageous man than a politician who defies the government. You are right in holding that caste will cease to be an operative force only when inter-dining and inter-marriage have become matters of common course. You have located the source of the disease.

But is your prescription the right prescription for the disease? Ask yourselves this question: why is it that a large majority of Hindus do not inter-dine and do not inter-marry? Why is it that your cause is not popular?

There can be only one answer to this question, and it is that inter-dining and inter-marriage are repugnant to the beliefs and dogmas which the Hindus regard as sacred. Caste is not a physical object like a wall of bricks or a line of barbed wire which prevents the Hindus from commingling and which has, therefore, to be pulled down. Caste is a notion, it is a state of the mind. The destruction of caste does not therefore mean the destruction of a physical barrier. It means a *notional* change.

Caste may be bad. Caste may lead to conduct so gross as to be called man's inhumanity to man. All the same, it must be recognized that the Hindus observe caste not because they are inhuman or wrongheaded. They observe caste because they are deeply religious. People are not wrong in observing caste. In my view, what is wrong is their religion, which has inculcated this notion of caste. If this is correct, then obviously the enemy you must grapple with is not the people who observe caste, but the Shastras which teach them this religion of caste. Criticizing and ridiculing people for not inter-dining or inter-marrying, or occasionally holding inter-caste dinners and celebrating inter-caste marriages, is a futile method of achieving the desired end. The real remedy is to destroy the belief in the sanctity of the Shastras.

How do you expect to succeed, if you allow the Shastras to continue to mould the beliefs and opinions of the people? Not to question the authority of the Shastras—to permit the people to believe in their sanctity and their sanctions, and then to blame the people and to criticize them for their acts as being irrational and inhuman—is an incongruous way of carrying on social reform. Reformers working for the removal of Untouchability, including Mahatma Gandhi, do not seem to realize that the acts of the people are merely the results of their beliefs inculcated in their minds by the Shastras, and that people will not change their conduct until they cease to believe in the sanctity of the Shastras on which their conduct is founded.

No wonder that such efforts have not produced any results. You also seem to be erring in the same way as the reformers working in the cause of removing Untouchability. To agitate for and to organise inter-caste dinners and inter-caste marriages is like forced feeding brought about by artificial means. Make every man and woman free from the thraldom of the Shastras, cleanse their minds of the pernicious notions founded on the Shastras, and he or she will inter-dine and inter-marry, without your telling him or her to do so.

It is no use seeking refuge in quibbles. It is no use telling people that the Shastras do not say what they are believed to say, if they are grammatically read or logically interpreted. What matters is how the Shastras have been understood by the people. You must take the stand that Buddha took. You must take the stand which Guru Nanak took.

You must not only discard the Shastras, you must deny their authority, as did Buddha and Nanak. You must have courage to tell the Hindus that what is wrong with them is their religion—the religion which has produced in them this notion of the sacredness of caste. Will you show that courage?

What are your chances of success?[254] Social reforms fall into different species. There is a species of reform which does not relate to the religious notions of a people, but is purely secular in character. There is also a species of reform which relates to the religious notions of a people. Of such a species of reform, there are two varieties. In one, the reform accords with the principles of the religion, and merely invites people who have departed from it, to revert to them and to follow them.

The second is a reform which not only touches the religious principles but is diametrically opposed to those principles, and invites people to depart from and to discard their authority, and to act contrary to those principles. Caste is the natural outcome of certain religious beliefs which have the sanction of the Shastras, which are believed to contain the command of divinely inspired sages who were endowed with a supernatural wisdom and whose commands, therefore, cannot be disobeyed without committing a sin.

The destruction of caste is a reform which falls under the third category [that is, the second variety of the second species]. To ask people to give up caste is to ask them to go contrary to their fundamental religious notions. It is obvious that the first and second species of reform are easy. But the third is a stupendous task, well-nigh impossible. The Hindus hold to the sacredness of the social order. Caste has a divine basis. You must therefore destroy the sacredness and divinity with which caste has become invested. In the last analysis, this means you must destroy the authority of the Shastras and the Vedas.

I have emphasized this question of the ways and means of destroying caste, because I think that knowing the proper ways and means is more important than knowing the ideal. If you do not know the real ways and means, all your shots are sure to be misfires. If my analysis

---

[254]'This is in bold in AoC 1936.

is correct, then your task is herculean. You alone can say whether you are capable of achieving it.

Speaking for myself, I see the task to be well-nigh impossible. Perhaps you would like to know why I think so. Out of the many reasons which have led me to take this view, I will mention some which I regard as most important. One of these reasons is the attitude of hostility which the Brahmins have shown towards this question. The Brahmins form the vanguard of the movement for political reform, and in some cases also of economic reform. But they are not to be found even as camp-followers in the army raised to break down the barricades of caste. Is there any hope of the Brahmins ever taking up a lead in the future in this matter? I say no.

You may ask why. You may argue that there is no reason why Brahmins should continue to shun social reform. You may argue that the Brahmins know that the bane of Hindu society is caste, and as an enlightened class they could not be expected to be indifferent to its consequences. You may argue that there are secular Brahmins and priestly Brahmins,[255] and if the latter do not take up the cudgels on

---

[255]There has been a conventionally regarded division of labour between the laukika Brahmin, the so-called secular Brahmin, and the shrotriya or vaidika Brahmin, the Brahmin well versed in the Vedas (the shruti tradition; from sru, to hear, srotriya; the oral tradition). The anthropologist M.N. Srinivas (1972, 8) uses these terms in this sense. The laukika—literally, those who concern themselves with this-worldly, temporal (loka) matters—is not secular in the Western Enlightenment sense of the term, as in those who disavow belief or are free from religious rules and teachings. The laukika Brahmin—the Brahmin as minister, bureaucrat, civil servant, writer—whom Ambedkar goes on to refer as the intellectual class of the Hindus, pursues a non-priestly career; priestly work is the preserve of the vaidika/shrotriya Brahmins (again, priests who perform only Vedic rites are to be distinguished from priests who officiate in temples, attending to post-Bhakti, post-Vedic gods). However, the laukika Brahmin does not undermine the significance or role of the shrotriya Brahmin. In fact, he deploys and legitimizes the services of the shrotriya Brahmin. The laukika Brahmin wields power Over this-worldly matters, the shrotriya's domain is other-worldly. All the same, the laukika would even look down upon the shrotriya as lower in the pecking order; someone whose services can be easily bought, for a price. In effect, they are two flanks of Brahminism. For a discussion on the etymology of laukika and vaidika in Sanskrit grammarian Panini's Ashtadhyayi (c. 400 BCE), see Patrick Olivelle (2008, 161–3).

behalf of those who want to break caste, the former will.

All this of course sounds very plausible. But in all this it is forgotten that the break-up of the caste system is bound to adversely affect the Brahmin caste. Having regard to this, is it reasonable to expect that the Brahmins will ever consent to lead a movement, the ultimate result of which is to destroy the power and prestige of the Brahmin caste? Is it reasonable to expect the secular Brahmins to take part in a movement directed against the priestly Brahmins? In my judgement, it is useless to make a distinction between the secular Brahmins and priestly Brahmins. Both are kith and kin. They are two arms of the same body, and one is bound to fight for the existence of the other.

In this connection, I am reminded of some very pregnant remarks made by Prof. Dicey in his English Constitution.[256] Speaking of the actual limitation on the legislative supremacy of parliament, Dicey says:

'The actual exercise of authority by any sovereign whatever, and notably by Parliament, is bounded or controlled by two limitations. Of these the one is an external, and the other is an internal limitation. The external limit to the real power of a sovereign consists in the possibility or certainty that his subjects or a large number of them possibility or certainty that his subjects or a large number of them will disobey or resist his laws....The internal limit to the exercise of sovereignty arises from the nature of the sovereign power itself. Even a despot exercises his powers in accordance with his character, which is itself moulded by the circumstance under which he lives, including under that head the moral feelings of the time and the society to which he belongs. The Sultan could not, if he would, change the religion of the Mohammedan world, but even if he could do so, it is in the very highest degree improbable that the head of Mohammedanism should wish to overthrow the religion of Mohammed; the internal check on the exercise of the Sultan's power is at least as strong as the external limitation. People sometimes

---

[256]124 Albert Venn Dicey (1835–1922) was a British jurist and constitutional theorist who expounded the theory of the 'rule of law' and popularised the term. The quote that follows is from Introduction to the Study of the Law of the Constitution (1885, 75–6) which forms a part of the unwritten British Constitution and is therefore also referred to as English Constitution.

ask the idle question, why the Pope does not introduce this or that reform? The true answer is that a revolutionist is not the kind of man who becomes a Pope and that a man who becomes a Pope has no wish to be a revolutionist.'

I think these remarks apply equally to the Brahmins of India, and one can say with equal truth that if a man who becomes a Pope has no wish to become a revolutionary, a man who is born a Brahmin has much less desire to become a revolutionary. Indeed, to expect a Brahmin to be a revolutionary in matters of social reform is as idle as to expect the British Parliament, as was said by Leslie Stephen,[257] to pass an Act requiring all blue-eyed babies to be murdered.

Some of you will say that it is a matter of small concern whether the Brahmins come forward to lead the movement against caste or whether they do not. To take this view is, in my judgement, to ignore the part played by the intellectual class in the community. Whether you accept the theory of the great man as the maker of history[258] or whether you do not, this much you will have to concede: that in every country the intellectual class is the most influential class, if not the governing class. The intellectual class is the class which can foresee, it is the class which can advise and give the lead. In no country does the mass of the people live the life of intelligent thought and action. It is largely imitative, and follows the intellectual class.

There is no exaggeration in saying that the entire destiny of a country depends upon its intellectual class. If the intellectual class

---

[257]Leslie Stephen (1832–1904) was a British philosopher, and literary and social critic. A reference to his comments on the prohibition of blue-eyed babies can be found in Dicey (1885, 78) cited above. Dicey is quoting Stephen from the Science of Ethics (1882), a work that sums up the ethical consequences of the theory of evolution.

[258]Ambedkar is referring to the concept popularised by Carlyle in the nineteenth century: the great man theory. Carlyle's *On Heroes, Hero-Worship and the Heroic in History* (1840) points out the essential role of great men in history, such as Muhammad, Luther, Rousseau, Cromwell and Napoleon among others, as the moving force of history. The main criticism of the great man theory was formulated by Herbert Spencer in The Study of Sociology (1873), but Carlyle's theory has occupied the mind of many an influential thinker, for example Leo Tolstoy.

is honest, independent, and disinterested, it can be trusted to take the initiative and give a proper lead when a crisis arises. It is true that intellect by itself is no virtue. It is only a means, and the use of means depends upon the ends which an intellectual person pursues. An intellectual man can be a good man, but he can easily be a rogue. Similarly an intellectual class may be a band of high-souled persons, ready to help, ready to emancipate erring humanity—or it may easily be a gang of crooks, or a body of advocates for a narrow clique from which it draws its support.

You may think it a pity that the intellectual class in India is simply another name for the Brahmin caste. You may regret that the two are one; that the existence of the intellectual class should be bound up with one single caste; that this intellectual class should share the interest and the aspirations of that Brahmin caste, and should be a class which has regarded itself as the custodian of the interest of that caste, rather than of the interests of the country. All this may be very regrettable. But the fact remains that the Brahmins form the intellectual class of the Hindus. It is not only an intellectual class, but it is a class which is held in great reverence by the rest of the Hindus.

The Hindus are taught that the Brahmins are Bhudevas (Gods on earth).[259] The Hindus are taught that Brahmins alone can be their teachers. Manu says, 'If it be asked how it should be with respect to points of the Dharma which have not been specially mentioned, the answer is, that which Brahmins who are Shishthas propound shall doubtless have legal force':[260]

अनाम्नातेषु धर्मेषु कथं स्वादिति चेवृभवेत।
सं शिष्टा ब्राह्मणा बूयु: स धर्म: रमादङ्क्षित:॥[261]

---

[259]This is the injunction from the Manusmriti that Ambedkar cites at the opening of AoC See Note 1 at 1.2.

[260]Shishthas: Brahmins educated in religious matters.

[261](*Anaamnaateshu dharmeshu katham syaaditi chedbhavet/ yam shishtaa braahmanaa bruuyuh sa dharmah syaadashadgkitah.*) Ambedkar first cites the translation of Manusmriti 12.108 from Buhler (1886/2004, 337) and then gives the Sanskrit verse. Bibek Debroy's translation: 'If asked about parts of Dharma that have not been stated, without a doubt, what learned/good Brahmins state is Dharma.'

When such an intellectual class, which holds the rest of the community in its grip, is opposed to the reform of caste, the chances of success in a movement for the break-up of the caste system appear to me very, very remote.

The second reason why I say the task is impossible will be clear, if you will bear in mind that the caste system has two aspects. In one of its aspects, it divides men into separate communities. In its second aspect, it places these communities in a graded order one above the other in social status. Each caste takes its pride and its consolation in the fact that in the scale of castes it is above some other caste. As an outward mark of this gradation, there is also a gradation of social and religious rights, technically spoken of as Ashtadhikaras[262] and Sanskaras.[263] The higher the grade of a caste, the greater the number of these rights; and the lower the grade, the lesser their number.

Now this gradation, this scaling of castes, makes it impossible to organize a common front against the caste system. If a caste claims the right to inter-dine and inter-marry with another caste placed above it, it is frozen the instant it is told[264] by mischief-mongers—and there are

---

[262]It is not clear what Ambedkar is referring to as the ashtadhikaras. Adhikara, in both Vedic Hinduism and tantra, refers to the religious qualification and eligibility to perform certain rituals. According to James Lochtefeld (2002, 6), 'This refers partly to knowing how to perform the ritual, and thus being "qualified"… More importantly, it refers to having gained the ritual status that entitles one to perform the ritual. This status is usually conferred by some sort of formal initiation…by one's teacher.' Thus we may say Shambuka, the pivotal Shudra in the Ramayana, does not have the adhikara to perform a Vedic rite, and is hence punished. For further discussion of the idea of adhikara, see Wilhelm Halbfass (1990, 67), where he says 'adhikara assumes such meanings as 'authority,' 'competence,' 'vocation,' but also 'obligation,' and 'responsibility.' It refers to 'governing' functions and elements not only in nature or society, but also in texts and teachings, where it may indicate a governing rule or dominant theme."

[263]Sanskaras (also samskaras) is the collective name given to various life-cycle sacrifices and rituals marking the different stages of human life; they are the rites that make people (or things) fit for a purpose (of performing rituals, taking one's rightful place in society), by removing taints and generating good qualities (Michaels, 2005, 74). Hindu Dharmashastras differ on the total number of sanskaras (twelve to eighteen) but sixteen sanskaras are generally agreed upon.

[264]The word used in AoC 1936 is 'silenced'; amended in 1937 and 1944 to 'frozen

many Brahmins amongst such mischief-mongers—that it will have to concede inter-dining and inter-marriage with castes below it! All are slaves of the caste system. But all the slaves are not equal in status.[265]

To excite the proletariat to bring about an economic revolution, Karl Marx told them: 'You have nothing to lose except your chains.'[266] But the artful way in which the social and religious rights are distributed among the different castes, whereby some have more and some have less, makes the slogan of Karl Marx quite useless[267] to excite the Hindus against the caste system. Castes form a graded system of sovereignties, high and low, which are jealous of their status and which know that if a general dissolution came, some of them stand to lose more of their prestige and power than others do.[268] You cannot, therefore, have a general mobilization of the Hindus (to use a military expression) for an attack on the caste system.

Can you appeal to reason, and ask the Hindus to discard caste as being contrary to reason? That raises the question: Is a Hindu free to follow his reason? Manu has laid down three sanctions to which every Hindu must conform in the matter of his behaviour:

वेद: स्मृति: सदाचर: स्वस्य च प्रियनात्मन:[269]

----

instantly it is told'. Edited here for clarity.

[265]In AoC 1936, this reads as 'do not suffer equally'; amended in 1937.

[266]This is the popularized version of one of the sentences from *The Communist Manifesto* (1848): 'The proletarians have nothing to lose but their chains. They have a world to win. Working Men of All Countries, Unite!'

[267]In AoC 1936: 'you cannot use the slogan which Karl Marx used'.

[268]In AoC 1936, this sentence reads: 'The Caste System is an imperium in imperio and in the general dissolution of Caste, some castes stand to lose more of their prestige and power than other castes.' Imperium in imperio means a state, power or sovereignty within a state, power or sovereignty.

[269](*Vedah smritih sadachara svasya cha priyamaatmanah.*) Debroy: 'For his own self and for those who are loved by him, the Vedas, the Smritis and good conduct...' This is a half of the shloka couplet. The complete shloka, from Manusmriti 2.12, is rendered by Buhler as: 'The Veda, the sacred tradition, the customs of virtuous men, and one's own pleasure, they declare to be visibly the fourfold means of defining the sacred law' (1886/2004, 19). The second line in Sanskrit reads as: एतज्ञचतुर्विधं प्राहु: साक्षाद्धर्मस्य लक्षणाम्। (*Etajna-chaturvidham praahu saakshadharmasya lakshanaam.*)

Here there is no place for reason to play its part. A Hindu must follow either Veda, Smriti or sadachar. He cannot follow anything else.

In the first place, how are the texts of the Vedas and Smritis to be interpreted whenever any doubt arises regarding their meaning? On this important question the view of Manu is quite definite. He says:

योऽवमन्येत ते मूल हेतुशास्त्राश्रयात् द्विज:।
स साधुभिर्वहिष्कार्यो नास्तिको वेदनिंदक:॥[270]

According to this rule, rationalism as a canon of interpreting the Vedas and Smritis is absolutely condemned. It is regarded to be as wicked as atheism, and the punishment provided for it is excommunication. Thus, where a matter is covered by the Veda or the Smriti, a Hindu cannot resort to rational thinking.

Even when there is a conflict between Vedas and Smritis on matters on which they have given a positive injunction, the solution is not left to reason. When there is a conflict between two Shrutis, both are to be regarded as of equal authority. Either of them may be followed. No attempt[271] is to be made to find out which of the two accords with reason. This is made clear by Manu:

श्रुसिद्धैध तु यत्र स्याप्तक धर्मांबुभौ स्मृतौ।[272]

---

[270] (*Yo-avamanyeta fey muule hetushaastraashrayaatdvijah/ sa saadhubhirbahish-kaaryo naastiko vedanindakah.*) Manusmriti 2.11. Debroy's translation: 'Every dwija [it can be rendered as either Brahmin or belonging to the first three varnas] who depends on texts of logic and ignores these two sources [the earlier shloka mentions] must be banished by virtuous people, as a person who is a non-believer and as one who criticises the Vedas.' Buhler's edition renders this as: 'Every twice-born man, who, relying on the Institutes of dialectics, treats with contempt those two sources (of the law), must be cast out by the virtuous, as an atheist and a scorner of the Veda' (1886/2004, 19).

[271] In AoC 1936, the two sentences are conjoined with a 'but', to read: 'Either of them may be followed but no attempt…' In 1937 and 1944, the 'but' is removed.

[272] (*Yaa vedavaahyaah smrutayo yaashcha kaashcha kudrishtayah/ Smritisarvaastaa nishphalaah pretya tamonishthaa hi tah smritaah.*) Manusmriti 12.95. Debroy: 'All the smriti and other texts which are based on wicked doctrines and are outside the Vedas, lead to no fruits after death. It is said that they are based on darkness.' Buhler renders this as: 'All those traditions (smriti) and those despicable systems of philosophy, which are not based on the Veda, produce no reward after death;

'When there is a conflict between Shruti and Smriti, the Shruti must prevail.' But here too, no attempt must be made to find out which of the two accords with reason. This is laid down by Manu in the following shloka:

या वेदबाह्या: समुतयो याश्च काश्च कुदृष्ट:
सर्वास्ता निष्फल: प्रेरय तमोनिष्ठा हित: स्मृता:॥

Again, when there is a conflict between two Smritis, the Manusmritii must prevail, but no attempt is to be made to find out which of the two accords with reason. This is the ruling given by Brihaspati:[273]

वेदायत्वोपनिबंधृत्वत् प्रमाम्यं हि गतो: स्मृतं।
मन्वर्थविपरीता तु या स्मृति: सा न शस्यते॥

It is, therefore, clear that in any matter on which the Shrutis and Smritis have given a positive direction, a Hindu is not free to use his reasoning faculty. The same rule is laid down in the Mahabharat:

पुराणं मानवो धनं: सांगो वेदश्चिकित्सितं।
अज्ञासिद्धानि चत्वारि न हन्तव्यानि हेतुधि:॥[274]

---

for they are declared to be founded on Darkness' (1886/2004, 335).

[273]Brihaspati was a Brahmin law-giver of the sixth or seventh century CE. Brihaspati's major work, the Brihaspati Smriti, survives only in fragments. It has been published in *The Minor Lawbooks* (1889), translated by Julius Jolly. Brihaspati is considered the first Hindu law-giver to separate civil law from criminal law, and his views concerning women's rights are considered liberal. Nonetheless, he confers the death sentence on a man who has a sexual relationship with a 'high'-caste woman, while merely assigning fines for men who have a sexual relationship with a woman of equal or of 'lower' caste. Consent (or the absence of it) on the woman's part does not alter the severity of the punishment. See G.S. Ghurye (1969, 245).

[274](*Puraanam maanavo dharmah saango vedashchikitsitam / Aajnaasiddhaani chatvaari na hantavyaani hetubhih.*) Debroy: 'This verse does not exist in the complete Critical Edition of the Mahabharata (Bhandarkar Oriental Research Institute, launched in 1966, ten years after Ambedkar's demise). Bhandarkar has it listed as 14.98–72 in the rejected texts, but there it occurs as the following, with a minor variation in the first word. That is, it is in Ashvamedhika parva, which does not figure in the Critical Edition:

भारतं मानवो धर्मों वेदा: साङ्गश्चिकित्सितम्।

He must abide by their directions. Caste and varna are matters which are dealt with by the Vedas and the Smritis, and consequently, appeal to reason can have no effect on a Hindu.

So far as caste and varna are concerned, not only the Shastras do not permit the Hindu to use his reason in the decision of the question, but they have taken care to see that no occasion is left to examine in a rational way the foundations of his belief in caste and varna. It must be a source of silent amusement to many a non-Hindu to find hundreds and thousands of Hindus breaking caste on certain occasions, such as railway journeys and foreign travel, and yet endeavouring to maintain caste for the rest of their lives!

The explanation of this phenomenon discloses another fetter on the reasoning faculties of the Hindus. Man's life is generally habitual and unreflective. Reflective thought—in the sense of active, persistent, and careful consideration of any belief or supposed form of knowledge, in the light of the grounds that support it and the further conclusions to which it tends—is quite rare, and arises only in a situation which presents a dilemma or a crisis. Railway journeys and foreign travels are really occasions of crisis in the life of a Hindu, and it is natural to expect a Hindu to ask himself why he should maintain caste at all, if he cannot maintain it at all times. But he does not. He breaks caste at one step, and proceeds to observe it at the next, without raising any question.[275]

The reason for this astonishing conduct is to be found in the rule of the Shastras, which directs him to maintain caste as far as possible and to undergo prayaschitta[276] when he cannot. By this theory of

आज्ञासिद्धानि चत्वारि न हन्तव्यानि हेतुभिः॥ (*Bhaaratam maanavo dharmo vedaah saadgaashchikitsitam/Aajnaasiddhaani chatvaari na hantavyaani hetubhih.*) A translation of the version Ambedkar uses: 'The Puranas, Manu's dharma, the Vedas and their limbs, and medicine—these four are in the nature of commandments. Under no circumstances must they be killed/destroyed.'

[275]Refer to the experiences of W.C. Bonnerjee discussed in Note 10 to AoC 2.6 as illustrative of Ambedkar's point.

[276]'Prayaschitta': Sanskrit for the purification rituals undertaken in penance after breaking caste taboos. It has also been variously understood as a combination of atonement, expiation and repentance. The Dharmashastras discuss prayaschitta

prayaschitta, the Shastras, by following a spirit of compromise, have given caste a perpetual lease on life, and have smothered the reflective thought which would have otherwise led to the destruction of the notion of caste.[277]

There have been many who have worked in the cause of the abolition of caste and Untouchability. Of those who can be mentioned,

---

(expiation) along with achara (ritual) and vyavahara (jurisprudence) as aspects of Hindu law.

[277] The Slovenian Marxist philosopher Slavoj Žižek says of the Manusmriti and the caste system that such a system can e sustained 'only by a complex panoply of tricks, displacements and compromises whose basic formula is that of universality with exceptions: in principle yes, but... *The Laws of Manu* demonstrates a breath-taking ingenuity in accomplishing this task.' Žižek believes that the true regulating power of the law does not reside in its 'direct prohibitions, in the division of our acts into permitted and prohibited, but in regulating the very violations of prohibitions: the law silently accepts that the basic prohibitions are violated (or even discreetly solicits us to violate them), and then, it tells us how to reconcile the violation with the law by way of violating the prohibition in a regulated way.' Cited in S. Anand (2010). Ambedkar deals with this aspect later in his discussion of Annihilation of Caste with Gandhi featured in 'A Reply to the Mahatma' (11.5), where he talks of how a Brahmin can remain a Brahmin irrespective of what he does: 'The number of Brahmins who sell shoes is far greater than those who practise priesthood. Not only have the Brahmins given up their ancestral calling of priesthood for trading, but they have entered trades which are prohibited to them by the shastras. Yet how many Brahmins who break caste every day will preach against caste and against the shastras?' Wendy Doniger, in the introduction to her translation of the Manusmriti (Doniger and Smith, 1991, liv), talks of how it was 'law in extremity', where every stringent rule has an exception that almost contradicts the rule; an emergency—apad—escape clause. 'The concept of apad recognises human fallibility: don't do this, says Manu, but if you do, this is what to do to fix it.'

Ramanuja,[278] Kabir,[279] and others stand out prominently. Can you appeal to the acts of these reformers and exhort the Hindus to follow them?

It is true that Manu has included *sadachar* as one of the sanctions along with Shruti and Smriti. Indeed, *sadachar* (सदाचार) has been given a higher place than Shastras:

यधद्माचर्यते येन धर्म्य वाऽधर्म्यमेव वा।
देशस्याचरणं नित्यं चरिवं तद्धिकीर्तितम्।।

According to this, sadachar, whether it is dharmya or adharmya,[280] in accordance with Shastras or contrary to Shastras, must be followed. But what is the meaning of sadachar? If anyone were to suppose that sadachar means right or good acts—i.e., acts of good and righteous men—he would find himself greatly mistaken. Sadachar does not means good acts or acts of good men. It means ancient custom, good or bad. The following verse makes this clear:

यधद्माचर्यते येन धर्म्य वाऽधर्म्यमेव वा।
देशस्याचरणं नित्यं चरिवं तद्धिकीर्तितम्।।

---

[278]Ramanuja, or Ramanujacharya, was a twelfth-century Brahmin philosopher, a proponent of the Vishishtadvaita, or qualified monism, school of thought. Coming as he did after the monotheistic Tamil Bhakti movements of the Saivite Nayanmars and Vaishnavite Alwars (sixth to eighth centuries), Ramanuja gave primacy to Bhakti or worship of a personal god. In his commentary of the Brahma Sutra, he declares the Shudra to be equally fit for studying the Vedas as the Brahmin and is said to have adopted a non-Brahmin as a guru. See Bartley (2002).

[279]Kabir was a fifteenth-century radical saint-poet who was born a weaver; the thousands of songs/poems attributed to him question the caste system, declare equality in the eyes of god and promote Bhakti. See Hess and Singh (2002), and Hess (2009) for translations of Kabir. See www.kabirproject.org, curated by Shabnam Virmani, for an audio and video documentation of various Kabir traditions across the subcontinent.

[280]Dharmya or adharmya. These terms broadly mean lawful/sacred and unlawful. According to the Kautilya's Arthashastra, there are eight types of marriage, of which four are accorded dharmya status and the other four adharmya (1992, 394-5). For Ambedkar's discussion of these marriages, see 'Riddle No. 19: The Change from Paternity to Maternity—What did the Brahmins Wish to Gain by it?' in Sharmila Rege (2013, 169–76).

As though to warn people against the view that sadachar means good acts or acts of good men, and fearing that people might understand it that way and follow the acts of good men, the Smritis have commanded the Hindus in people might understand it that way and follow the acts of good men, the Smritis have commanded the Hindus in unmistakable terms not to follow even Gods in their good deeds, if they are contrary to Shruti, Smriti, and sadachar. This may sound to be most extraordinary, most perverse, but the fact remains that is an injunction issued to the Hindus by their Shastras.[281]

Reason and morality are the two most powerful weapons in the armoury of a reformer. To deprive him of the use of these weapons is to disable him for action. How are you going to break up caste, if people are not free to consider whether it accords with reason? How are you going to break up caste, if people are not free to consider whether it accords with morality? The wall built around caste is impregnable, and the material of which it is built contains none of the combustible stuff of reason and morality. Add to this the fact that inside this wall stands the army of Brahmins who form the intellectual class, Brahmins who are the natural leaders of the Hindus, Brahmins who are there not as mere mercenary soldiers but as an army fighting for its homeland, and you will get an idea why I think that the breaking up of caste among the Hindus is well-nigh impossible. At any rate, it would take ages before a breach is made.

But whether the doing of the deed takes time or whether it can be done quickly, you must not forget that if you wish to bring about a breach in the system, then you have got to apply the dynamite to the Vedas and the Shastras, which deny any part to reason; to the Vedas and Shastras, which deny any part to morality. You must destroy the religion of the Shrutis and the Smritis. Nothing else will avail. This is my considered view of the matter.

Some may not understand what I mean by destruction of religion; some may find the idea revolting to them, and some may find it revolutionary. Let me therefore explain my position. I do not know

---

[281](Na deva charitamam charet.) Debroy: 'One should not follow the conduct of the gods.'

whether you draw a distinction between principles and rules. But I do. Not only do I make a distinction, but I say that this distinction is real and important. Rules are practical; they are habitual ways of doing things according to prescription. But principles are intellectual; they are useful methods of judging things. Rules seek to tell an agent just what course of action to pursue. Principles do not prescribe a specific course of action. Rules, like cooking recipes, do tell just what to do and how to do it. A principle, such as that of justice, supplies a main heading by reference to which he is to consider the bearings of his desires and purposes; it guides him in his thinking by suggesting to him the important consideration which he should bear in mind.

This difference between rules and principles makes the acts done in pursuit of them different in quality and in content. Doing what is said to be good by virtue of a rule, and doing good in the light of a principle, are two different things. The principle may be wrong, but the act is conscious and responsible. The rule may be right, but the act is mechanical. A religious act may not be a correct act, but must at least be a responsible act. To permit of this responsibility, religion must mainly be a matter of principles only. It cannot be a matter of rules. The moment it degenerates into rules, it ceases to be religion, as it kills the responsibility which is the essence of a truly religious act.

What is this Hindu religion? Is it a set of principles, or is it a code of rules? Now the Hindu religion, as contained in the Vedas and the Smritis, is nothing but a mass of sacrificial, social, political, and sanitary rules and regulations, all mixed up. What is called religion by the Hindus is nothing but a multitude of commands and prohibitions. Religion, in the sense of spiritual principles, truly universal, applicable to all races, to all countries, to all times, is not to be found in them; and if it is, it does not form the governing part of a Hindu's life. That for a Hindu, Dharma means commands and prohibitions, is clear from the way the word Dharma is used in the Vedas and the Smritis and understood by the commentators. The word Dharma as used in the Vedas in most cases means religious ordinances or rites. Even Jaimini in his Purva-Mimamsa defines Dharma as 'a desirable goal or result that is indicated by injunctive (Vedic) passages.'

To put it in plain language, what the Hindus call religion is really law, or at best legalized class-ethics. Frankly, I refuse to call this code of ordinances as religion. The first evil of such a code of ordinances, misrepresented to the people refuse to call this code of ordinances as religion. The first evil of such a code of ordinances, misrepresented to the people as religion, is that it tends to deprive moral life of freedom and spontaneity, and to reduce it (for the conscientious, at any rate) to a more or less anxious and servile conformity to externally imposed rules. Under it, there is no loyalty to ideals; there is only conformity to commands.

But the worst evil of this code of ordinances is that the laws it contains must be the same yesterday, today and forever. They are iniquitous in that they are not the same for one class as for another. But this iniquity is made perpetual in that they are prescribed to be the same for all generations. The objectionable part of such a scheme is not that they are made by certain persons called Prophets or law-givers. The objectionable part is that this code has been invested with the character of finality and fixity. Happiness notoriously varies with the conditions and circumstances of a person, as well as with the conditions of different people and epochs. That being the case, how can humanity endure this code of eternal laws, without being cramped and without being crippled?

I have, therefore, no hesitation in saying that such a religion must be destroyed, and I say there is nothing irreligious in working for the destruction of such a religion. Indeed I hold that it is your bounden duty to tear off the mask, to remove the misrepresentation that is caused by misnaming this law as religion. This is an essential step for you. Once you clear the minds of the people of this misconception, and enable them to realize that what they are told is religion is not religion, but that it is really law, you will be in a position to urge its amendment or abolition.

So long as people look upon it as religion they will not be ready for a change, because the idea of religion is generally speaking not associated with the idea of change. But the idea of law is associated with the idea of change, and when people come to know that what is called religion is really law, old and archaic, they will be ready for a change, for people know and accept that law can be changed.

While I condemn a religion of rules, I must not be understood to hold the opinion that there is no necessity for a religion. On the contrary, I agree with Burke when he says that 'True religion is the foundation of society, the basis on which all true Civil Government rests, and both their sanction.'[282] Consequently, when I urge that these ancient rules of life be annulled, I am anxious that their place shall be taken by a religion of principles, which alone can lay claim to being a true religion. Indeed, I am so convinced of the necessity of religion that I feel I ought to tell you in outline what I regard as necessary items in this religious reform. The following, in my opinion, should be the cardinal items in this reform:

1. There should be one and only one standard book of Hindu religion, acceptable to all Hindus and recognized by all Hindus. This of course means that all other books of Hindu religion such as Vedas, Shastras and Puranas, which are treated as sacred and authoritative, must by law cease to be so, and the preaching of any doctrine, religious or social, contained in these books should be penalized.

2. It would be better if priesthood among Hindus were abolished. But as this seems to be impossible, the priesthood must at least cease to be hereditary. Every person who professes to be a Hindu must be eligible for being a priest. It should be provided by law that no Hindu shall be entitled to be a priest unless he has passed an examination prescribed by the State, and holds a sanad[283]

---

[282]Edmund Burke (1729–97) was a British statesman, orator and political thinker of Irish origin. A staunch supporter of the American Revolution, he opposed the French Revolution in his work Reflections on the Revolution in France (1790). Ambedkar cites him often, especially during his interventions at the Round Table Conference (see Das 2010b). Though the source of this quotation has been difficult to trace, a fuller version of it has been widely cited. See O'Brien (1947, 191): 'True religion is the foundation of society, the basis on which all true Civil Government rests and from which power derives its authority, laws their efficacy, and both their sanction. If it is once shaken by contempt, the whole fabric cannot be stable or lasting.'

[283]Sanad: Hindi for certificate or diploma. The Merriam-Webster dictionary gives the meaning of sanad as 'an Indian government charter, warrant, diploma, patent

from the State permitting him to practise.

3. No ceremony performed by a priest who does not hold a sanad shall be deemed to be valid in law, and it should be made penal [punishable] for a person who has no sanad to officiate as a priest.

4. A priest should be the servant of the State,[284] and should be subject to the disciplinary action of the State in the matter of his morals, beliefs, and worship, in addition to his being subject along with other citizens to the ordinary law of the land.

5. The number of priests should be limited by law according to the requirements of the State, as is done in the case of the I.C.S.

To some, this may sound radical. But to my mind there is nothing revolutionary in this. Every profession in India is regulated. Engineers must show proficiency, doctors must show proficiency, lawyers must show proficiency, before they regulated. Engineers must show proficiency, doctors must show proficiency, lawyers must show proficiency, before they are allowed to practise their professions. During the whole of their career, they must not only obey the law of the land, civil as well as criminal, but they must also obey the special code of morals prescribed by their respective professions. The priest's is the only profession where proficiency is not required. The profession of a Hindu priest is the

or deed'. Ambedkar's thoughts here on reform, and on giving a semblance of meritocracy to the institution of priesthood, gesture towards an alternate meaning of sanad as well. Isnaad (from Arabic sanad, 'support') in Islam is a list of authorities who have transmitted a report (hadith, also hadees) of a statement, action or approbation of Muhammad, one of his companions (sahaabah), or of a later authority (tabee); its reliability determines the validity of a hadith. The isnaad precedes the actual text (matn) and takes the form, 'It has been related to me by A on the authority of B on the authority of C on the authority of D (usually a Companion of the Prophet) that Muhammad said...' A careful scrutiny of the isnaads, rating each hadith according to the completeness of its chain of transmitters, and the reliability and orthodoxy of its authorities, was done in the second century AD (after 720 CE) to avoid confusion and multiple narrations, and to assist in giving precedence to the ahadith (the total body of hadith) over whatever local customs might have developed in Muslim communities (Scott 2004).
[284]In AoC 1936 and 1937, this reads: 'A priest should be the servant of the state like any civil servant and should be paid by the state.' The italicised words are edited out in 1944.

only profession which is not subject to any code.

Mentally a priest may be an idiot, physically a priest may be suffering from a foul disease such as syphilis or gonorrhea, morally he may be a wreck. But he is fit to officiate at solemn ceremonies, to enter the sanctum sanctorum [holiest part] of a Hindu temple, and to worship the Hindu God. All this becomes possible among the Hindus because for a priest it is enough to be born in a priestly caste. The whole thing is abominable, and is due to the fact that the priestly class among Hindus is subject neither to law nor to morality. It recognizes no duties. It knows only of rights and privileges. It is a pest which divinity seems to have let loose on the masses for their mental and moral degradation.

The priestly class must be brought under control by some such legislation as I have outlined above. This will prevent it from doing mischief and from misguiding people. It will democratize it by throwing it open to everyone. It will certainly help to kill the Brahminism and will also help to kill caste, which is nothing but Brahminism incarnate. Brahminism is the poison which has spoiled Hinduism. You will succeed in saving Hinduism if you will kill Brahminism. There should be no opposition to this reform from any quarter. It should be welcomed even by the Arya Samajists, because this is merely an application of their own doctrine of guna-karma.

Whether you do that or you do not, you must give a new doctrinal basis to your religion—a basis that will be in consonance with Liberty, Equality and Fraternity; in short, with Democracy. I am no authority on the subject. But I am told that for such religious principles as will be in consonance with Liberty, Equality and Fraternity, it may not be necessary for you to borrow from foreign sources, and that you could draw for such principles on the Upanishads.

Whether you could do so without a complete remoulding, a considerable scraping and chipping off from the ore they contain, is more than I can say. This means a complete change in the fundamental notions of life. It means a complete change in the values of life. It means a complete change in outlook and in attitude towards men and things.

It means conversion—but if you do not like the word, I will say it means new life. But a new life cannot enter a body that is dead. New life can enter only into a new body. The old body must die before a new body can come into existence and a new life can enter into it. To put it simply: the old must cease to be operative before the new can begin to enliven [to live] and to pulsate. This is what I meant when I said you must discard the authority of the Shastras, and destroy the religion of the Shastras.

I have kept you too long. It is time I brought this address to a close. This would have been a convenient point for me to have stopped. But this would probably be my last address to a Hindu audience, on a subject vitally concerning the Hindus. I would therefore like, before I close, to place before the Hindus, if they will allow me, some questions which I regard as vital, and invite them seriously to consider the same.

In the first place, the Hindus must consider whether it is sufficient to take the placid view of the anthropologist that there is nothing to be said about the beliefs, habits, morals, and outlooks on life which obtain among the different peoples of the world, except that they often differ; or whether it is not necessary to make an attempt to find out what kind of morality, beliefs, habits, and outlook have worked best and have enabled those who possessed them to flourish, to grow strong, to people the earth and to have dominion over it. As is observed by Prof. Carver:

'Morality and religion, as the organised expression of moral approval and disapproval, must be regarded as factors in the struggle for and disapproval, must be regarded as factors in the struggle for existence as truly as are weapons for offence and defence, teeth and claws, horns and hoofs, furs and feathers. The social group, community, tribe, or nation, which develops an unworkable scheme of morality or within which those social acts which weaken it and unfit it for survival, habitually create the sentiment of approval, while those which would strengthen and enable it to be expanded habitually create the sentiment of disapproval, will eventually be eliminated. It is its habits of approval or disapproval (these are the results of religion and morality) that handicap it, as really as the possession of two wings on one side with none on the other will handicap the colony of flies. It would be as futile in the one case as in the other to argue, that one system is just as good as another.'[285]

Morality and religion, therefore, are not mere matters of likes and dislikes. You may dislike exceedingly a scheme of morality which, if universally practised within a nation, would make that nation the strongest nation on the face of the earth. Yet in spite of your dislike, such a nation will become strong. You may like exceedingly a scheme of morality and an ideal of justice which, if universally practised within a nation, would make it unable to hold its own in the struggle with other nations. Yet in spite of your admiration, this nation will eventually disappear. The Hindus must, therefore, examine their religion and their morality in terms of their survival value.

Secondly, the Hindus must consider whether they should conserve the whole of their social heritage, or select what is helpful and transmit to future generations only that much and no more. Prof. John Dewey, who was my teacher and to whom I owe so much, has said: 'Every society gets encumbered with what is trivial, with dead wood from the past, and with what is positively perverse… As a society becomes more enlightened, it realizes that it is responsible *not* to conserve and transmit the whole of its existing achievements, but only such as make for a better future society.'[286] Even Burke, in spite of the vehemence with which he opposed the principle of change embodied in the French Revolution, was compelled to admit that 'a State without the means

---

[285]This excerpt is from the first chapter, 'What is Justice?', of Thomas Nixon Carver's Essays in Social Justice (1915, 20). Carver (1865–1961) was a neoclassical American economist who wrote on a wide array of topics such as rural economics, the problems of distribution of wealth, social justice, the place of religion in society, and social evolution. He was professor of economics and sociology at Harvard University from 1900 to 1932. Minor errors in Ambedkar's quotation of Carver—that perist in the 1936, 1937 and 1944 editions—have been corrected.
[286]Towards the close of his address, Ambedkar records his debt to John Dewey from whose work, as has been shown, he draws extensively. This being a presidential address at a conference it is understandable that Ambedkar does not always cite references—not just from Dewey but for various other materials he marshals to make his case. This quote is from the second chapter of *Democracy and Education: An Introduction to the Philosophy of Education* (1916), concerning the role of the school in implementing social change.

of some change is without the means of its conservation. Without such means it might even risk the loss of that part of the constitution which it wished the most religiously to preserve.'[287] What Burke said of a State applies equally to a society.

Thirdly, the Hindus must consider whether they must not cease to worship the past as supplying their ideals. The baneful effects of this worship of the past are best summed up by Prof. Dewey when he says:

'An individual can live only in the present. The present is not just something which comes after the past; much less something produced by it. It is what life is in leaving the past behind it. The study of past products will not help us to understand the present. A knowledge of the past and its heritage is of great significance when it enters into the present, but not otherwise. And the mistake of making the records and remains of the past the main material of education is that it tends to make the past a rival of the present and the present a more or less futile imitation of the past.'[288]

The principle which makes little of the present act of living and growing, naturally looks upon the present as empty and upon the future as remote. Such a principle is inimical to progress, and is a hindrance to a strong and a steady current of life.

Fourthly, the Hindus must consider whether the time has not come for them to recognize that there is nothing fixed, nothing eternal, nothing sanatan;[289] that everything is changing, that change is the law of life for individuals as well as for society. In a changing society,

---

[287]Quote from Burke's *Reflections on the Revolution in France* (1790), in which he launched a bitter attack on the French Revolution.

[288]Dewey, *Democracy and Education*, chapter 7.

[289]Sanatan literally means eternal, everlasting; sanatan dharm (also rendered as sanatana dharma) is the religion that is said to have no beginning nor end. An orthodox person in the nationalist period would prefer to describe himself as someone who belonged to the 'sanatan dharm', the ever-lasting religion. The Anglicized terms 'Hindu' and 'Hinduism' do not capture the conservative fundamentalism inherent in sanatan dharm. While the Arya Samaj or Brahmo Samaj advocated reforms, the sanatani Hindus (the orthodoxy) believed in an eternal/sanatan Hinduism without any need for reforms.

there must be a constant revolution of old values; and the Hindus must realize that if there must be standards to measure the acts of men, there must also be a readiness to revise those standards.

I have to confess that this address has become too lengthy. Whether this fault is compensated to any extent by breadth or depth is a matter for you to judge. All I claim is to have told you candidly my views. I have little to recommend them but some study and a deep concern in your destiny. If you will allow me to say it, these views are the views of a man who has been no tool of power, no flatterer of greatness. They come from one, almost the whole of whose public exertion has been one continuous struggle for liberty for the poor and for the oppressed, and whose only reward has been a continuous shower of calumny and abuse from national journals and national leaders,[290] for no other reason except that I refuse to join with them in performing the miracle—I will not say trick—of liberating the oppressed with the gold of the tyrant, and raising the poor with the cash of the rich.

All this may not be enough to commend my views. I think they [Dr Ambedkar's views] are not likely to alter yours. But whether they do or do not, the responsibility is entirely yours. You must make your efforts to uproot caste, if not in my way, then in your way.

I am sorry, I will not be with you. I have decided to change. This is not the place for giving reasons. But even when I am gone out of your fold, I will watch your movement with active sympathy, and you

---

[290]Much before right-wing Hindutva ideologue Arun Shourie (1997) suggested that Ambedkar was a 'stooge' of the British and cast aspersions on his 'nationalist' credentials, the newspapers of Ambedkar's time constantly doubted his credentials. *In What Congress and Gandhi Have Done to the Untouchables* (BAWS 9, 200), Ambedkar writes: '[The Untouchables] have no Press and the Congress Press is closed to them. It is determined not to give them the slightest publicity. They cannot have their own Press. It is obvious that no paper can survive without advertisement revenue… The staff of the Associated Press in India, which is the main news distributing agency in India, is entirely drawn from Madras Brahmins—indeed the whole of the Press in India is in their hands and who for well-known reasons are entirely pro-Congress and will not allow any news hostile to the Congress to get publicity. These are reasons beyond the control of the Untouchables.' For a documentation of the insensitive way in which the so-called nationalist press reported on Ambedkar, see Ramnarayan Rawat (2001, 128–9).

will have my assistance for what it may be worth. Yours is a national cause. Caste is no doubt primarily the breath of the Hindus. But the Hindus have fouled the air all over, and everybody is infected—Sikh, Muslim and Christian.[291] You, therefore, deserve the support of all those who are suffering from this infection—Sikh, Muslim and Christian.

Yours is more difficult than the other national cause, namely Swaraj. In the fight for Swaraj[292] you fight with the whole nation on your side. In this, you have to fight against the whole nation—and that too, your own.[293] But it is more important than Swaraj. There is no use having Swaraj, if you cannot defend it. More important than the question of defending Swaraj is the question of defending the Hindus

---

[291]The import here is that caste has contaminated even the new faiths that emerged from within India (such as Sikhism) as it did religions that came to India (Islam and Christianity). For an account of how caste affects Sikhism, see Mark Juergensmeyer (2009); on caste among Muslims in India, see Imtiaz Ahmad (1978); and among Christians, see Kenneth Ballhatchet (1998), and the more recent study focused on Tamil Nadu by David Mosse (2012).

[292]Swaraj, literally 'self-rule', was the term used by the Congress party and other nationalist leaders to refer to the struggle for independence from British rule. The conservative leader Bal Gangadhar Tilak famously declared in 1899: 'Swaraj is my birthright, and I shall have it!' However, it was Gandhi who popularized the term, especially with his manifesto-like Hind Swaraj or Indian Home Rule (1909). According to Gandhi, 'It is swaraj when we learn to rule ourselves.' For an annotated edition of Hind Swaraj, see Parel (1997). According to Lelyveld (2011, xiv), swaraj for Gandhi was bigger than the struggle for mere independence from British rule. 'As used by Gandhi, poorna [complete] swaraj put the goal on yet a higher plane. At his most Utopian, it was a goal not just for India but for each individual Indian; only then could it be poorna, or complete. It meant a sloughing not only of British rule but of British ways, a rejection of modern industrial society in favor of a bottom-up renewal of India, starting in its villages...'

[293]Echoing a similar sentiment in 1927, when he led the civil rights struggle for Untouchables' access to the Chavadar Tank in Mahad, Ambedkar said: 'The satyagraha movement started by Gandhi was backed by the people as it was against foreign domination. Our struggle is against the mass of caste Hindus and naturally we have little support from outside.' Excerpts of Ambedkar's speech in Mahad, where he compares the event to the storming of the Bastille, can be found in Arjun Dangle (1992, 223–33) and in Satyanarayana and Tharu (2013, 22–31). For an account of the Mahad struggle, see Zelliot (2013, 78–82) and Rao (2009, 83–8).

under the Swaraj. In my opinion, it is only when Hindu Society becomes a casteless society that it can hope to have strength enough to defend itself. Without such internal strength, Swaraj for Hindus may turn out to be only a step towards slavery. Goodbye, and good wishes for your success.

◆

Dr Ambedkar's Indictment (I)

The readers will recall the fact that Dr Ambedkar was to have presided last May at the annual conference of the Jat-Pat-Todak Mandal of Lahore. But the conference itself was cancelled because Dr Ambedkar's address was found by the Reception Committee to be unacceptable. How far a Reception Committee is justified in rejecting a President of its choice because of his address that may be objectionable to it is open to question. The Committee knew Dr Ambedkar's views on caste and the Hindu scriptures. They knew also that he had in unequivocal terms decided to give up Hinduism. Nothing less than the address that Dr Ambedkar had prepared was to be expected from him. The committee appears to have deprived the public of an opportunity of listening to the original views of a man who has carved out for himself a unique position in society. Whatever label he wears in future, Dr Ambedkar is not the man to allow himself to be forgotten.

Dr Ambedkar was not going to be beaten by the Reception Committee. He has answered their rejection of him by publishing the address at his own expense. He has priced it at 8 annas, I would suggest a reduction to 2 annas or at least [at most] 4 annas.

No reformer can ignore the address. The orthodox will gain by reading it. This is not to say that the address is not open to objection. It has to be read only because it is open to serious objection. Dr Ambedkar is a challenge to Hinduism. Brought up as a Hindu, educated by a Hindu potentate, he has become so disgusted with the so-called Savarna Hindus or the treatment that he and his people have received at their hands that he proposes to leave not only them but the very religion that is his and their common heritage. He has transferred to that religion, his disgust against a part of its professors [believers].

But this is not to be wondered at. After all, one can only judge a system or an institution by the conduct of its representatives. What is more, Dr Ambedkar found that the vast majority of Savarna Hindus had not only conducted themselves inhumanly against those of their fellow religionists whom they classed as Untouchables, but they had based their conduct on the authority of their scriptures, and when he began to search them he had found ample warrant for their beliefs in Untouchability and all its implications. The author of the address has quoted chapter and verse in proof of his three-fold indictment—inhuman conduct itself, the unabashed justification for it on the part of the perpetrators, and the subsequent discovery that the justification was warranted by their scriptures.

No Hindu who prizes his faith above life itself can afford to underrate the importance of this indictment. Dr Ambedkar is not alone in his disgust. He is its most uncompromising exponent and one of the ablest among them. He is certainly the most irreconcilable among them. Thank God, in the front rank of the leaders he is singularly alone, and as yet but a representative of a very small minority. But what he says is voiced with more or less vehemence by many leaders belonging to the depressed classes. Only the latter, for instance Rao Bahadur M.C. Rajah and Dewan Bahadur Srinivasan, not only do not threaten to give up Hinduism, but find enough warmth in it to compensate for the shameful persecution to which the vast mass of Harijans are exposed.

But the fact of many leaders remaining in the Hindu fold is no warrant for disregarding what Dr Ambedkar has to say. The Savarnas have to correct their belief and their conduct. Above all, those who are [preeminent] by their learning and influence among the Savarnas have to give an authoritative interpretation of the scriptures. The questions that Dr Ambedkar's indictment suggests are:

1. What are the scriptures?
2. Are all the printed texts to be regarded as an integral part of them, or is any part of them to be rejected as unauthorized interpolation?
3. What is the answer of such accepted and expurgated scriptures on the question of Untouchability, caste, equality of status,

inter-dining and inter-marriages? (These have been all examined by Dr Ambedkar in his address.)

4. I must reserve for the next issue my own answer to these questions and a statement of the (at least some) manifest flaws in Dr Ambedkar's thesis.

Dr Ambedkar's Indictment (II)

The Vedas, Upanishads, Smritis and Puranas, including the Ramayana and the Mahabharata, are the Hindu Scriptures. Nor is this a finite list. Every age or even generation has added to the list. It follows, therefore, that everything printed or even found handwritten is not scripture. The Smritis, for instance, contain much that can never be accepted as the word of God. Thus many of the texts that Dr Ambedkar quotes from the Smritis cannot be accepted as authentic. The scriptures, properly so-called, can only be concerned with eternal verities and must appeal to any conscience, i.e. any heart whose eyes of understanding are opened. Nothing can be accepted as the word of God which cannot be tested by reason or be capable of being spiritually experienced. And even when you have an expurgated edition of the scriptures, you will need their interpretation. Who is the best interpreter? Not learned men surely. Learning there must be. But religion does not live by it. It lives in the experiences of its saints and seers, in their lives and sayings. When all the most learned commentators of the scriptures are utterly forgotten, the accumulated experience of the sages and saints will abide and be an inspiration for ages to come saints will abide and be an inspiration for ages to come.

Caste has nothing to do with religion. It is a custom whose origin I do not know, and do not need to know for the satisfaction of my spiritual hunger. But I do know that it is harmful both to spiritual and national growth. Varna and Ashrama are institutions which have nothing to do with castes. The law of varna teaches us that we have each one of us to earn our bread by following the ancestral calling. It defines not our rights but our duties. It necessarily has reference to callings that are conducive to the welfare of humanity and to no other. It also follows that there is no calling too low and none too high. All are good, lawful and absolutely equal in status. The callings of a

Brahmin—spiritual teacher—and a scavenger are equal, and their due performance carries equal merit before God, and at one time seems to have carried identical reward before man. Both were entitled to their livelihood and no more. Indeed one traces even now in the villages the faint lines of this healthy operation of the law.

Living in Segaon with its population of 600, I do not find a great disparity between the earnings of different tradesmen, including Brahmins. I find too that real Brahmins are to be found, even in these degenerate days, who are living on alms freely given to them and are giving freely of what they have of spiritual treasures. It would be wrong and improper to judge the law of varna by its caricature in the lives of men who profess to belong to a varna, whilst they openly commit a breach of its only operative rule. Arrogation of a superior status by and of the varna over another is a denial of the law. And there is nothing in the law of varna to warrant a belief in Untouchability. (The essence of Hinduism is contained in its enunciation of one and only [one] God as Truth and its bold acceptance of Ahimsa as the law of the human family.)

I am aware that my interpretation of Hinduism will be disputed by many besides Dr Ambedkar. That does not affect my position. It is an interpretation by which I have lived for nearly half a century, and according to which I have endeavoured to the best of my ability to regulate my life.

In my opinion the profound mistake that Dr Ambedkar has made in his address is to pick out the texts of doubtful authenticity and value, and the state of degraded Hindus who are no fit specimens of the faith they so woefully misrepresent. Judged by the standard applied by Dr Ambedkar, every known living faith will probably fail.

In his able address, the learned Doctor has overproved his case. Can a religion that was professed by Chaitanya, Jnyandeo, Tukaram, Tiruvalluvar, Ramakrishna Paramahansa, Raja Ram Mohan Roy, Maharshi Devendranath Tagore, Vivekanand, and a host of others who might be easily mentioned, be so utterly devoid of merit as is made out in Dr Ambedkar's address? A religion has to be judged not by its worst specimens, but by the best it might have produced. For that and that alone can be used as the standard to aspire to, if not to improve upon.

III: Varna versus Caste

Shri Sant Ramji of the Jat-Pat-Todak Mandal of Lahore wants me to publish the following:

'I have read your remarks about Dr Ambedkar and the Jat-Pat-Todak Mandal, Lahore. In that connection I beg to submit as follows:

We did not invite Dr Ambedkar to preside over our conference because he belonged to the Depressed Classes, for we do not distinguish between a touchable and an Untouchable Hindu. On the contrary our choice fell on him simply because his diagnosis of the fatal disease of the Hindu community was the same as ours; i.e., he too was of the opinion that the caste system was the root cause of the disruption and downfall of the Hindus. The subject of the Doctor's thesis for his Doctorate being the caste system, he has studied the subject thoroughly. Now the object of our conference was to persuade the Hindus to annihilate castes, but the advice of a non-Hindu in social and religious matters can have no effect on them. The Doctor in the supplementary portion of his address insisted on saying that that was his last speech as a Hindu, which was irrelevant as well as pernicious to the interests of the conference. So we requested him to expunge that sentence, for he could easily say the same thing on any other occasion. But he refused, and we saw no utility in making merely a show of our function. In spite of all this, I cannot help praising his address, which is, as far as I know, the most learned thesis on the subject and worth translating into every vernacular of India.

Moreover, I want to bring to your notice that your philosophical difference between caste and varna is too subtle to be grasped by people in general, because for all practical purposes in the Hindu society caste and varna are one and the be grasped by people in general, because for all practical purposes in the Hindu society caste and varna are one and the same thing, for the function of both of them is one and the same, i.e. to restrict inter-caste marriages and inter-dining. Your theory of Varnavyavastha is impracticable in this age, and there is no hope of its revival in the near future. But Hindus are slaves of caste, and do not want to destroy it. So when you advocate your ideal of imaginary Varnavyavastha, they find justification for clinging to caste. Thus you are doing a great disservice to social reform by advocating your imaginary utility of the division of varnas, for it creates a hindrance in our way. To try to remove Untouchability without striking at the root of Varnavyavastha is simply to treat the outward symptoms of a disease, or to draw a line on the surface of water. As in the heart of their hearts Dvijas do not want to give social equality to the so-called touchable and untouchable Shudras, so they refuse to break caste—and give liberal donations for the removal of Untouchability simply to evade the issue. To seek the help of the Shastras for the removal of Untouchability and caste is simply to wash mud with mud.'

The last paragraph of the letter surely cancels the first. If the Mandal rejects the help of the Shastras, they do exactly what Dr Ambedkar does, i.e. cease to be Hindus. How then can they object to Dr Ambedkar's address merely because he said that that was his last speech as a Hindu? The position appears to be wholly untenable, especially when the Mandal, for which Shri Sant Ram claims to speak, applauds the whole argument of Dr Ambedkar's address.

But it is pertinent to ask what the Mandal believes, if it rejects the Shastras. How can a Muslim remain one if he rejects the Quran, or a Christian remain Christian if he rejects the Bible? If caste and varna are convertible terms, and if varna is an integral part of the Shastras which define Hinduism, I do not know how a person who rejects caste, i.e. varna, can call himself a Hindu.

Shri Sant Ram likens the Shastras to mud. Dr Ambedkar has not, so far as I remember, given any such picturesque name to the Shastras. I have certainly meant when I have said: that if Shastras support the existing Untouchability I should cease to call myself a Hindu. Similarly, if the Shastras support caste as we know it today in all its hideousness, I may not call myself or remain a Hindu, since I have no scruples about inter-dining or inter-marriage. I need not repeat my position regarding Shastras and their interpretation. I venture to suggest to Shri Sant Ram that it is the only rational and correct and morally defensible position, and it has ample warrant in Hindu tradition.

(Harijan, August 15, 1936)